STUDIES IN BAPTIST
VO

MW01711191

The European Baptist Federation

A Case Study in European Baptist Interdependency

1950 – 2006

STUDIES IN BAPTIST HISTORY AND THOUGHT
VOLUME 43

A full listing of titles in this series
appears at the end of this book

This volume is published in co-operation with the
International Baptist Theological Seminary, Prague,
Czech Republic

STUDIES IN BAPTIST HISTORY AND THOUGHT
VOLUME 43

The European Baptist Federation

A Case Study in European Baptist Interdependency

1950 – 2006

Keith G. Jones

Foreword by Ian M. Randall

Paternoster:
thinking faith

MILTON KEYNES • COLORADO SPRINGS • HYDERABAD

International Baptist Theological Seminary of the EBF

First published 2009 by Paternoster

Paternoster is an imprint of Authentic Media
9 Holdom Avenue, Bletchley, Milton Keynes, Bucks, MK1 1QR
1820 Jet Stream Drive, Colorado Springs, CO 80921, USA
OM Authentic Media, Medchal Road, Jeedimetla Village,
Secunderabad 500 055, A.P., India
www.authenticmedia.co.uk
Authentic Media is a division of IBS-STL UK, a company limited by guarantee
(registered charity no. 270162)

15 14 13 12 11 10 09   7 6 5 4 3 2 1

British Library Cataloguing in Publication Data
A catalogue record for this book is available from the British Library

ISBN 978–1–84227–639–6

Typeset by Philip Alexander
Printed and bound in Great Britain
by Alpha Graphics Nottingham

Series Preface

Baptists form one of the largest Christian communities in the world, and while they hold the historic faith in common with other mainstream Christian traditions, they nevertheless have important insights which they can offer to the worldwide church. Studies in Baptist History and Thought will be one means towards this end. It is an international series of academic studies which includes original monographs, revised dissertations, collections of essays and conference papers, and aims to cover any aspect of Baptist history and thought. While not all the authors are themselves Baptists, they nevertheless share an interest in relating Baptist history and thought to the other branches of the Christian church and to the wider life of the world.

The series includes studies in various aspects of Baptist history from the seventeenth century down to the present day, including biographical works, and Baptist thought is understood as covering the subject-matter of theology (including interdisciplinary studies embracing biblical studies, philosophy, sociology, practical theology, liturgy and women's studies). The diverse streams of Baptist life throughout the world are all within the scope of these volumes.

The series editors and consultants believe that the academic disciplines of history and theology are of vital importance to the spiritual vitality of the churches of the Baptist faith and order. The series sets out to discuss, examine and explore the many dimensions of their tradition and so to contribute to their on-going intellectual vigour.

A brief word of explanation is due for the series identifier on the front cover. The fountains, taken from heraldry, represent the Baptist distinctive of believer's baptism and, at the same time, the source of the water of life. There are three of them because they symbolize the Trinitarian basis of Baptist life and faith. Those who are redeemed by the Lamb, the book of Revelation reminds us, will be led to 'fountains of living waters' (Rev. 7.17).

This book is dedicated to the churches and communities of the Yorkshire Baptist Association who nurtured me in baptistic ways in the first forty years of my life.

Contents

Foreword

This is a ground-breaking book on Baptist ecclesiology. Keith Jones examines and argues for the conviction that Baptist congregations are ecclesiologically interdependent. The examination is undertaken, in proper Baptist fashion, not by a theoretical enquiry but by looking at important dimensions of the life of Baptists in Europe. This book takes the European Baptist Federation as a case study and shows that the EBF arose out of an understanding that each local community of believers (gathering churches) should engage with and relate to other like-minded communities for a range of ecclesial purposes.

I see the ground-breaking nature of this book as having a number of aspects. It is thoroughly absorbing as a historical analysis. Each chapter takes the reader on a historical journey which opens up many areas of Baptist history in Europe. This is a book which will help Baptists across Europe to understand one another's stories at a depth that has not been attempted in any study up to this point.

In addition, this is an ecumenical volume. It contains insights into ecumenical relationships in Europe which are invaluable not only for Baptists but for others who want to understand the diverse forms of Christian life across our continent. Both those who are committed to ecumenical fellowship and those who have reservations – for whatever reason – will find material here that offers them challenging new perspectives.

Keith Jones has also written a deeply theological work. It is fascinating to read here that Henry Cook from Great Britain, one of the prime movers in the formation of the EBF, spoke in 1950 (as moves were being made to establish the EBF) about the strength of the interdependent principle, for example in the 1664 Confession of Faith of the London Particular Baptists. Cook argued that both General and Particular Baptists, 'deliberately linked their churches, both to steady one another in doctrine and explain themselves unitedly to the world, to aid one another in time of need and especially to propagate their views'. Within the longer Baptist tradition there was never a desire to have churches that were simply independent. This book argues that such interdependency did not and does not spring from pragmatism, but from a thoughtful ecclesial vision.

There is, in addition, much robust argument in this book. The arguments are based on and show evidence of very detailed engagement with a wider range of primary and secondary sources, but such engagement is never dry and lifeless. The reverse is the case. Personalities and issues are brought to life in a splendidly vivid way through the descriptions and the fresh interpretations offered here. Controversial events are not avoided but are given appropriate treatment.

A number of the significant developments within the EBF story, not least those associated with the International Baptist Theological Seminary, have been connected with Baptist life in North America. In tracing these connections this book will, therefore, make a major contribution to the international Baptist community. Many Baptist groups world-wide have been influenced – primarily from North America – by a very different model to the interdependent one that has been espoused in Europe. The differences in perspective are portrayed with precision and clarity in this book. Instead of the path of ideological isolationism, Keith Jones argues in favour of the path mapped out by many European Baptists, in which there is an acknowledgement of the need of gathering churches to find unity within diversity. This book is a powerful resource for those within the baptistic tradition who are committed to that task and is a powerful challenge to those who may not, as yet, espouse those convictions.

Ian M. Randall
Cambridge
Lent 2009

Acknowledgements

I am deeply indebted to many people who have encouraged me in various ways during the research and writing of this book. The Revd Dr Ian M. Randall has been a source of constant encouragement and of many valuable insights. His critical engagement with the enterprise was of assistance to me in stimulating my own thinking and in enabling me to reflect cogently on many of the source materials I have reviewed. Over the period of five years as this work took shape, his enthusiasm for the task never wavered and he has been so much more than a formal supervisor of a doctoral dissertation but he has engaged with me as a conversation partner in questions of baptistic ecclesiology and identity beyond the local. Professor John H.Y. Briggs also read the text and his comments and insights helped me in further research and clarification of certain issues, especially in regard to the Christian World Communions.

I am thankful to those who developed in me both the desire to engage critically in history and in theology. To Professor David G. Wright for awakening a sense of the importance of historical analysis at an early age, and to the Revd Professor Michael H. Taylor for providing the groundwork in theological reflection and the constant encouragement to believe I could aim for more.

To my academic colleagues at the International Baptist Theological Seminary I owe a profound debt of gratitude for providing a supportive and collegial academic community in which to work. Within that community I want to mention specifically my colleague the Revd Docent Dr Parush R. Parushev, who had to bear extra responsibilities when I was engaged in sabbatical study leave; my Kvestor JUDr Petra Veselá, who similarly was a source of encouragement and relieved me of responsibilities at a key point to allow the work to continue; and Lina Andronovienė, who was my personal assistant for the period of the early research and then supported me in my endeavours as the project developed, not least in unravelling some of the vagaries of computer programmes. To my present personal assistant, Vanessa L. Lake, I offer my thanks for her support, guarding my door when research was in progress, and assisting by taking my diagrams and turning them into presentable graphics.

From beginning to end, my wife, Denise, has been a tower of strength. She has supported the research throughout, coping with my absences researching in

Philadelphia, Virginia and Oxford and been of immense help in reading and offering suggestions on layout, language and punctuation. I am grateful to my friend, Bill Lively, for work on the index and to my colleague, Philip Alexander for sub-editing and typesetting work.

In searching through archive material I have received invaluable cooperation from Susan J. Mills and Jennifer Thorpe at the Angus Library, Regent's Park College. Deborah Van Broekhoven, Betty Layton and their colleagues at the American Baptist Historical Society, then at Valley Forge, Pennsylvania, went out of their way to trace material in response to my enquiries and provided me with a good base in their offices for my researches. Malcolm and Ann Goodspeed provided hospitality for my sojourns at Regent's Park and John and Carol Sundquist for my time at Valley Forge. For their friendship, interest and assistance I thank them most sincerely. Alec Gilmore, Katharina Penner, Nancy Lively, Daily Adam and the IBTS archive and library team assisted me in my searchings amongst the materials located in Prague with cheerfulness and perseverance. The staff of the EBF office in Prague – Helle Liht, Timofey Cheprasov and Alexandra Alexander – all assisted in my researches for documents of the EBF General Council.

Many individuals responded to my questions and recalled key points of the story for me, but I am especially grateful to successive EBF General Secretaries Knud Wümplemann, Karl Heinz Walter, Theo Angelov and Tony Peck for answering my questions and engaging in conversation about the enterprise. Former Southern Baptist Foreign Mission personnel Isam Ballenger, G. Keith Parker, John W. Merritt, John David Hopper and JoAnn Hopper all willingly responded to my desire for more information or where certain documents might be located. I remain grateful to them for their commitment to Europe, to the EBF and to their interest in my work. Archie Goldie kindly answered my queries on the early days of Baptist World Aid. Carol Woodfin assisted me in identifying key resources in the history of IBTS.

The Board of Trustees of the International Baptist Theological Seminary (IBTS) granted me a sabbatical in two halves enabling visits to various archives and sustained writing time, for which I am very grateful. The community of IBTS has been supportive in understanding that sometimes the Rector was immersed in research and not immediately available to respond to questions and queries, and I thank them for their accompaniment on this journey.

Keith G. Jones
IBTS, Prague
Epiphany 2009

Abbreviations

ABC	American Baptist Churches, USA
ABQ	American Baptist Quarterly
AUCECB	All Union Council of Evangelical Christian Baptists in the Soviet Union
BEM	*Baptism, Eucharist and Ministry*
BICTE	Baptist International Conference for Theological Educators
BMS	Baptist Missionary Society, United Kingdom From 2000 known as BMS World Mission.
BQ	Baptist Quarterly, United Kingdom
BRE	Baptist Response-Europe, the EBF relief and development fund
BTS	Baptist Theological Seminary, Rüschlikon
BUGB	Baptist Union of Great Britain
BUGBI	Baptist Union of Great Britain and Ireland (title until 1985)
BWA	Baptist World Alliance
CBF	Cooperative Baptist Fellowship, USA
CCEE	Council of European Bishops' Conferences
CEC/KEK	Conference of European Churches
CEO	Chief Executive Officer, as used in some US denominational organisations
CMS	Church Missionary Society
CPC	Christian Peace Conference
CPCE	Community of Protestant Churches in Europe
CWC	Christian World Communions
DDR	German Democratic Republic (communist East Germany)
DM	Deutschmark (German currency until the adoption of the Euro in 2000)

EBC	European Baptist Convention (Now International Baptist Convention)
EBF	European Baptist Federation
EBM	European Baptist Mission
EBPS	European Baptist Press Service
EBWU	European Baptist Women's Union
EBYC	European Baptist Youth Committee
EEA	European Evangelical Alliance
EKD	Evangelical Church in Germany
FMB	Foreign Mission Board of the Southern Baptist Convention
FMS	Foreign Mission Society of the American Baptist Churches
IBCA	International Baptist Cooperation in Albania
IBLA	International Baptist Lay Academy
IBTS	International Baptist Theological Seminary
IMB	International Mission Board (used by both ABC and SBC)
IMP	Indigenous Missionary Project
JEBS	Journal of European Baptist Studies
LWF	Lutheran World Federation
MTh	Master of Theology
NABF	North American Baptist Fellowship
OSCE	Organisation for Security and Cooperation in Europe
SBC	Southern Baptist Convention, USA
SRC	Structure Review Committee
TFHRRL	Task Force on Human Rights and Religious Freedom, EBF
USA	United States of America
USSR	Union of Soviet Socialist Republics
WARC	World Alliance of Reformed Churches
WCC	World Council of Churches
WCF	World Confessional Families
WEF	World Evangelical Fellowship
WMC	World Methodist Council
WMU	Women's Missionary Union – an auxiliary of the Southern Baptist Convention

CHAPTER 1

Baptists and Interdependency

The famous Baptist historian, W.T. Whitley,[1] always started any survey about Baptists with the remark 'the distinctive feature about Baptists is their doctrine of the Church'.[2] In recent times various Baptist theologians have sought to identify and mark out a combination of theological assertions which might be said to characterise the people called Baptists.[3] Alan P.F. Sell from the Reformed tradition echoes Whitley in commenting: 'Baptist polity has been determined by the doctrine of the Church... the organs of polity – Church Meeting, Association – have stated those doctrines commonly believed'.[4] One such assertion, which is not always given emphasis in Baptist life outside of Europe,[5] is that Baptists are not ecclesiologically independent, but interdependent. That is to say, although Baptist ecclesiology is founded on the theological assertion that each local church or, to use more specifically Baptist terminology, each local community of believers, has full authority to interpret the mind of Christ, nevertheless there is an understanding that each local community of believers should engage with and relate to other like-minded communities for a whole variety of ecclesial purposes. Indeed, it is not always so apparent that, even within Europe, Baptists take this issue seriously and they certainly do not engage much in critical reflection upon it. As Alan Sell comments, 'until recently, as far as I have been able to discover, there has been little detailed *theological* writing upon Baptist associations and the Baptist Union in so far as these have significance in a communion which prizes local

---

[1] On W.T. Whitley see I. Sellers, 'W.T. Whitley – A Commemorative Essay' and K. Manley, 'The Right Man in the Right Place: W.T. Whitley in Australia (1891-1901)', both in *The Baptist Quarterly (BQ)*, Vol. XXXVII, No. 4 (Oct. 1997), pp. 159-92.

[2] W.T. Whitley, *A History of British Baptists*, rev. ed. (London: Kingsgate, 1932), p. 4.

[3] By Baptists it is assumed those within the believers' church tradition who are identified with the Baptist World Alliance. See A.W. Wardin (ed.), *Baptists Around the World* (Nashville, Tenn.: Broadman and Holman, 1995).

[4] A.P.F. Sell, *Testimony and Tradition: Studies in Reformed and Dissenting Thought* (Aldershot: Ashgate Press, 2005) p. 50.

[5] For an American perspective see D.K. McCall with A.R. Tonks, *Duke McCall: An Oral History* (Brentwood, Tenn: Baptist History and Heritage Society/Nashville: Fields, 2001).

autonomy'.[6] This work seeks to redress that balance and make assertions about the importance of the more-than-local expressions of ecclesial reality amongst Baptists within a continental framework.

It is necessary at this point for me to indicate that I am working with the notion of the basic unit of ecclesiology as the gathering, intentional, convictional community of believers. This perspective belongs to the fourth great stream of Christianity, described by Lesslie Newbigin as the 'pneumatic type';[7] by Donald Durnbaugh and others as the 'believers' churches;[8] by James Wm. McClendon, Jr. as the 'baptistic' grouping of 'baptists with a small b';[9] or by Nigel G. Wright and myself as the 'gathering church' grouping.[10] The importance of the notion of 'gathering', rather than the older terminology of 'gathered',[11] is found in both the intransitive sense, that the community gathers as it worships, and in the transitive sense, that it gathers people into itself. Such a relationship – people gathering and being gathered by God's divine activity through the Holy Spirit – is not simply pragmatic, but is at the heart of the theology and mission appropriate to the believers' church tradition in which believers covenant together and churches also covenant with each other. Furthermore, such relationships, entered into by local covenanted communities of believers, are not bound to a specific micro-geographical area, but can be regional, national, continental and international.

'Members of one body': Baptists and Interdependency

I will seek, using a specific case study – the European Baptist Federation (EBF) – to advance an argument for trans-local interdependency as integral to any full-orbed baptistic ecclesiology. There is a fine history of the EBF by Bernard Green.[12] However, the purpose of this work is to analyse the EBF as an

---

[6] A.P.F. Sell, *Nonconformist Theology in the Twentieth Century* (Milton Keynes: Paternoster, 2006), p. 106. Pp. 91-145 survey the theological reflection on ecclesiology within the British gathering church traditions.

[7] L. Newbigin, *The Household of God* (New York: Friendship, 1954), pp. 105-106.

[8] Believers' church is used here as defined by D.F. Durnbaugh in *The Believers' Church: the History and Character of Radical Protestantism* (New York: The MacMillan Company, 1968).

[9] J.W. McClendon, Jr., *Systematic Theology: Ethics*, vol. 1 (Nashville, Tenn.: Abingdon, 1986), pp. 19- 41.

[10] N.G. Wright, *New Baptists, New Agenda* (Carlisle: Paternoster, 2002); N.G. Wright, *Free Church Free State* (Milton Keynes: Paternoster, 2005); K.G. Jones, *A Believing Church: learning from some contemporary Anabaptist and Baptist perspectives* (Didcot: Baptist Union of Great Britain, 1998).

[11] D. Davie, *A Gathered Church: The Literature of the English Dissenting Interest, 1700-1930* (London: Routledge and Kegan Paul, 1978).

[12] B. Green, *Crossing the boundaries: a history of the European Baptist Federation* (Didcot: The Baptist Historical Society, 1999).

ecclesial body. Although some in the baptistic tradition have seen ecclesial links beyond the local as optional, I will seek to show that a wider ecclesial view has been at the heart of the thinking of those involved in seeking to shape the various Baptist communities in the nations of Europe.[13] This ecclesial reality has encompassed both personal and corporate elements and those involved have been committed, not only to fostering *koinonia*,[14] but also to mission, to issues of society and politics, and to working out the cross-cultural dimensions of such interaction. It is important to continue the process of reflecting upon these dimensions theologically. The ecclesial basis and significance of the EBF, which was founded in 1949 and has continued to grow and develop until the present day, has many facets, not only in terms of relationships between Baptist communities in Europe but also in the way the EBF has interacted with mission organisations beyond Europe. These various facets deserve careful analysis, which will be undertaken, not only by means of historical investigation, but also by engaging with the wider discussion on Baptist and baptistic ecclesiology as it has been undertaken principally in Europe and the USA, and by looking at the models of ecclesial associating that have developed within defined geographic areas, nations and continents.

For European Baptists, the desire to associate together has been part of the story of Baptist life since the seventeenth century. It is true that when John Smyth and Thomas Helwys began what was the first English-speaking Baptist Church in Amsterdam in 1609, and produced their Confession of 1611,[15] they could not immediately form wider links. However, the subsequent commitment among English Baptists to inter-congregational relationships was strong. English Baptists also saw themselves as being part of a wider community in Europe that stretched beyond those who used the name 'Baptist'. The early link with the Netherlands was also noted. Thus the English Particular Baptist leader, John Rippon, in his important *Baptist Annual Register* of 1793, produced a

---

[13] The EBF currently includes the whole of Europe, middle Asia, the Middle East, parts of north Africa and all of Russia. Whilst the focus of the work is on the classic geographical expression of Europe – from the Atlantic isles to the Bosphorus, from the Azores to the Urals – inevitably some aspects will refer to this greater baptistic 'Europe'.

[14] I use *koinonia* in that rich theological sense expressed in much ecumenical theology, which is inadequately rendered as 'fellowship' in English. For an exposition of *koinonia* and the depth of its meaning as communion, fellowship and community see T.F. Best and G. Gassman (eds.), *On the Way to Fuller Koinonia* (Geneva: WCC, 1994).

[15] The date is generally credited as being 1609. The EBF are planning a 400th anniversary event in Amsterdam in July 2009. This book celebrates that event. On John Smyth see J.R. Coggins, *John Smyth's Congregation: English Separatism, Mennonite influence and the Elect Nation* (Scottdale, Pa: Herald, 1991), and J.K. Lee, *The Theology of John Smyth: Puritan, Separatist, Baptist, Mennonite* (Macon: Mercer University Press, 2003).

'Catalogue of the Professors and Ministers among the Baptists within, and out of the United Netherlands.... for 1791'.[16] Rippon added, for good measure, details of what he assumed to be Baptist churches in Prussia, Poland, Lithuania, Saxony, the Rhineland, Switzerland, France and Russia. Most of these churches were affiliated to the Mennonite family of churches or to some form of Anabaptist life, but for Rippon, as for many contemporary Baptist theologians, there is a wider baptistic community holding certain common virtues and practices. Indeed Rippon printed a dedication:

> To all the baptized ministers and people in America, England, Ireland, Scotland, Wales, the United Netherlands, France, Switzerland, Poland, Russia and elsewhere... in serious expectation that before many years elapse (in imitation of other wise men) a deputation from all these climes will meet probably in London to consult the ecclesiastical good to the whole.[17]

For Rippon, associating for the purposes of *koinonia* and for mission was clearly very important and it is this theme that will be pursued in this book.

The vision expressed by Rippon was and is influential for many Baptists, but not for all. It is a wider and more comprehensive vision than that of many in the Baptist World Alliance (BWA), which was founded in 1905. However, the importance of associating beyond national boundaries, with like-minded believers, is a clear and consistent principle that is to be found throughout the story of Baptist life in Europe, as British Baptists maintained in the mid-twentieth century in a key statement (in 1948) on the Doctrine of the Church:

> Although Baptists have for so long held a position separate from that of other communions, they have always claimed to be part of the one holy catholic Church. They believe in the catholic Church as the holy society of believers in our Lord Jesus Christ, which He founded, of which He is the only Head, and in which He dwells by His Spirit, so that though manifested in many communions, organized in many modes and scattered throughout the world, it is yet one in Him. The Church is the Body of Christ and a chosen instrument of the divine purpose in history.[18]

The themes in this crucial ecclesiological statement, which in terms of its authorship owed much to some who would be instrumental in shaping the ecclesial reality of the EBF, are themes to which we shall keep returning. Such a statement is in sharp contrast to the movement among Baptists for local

---

[16] J. Rippon, *Baptist Annual Register 1 (1790-1793)* (London: Dilly, Button and Thomas, 1793).

[17] *Ibid.,* inside page immediately after cover page, unnumbered.

[18] The report was selected for a series of key Baptist Union statements and introduced by Roger Hayden, 'The Baptist Doctrine of the Church', Baptist Union Council, 1948, in *Baptist Union Documents 1948-1977* (London: Baptist Historical Society, 1980), p. 5.

church autonomy.[19] This pressure for 'independence', that has come especially from the strong North American Baptist world,[20] is referred to by Stanley Fowler as a view that tends to play down the universal Church, although it must be noted that in such thinking the place of the wider Church is not denied. Nonetheless, Fowler sees 'the trajectory of Baptist ecclesiology in North America' as illustrating how the universal Church can end up being in a position of functional insignificance.[21]

A study of Baptist ecclesiology has to be set within the context of more recent wider theological studies: ecclesiology remains a productive area of primary theological exploration in the twentieth and twenty-first centuries,[22] not least in the area of reflection on the interaction between local congregations, regional bodies (diocesan, associational, provincial), and, more widely, continental and intercontinental structures. It is not the purpose of this book to explore in detail the various traditions. However, it is important to note some of the key theologians who have been reflecting ecclesiologically in the other traditions. More recent Roman Catholic theological reflection on ecclesiology owes a great deal to Avery Dulles. His book, *The Catholicity of the Church*,[23] perhaps marks the starting point of the current period of reflection on ecclesiology. From the non-Western world, writers such as Leonardo Boff in *Church, Charism and Power*,[24] have opened up the whole debate about the relationships between the local, regional and inter-continental aspects of the Church and the relationship of the Church to the surrounding society. Such studies place firmly on the agenda many of the concerns explored in this work. From within the Orthodox tradition, John D. Zizioulas has been at the forefront

---

[19] W.H. Brackney, 'An Historical Theologian looks anew at Autonomy', at www.bwanet/media/documents/Elstal, accessed 23 April 2007.

[20] Baptist statistics are difficult to present carefully and honestly. However, if there are at least 48 million baptised believers belonging to churches which were in membership with the Baptist World Alliance [BWA] in 2004, then approximately 33 million of them have their home in the USA.

[21] S.K. Fowler, 'Churches and the Church', in P.E. Thompson and A.R. Cross (eds.), *Recycling the Past or Researching History? Studies in Baptist Historiography and Myths* (Milton Keynes: Paternoster, 2005), p. 37.

[22] In speaking of primary theology I am following the insights of my colleague, P.R. Parushev, seeing the gathering churches as doing theology in the community. For him secondary theology is the theology of the study and academia. He explains his ideas in P.R. Parushev (ed.), *Primary and Secondary Theologies in Baptistic Communities* (Prague, IBTS, forthcoming). This insight will determine some of my theological conversation partners. The most fruitful conversation is with those who are more interested in the theology of the community rather than academic systematic theology.

[23] A. Dulles, *The Catholicity of the Church* (Oxford: Clarendon, 1985). More recently Richard R. Gaillardetz, *Ecclesiology for a global Church* (Maryknoll: Orbis, 2008).

[24] L. Boff, *Church Charism and Power: Liberation Theology and the Institutional Church* (London: SCM, 1985).

of those seeking to stimulate debate about the nature of the Church and its ecclesiology in the first three centuries, especially as a challenge to some of the current patterns of the life of the Orthodox autocephalus Churches.[25] Baptist theologians in Europe have been engaging in theological conversation on ecclesial issues with Catholic and Orthodox thinkers.[26]

Turning to mainstream Protestantism, leading theologians have been and are debating ecclesiology. Often Baptists have seen themselves as most closely related to this ecclesial stream. Within European Protestantism there has been a deep concern for an authentic expression of the Church, a concern that was especially acute in the light of events in Europe in the twentieth century. Theologians such as Karl Barth,[27] from the Protestant mainstream in Germany, sought to argue for a clear ecclesiology, particularly in the 1930s when the relationship of national and folk churches to nations and culture was a cause for serious reflection. To take another notable example, in response to the policies of the Nazis, Dietrich Bonhoeffer and others formed the Confessing Church and struggled to offer a credible, corporate witness to Christ within their context. The Confessing Church remains a powerful instance of the crucial importance of ecclesial theology.[28] It is especially important to this study because of the reflection on the reality of Christians relating to each other as a source of spiritual renewal and service. For Bonhoeffer the relationship of believers to each other was mediated through Christ, involving a call to costly service,[29] and was also expressed in community.[30] More recently Jürgen Moltmann has shown a concern for ecclesiology[31] and, within Anglicanism,

---

[25] J.D. Zizioulas, *Eucharist, Bishop, Church: The Unity of the Church in the Divine Eucharist and the Bishop during the first three centuries* (ET, Elizabeth Theoritoff, Brookline, Ma: Holy Cross Orthodox Press, 2001).

[26] See J.E. Colwell, *Promise and Presence: An Exploration of Sacramental Theology* (Milton Keynes: Paternoster, 2005) and I.M. Randall (ed.) *Baptists and Orthodoxy: On the way to understanding* (Prague: IBTS, 2003).

[27] K. Barth, *Church Dogmatics,* vol. IV (ET G.W. Bromiley and T.F. Torrance (eds.), Edinburgh: T&T Clark, 1960). See, more recently, N.M. Healy, 'Karl Barth's Ecclesiology Reconsidered' in *Scottish Journal of Theology* 57 (2004), pp. 287-299.

[28] On Bonhoeffer see K.W. Clements, *What Freedom? The Persistent challenge of Dietrich Bonhoeffer* (Bristol: Bristol Baptist College, 1990), K.W. Clements, *A Patriotism for Today: Dialogue with Dietrich Bonhoeffer* (Bristol: Bristol Baptist College, 1984) E. Bethge, *Dietrich Bonhoeffer* (London: Collins, 1970) and Stephen Plant, *Bonhoeffer* (London: Continuum, 2004).

[29] D. Bonhoeffer, *The Cost of Discipleship* (English Translation from German original *Nachfolge,* Münich: Kaiser Verlag, 1937; London: SCM, 1948).

[30] D. Bonhoeffer, *Life Together* (ET from German original *Gemeinsames Leben,* Münich: Kaiser Verlag, 1937; London: SCM, 1954).

[31] J. Moltmann, *The Church in the Power of the Spirit: A Contribution to Messianic Ecclesiology* (New York: Harper and Row, 1977).

Paul Avis has written widely about ecclesiology.[32] There has also been the development of journals, such as *Pro Ecclesia* and *Ecclesiology*, strengthening the sense that ecclesiology is firmly on the agenda.

The major twentieth-century European theologian from within the gathering church tradition who has addressed these issues is Miroslav Volf. In *After Our Likeness: The Church as the Image of the Trinity*, [33] Volf asserts that there is 'no church without the reign of God' and that there is 'no reign of God without the Church'.[34] The idea that the Church is God's and that it lives from something and towards something greater than itself is a theme which has motivated the present study. The move towards 'something greater' is taken up as a model by another gathering church theologian, Stanley Grenz, in his reflection on the Church as an eschatological community.[35] Grenz joins with J.D. Zizioulas, in recognising that, in the New Testament and during the first three centuries of Christian history, the local church was the prime ecclesial community.[36] This perspective on the Church has been worked out by, amongst others, J.W. McClendon,[37] though, like a number of Baptists working in a North American context, he offers a less adequate understanding of the Church as trans-local. For this we must turn primarily to European baptistic experience and theology.

Following Miroslav Volf, who is Croatian, I wish to focus, from a European perspective, not only on how inter-congregational relationships work out pragmatically, but also on wider theological issues. I wish to argue (as Volf has done) that a crucial calling for the Church – or for churches/ecclesial bodies such as the EBF – is to 'reflect in and of itself the eschatological catholicity of the people of God (albeit in a broken fashion) because it is itself a communion'.[38] Indeed both Bonhoeffer, from the national Confessing Church perspective, and Volf, as a gathering church theologian, portray a theological vision that has little to do with the many mundane issues that often occupy church leaders, such as juridical authority or effective management of church funds, but go right to the heart of what it is to be the Church. This has to do

---

[32] See, for instance, P. Avis, *A Church Drawing Near: Spirituality and Mission in a Post-Christian Culture* (London: T&T Clark, 2003).

[33] M. Volf, *After Our Likeness: The Church as the Image of the Trinity* (Cambridge and Grand Rapids, Mich: Eerdmans, 1998).

[34] *Ibid.*, p. x.

[35] S.J. Grenz, *Theology for the Community of God* (Carlisle: Paternoster, 1994), pp. 603-610.

[36] J.D. Zizioulas, *Being and Community: Studies in Personhood and the Church* (Crestwood, NY: St Vladimir's Seminary Press,1985), pp. 148-154. By 'local' I understand Zizioulas to mean a city.

[37] J.W. McClendon, Jr., *Systematic Theology: Doctrine*, vol. 2 (Nashville, Tenn.: Abingdon, 1994), pp. 331-372.

[38] *Ibid.*, p. 280.

with nothing less than the nature and purpose of the Triune God, the God who is community,[39] and in such heady waters the Church may be seen as a divinely-called organism which has significance in the proclamation of the Gospel. The call is to seek to identify with the *Missio Dei*.[40] Any ecclesial reality – such as the EBF – has to be rooted in an understanding of the Trinity and has, in the light of this, to have its place within the orthodoxy and orthopraxy of the larger Christian community.

Flowing from the idea of the Church being caught up with the purposes of God, another key concept for baptistic believers has been that of covenant. The British Baptist theologian, Paul Fiddes, with other colleagues, has been concerned to explore the idea of covenant as expressive of the divine purpose for humankind and also as a key ecclesial reality.[41] Drawing on seventeenth-century Baptist history in England, Fiddes takes up the Abingdon Association's argument of 1652 that there is the same relationship between a number of local churches associating together as there is between the different members of one local church.[42] Baptist theologians in Britain have explored this covenantal relationship, from the local to the inter-continental, in a succession of tracts offering reflections on the British Baptist Union's *Declaration of Principle* and on the theological nature of gatherings which draw together people from local churches into assemblies and councils of the wider Church.[43] Indeed, since the mid 1990s it has been clear that there has been a renewed interest among Baptists in the study of ecclesiology and the ecclesial nature of the more-than-local[44] which is at the heart of this exploration of the EBF.

'Help one another': Associating Together, 1596-1891

Although this study will range across Europe, the English Baptist tradition has contributed significantly to the concept of churches associating together. The 'catholic' view expressed in 'The Baptist Doctrine of the Church',[45] echoes

---

[39] Volf, *After Our Likeness*, especially chapters V and VI.

[40] D.J. Bosch, *Transforming Mission: Paradigm Shifts in Theology of Mission* (Maryknoll, New York: Orbis, 1991) pp. 10, 389-393.

[41] P. Fiddes, *Tracks and Traces: Baptist Identity in Church and Theology* (Carlisle: Paternoster, 2003), especially pp. 197-227.

[42] *Ibid.*, p. 199.

[43] The Baptist Union of Great Britain, Doctrine and Worship Committee, 'The Nature of the Assembly and the Council of the Baptist Union of Great Britain' (Didcot, 1994); R.L. Kidd (ed.), *Something to Declare* (Oxford: Whitley Publications, 1996); R.L. Kidd (ed.), *On the Way of Trust* (Oxford: Whitley Publications, 1997).

[44] For instance, the BWA and the German Baptist Union organised a Symposium on Baptist Ecclesial Identity Beyond the Local Church in March 2007.

[45] Hayden, 'The Baptist Doctrine of the Church'.

earlier Confessions of Faith produced by English Baptists.[46] The idea of local congregations associating together was set out in some of the earliest statements by the English Separatist Churches – out of which Baptist and Congregational communities emerged in England and Holland. One such document was *A True Confession*, produced in 1596 and emanating from one of these separatist communities, part of which was located in London and part in Amsterdam. The preface to the confession indicates that it was chiefly the work of the Amsterdam group and possibly of Henry Ainsworth, the pastor. Clause 38 states:

> That though Congregations bee thus distinct and severall bodyes, every one as a compact Citie in it self, yet are they all to walke by one and the same rule, and by all meanes convenient to have counsell and help one of another in all needfull affayres of the church, as members of one body in the common Faith, under Christ their head.[47]

The first Baptist Confession to offer an unambiguous statement of interdependency was the 1644 Confession, produced by seven Particular Baptist congregations in London. It has this section, which follows almost word for word the 1596 Separatist statement:

> Article XLVII
>
> And although the particular Congregations be distinct and several bodies, every one a compact and knit Citie in itselfe; yet are they all to walk by one and the same Rule, and by all meanes convenient to have counsel and help one another in all needfull affaires of the Church, as members of one body in the common faith under Christ their onley head.[48]

Thus, in one of the earliest English Baptist confessions there is a clear statement about the 'more-than-local relationship' between congregations holding to what the 1644 Confession describes as 'the same Rule'. They are to

---

[46] For purposes of brevity I deal here with statements by Baptists. These could be supplemented by examples from Anabaptists and other gathering or believer-church groupings in Europe who had a theology of the more-than-local interdependency of gathering congregations. On this see Durnbaugh, *The Believers' Church*, especially chapter XI; C.A. Snyder, *Anabaptist History and Theology: An Introduction* (Kitchener, Ont: Pandora, 1995); and G.H. Williams, *The Radical Reformation* (Philadelphia: Westminster, 1962).

[47] 'A True Confession' of 1596. Found in W.L. Lumpkin, *Baptist Confessions of Faith* (Valley Forge, Pa: Judson Press, 1969), p. 94. See also B.R. White, *The English Separatist Tradition* (London: Oxford University Press, 1971).

[48] Texts quoted are 1 Cor. 4:17, 14:33,36; Matt.8:20; 1 Tim. 3:15, 6:13-14; Rev. 22:18,19; Col. 2:6,19 and 4:16. The 1644 Confession of Faith is found in Lumpkin, *Baptist Confessions of Faith*, pp. 168-169.

discuss issues together and assist one another in all appropriate areas as part of one 'body' in a common faith.[49]

The next stage in the development of an ecclesial view that gave a significant place to the 'more-than-local' came through the life of the increasing number of local Baptist churches in England in the seventeenth century, both Particular and General Baptist Churches,[50] as they associated together. That Baptists have always been associational in nature and not strict independents is shown by the way in which, as persecution ceased for a time during the Cromwellian period in the mid 1600s in England, they took the opportunity to develop what were to be more permanent regional associations. This led to a flowering of documents describing the faith of the Baptist churches covenanting together within an association. Some of these associations were based on historic counties, but many were not tied to what might be seen as bounded geo-political areas; rather they came into being through the experiences of *koinonia* among the churches and also from missional developments. So ecclesial bodies comprising several churches soon emerged as a normal part of Baptist community life, for example among the General Baptists in areas such as Lincolnshire and Leicestershire in the English Midlands.[51]

As a result of a meeting of General Baptist communities in Lincolnshire, Leicestershire, and adjacent counties, a document was issued in 1651, *The Faith and Practice of Thirty Congregations, Gathered According to the Primitive Pattern.*[52] On a wider front, the Minutes of the (national) General Assembly of General Baptists date from 1654.[53] Thus, from the earliest days of the existence of Baptist congregations, the associational principle was not merely a pragmatic development, but a foundational point of ecclesial theology.[54] *The Faith and Practice of Thirty Congregations* reveals something of the nature of associating as an initiative from a group of local congregations.

---

[49] Fiddes uses the 1644 Confession to affirm the theology of associating in *Tracks and Traces*, pp. 6-10, 44, 55, 199-201, as does N.G. Wright, *Free Church: Free State* (Milton Keynes: Paternoster, 2005), p. 187.

[50] S. Wright, *The Early English Baptists, 1603-1649* (Woodbridge, Suffolk: The Boydell Press, 2006).

[51] See, for instance, I. Sellers (ed.), *Our Heritage: The Baptists of Yorkshire, Lancashire and Cheshire 1647-1987* (Leeds: Yorkshire Baptist Association and Lancashire & Cheshire Baptist Association, 1987).

[52] Lumpkin, *Baptist Confessions of Faith*, p. 171.

[53] W.T. Whitley (ed.), *Minutes of the General Assembly of General Baptists*, 2 vols. (London, 1910).

[54] Whitley, *A History of the British Baptists*, pp. 53-60. See also B.R. White, *The English Baptists of the 17th Century* (London: The Baptist Historical Society, 1983), pp. 51- 55; F.M.W. Harrison, *It All Began Here* (London: East Midland Baptist Association (Inc.), 1986), pp.13-29.

In the case of the General Assembly there was a clear desire to express ecclesial reality within a still wider grouping of churches. There were differences between the General and Particular Baptists[55] in terms of the authority that they gave to trans-local gatherings,[56] but, in declaring their beliefs, both strands of Baptist life were committed to a view of the church 'beyond the local'. The Confession of 1651 is important as it might be regarded as the first General Baptist statement representing more than one church. It shows essential theological agreement with the General Baptist Confession of 1611 from the Amsterdam congregation. The frontispiece of the 1651 document is of significance,[57] stating, as it does, that it is published 'by consent of two from each Congregation appointed for that purpose' and that its purpose was that the congregations 'may in love, and the spirit of Meekness, be informed by any that conceive they walk amiss'. The statement refers to the importance of a local congregation relating to other congregations in 'informing other congregations about poor people in need of help and about anyone who has been excommunicated from a local congregation'.[58] Paragraph 65 reads:

> That if the poor fearing God, cannot conveniently have a competent maintenance, for the supply of their necessities in that society whereunto they must commonly resort, that then those men [sic] that have the care laid upon them, send or give intelligence to the other Churches or saints of God, who have ingaged [sic] themselves by declaring their willingness towards the relief of such a distressed people, Rom. 15:26.[59]

Here we have a sense of mutual accountability that is both theological and practical.

The influential Particular Baptist *Second London Confession* of 1677 has two paragraphs on the relationship between the various local congregations:[60]

> 14. As each Church and all the Members of it, are bound to pray continually, for the good and prosperity of all the Churches of Christ, in all places; and upon all occasions to further it (every one within the bounds of their places, and callings, in the exercise of their Gifts and Graces) so the churches (when planted by the providence of God so as they may enjoy opportunity and advantage of it) ought to

---

55 For a re-examination of the similarities and differences between General and Particular Baptists see Wright, *The Early English Baptists*.

56 See White, *The English Separatist Tradition,* and Wright, *The Early English Baptists*.

57 Lumpkin, *Baptist Confessions of Faith*, p.174.

58 *Ibid.,* pp. 174-87.

59 *Ibid.,* p. 185, 'The Faith and Practice of thirty congregations Gathered According to the Primitive Pattern'.

60 *Ibid.,* p. 288.

hold communion amongst themselves for their peace, increase of love and mutual edification.

15. In cases of difficulties or differences, either in point of Doctrine, or administration; wherein either the Churches in general are concerned, or any one Church in their peace, union, and edification; or any member, or members, of any Church are injured, in or by any proceedings in censures not agreeable to truth, and order: it is according to the mind of Christ, that many Churches holding communion together, do by their messengers meet to consider, and give their advice in difference, to be reported to all the Churches concerned; howbeit these messengers assembled, are not entrusted with any Church-power properly so called; or with any jurisdiction over the Churches themselves, to exercise any censures either over any Churches or Persons: or to impose their determination on the Churches or Officers.

These paragraphs call upon the churches to be in a relationship of communion with each other, to hold meetings at which each member church sends Messengers to consider matters of mutual concern, and to give advice, with the advice being reported to all the churches within the communion. But such gatherings, for the Particular Baptist churches, were to issue advice, and this does not imply a jurisdiction over the congregations or the ability to impose a determination from the larger gathering on a particular congregation. Here we see the wider ecclesial understanding of early Particular Baptists. This would later be modified in some of the emerging Baptist Unions and Conventions elsewhere in the world. Nevertheless, the *Second London Confession* is an important reference point in building the theological framework of early – and later – Baptist understanding in Europe, an understanding out of which the EBF was to be formed.[61]

The emphasis on a deeper form of communion as an aspect of the associational principle was taken in a different direction by the Orthodox Creed of 1678/1679.[62] This Creed was developed within the General Baptist churches and especially a group in the south midland counties of Buckinghamshire, Hertfordshire, Bedfordshire and Oxfordshire. On 30 January 1678 fifty-four Messengers, Elders and Brethren met. Lumpkin[63] claims that the work was principally that of Thomas Monck, a farmer and Messenger of Buckinghamshire. This creed was aimed at establishing the orthodoxy of the English General Baptists, but it is noteworthy for the way it sets out the

[61] H. Cook and E.A. Payne, key figures in developing the ecclesial reality and theology of the EBF, were much influenced from their historical studies by this Confession, and the later EBF document, *What are Baptists? (*Hamburg, European Baptist Federation, 1993) draws attention to this historic background.

[62] Lumpkin, *Baptist Confessions of Faith,* pp. 295-334.

[63] *Ibid.,* p. 295.

ecclesial reality of churches associating together. Article XXXIX reads:[64]

> General councils, or assemblies, consisting of Bishops, Elders and Brethren, of the several churches of Christ, and being legally convened, and met together out of all the churches, and the churches appearing there by their representatives, make but one church, and have lawful right, and suffrage, in this general meeting, or assembly, to act in the name of Christ; it being of divine authority, and is the best means under heaven to preserve unity, to prevent heresy, and superintendency among, or in any congregation whatsoever within its own limits, or jurisdiction. And to such a meeting, or assembly, appeals ought to be made, in case any injustice be done, or heresy, and schism countenanced, in any particular congregation of Christ, and the decisive voice in such general assemblies is the major part, and such general assemblies have lawful power to hear, and determine, as also to excommunicate.

Here the claim is made that such general assemblies, being lawfully convened, can have a deeper form of communion by making common decisions together and that they have an ecclesial function given to them in preserving the unity of the believers, preventing heresy and providing a form of oversight, or *episkope*.

The idea of interdependency being sustained by real *koinonia* between local churches and their pastors has been a recurrent ecclesiological theme amongst English Baptists. An example is the case of Dan Taylor, who became the leading figure in the New Connexion of General Baptists (formed in 1770), and his Birchcliffe church in Yorkshire. Taylor became concerned in the late 1760s about the theological views of some of the General Baptist churches within the Lincolnshire Association and the London General Assembly, of which they were members. The General Baptist Messenger, Gilbert Boyce (exercising a form of *episkope*), wrote to Taylor as follows:

> Do, my brother, carefully weigh and seriously consider the vast importance of peace and unity, and whether there is sufficient reason for the separation now in agitation.... If once we begin to divide and separate, away fly love and christian affection; shyness, indifferency and evil-surmisings enter in and make way, not to bring us nearer, but to keep us at a greater distance from one another.[65]

Though Dan Taylor did later separate from the old General Baptists, who increasingly displayed features of a unitarian, rather than a trinitarian understanding in theology, Taylor was very conscious of the place of a depth of relationship between churches and pastors, and his New Connexion of General

[64] *Ibid.*, p. 327.

[65] Dan Taylor was to lead the New Connexion of General Baptists, formed in 1770. This united with the Particular Baptists in 1891 to form the Baptist Union of Great Britain and Ireland. The letter of Boyce is quoted in A. Taylor, *Memoirs of Dan Taylor* (London: Baynes and Son, 1820), p. 75.

Baptists retained much of the old General Baptist emphasis on the churches working together.[66] Indeed, like many other Baptists in Europe since then, he was concerned to foster good fellowship with others who basically shared his evangelical tenets. Thus, in his home community of Hebden Bridge, he enjoyed close fellowship with his neighbour, the Particular Baptist, John Fawcett. As Adam Taylor notes:

> Dr Fawcett accepted the office of pastor over the Particular Baptist Church at Wainsgate. A congenial taste for literature and equal zeal for religion soon produced an intimacy between these two ministers [Fawcett and Taylor], which, notwithstanding their differences of sentiments on points of doctrine, ripened into a friendship that was never interrupted through the course of their long lives... three young men were in the habit of meeting regularly, three or four times a week, either at Mr Fawcett's or Mr Taylor's to improve their knowledge of divinity, read the classics and cultivate other branches of learning.[67]

J.H.Y. Briggs argues that though there was some isolationism amongst certain Baptists in the second half of the 1700s, commitment to associating and interdependency re-asserted itself in strength during the 1800s, partly as a feature of the Evangelical Revival. [68] As new associational structures developed,[69] they had an urgent missionary purpose.[70] This aspect of interdependency will feature prominently in our study of the EBF. In the context of social and political turmoil in Europe, not least the French Revolution, associating together for mission, for mutual support and for encouragement became a high priority for Baptists.[71] The Associations became prime promoters of mission endeavour, especially in making a response to the expanding towns of the industrial revolution.[72] The work of overseas mission grew apace.[73] The challenges of the expanding mission fields at home and overseas meant that associations were drawn into new responsibilities – raising funds for the erection of buildings, helping to support poorly paid pastors,

---

[66] See F. Rinaldi, *The Tribe of Dan: The New Connexion of General Baptists 1770-1891* (Carlisle: Paternoster, 2008).

[67] Taylor, *Memoirs of Dan Taylor*, pp. 31, 32. The third person referred to is the Revd H. Foster, later a celebrated divine of the Church of England.

[68] J.H.Y. Briggs, *The English Baptists of the 19th Century* (Didcot: The Baptist Historical Society, 1994), pp. 199-204.

[69] J.H.Y. Briggs, 'Confessional Identity, Denominational Institutions and Relations with Others: A Study in Changing Contexts', in Thompson and Cross, *Recycling the Past or Researching History?*, pp. 1-24.

[70] See G.F. Nuttall, 'Assemblies and Associations in Dissent', *Studies in Church History* 7 (1971), pp. 304-5.

[71] As an example see Sellers, *Our Heritage*, p. 21-38.

[72] Briggs, *The English Baptists of the 19th Century*, p. 207-47.

[73] B. Stanley, *The Baptist Missionary Society 1792-1992* (Edinburgh: T&T Clark, 1992).

beginning the modest development of retirement funds, and raising money for overseas missionaries. Nationally, associating strengthened with the development of a Baptist Union. Though at first it was minimal in nature, by 1832 a more substantial development occurred,[74] and this national organisation began to engage in commenting on issues in society, for example passing resolutions on such issues as slavery, including addressing these concerns to the American Triennial Convention of Baptist Churches.[75] Most significantly, during the nineteenth century General and Particular Baptists worked together and interchanged ministers and mission resources. This almost naturally culminated, at the meetings of the General Baptist Association of the New Connexion at Burnley in 1891 under the presidency of John Clifford, in an agreement to respond to an invitation of the Baptist Union which enabled Particular and General Baptists to associate formally around a broad evangelical theology and without narrow doctrinal tests.[76]

'Mutual participation': Wider European Developments

The development of Baptist life in continental Europe in the nineteenth century was initially on a very small scale, with a few pockets of indigenous growth and missionary impetus, for example in France.[77] In some places Baptists were indebted to Pietism,[78] whilst in other places Baptists grew out of existing different types of evangelical renewal groups which had no contact with Germany.[79] However, a hugely important step forward was taken following the adoption of a Baptist form of church life by Johann Gerhard Oncken (1800-1884), who was baptised by the American Baptist, Barnabas Sears, in the Elbe at Hamburg on 22 April 1834. The vigorous church that Oncken developed in Hamburg, though persecuted, made contact with many German merchants and tradesmen from all over Europe who were working in the city, and a whole pattern of German-speaking Baptist churches was established throughout Europe in the succeeding years.[80] In 1849 fifty-six Baptist representatives met

---

[74] Briggs, *The English Baptists of the 19th Century*, p. 214.

[75] See W.H. Brackney, *The Baptists* (New York: Greenwood Press, 1988), pp. 15-17.

[76] Here it is safer to trust the analysis of J.H.Y. Briggs than the comments of H.L. McBeth in *The Baptist Heritage* (Nashville, Tenn., 1987), pp. 510, 517.

[77] See, for instance, S. Fath 'A Forgotten Missionary Link: The Baptist Continental Society in France (1831-1936)', *BQ*, Vol. 40, No. 3 (July 2003), pp. 133-51.

[78] W.R. Ward, *Early Evangelicalism: a global intellectual history, 1670-1789* (Cambridge: Cambridge University Press, 2006).

[79] See I.M. Randall, '"Pious Wishes": Baptists and wider renewal movements in nineteenth-century Europe', *BQ*, Vol. XXXVIII, No. 7 (July 2000), pp. 316-31.

[80] The most comprehensive account of the life and work of Oncken is by the German Baptist historian G. Balders, *Theurer Bruder Oncken: Das Leben Johann Gerhard Onckens* (Kassel, Wuppertal: Oncken Verlag, 1978).

in Hamburg and organised what was called the Union of Associated Churches of Baptised Christians in Germany and Denmark. The reason given by Oncken for the creation of the Union was theological and missiological: 'Every apostolic Christian church must be a Mission Society... but the mission work must be furthered by the joining together of more churches'.[81] Oncken himself conducted preaching tours in the Balkans, France, Hungary, Prussia and Russia. Churches which were to become very important in the establishment of national Baptist groupings, including what became a very large congregation in Memel, Lithuania,[82] and a church in Prague,[83] came out of the work of Oncken and his colleagues. Oncken and his missionaries had a hand in the formation of other Baptist leaders, such as Gottfried F. Alf,[84] in Poland, who were significant church-planting missionaries. Oncken baptised several carpenters working in Hamburg and, as they went back to German-speaking communities elsewhere in Europe, so the connectedness of Baptists engaged in church planting existed like a web across the continent. Friedrich Mayer started work in Switzerland, Joseph Rottmaier in Hungary and Karl Johann Scharschmidt in Romania. All remained interconnected in the development of Baptist life and witness.[85]

Throughout this development of early continental Baptist communities using the German language, there was an importance placed on interdependency and on *koinonia* and this can be detected in the Confession of Faith drawn up in 1913 by Johann Kargel, who had trained in Oncken's Baptist Seminary in Hamburg and who became a leading figure in the Russian Baptist community. His Confession was used as a statement of faith by Russian Baptists through to the 1980s. This Confession reads:

> The universal Church of Christ is built upon the foundation of the apostles and prophets, Christ Jesus Himself being the cornerstone. She consists of those who are saved, who believe, who are called to be saints, who are in this world as well as the saved ones who have gone to be with the Lord. Those and these are

---

[81] W.L. Wagner, *New Move Forward in Europe* (South Pasadena, Ca.: William Carey Library, 1978), p. 13, from the Union 'Protokol' of 1849; *cf.* I.M. Randall, '"Every Apostolic Church a Mission Society": European Baptist Origins and Identity', in A.R. Cross (ed.), *Ecumenism and History: Studies in Honour of John H. Y. Briggs* (Carlisle: Paternoster, 2002), pp. 281-301.

[82] Memel (1841), now called Klaipeda, in Lithuania, formerly Prussia. See also R. Lysenkaite 'The Place of Cultural Heritage in the Context of Contemporary Baptist Identity: A Case Study of Klaipeda Baptist Church', unpubl. MTh dissertation (International Baptist Theological Seminary, Prague, 2003).

[83] J. Novotny, *The Baptist Romance in the Heart of Europe: The Life and Times of Henry Novotny* (New York: Czechoslovak Baptist Convention in America and Canada, undated).

[84] A.W. Wardin, Jr., *Gottfried F Alf: Pioneer of the Baptist Movement in Poland* (Nashville Tenn.: Baptist History and Heritage, 2003).

[85] See Randall 'Every Apostolic Church a Mission Society', pp. 281-301.

> constituting one body whose head is Christ. And although the members of this church are from different nations, different situations and have different gifts, they all are one in Christ and individually members one with another.
>
> The single local churches [gathering communities] are only part of one universal Church; they are built by the Lord in different countries, cities and local places for the uniting of the saved children of God on earth, for the unified praising of God, for the growth of the members in the knowledge of God and Christ, for upbuilding in the life of faith after the image of Christ, for the mutual participation in all this and for the spreading of the Kingdom of God on earth.[86]

Although the German Baptists offer the clearest example of a union of Baptists with 'mutual participation' across national boundaries, the experience of networking around a common *koinonia* was also to be found in Europe by the 1930s in other groups, such as a Latin group (Belgium, France, Spain, Portugal and Italy) which met together and which also incorporated delegates from the Anglo-Saxon world.[87]

European Baptists, therefore, developed an ecclesiology that embraced a concept of interdependency and gave a central place to 'apostolicity' expressed through the local community, through individuals and in the wider church, especially in its mission. This view is in contrast to that held by some Baptists in other parts of the world, especially Baptists in the southern states of the USA. Organisationally, however, the world family of Baptists came into being before the EBF, through the formation in 1905 of the BWA, and Baptists from America were deeply involved.[88] The relationship between the EBF and the BWA will be examined throughout this work, as there have been periods of disagreement about the nature of the relationship and which has the greater ecclesial reality. These issues relate to differing theological presuppositions as well as issues of personality and history, and taken as whole, they are of great significance. The BWA, having celebrated one hundred years of existence in 2005, has been undertaking a structural review and one element is the relationship between what the BWA calls the 'regions' (geographical regions) and the BWA itself. One key factor is that the General Secretary of each of the bodies equivalent to the EBF in Africa, Asia, the Americas and the Caribbean also has a role as a staff member of the BWA, with the title Regional Secretary.

---

[86] G.K. Parker, *Baptists in Europe: History and Confessions of Faith* (Nashville, Tenn.: Broadman, 1982), pp. 149-158.

[87] See S. Fath, 'The Impact of Charismatic Christianity on Traditional French Baptist Identity', in I.M. Randall, T. Pilli and A.R. Cross (eds.), *Baptist Identities: International Studies from the Seventeenth to the Twentieth Centuries* (Carlisle: Paternoster, 2006), pp. 77-91.

[88] The story of the BWA is told in R.V. Pierard (ed.), *Baptists Together in Christ 1905-2005: A Hundred-year History of the Baptist World Alliance* (Birmingham, Al.: Samford University Press, 2005).

This book will explore the tensions associated with this arrangement as they emerged in the early period of the development of the EBF and as they have become more apparent recently. The BWA has been seeking to map out clearly where it intends to go and whether the regions 'follow' the lead of the Alliance, or whether they are subject to the decisions of their member bodies in Council.[89]

Given that European Baptists have taken associating together, or interdependency, as a serious matter,[90] they have constructed, in the EBF, an ecclesial reality which displays aspects of the individual, corporate and translocal understanding of the community of faith. Membership of the organisation cannot be by individuals, but is based around the concept of covenanted bodies. Local churches associate together in national bodies – the Conventions, Unions or Fellowships[91] – and these bodies are given authority to join the EBF. It should be noted here that some bodies join the EBF but do not join the BWA and there have been bodies within the geographical area of the EBF in the past who were in membership with the BWA but not the EBF. There is no absolute consequential pattern of membership. The ecclesial community itself takes the decision to apply and the wider body accepts or rejects that application. The BWA, in the past, has attempted to suggest that membership of a continental grouping must always include membership of the world grouping, but for baptistic communities, associating has to have a value in terms of *koinonia* and mission. For example, the Swedish body, Interact (at one time known as the Őrebro Mission), which grew out of a radical

[89] Amongst the BWA regional bodies the EBF is unique in having legal status as a Swiss Verein, or association, and this is independent of any reference to the BWA. The achievement of this status in 2002 will be explored; it should not be underestimated.

[90] This assertion will be explored in subsequent chapters, but certainly the spread of Anabaptist communities and later baptistic churches across Europe has been driven by the twin Baptist features of associating and mission. From William Carey, of the Baptist Missionary Society, and Johann Oncken onwards, Baptist mission has been cooperative. The expansion of baptistic communities across Europe has relied on local churches in Europe associating together and driven by a missionary imperative, and when additional support has been needed (principally, though not exclusively, this has come from America) the vast majority of such support has been in the form of an associational, mission agency. On Carey see Mary Drewery, *William Carey* (London: Hodder & Stoughton, 1978).

[91] All three words are used within the EBF community. Union is a word which is linked with the development of Particular Baptist life and in communities influenced by English Baptists. Convention is a word which grew in prominence within North American Baptist life. Association or Fellowship are words that have been used within the European context and might generally be thought to denote a less covenantal theology.

evangelical movement in Sweden that in part had Baptist roots,[92] applied to join the EBF in 2005. It did so with the encouragement and support of the Baptist Union of Sweden and the application was accepted. The BWA asked why Interact did not also apply to join the BWA, but Interact made it plain that they had good *koinonia* with many communities in the EBF family and saw EBF membership as being important in their sense of mission. However, they could not immediately see these elements present when they considered a possible relationship with the BWA.[93]

The official Statutes of the EBF, dating from 2001, make clear that the purpose of the EBF is to:

> strengthen and draw together Baptists in Europe and the Middle East on the basis of their Christian witness and distinctive conviction, to encourage and inspire them in faith and fellowship and shared responsibility and to seek in all its endeavours to fulfil the will of Jesus Christ, Lord and Saviour.[94]

The relationship of the EBF to the BWA is also made clear, as is the role of the EBF as owner and operator of the International Baptist Theological Seminary (IBTS) in Prague, Czech Republic:

> The Association (EBF) is a body affiliated to the 'Baptist World Alliance'. It seeks to share its concerns and further its purposes.
>
> The EBF owns and operates the 'International Baptist Theological Seminary of the European Baptist Federation', located in Prague.[95]

These statements show that the EBF is an organisation which has its own life and purpose. Its member bodies are the framers of the statements. Currently, in 2009, there are over fifty member bodies.[96] The Statutes make clear that the EBF has not understood itself and does not believe itself to be an integrated 'region' of the BWA. Rather the EBF is affiliated to the BWA while at the same time having its own activities, operations and purpose as determined by

---

[92] E. Rudén, 'The Baptist Witness in Scandinavia and the North', *BQ*, Vol. XXVII, No. 2 (April 1979), p. 78.

[93] Verbal report of the EBF General Secretary to the EBF Executive Committee, March 2005, Prague, confirmed by the fact that Interact joined the EBF at the Council meeting later that year, but not the BWA. EBF General Council Minutes, September 2005 (Prague: EBF Archive).

[94] EBF Statutes, Article 2 on purpose (*European Baptist Federation Directory*, 2006).

[95] *Ibid.*

[96] The EBF works with a membership basis of associations – unions, conventions or similar. These are generally national entities. Membership is open in a limited way to individual local churches in situations where, currently, a wider grouping either does not exist or is not possible. Examples of this are a church on the island of Malta and the Baptist Church in Baghdad.

the membership, who meet annually in Council. It is the member bodies acting together that constitute the ecclesial identity of the EBF. This leads to a consideration of the member bodies.

'Member bodies': The Structure of the EBF

More will follow about the history and development of the EBF, but at this point something should be said about the current structure of the body being studied. The structure of the EBF, typical of Baptist ecclesiology, lays decision-making power within an assembly, or Council, of the member bodies.[97] The attendance at Council meetings is not limited, but there is a scheme giving votes to the member bodies and this scheme relates to the size of the bodies. So, automatically, either the President or the General Secretary of a member body[98] is present and, if present, has a vote, and additional representatives from that member body can have voting rights on the following scale:

Up to 10,000 members in a member body	1 additional representative
10,000 – 50,000 members	2 additional representatives
50,000 – 100,000 members	3 additional representatives
More than 100,000 members[99]	4 additional representatives.

In 2006 only the Baptist Unions of the Ukraine and Great Britain[100] fell into the

[97] I will use 'member bodies' henceforth to describe 'Union, Convention, Fellowship or Association' where organisations having one of these titles exist together in another structure such as the EBF or BWA.

[98] Historically Baptist bodies seem normally to have appointed a pastor to be the administrative and chief operating officer of a member body. The General Secretary is often the 'permanent' senior leader within a member body. It is a title people have struggled to equate with an 'office' in the New Testament and increasingly Baptist bodies throughout the world have been experimenting with other designations. So the Baptist Union of New Zealand has a 'National Leader' and the Baptist Union of Scotland a 'General Director'. The word 'Bishop' has been introduced in some Unions in place of 'President'. This is an on-going fluid situation amongst Baptists.

[99] For this purpose 'member' means a member of a local Baptist church in membership with the member body. It has its own theological problems as some member bodies have closed membership and some member bodies have within them believers who have not been baptised as believers, but perhaps have joined by transfer from another Christian church. The EBF has not sought to define tightly a member of a local church, leaving such definition to the member body.

[100] The Baptist Union of Great Britain has a rather anomalous name as there is a Baptist Union of Scotland and a Baptist Union of Wales. The Baptist Union of Great Britain is principally made up of Baptist churches in England and some English-speaking Baptist churches in Wales. Some of the churches in Wales are also aligned with the Baptist Union of Wales. The reasons for this complex situation are historic and outwith the scope of this study.

last category. The smallest member body in 2006 was the Union of Baptist Christians in the Republic of Macedonia, with two churches and a total of 70 members.[101]

Alongside these representatives of the member bodies, there is an element of the personal within the corporate; that is, those who hold special responsibility within the EBF for a specific task, committee or leadership role are given membership of the EBF Council in their own right while they hold such a position. Under the arrangements currently in force these people are: the EBF President; the Vice-President; the General Secretary; the Chairpersons of the Finance and Nominations Committees; the Chairpersons of the Divisions of Theology and Education; Communication; Mission and Evangelism and External Relations (four divisions); the Chairperson of the Board of Trustees of IBTS; the Rector of IBTS; the President of the European Baptist Women's Union; and the Chairperson of the EBF Youth Committee. In recent years others serving on the EBF Executive and thereby becoming voting members of Council have been a representative of the Middle East Unions and one person representing the Slavic Unions.[102] These are not fixed, but can vary from time to time. In addition the Women's Union and the Youth Committee are each allowed two additional Council members and the Nominations Committee suggest to Council up to four lay members (that is to say non-ordained)[103] whom Council appoints for a two-year period. The Council meets annually: every three to four years the meeting takes place at the European Baptist Centre in Prague;[104] otherwise the Council responds to any invitations received from member bodies. The Council elects and appoints EBF officers, the IBTS Rector and those with special responsibilities for committees and members of committees. It receives reports, makes resolutions, approves a budget and accounts and discusses in plenary and group sessions issues affecting Baptist life and mission. This is the present situation, but in the next chapter I shall seek to explain how this came to be developed over the course of fifty years.

---

[101] *EBF Directory*, 2006, p. 26.

[102] Though the EBF originally envisaged members being from the historic Europe west of the Urals and north of the Bosphorus, because of the collapse of the old political reality of the USSR and the need for Baptists in the Middle East to be part of a larger body which could strengthen them and support them, the boundaries of the EBF now extend far beyond Europe to north Africa, Iraq, and the areas bordering China including Kyrgystan, Tajikistan and Uzbekistan. This will be discussed further.

[103] There has been a concern that as the Council consists principally of 'officers' of member bodies these will generally be ordained pastors, with a male majority. To attempt to offset this, there is the possibility of the Nominations Committee proposing additional lay people.

[104] The European Baptist Centre campus includes the offices of the EBF, IBTS, Hotel Jenerálka (which is owned by the EBF IBTS Verein), and offices of American Baptist Churches USA (Europe region) and Canadian Baptist Ministries (Europe region).

The role of the officers of the EBF is vital and holds within it the outline shape and form of a translocal *episkope*. The President serves for a two-year term. The post is honorary. The President is normally a senior Baptist leader from a member body – a General Secretary, President or Rector of a seminary. The position traditionally moves around the parts of the EBF constituency, though not in an organised or definable way. A Vice-President is appointed for two years with the assumption of acceding to the Presidency.[105] The General Secretary is appointed by the Council and this post is full-time and salaried.[106] The General Secretary serves for a period of five years, which is renewable.[107] This aspect of the work of the EBF will also be examined fully in a later chapter. The General Secretary exercises a significant measure of personal oversight within the Baptist community in Europe and represents the European Baptist family to the BWA, to the Conference of European Churches and in other significant ecumenical ways. Whilst neither the Statutes nor the General Secretary's Job Description set these things out in detail, within the EBF family the General Secretary acquires a trust and influence of great weight. So, for instance, Unions will expect the General Secretary to visit their annual assemblies and give an address, be present at graduation ceremonies in the national seminaries, and in other ways being a representative trans-local figure.

The other full-time salaried post, with the appointment being the responsibility of the EBF Council, is the Rector of IBTS. Since the EBF acquired the seminary in 1988 there has been a parallel structure of an Executive Committee (Board of Trustees) for the seminary alongside the Executive Committee for the general work of the EBF. The General Secretary of the EBF serves on the IBTS Board of Trustees and the Rector of IBTS serves on the EBF Executive.[108] Thus IBTS is seen as a major component of the life and work of the EBF and merits its own chapter. Important issues of oversight and mission amongst European Baptists have found their focus in the life and affairs of the seminary. Indeed, the seminary was founded just before the EBF, and the EBF was founded out of meetings held in the seminary, so the two stories are inevitably and powerfully intertwined. The seminary will be seen to have been one of the essential defining strands of *koinonia* within the EBF as its alumni are to be found throughout the EBF family, and the work of the

---

[105] EBF Statutes, Articles 18, 19, 20 (*EBF Directory*, 2006).

[106] This was not so from the very beginning, but soon became so. It is totally funded by the member bodies through the annual budget.

[107] Most General Secretaries since the 1980s have served until retirement.

[108] Whilst the EBF Statutes make clear that the EBF Executive and the Board of Trustees are appointed by Council and directly answerable to the EBF Council, this device of having the chief executives of both organisations serve on the executive of the other organisation is intended to promote ease of communication and a common overall strategy. In the period 1988 to 2000 this was not always easy to obtain as subsequent chapters will show.

seminary is a matter of great interest to the Unions.

From the earliest days of the development of Baptist life in mainland Europe, there has been particular and sustained support for Baptists in Europe from Baptists in North America. In the case of the American Baptist Churches this interaction commenced when they assisted Johann Oncken with his salary as Baptist pastor in Hamburg. Today the EBF Constitution has, as non-voting members of Council, representatives of the following North American bodies:

> Canadian Baptist International Ministries, International Ministries of American Baptist Churches-USA, The International Mission Board of the Southern Baptist Convention, the North American Baptist Conference International Ministries and the Cooperative Baptist Fellowship.[109]

These bodies are not there because of some polite desire to have international guests at the Council, but because these are organisations who have been working intimately with Europeans in their life and mission over many years. The European desire to be in wider association, as expressed in the EBF, is deeply rooted. There are signs that the European perspective is being heard. Thus the 'Message from the Centenary Congress' of the BWA (2005), produced by a global team of scholars over a two-year period and accepted without dissent by the General Council of the BWA, states:

> Those assembled [at the Centenary Congress] believe our gathering churches, with other true Christian churches, are called to be witnesses to the Kingdom of God… Repent for not having prayed and worked hard enough to fulfil the prayer of Christ for the church's unity. We commit ourselves to pray and work to further the unity of Christian Believers. [110]

To this statement should be added a more explicit BWA commitment to interdependency, ecumenism and associating found in a longer study document.[111] This represents, to a large extent, the European Baptist view.

---

[109] EBF Statutes Article 8. 2 (*EBF Directory*, 2006).

[110] Paragraphs 7 and 9 of the BWA 'Message from the Centenary Congress', Birmingham, England, July 2005. The full text, in several languages, at http://www.bwanet.org/congress, accessed 18 January 2007.

[111] 'The Message from the Centenary Congress', BWA, 2005, has a whole section on the ecumenical movement and the dialogue with other Christian traditions. This suggests that the wider Baptist family, excluding the southern states of the USA, has no desire to be caught in some narrow ghetto, but to take interdependency beyond the boundaries of the Baptist world into a wider ecumenism.

Conclusion

The European Baptist belief in associating has been introduced and briefly explored in this chapter. This belief in interdependency between local gathering communities has been part of the Baptist story from the seventeenth century onwards. The way in which this has been worked out in the EBF will be investigated in detail in the course of this book. Chapter 2 will expand on the initial analysis that has been undertaken in this chapter, of the nature of Baptist ecclesiology and its expression in the EBF. Chapter 3 will seek to explore the EBF and its ecclesial reality in relation to the wider community of Christians in Europe in the historic Catholic, Orthodox, Protestant and evangelical traditions. This will include the part the EBF has played in talks with the community of Protestant churches in Europe as to whether there could be a real possibility of 'church fellowship'. The next chapter, 4, dissects the history and experience of one key element in the life of the EBF: IBTS. Chapter 5 explores the nature of personal oversight that has been exercised through the ministries of the EBF General Secretaries. Questions are pursued about the role of the concept of *episkope* in wider associating. Then follows a chapter (6) reflecting on the engagement of the EBF with mission agencies in the USA, particularly those of the American Baptist Churches-USA and the Southern Baptist Convention. Although basic baptistic theology asserts that associating is done between communities of believers, there are links with mission agencies that do not fit so neatly into an ecclesial model. Chapter 7 explores the cross-cultural effectiveness and the holistic mission vision of the EBF. Finally, the arguments of this book are brought to a conclusion.

CHAPTER 2

'Beyond the Local': The Ecclesiological Basis of the European Baptist Federation

In this chapter I am using, as an ecclesiological basis, a Baptist understanding of the prime ecclesial unit as the local gathering, convictional, intentional community of believers.[1] In historic Baptist thought, however, as has been seen, this kind of community is not independent, but interdependent, connected with other similar communities around a covenantal and intentional relationship and associating in trans-local ways – national, continental and international. This might be described as an ecclesiology from below, which has both corporate and individual aspects. I will set out briefly such a Baptist approach to ecclesiology specifically from a European perspective, noting, *inter alia*, the contrasts with some other baptistic communities in the world, and will then seek to show in detail how this is the ecclesial understanding of the European Baptist Federation (EBF). In the course of examining issues discussed during the formation of the EBF, I will make comparisons with other regional fellowships of the Baptist World Alliance (BWA), such as the North American Baptist Fellowship (NABF). It is significant that in *Baptists in America*[2] B.J. Leonard, a leading North American Baptist historian, makes no reference to the NABF (the North American 'equivalent' of the EBF), only to the BWA. The same is true of works by another leading North American Baptist historian, W.H. Brackney, in *The Baptists* and in *A Genetic History of Baptist Thought*.[3] Thus this chapter explores a particular expression of Baptist life – that found in Europe – to illuminate issues of Baptist ecclesiology.[4] The intention is to

---

[1] I have argued this particular formula in various publications, but most succinctly in 'Towards a Model of Mission for Gathering, Intentional, Convictional *Koinonia*', *Journal of European Baptist Studies*, Vol. 4, No. 2 (January 2004), pp. 5-13.

[2] B.J. Leonard, *Baptists in America* (New York: Columbia Press, 2005).

[3] W.H. Brackney, *The Baptists* (New York: Greenwood Press, 1988); W.H. Brackney, *A Genetic History of Baptist Thought* (Macon, Georgia: Mercer University Press, 2004).

[4] There will be a comparison later with similar groupings in other 'Christian World Communions'. This is the title used to describe the different Christian traditions which are seen to be orthodox and within what might be described as mainstream Christianity.

explore the way in which this type of ecclesiological reality developed in Europe and how far this informs aspects of Baptist ecclesiology.

'We experience interdependence': Baptist Ecclesiology

As has been argued earlier, I subscribe to the view that 'the distinctive feature about Baptists is their doctrine of the Church'.[5] In recent times various Baptist theologians have sought to identify and mark out a combination of theological assertions which might be said to characterise Baptists. One key declaration, not commonly featured amongst Baptists in the USA,[6] as I have argued earlier in Chapter One, is that Baptists are intentionally interdependent. Such an interdependent relationship is not simply pragmatic, but is of the essence of the theology appropriate to the believers' church tradition.[7] Some have accused those who advocate such an ecclesiology of adopting an incipiently sectarian stance, but, as Alan Sell comments 'while this is an ever present danger, if the concepts of discipleship and mission are to the fore in the community of faith, sectarian ghettoization will not be a necessary result'.[8] This point was emphasised in the 2005 BWA Centenary Congress message in the paragraph on the Church and the Kingdom, which reads:

> [We] 8. Declare that through the Holy Spirit we experience interdependence with those who share this dynamic discipleship of the church as the people of God.[9]

The whole of this statement expresses the thinking that has had a shaping influence on European Baptists.

Interdependent relationships, entered into by local covenanted communities of believers, are not bound to a specific micro-geographical area, but can be recognised in regional, national, continental and international arenas, as the BWA Centenary Congress Message makes clear. The basic model is of the local covenanted gathering church being driven by the Holy Spirit to participate in such trans-local relationships freely and for theological and missiological

---

The General Secretaries (or equivalents) of the world expressions of these various denominations meet annually and are a recognised grouping to which the World Council of Churches, World Evangelical Alliance and others relate.

[5] W.T. Whitley, *A History of British Baptists*, rev. ed. (London: Kingsgate, 1932), p. 4.

[6] See, for instance, D.K. McCall with A.R. Tonks, *Duke McCall: An Oral History* (Brentwood, Tenn.: Baptist History and Heritage Society/Nashville: Fields, 2001).

[7] Believers' church is used here as defined by D.F. Durnbaugh in *The Believers' Church: the History and Character of Radical Protestantism* (New York: The MacMillan Company, 1968).

[8] A.P.F. Sell, *Confessing and Commending the Faith* (Cardiff: University of Wales Press, 2002), p. 45.

[9] BWA 'Message from the Centenary Congress', Birmingham, England, July 2005 at http://www.bwanet.org/congress, para. 8, accessed 20 January 2007.

reasons, as an outcome of their worship of the Triune God. For local gathering communities, which then directly understand the Holy Spirit to be encouraging them to recognise they already participate in the one holy catholic and orthodox church and should therefore join and participate in regional and national Baptist ecclesial groupings, there is also a covenant of trust,[10] that empowers and permits the national officers and councils of these groupings to join continental and intercontinental ecclesial-like groupings as if the local church itself made the move towards such wide-scale interdependency. The ecclesial form thus described places the weight of ecclesiology on the local, as opposed to the international, continental, national or regional bodies (in contradistinction to many other Christian traditions), but I will argue that it gives real substance to the ecclesial nature of the 'more-than-local', trans-local, trans-national and trans-continental elements and, though it is principally an ecclesiology from below, it is not vacuous in the other spheres of the more-than-local.

This is a key theological point, because it places the formation of the EBF within a historic Baptist pattern of always seeking to build ecclesial trans-local life outwards from the prime notion of the local church as the base ecclesiological unit, with all other structures being derived in a pyramidical way from the core ecclesial reality. The different ways of conceiving Baptist ecclesial life can be considered diagrammatically.

The Baptist Pyramid
(Diagram 1)

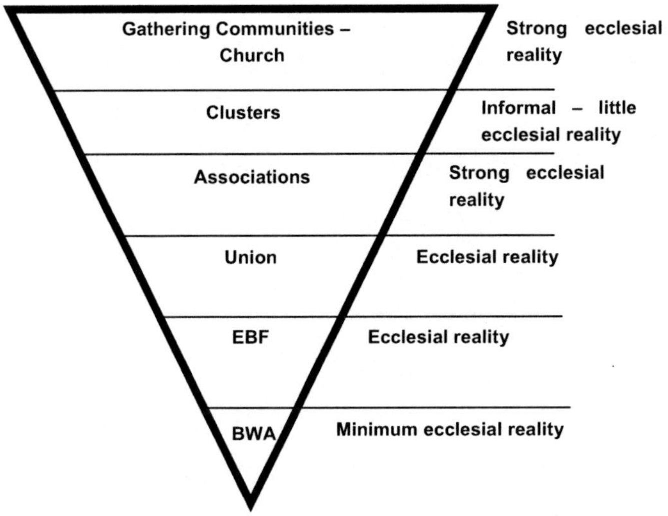

[10] See R. Kidd (ed.), *On the Way of Trust* (Oxford: Whitley Publications, 1997), pp. 22-

In contrast to this model of ecclesial relationships, Jonathan Edwards, the General Secretary of the Baptist Union of Great Britain, argues for a series of concentric circles and this is the view of some other leading European Baptists.[11]

The Baptist Concentric Circles
(Diagram 2)

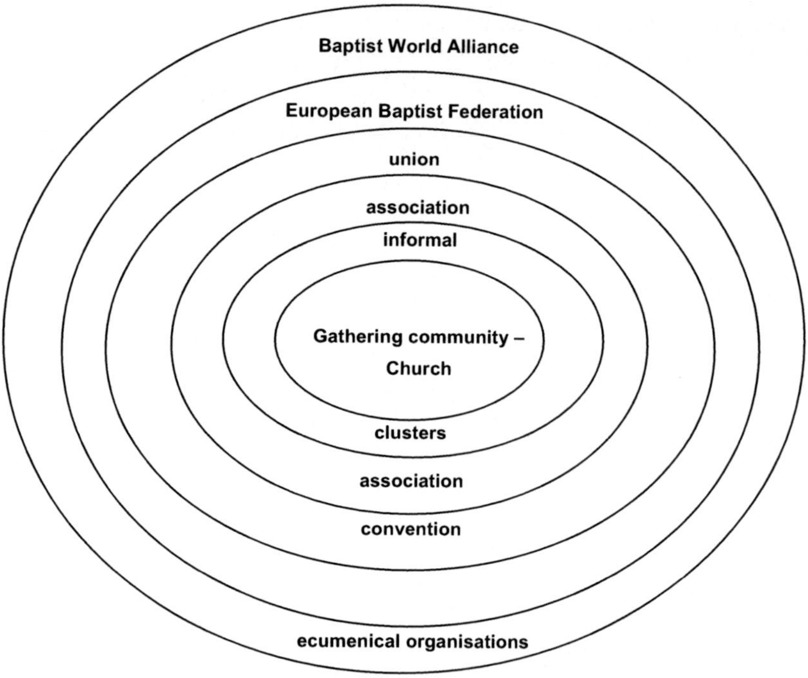

4, on 'covenant, union and alliance'.

[11] Jonathan Edwards expressed this point of view at a Workshop on the future structure of the BWA on 30 September 2006 at Valpre, Lyon, France. Personal recollection of the author.

My view is that in contemporary Baptist life the gathering baptistic churches best relate and resource each other in something more akin to a web than either a pyramid or concentric circles, and the theologising behind such an approach is spelt out by N.G. Wright.[12]

The Baptistic Web
(Diagram 3)

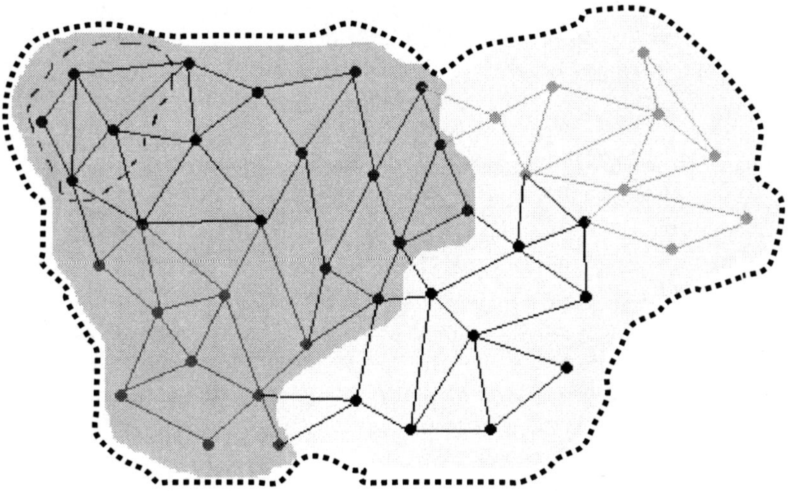

Note: Some gathering communities have connections beyond their clusters and out of their associations. There are cross-cultural links between gathering communities across the boundaries of union through church partnerships. Some have an ecumenical dimension, especially in the clusters.

Dots:	gathering communities
Lines:	association(s)
▬ ▬ ▬ ▬ ▬	cluster(s)
Shaded regions:	union(s)
•••••••••••	continental federation

[12] N.G. Wright, *Free Church, Free State: The Positive Baptist View* (Milton Keynes: Paternoster, 2005).

In whatever way we try to express diagrammatically the ecclesial nature of baptistic communities, what is very clear is that, for Europeans, there is an ecclesial life and reality beyond the local and that normally this is by gathering communities associating together and then by those bodies associating with one another.

This issue of wider partnerships between Baptists will be explored by looking in detail at the development of the EBF from the 1940s, but it is important to note that this issue is a matter of ongoing discussion among European Baptists. The question of Baptist ecclesiology as expressed in a pan-European context was examined in a Study Paper which arose out of an EBF Consultation on Baptist Mission held in Dorfweil, Germany, 26-29 January 1992.[13] A draft document produced on that occasion was handed to the members of the EBF Theology and Education Division who prepared explanatory clauses. The draft document was circulated amongst the Baptist Unions of Europe, and their responses were carefully considered by the core group of the Division, then reported to a meeting of Baptist Theological Teachers in Europe held in July 1992, where the document was discussed and refined. The EBF Council, meeting in High Leigh, Hertfordshire, England, in September 1992, asked the Theology and Education Division to reflect further on the topic and issue a paper 'in process' to the wider European family. Paul Fiddes, the Principal of Regent's Park College, Oxford, and a leading European Baptist theologian, was deeply involved in this process. The minutes of the EBF Council meeting record:

> Dr Paul Fiddes… spoke of the statement on Baptist identity which was circulated to members. He pointed out that this was not a formal Confession of faith, but rather a statement of theological viewpoints, reflecting diversity and unity among Baptists in Europe. The target audience, he said, was members and especially leaders of other churches and denominations, and for our own members to raise awareness of their identity. It was meant also to help in mission and arose out of the Dorfweil Consultation on Mission. As we evangelise we need to explain who we are.[14]

In the discussion which followed the presentation by Paul Fiddes, Council members asked a number of questions for clarification, and suggestions were made as to how the document could be strengthened. One of the issues was that of associations that were 'beyond the local'. By a show of hands it was agreed to refer the document back to the Division to take account of the points made

---

[13] 'What are Baptists? On the way to expressing Baptist Identity in a Changing Europe', Study Paper issued by the Division for Theology and Education of the EBF, Oxford, 1993.

[14] Minutes of the EBF Council, October 1992, p. 8, minute 17.11, EBF Archive, IBTS Library, Prague.

and then issue the document as a Study Paper in process.[15]

After the Theology and Education Division had met again in Moldova in 1993, the paper was issued and has continued to form an important document seeking to express who European Baptists are and to promote dialogue amongst the churches and unions about European Baptist theology, ecclesiology and identity. The document states that in associating beyond the local:

> We believe that the mutual commitment expressed in baptism and in membership of the local church should lead to wider partnerships between churches wherever possible.[16]

The explanatory text of this study document goes on to comment in a highly significant way:

> From the very beginning of their history, local Baptist churches have sought fellowship with other churches, for mutual encouragement, guidance, sharing of mission and as a sign of reconciliation for the world. Baptist churches form local associations with other Baptist churches, coming together into a Union of churches at national level.[17]

This document, coming out of the life of the EBF, more than forty years after its founding, exhibits two cardinal ecclesiological points which European Baptists appear to hold to and which, as will be demonstrated, belong to the foundation of the EBF.

'To further Baptist work': The Founding of the EBF

The founding of the EBF took place in the aftermath of the Second World War. There had, of course, been many earlier contacts between Baptists in Europe, and several unions belonged to the BWA, which was founded in 1905.[18] However, the long-standing desire of churches and unions in Europe to have a pan-European organisation with a specific European identity, pattern and vision was brought into focus in the context of a BWA European Conference held in London from 13-17 August 1948. At this Conference a sub-committee was appointed to look at closer cooperation in Europe, and this sub-committee recommended:

---

[15] *Ibid.*

[16] 'What are Baptists?', Study Paper, p. 3.

[17] *Ibid.*, p. 1.

[18] The BWA, founded in 1905, now consists of over 200 Unions and Conventions with 43 million church members and an estimated community strength of more than 100 million. These figures are based on the work of the Study and Research Division presented to the BWA General Council, July 2001, in Canada and are contained in the official Report Book of the Council (Falls Church, Virginia: BWA Archive).

> That the Baptists of Europe be encouraged to plan for a closer fellowship between the various national Baptist bodies, and that the European members of the Executive Committee of the BWA constitute a planning committee to form a European Baptist Committee on Co-operation to further Baptist work in Europe.[19]

In fact, the Committee of Seven, as it came to be known, recommended to the unions in Europe rather more than a 'Committee on Co-operation'. They proposed an organisation with a real measure of ecclesial life to it.

This 1948 conference spoke about a model in which the European organisation would, in effect, be created out of the BWA.[20] However, the Committee of Seven (followed by a later group which prepared an appropriate Constitution and Bye-Laws), proposed a European body with obvious resonance with the theology and structures of the national unions. This was in contrast to the pragmatic cooperation of the BWA, which was, at that time (and has increasingly become) more of a mixed society of unions or conventions of churches, representatives of mission agencies, and individuals, and much less a gathering of representatives of national unions elected to that task and operating through a council in an ecclesial way. This can be clearly seen in the current BWA Bye-Laws, as amended in Spain in 2002, where – though the membership is of '[a] Baptist body… [which] shall have an identity of its own and shall not exist as an integral part of some other union or convention'[21] – there is a whole section[22] providing for any Baptist church, organised group (university, college, seminary, mission organisation, social welfare or diakonic society) or individual to become an associate or personal member, providing they pay an appropriate membership fee. This approach is rejected in the Constitution of the EBF which declares in its Statutes[23] that only Unions, Conventions or similar Baptist bodies can be members. Here the ecclesial thinking of the EBF, by contrast with the BWA, is clearly expressed. The BWA appears to take the form of the missionary or voluntary society model, rather than the ecclesial case I am arguing for the EBF.[24]

The Committee of Seven which was established to create the EBF was drawn from Great Britain, Denmark, Germany, Italy, France, Switzerland and Holland, thus representing several significant streams of Baptist life in Europe – English General Baptist, Particular Baptist, churches across Europe stemming from the work of Oncken in the nineteenth century, and those who valued the

---

[19] Minutes of the EBF Council, 1950, p. 1, Box 801, EBF Archive, Prague.

[20] *Ibid.,* p. 2.

[21] BWA Bye-Law I.1 and 2, *2005 Yearbook of the Baptist World Alliance* (BWA Archive, Falls Church, Virginia, 2005), p. 110.

[22] *Ibid.,* p. 111.

[23] EBF Statutes, Article 3 on Membership (*EBF Directory,* 2006), p. 3.

[24] This point of view is argued by J.H.Y. Briggs in an unpublished paper on the BWA revised constitution prepared for BWA General Secretary, Denton Lotz, in 2002.

heritage of the Anabaptists, especially the Swiss and the Dutch. The Committee of Seven thus reflected the mixed heritage of European Baptist life from the seventeenth to the nineteenth centuries. At their first meeting in Switzerland on 8th October 1949 they moved away from the BWA Conference's suggestion for a European Baptist Committee of Co-operation, and instead proposed that the title of the new organisation should be the European Baptist Federation.[25] This clearly expressed their desire, after starting with the local gathering community of believers as the heart of an ecclesial expression, to spread outwards in relationship to other communities. It should be noted that though the first initiative had, no doubt realistically, come from within the BWA,[26] it was not seen by European Baptists to be theologically correct or appropriate for this group to be a regional sub-division of the BWA.[27] This contrasts with other regions of the BWA, for instance the North American Baptist Fellowship (NABF), which, as one of their leaders commented to me recently, 'would not exist if it were not for the prior existence of the Baptist World Alliance'.[28] For theological and ecclesial reasons, such a view would be anathema to the majority of European Baptists, although it has to be acknowledged that a minority of European leaders, such as Hans Luckey of Germany, intended that the EBF should be 'a finger which the hand of the Alliance can use in Europe'.[29]

It is noteworthy that the three members of the initial Committee of Seven who were asked to meet to produce the final detail of the first Constitution of the EBF were Henry Cook from Great Britain – who had given particular attention to Baptist ecclesiology,[30] – Bredhal Petersen of Denmark[31] and W.O. Lewis[32] of the BWA staff. They met in Copenhagen on 23 February 1950 to

---

[25] Minutes of the EBF Council, 8 October 1949, p. 1, Box 801, EBF Archive.

[26] Pierard (ed.), *Baptists Together in Christ 1905-2005*. Full details of the work of the BWA can be found on their website: http://www.bwanet.org.

[27] Minutes of the EBF Council, 8 October 1949, p. 1, Box 801, EBF Archive, Prague.

[28] Personal comment made to me by Gary Nelson, General Secretary, Canadian Baptist Ministries, Mexico City, July 2006.

[29] Quoted in a letter from H. Cook to W.O. Lewis, 29 December 1955 (BWA/EBF Letters Box 27, Angus Library, Regent's Park College, Oxford).

[30] H. Cook, *What Baptists Stand For* (London: Carey Kingsgate Press, 1947), Chapter II, 'The Nature of the Church'.

[31] B. Petersen was a well-travelled pastor of one of the main churches in Copenhagen. At this time he was joined by an assistant pastor, Knud Wümpelmann, who was later to be EBF General Secretary. See B. Hylleberg, 'Knud Wümplemann', *Journal of European Baptist Studies*, Vol. 2, No. 3 (Prague: IBTS, May 2002), pp. 5-20.

[32] W.O. Lewis was Associate General Secretary of the BWA based at Baptist Church House in London. He served as Director of Relief work as well as taking care of Baptist issues in the eastern hemisphere.

plan the launch of the EBF.[33] Cook's view was that Baptists begin with the doctrine of the Church and their view of baptism arises directly out of it, expressed in *What Baptists Stand For*,[34] in which he noted, with approval,[35] Whitley's emphasis on the fact that the importance of the local church should never be stressed in such a way as to deny the importance of 'sisterly intercourse' with other churches.[36] Cook went on to note the strength of the interdependent principle elucidated in the 1664 Confession of Faith of the London Particular Baptists, and then he commented that both General and Particular Baptists, 'deliberately linked their churches, both to steady one another in doctrine and explain themselves unitedly to the world, to aid one another in time of need and especially to propagate their views'.[37] Further, Cook argued:

> It is interesting to note that this sense of unity that was so conspicuous a mark of early Baptist churches in England was even more strongly emphasised by the Anabaptist communities on the Continent. They never were and never sought to be Independents; on the contrary, whenever they were free enough from persecution to create an organization, they never failed to institute, after the example of the Waldenses and the Bohemian Brethren, a system with a general superintendency, an itinerant ministry, and a clearly defined interdependency of the local congregations.[38]

To make the point absolutely clear (and no doubt take the strength of his conviction into the committee which established the EBF), Henry Cook made the following claim:

> It comes then to this, that Baptists at the beginning were Congregationalists, but not Independents; that is to say, they believed in the gathered church.... But they set their faces against isolationism, and they regarded local churches as livingly related for the common ends of the Gospel.[39]

Cook, Petersen and Lewis gathered with representatives from ten countries,[40]

---

33 Minutes of the EBF Council, 23 February 1950, Box 801, EBF Archive.
34 Cook, *What Baptists Stand For*, p.113.
35 *Ibid.*, p. 84.
36 Whitley, *A History of British Baptists*, p. 86-87.
37 Cook, *What Baptists Stand For*, p. 85.
38 *Ibid.*, p. 85.
39 *Ibid.*, p. 85.
40 Representatives from Spain, Portugal and Finland had also expressed a strong desire to be present, but had no funds for travel. They appealed to W. O. Lewis for travel assistance, but he had to decline as travel funds had been fully exhausted on the BWA Congress in Cleveland in July 1950 (Post office telegrams in BWA Correspondence Box 23, Angus Library, Regent's Park College, Oxford).

all Western European, at 48 Rue de Lille, Paris, on 21 October 1950,[41] to take part in the formation of the EBF. Exchanging correspondence with British Baptist General Secretary, M.E. Aubrey, at the end of September 1950, Lewis wrote:

> I hope the European Baptist Federation which will soon be launched may contribute to the unification of the Baptist work in Spain as well as in all of Europe. The first meeting of the Council of the Federation will take place in Paris October 19-22. It is understood that this Federation will be made up of representatives of Baptist Churches of all of Europe when it is fully organised. We are at present in need of a little money to launch the scheme. If the Continental Committee feels that it would be a legitimate use of its money to promote the Federation, such help would be greatly appreciated.[42]

In the exchange between Lewis and Aubrey there is an optimism that the new Federation would contribute to unification amongst Baptists, but also the modesty of the original enterprise with the plea to the British Baptist Continental Fund for some financial support. Yet here again there was an acknowledgement of interdependency. It may be thought surprising that neither the General Secretary of the British Baptists, M.E. Aubrey, nor his colleague, O.D. Wiles, were part of the inaugural meeting in Paris. However, in a letter of 21 September 1950, W.O. Lewis explained to Edwin A. Bell, of the American Baptist Churches, that:

> He [M.E. Aubrey] is travelling all over the country this year and is not likely to be free for very many months. And Mr Wiles is supposed to stay in the office when Aubrey is away.... When Payne becomes Secretary here he may be able to get into Germany.... But Payne will not be in office until next May.[43]

So, Cook, who was later to serve as interim Associate Secretary of the BWA for Europe, remained the key British Baptist involved in the EBF until E.A. Payne came into office. Gradually Payne's skills were utilised by the EBF as British Baptist officer influence began to be experienced within the counsels of the EBF. Payne was probably the most creative thinker of the period in setting out Baptist ecclesiology, and his own emphasis was on fellowship, as seen in his book, *The Fellowship of Believers*.[44] Payne was also a prime mover in the formulation of the British Baptist Union Statement on the Doctrine of the

---

[41] Minutes of the EBF Council, 21 October 1950, p. 2, Box 80, EBF Archive.

[42] Letter from W.O. Lewis to M.E. Aubrey, 29 September 1950 (BWA Correspondence Box 23).

[43] Letter from W.O. Lewis to E.A. Bell, 21 September 1950 (BWA Correspondence Box 23).

[44] E.A. Payne, *The Fellowship of Believers* (London: Kingsgate Press, 1944).

Church (issued in 1948).[45] The definition of the Church in this document hints at the wider ecclesiology which would influence the formation of the EBF. Clause 3 (c) asserts:

> Although each local church is held to be competent, under Christ, to rule its own life, Baptists, throughout their history, have been aware of the perils of isolationism and have sought safeguards against exaggerated individualism. From the seventeenth century there have been 'Associations' of Baptist churches which sometimes appointed Messengers; more recently their fellowship with one another has been greatly strengthened by the Baptist Union, the Baptist Missionary Society [BMS] and the Baptist World Alliance .... Indeed, we believe that a local church lacks one of the marks of a truly Christian community if it does not seek the fellowship of other Baptist churches, does not seek a true relationship with Christians and churches of other communions and is not conscious of its place in the one catholic Church.[46]

The aims of the new Europe-wide body, and some of the ways in which these aims were to be achieved, reflected this concern for wider Christian community. Petersen and Cook, who had been leading lights in the Committee of Seven and who had formed, with Lewis, the core group that made the arrangements for the inauguration of the EBF, were elected President and Vice-President respectively. The Constitution, in contrast to that of the BWA at the time, made clear that membership was open *only* to Baptist Unions of Churches. The purpose of the EBF was:

> (1) To promote fellowship amongst Baptists in Europe;
> (2) To stimulate and co-ordinate evangelism in Europe;
> (3) To provide a board of consultation and planning for Baptist mission work in Europe;
> (4) To stimulate and co-ordinate where desirable foreign missionary work of European Baptists who have no field of their own;
> (5) To promote such Baptist relief work as may be needed in Europe.[47]

These aims show a classic reflection of the interdependent ecclesial concerns which have been present from the earliest associations of Baptists onwards. Principally, there is the desire for true *koinonia* amongst like-minded Christians. Out of this spiritual and theological reality the emphasis turns to the missionary enterprise, which has been at the centre of most associational quasi-ecclesial activity from the first gathering of General Baptist Messengers in the

---

[45] 'The Doctrine of the Church', Statement agreed by the Council of The Baptist Union of Great Britain and Ireland, in *Baptist Union Documents 1948-1977* (London: Baptist Historical Society, 1980), pp. 5-11.

[46] *Ibid.*, p 8.

[47] Minutes of the EBF Council, October 1950, pp. 2-3, Box 801, EBF Archive.

seventeenth century; through the development of the Northamptonshire Association, formed in 1764 (and never confined simply to the churches of that county) to the formation of a Missionary Society[48] arising out of the address of William Carey in 1792.[49] In later years the churches and associations in England developed a national Union. The purposes of the EBF were similar, but the operation went beyond the national for the EBF set out to include the coordination of foreign mission work beyond Europe, supporting those member Unions who had no mission agency of their own. The translocal ecclesiology, lying at the heart of this vision 'to further Baptist work', was unmistakeable.

'To promote fellowship': The Development of the EBF

The theme of ecclesial fellowship was central to the life of the EBF. In 1956, at the EBF Council meeting held in Langesund, Norway,[50] a Committee on the Constitution was established, chaired by Payne, then General Secretary of the Baptist Union of Great Britain. Bredhal Petersen, who had served as first President of the EBF and, with Henry Cook, had devised and promoted the first Constitution, also served. Edwin Bell, writing to his colleagues in New York reflected:

> In many ways this meeting of the EBF Council was the best which has taken place so far in that there was the very definite disposition to look at the future of the Federation and its possibilities. This restatement of the functions of the organization came pretty much as the result of a rather long discussion on the future of the Federation and what it really ought to plan to do.[51]

However, there were some tensions in the fellowship. The new President of the EBF was Hans Luckey from the Baptist Seminary at Hamburg, but Bell thought he might not be completely effective because he could only speak German fluently and 'he is inhibited also by the memories which some of the people have of his attitudes during the Hitler era'.[52] Nonetheless, progress was made. The Committee worked in parallel with the Council and presented a report for consideration by the member bodies, the Unions, with a view to the Constitution being revised at a European Baptist Conference to be held in 1958. The right of each Council meeting of representatives of the member bodies to

---

[48] See B. Stanley, *The History of the Baptist Missionary Society 1792-1992* (Edinburgh: T&T Clark, 1992).

[49] See T.G. Carter, *The Journal and Selected Letters of William Carey* (Macon, Ga.: Smyth & Helwys, 1999).

[50] Minutes of the EBF Council, September 1956, pp. 30-2, Box 801, EBF Archive.

[51] Letter from E.A. Bell to J.L. Sprigg, 13 October 1956 (American Baptist Foreign Mission Society, ABFMS Archives, Box 476, American Baptist Historical Society, Valley Forge, Pa.).

[52] *Ibid.*

meet, discuss and discern the mind of Christ together seems to have been behind a comment on decisions that had been taken at a meeting of the Council in Copenhagen in 1952, where it had been suggested that a Vice-President of the Council should automatically succeed to the Presidency.[53] Payne stated that the Committee on the Constitution was 'unanimously opposed to any such rule and recommends that each Council meeting should be entirely free in its choice of President. It was agreed that this should be stated in the Minutes of the Council meeting.'[54]

This statement by Payne might be properly thought to reflect Baptist ecclesiology, where it is understood that the gathering of believers is for the discernment of the Holy Spirit, classically expressed as 'it seemed good to the Holy Spirit and to us'[55] and the desire to leave each Council meeting open to fresh insights. The rights of Unions were further clarified in discussions held during a meeting of the EBF Executive Committee in Berlin in September 1957.[56] The Dutch Baptist Union had written with regard to the Constitution article on membership.[57] The first Constitution had said that membership of the EBF was open to Unions in Europe that were members of the BWA. The Dutch Union commented that, 'It ought to be left to the decision and freedom of the European Unions whether they will take up membership with the Federation or not.'[58] The Secretary, Henry Cook, had consulted with the Chairman of the Committee on the Constitution, Ernest Payne, and there was no hesitation in agreeing this point. Again, this reinforces the baptistic ecclesial model contended for in this chapter. Payne suggested the point could be clarified in the Constitution by some such phrase as, 'unless they formally decide to withdraw therefrom'.[59] However, the Executive decided to clarify matters further so that there would be no doubt about the ecclesiological point by stating that Unions in Europe had the right to take up membership, but they themselves were free to decide whether they did so or not.[60] There was to be no forced fellowship.

The Dutch Union had a second concern, which again sprang from the desire to leave no doubt as to the proper understanding of ecclesial reality amongst European Baptists. From the beginning of the EBF the first secretary to serve had been W.O. Lewis, an Associate General Secretary of the BWA responsible

---

[53] Minutes of the EBF Council, September 1952, p. 35, Box 801, EBF Archive.
[54] *Ibid.,* p 36.
[55] Acts 15:28.
[56] Minutes of the EBF Council, 1957, p. 41, EBF Archive.
[57] *Ibid.,* p. 42.
[58] *Ibid.,* p. 47.
[59] *Ibid.,* p. 47.
[60] *Ibid.,* p. 47.

for Europe.[61] On Lewis' appointment as General Secretary of the BWA, Henry Cook had assumed the secretaryship of the EBF. Now, a search was in hand to find a new BWA staff member. Some had hopes that the BWA staff member for Europe could also serve as EBF General Secretary. At this crucial point in the developing life of the EBF it was clear, however, that many were concerned to ensure that the EBF had a structure of its own and a responsibility for its own life as determined by the Unions in Europe and not the BWA. Here arose a crucial difference between the EBF and some of the other continental expressions of Baptist life. In other parts of the world the regional expression of Baptist life was shaped by the world body, and this body has had a significant ongoing role in determining how regional Baptist life operates. This has not been the case in Europe. In expressing what was seen as a proper Baptist ecclesial position, the letter from the Dutch Union said:

> It ought to be stressed that the election of the Secretary or Secretary-Treasurer [of the EBF] is the perogative of the General Council of the Federation, and that, in case the Baptist World Alliance wants to combine with that position the Associate Secretaryship of the BWA in Europe, the BWA should consult with the Federation.[62]

Ernest Payne, with characteristic clarity, pointed out:

> That the question does not arise in the Constitution itself, which makes it plain that the Secretary of the Federation must be appointed by the [EBF] General Council. In practice he *may* also be a secretary of the Baptist World Alliance, but again he may not, and that is a matter for consultation.[63]

This point has caused some disputes and concerns during the fifty years of the EBF. The EBF Council members have been quite clear about the relationship between their General Secretary and themselves, but successive General Secretaries, who have also served as BWA Regional Secretaries for Europe, have had to contend with some issues of responsibility and loyalty which have not been without tension.[64] Theologically, however, the importance of the principle that the Council has a clear and unrestricted right in dealing with these matters was affirmed in 1957. It is clear that, from the beginning, the EBF has sought to understand itself as embodying an ecclesial reality based on historic Baptist understandings of associating together in fellowship. At the

[61] W.O. Lewis was originally a Southern Baptist Missionary, who was subsequently seconded to the BWA as Associate Secretary for Europe, then became full-time General Secretary of the BWA.

[62] Minutes of the EBF Council, September 1957, p. 47, Box 801, EBF Archive.

[63] *Ibid.*, p. 48.

[64] These will be explored when looking at the leadership roles of Knud Wümplemann and Karl Heinz Walter.

same time it can readily be recognised that not all Baptists in the world have stressed the centrality of wider fellowship 'from below'. Among European Baptists the wider interdependency of the churches and their covenanting together in faith and life has generally been seen as a defining conviction around which much of Baptist identity is focused.

There is, however, continuing debate about how such fellowship operates. The thinking of the 1948 British Baptist Statement has clearly been significant for European Baptist life. It has also been recognised as a statement that still informs debates about fellowship among Baptists, including debates taking place currently in the USA. Walter Shurden, a Professor at Mercer (Baptist) University in Georgia, writing on the Baptist vision of the Church,[65] quotes the British Baptist Statement,[66] commenting that it is a 'magnificent statement... Do not let the fact that this essay is fifty-years old keep you from a careful and critical study. It is one of the clearest statements on a Baptist perspective of the church available.'[67]

Documents on this topic have been produced in the USA.[68] However, there is a tendency in the USA not to appreciate the strong sense of European identity felt by many Baptists involved in the wider fellowship of the EBF. Thus former BWA President, D.K. McCall, a former Executive Secretary of the Southern Baptist Convention and President of the Southern Seminary in Louisville, Kentucky, writes of the EBF as being a 'sub-division of the BWA'. He says that:

> Some other groups, such as the American Baptists and the Canadian Baptists, give very large gifts to the BWA on a per-capita basis. But they also designate a lot of their gifts for relief. This means their gifts are not available for the BWA programs or operating expense. Then Baptist groups in Europe give generously to the support of the subdivision of the BWA the European Baptist Federation – and thereby feel they have given to the Alliance.[69]

Nowhere would any European Baptist accept that the EBF is or was ever a 'sub division of the BWA'; in fact, there has been and is a much stronger sense of identity and community within the EBF than within the BWA.

This vision for wider fellowship was reaffirmed in a Baptist Union of Great Britain Doctrine and Worship Committee Report which was presented to the

---

65 W.B. Shurden, *Proclaiming the Baptist Vision* (Macon, Ga.: Smyth and Helwys, 1996), p. 4.

66 'The Doctrine of the Church' in *Baptist Union Documents 1948-1977*, pp. 5-7.

67 Shurden, *Proclaiming the Baptist Vision*, p. 4.

68 Such statements can be found in W.L. Lumpkin, *Baptist Confessions of Faith* (Valley Forge, Pa.: Judson Press, 1959) and W.H. Brackney (ed.), *Baptist Life and Thought*, rev. ed. (Valley Forge, Pa.: Judson Press, 1998).

69 In McCall and Tonks, *Duke K McCall: An oral history*, p. 388.

Council of the Baptist Union of Great Britain in 1994. This set out again some basic principles of local churches associating together in relationships which have a covenantal aspect and suggested aspects of 'being church' beyond the local church, association and union. Thus, on wider associating, such as that of the EBF, this important theological report states:

> All this gives a local church a vision of the Church Universal, a glimpse into the reality of the whole Body of Christ in the world. Through such fellowship it finds mutual support, a sharing in mission (including world movements for peace, justice and care of the environment) and clearer insight into the Mind of Christ.[70]

It is this perspective which appears to be most favoured amongst the Baptist groups to be found across Europe. Associating together in the EBF is not simply a pragmatic attempt to address certain matters where mutual assistance might be of benefit, but has deeply imbedded within it, from the foundation of the EBF until today, a desire to experience a *koinonia* beyond the local and, as the British Baptist Report on their own Assembly and Council makes clear, to give the primary ecclesial unit, the local church 'a vision of the Church Universal, a glimpse into the reality of the whole body of Christ in the world'.[71] Nowhere is this language mirrored in the documentation or language of the BWA in the period 1950-2005, where a much looser pragmatic construct – one associated with the theology and ecclesiology of the Southern Baptist Convention – has held sway.[72] The European vision has been for meaningful Baptist commitment across the continent.

'One family': Organisational Structure

In Baptist thinking, the reality of being called into fellowship, although primary, has to be expressed in structures. When the EBF was established to promote fellowship, stimulate and coordinate evangelism, plan mission work,

---

[70] In the Report of The Baptist Union of Great Britain, Doctrine and Worship Committee, 'The Nature of the Assembly and the Council of the Baptist Union of Great Britain' (Didcot, 1994), p. 13.

[71] *Ibid.*, p. 13.

[72] Whilst this work is not principally concerned with the BWA, it might be noted that with the departure from the BWA of the Southern Baptist Convention in 2004, there has been some modest movement by European Baptists to argue the case within the BWA for a more theological and covenanted understanding of relationships within the BWA, and it might be thought there could be some modest shift in the language and style of the BWA in the future. A recent initiative of former US Presidents, Jimmy Carter and Bill Clinton, announced in January 2007, aims to bring together all Baptists in North America and talks about a 'Covenant Relationship' in a press release of Associated Baptist Press, 13 January 2007. So, there may be future movement towards the approach which has been pioneered by the Europeans.

coordinate foreign mission work and promote Baptist relief work,[73] the structure determined was simply that of a General Council, with representatives appointed from the member Unions, and an Executive consisting of seven members including the officers.[74]

However, in parallel to this there existed two earlier groupings. These have never been fully part of the EBF, though the officers have had representation on the EBF Council (later also direct representation on the Executive) and make reports to the Council. The first of these, the European Baptist Women's Union (EBWU), was established in 1948 at a meeting of the BWA held in England.[75] No parallel organisation for men has ever been sustained within the EBF, though there have been various conferences for men and attempts to found an EBF organisation in the 1960s and 1990s. For a short period in the early 1970s a representative of the EBF Men's Committee served on the EBF Executive. A youth organisation came into being about the same time as the EBWU, formed principally out of Europeans involved in the already existing Young People's Department of the BWA. This basic structure of a Council, with a small Executive acting between Councils, and related sectional groupings having a place on the General Council, operated without significant modification for several years, though there were various developmental changes which appear to have occurred in a natural way. So, for instance, with the youth involvement: originally a member of the BWA Youth Committee from Europe attended the General Council. Joel Sorenson is so described at the 1953 Council held in Rome.[76] In 1954 Sorenson again attended, but his description was changed to a representative of the Youth Committee of the European Baptist Federation.[77] There were ongoing struggles to reflect the fellowship in an appropriately structured way.

In 1956, the Report of the Nominating Committee to the Council Meeting in Langesund, Norway, appeared to expand the Executive Committee of the EBF from the original seven, including four officers, to the following:

---

[73] These were the five basic purposes of the EBF agreed in the original Constitution, Minutes of the EBF Council, Paris, 1950, p. 8, Box 801, EBF Archive.

[74] The EBF Officers, according to the 1950 Constitution, were President, Vice-President, Secretary and Treasurer elected by and from the General Council, EBF Constitution, Box 801, EBF Archive.

[75] The story of the European Baptist Women's Union [EBWU] is recorded in Y. Pusey, *Our Story 1948-1998* (Oakham, Rutland: EBWU, 1998).

[76] Minutes of the EBF Council, Rome, 1953, p. 20, Box 801, EBF Archive.

[77] Minutes of the EBF Council, München, 1954, p. 25, Box 801, EBF Archive.

President
Vice-President
Past-President
Secretary/Treasurer
President of the EBWU
President of the Youth Committee
President of the European Baptist Mission [EBM][78]
Three other members of Council.[79]

This was an increase from seven to ten members. Also to be noted was the joining together of the posts of Secretary and Treasurer, in contradistinction to the original Constitution and the general European model and in greater conformity to the North American pattern seen in the BWA. This particular change was to have unhappy consequences at a later stage in the story of the EBF.[80] At this same meeting a Committee on the Constitution was appointed to examine some of these developing practices. This group was chaired by E.A. Payne and it is clear they did not approve of some of the unofficial developments. Particular criticism was made of the idea emerging of Vice-Presidents succeeding automatically to the Presidency, though that, in fact, became the norm as the EBF developed. In the early 1970s it was suggested, at the EBF Council in Scotland, that two Vice-Presidents might be elected, one from Western Europe and one from Eastern Europe. The Executive Committee considered this in Tølløse, Denmark, in July 1971 and agreed that:

> The danger of making too great a distinction between eastern and western Europe and ... the Executive agreed that the Federation should consider its field as one field and as one family. It was generally considered that in appointing two Vice-Presidents the problems of succession to the Presidency would necessitate a choice which would be embarrassing. The Executive agreed that eastern Europe should have full representation on the Executive by normal election.[81]

This report was accepted by the Council when it met in Novi Sad in 1972.[82] It is significant that the aim was to embody the ideal of 'one family' in structural terms.

In time, the EBF recognised further Departments, and the Executive Committee, meeting in Sweden in 1959, created a Commission on Bible Study

---

[78] The European Baptist Mission [EBM] came out of the formation of the EBF. It is a cross-cultural mission agency supported by many of the Baptist Unions in the EBF. For the EBM see Chapter 7.
[79] Minutes of the EBF Council, Norway, 1956, pp. 35-6, EBF Archive.
[80] On this point see Chapter 5 on the role of EBF General Secretaries.
[81] Minutes of the EBF Executive, 1971, p. 2, Box 801, EBF Archive.
[82] Minutes of the EBF Council, 1972, p. 12, Box 801, EBF Archive.

and Membership Training, with B.B. Eriksson as Secretary.[83] The 1960 Council was asked to accept the Committee as a permanent part of the EBF structures as they sought to produce material on Baptist principles, life and mission of European Baptists, Baptist Missions around the world and various Bible topics for both young people and adults. However, this Committee, unlike the Women, Youth and EBM, was not given a place on the Executive Committee. It later became known as the Christian Education Committee. Similar Committees were developed on Evangelism and Media (Radio and Television), which was then connected to the studio established by the Southern Baptist Convention Foreign Mission Board (FMB) at Rüschlikon, Switzerland, in 1964. It was at that same Council meeting in 1960 that the decision was taken to establish a European Baptist Press Service (EBPS), with J.A. Moore, a Southern Baptist missionary working out of the Southern Baptist established Seminary at Rüschlikon[84] as part-time Director.[85] Whilst the Director was not made a member of the EBF Executive Committee, the two North American mission agencies were invited to have observers at the Executive and J.A. Moore became the Southern Baptist FMB observer on the Executive.[86] All of these developments were intended to strengthen the sense of a European Baptist identity.

There was also a concern to articulate Baptist convictions. In the 1960s some discussions took place about the possibility of the EBF establishing a European Baptist Theological Journal and there was a positive feeling that this could happen, though the project did not get off the ground. It was not until the International Baptist Theological Seminary became wholly owned by the EBF in 1988, relocated to Prague in 1996 and had come under European Baptist leadership in 1998 that the *Journal of European Baptist Studies* (JEBS) was born.[87] In order to make Baptist convictions more widely known, from 1969 onwards the Council began to produce and pass Resolutions on important issues. These were generally facilitated by a Resolutions Committee formed at each Council meeting, who would work on topics presented to them by member Unions, and submit a proposed text to the full Council. Topics for such

---

[83] Minutes of the EBF Council, Vienna, 1960, p. 70, Box 801, EBF Archive.

[84] On IBTS Rüschlikon, see Chapter 4.

[85] Minutes of the EBF Council, 1960, p. 81, Box 801, EBF Archive. The EBPS has continued from 1960 until the present and their News Archive on the EBF web site www.ebf.org, accessed 26 January 2007, is an important source of information on the work of the EBF. The Southern Baptist Convention Foreign Mission Board (now International Mission Board) continued to fund this until 2002. The relationship between the FMB and the EBF will be examined in Chapter 4.

[86] See, for instance, Minutes of the EBF Executive, Belgium, 1961, Box 801, EBF Archive.

[87] *The Journal of European Baptist Studies*, published three times per year by the International Baptist Theological Seminary of the European Baptist Federation o.p.s.

resolutions have included:

> Peace and Reconciliation amongst peoples (1969, 1975, 1979, 1982, 1984, 1986);
> Freedom of Religion (1969, 1977, 1992, 1997, 1999);
> Justice and Human Rights (1980, 1984, 1991, 1998);
> Suffering, dispossessed and homeless people in the world (1969, 1975, 1979);
> Rwanda and Burundi (1972);
> Helsinki Final Act (1975, 1977, 1980, 1984, 1985);
> Migrants and Immigrant workers (1975, 1987);
> Evangelistic task (1975, 1978, 1983, 1990, 2003);
> Nuclear Disarmament (1977, 1979, 1981, 1983, 1985, 1987);
> Middle East (1978, 1982, 2006);
> International Year of the Child (1978, 1979);
> International Youth Year (1984, 1985);
> Racism (1985);
> Dignity as human beings (1981);
> Unemployment (1983);
> Interchurch conversations (1982);
> The European vision and structures (1979, 1990);
> Women and Christian Leadership (1987);
> Human Trafficking (2003);
> Eradication of Poverty and Forgiveness of Debts of Poorest Nations (1998, 1999 - Jubilee 2000; 2005 - Micah Challenge);
> Millennium – proclamation of the Good News (1998);
> Caucasus Conflict (1999);
> Balkan conflict (1999);
> Terrorist attacks in USA, 9/11 (2001);
> War in Iraq (2002, 2004).

How these themes were tackled will be examined later.

By 1971 it was clear that the EBF was growing in shape and tasks, and a clearer distinction needed to be made between Standing Committees and ad hoc committees. The Executive took the view that Standing Committees should have a place on the Executive Committee. Meanwhile, within the wider world of the BWA, other regional fellowships were beginning to emerge and become organised, and at the 1974 EBF Council in Norway, Carl Tiller from the BWA reported on some of the developments in Asia, Africa and the Caribbean. The EBF Executive had discussed the position earlier and proposed the following:

> The Constitution of the European Baptist Federation should be re-written in the light of considerable changes which have taken place in the work of the Federation since the previous constitution was written and also because of certain

> changes which were envisaged in the light of the proposed Baptist World Alliance re-structuring.[88]

Amongst the main proposals to be considered was a plan to move to annual meetings of the Council (for some years the Council met only every second year); the number of delegates per member body should increase from one to two, with the Officers and Executive members also being members of the Council; and, whilst other Committees would continue (especially the Committee on Education and Evangelism), only the Youth Committee and the EBWU would have a place by right on the Executive.[89] Ronald Goulding, then General Secretary of the EBF, prepared a report outlining the issues faced by the EBF and recognised that the original vision for the work of the EBF was, as so often in Baptist life, constricted by lack of resources. However, he went on to say, from the crucial concept of *koinonia*:

> Where have we been most successful? In my opinion in bringing together regularly the leadership of the member Unions and Conventions. This has led to a deeper understanding and appreciation of our essential unity and of the problems and opportunities common to our work.[90]

He also identified success in the work of the Committees on evangelism, education, and media, but acknowledged the difficulty of communicating the vitality of European Baptist interdependency to local church members and in having the full involvement of those Unions which lacked financial resources.[91] This has been a continuing challenge for the EBF. The vision of some within the churches has not been fully shared, or at least not fully implemented by all.

At the 1975 EBF General Council in Holland a new Constitution was adopted, which took on board most of the recommendations from the General Secretary and the Executive and made clear that the EBF was an affiliated organisation of the BWA. The EBF had, nonetheless, its own distinct identity. In this Constitution, for the first time, a place on the Council was given to a representative of the Baptist Theological Seminary in Rüschlikon, Switzerland. Within fifteen years this Seminary was to be wholly owned by the EBF, but at that stage it was still owned by the Southern Baptist Convention FMB, but at the service of the EBF.[92] The size of the Executive was reduced by removing

---

[88] Minutes of the EBF Council, 1974, p. 4, Box 803, EBF Archive.

[89] *Ibid.,* p. 5.

[90] Report of the EBF General Secretary, C.R. Goulding, to the EBF Council, 1974. Appended to the Council Minutes of the EBF, 1974, Box 803, EBF Archive.

[91] *Ibid.*

[92] The relationship of this Seminary to European Baptists and the role of the Southern Baptist Convention FMB in both giving it to Europeans and defunding it will be examined in Chapter 4.

the automatic right of the EBWU and Youth Committee to be represented, though a power to co-opt for specific purposes was given and, as will be seen, the relationship with the EBWU and the Youth Committee remained a very specific focus within the EBF Executive. The Officers of the EBF were clarified in the Constitution as being a President, a Vice-President and the Past-President (all serving for two years), and the General Secretary. All reference to a Treasurer was dropped from the Constitution.[93] Further tidying up of the Bye-Laws took place in 1983, clarifying who could serve on the Council as non-voting members (BWA Vice-Presidents in Europe, the Director of the EBPS, one representative each of the EBM, the BMS of Great Britain, American Baptist Churches International Mission Board and the Southern Baptist Convention FMB).[94] In certain respects the connections were being broadened. The intention was to have an inclusive fellowship while retaining the ecclesial integrity of the EBF.

'An episkopal function': The Development of the EBF

Although the structures have been and are necessary, the intention has been that they should be structures that enable people to be involved in ministry, rather than restricting that ministry. At the first formal meeting of what later became the Executive Committee of the Council, discussion took place about strategic church planting. Noting discussions on 21 October 1950 in Paris, the minutes record:[95]

> W.T. Cowlan reported that at a recent meeting of Baptist youth leaders in Holland, the hope was expressed that the European Baptist Federation would sponsor youth camps, and they were interested in establishing a Baptist church in Strasbourg.

The emerging Youth Committee and the EBWU were not invited to this inaugural meeting of the EBF in Paris and this fact is noted in a letter dated 12 October 1950 of W.O. Lewis, to his Secretary, Mabel Nisted, whilst in Stuttgart:

> I think you did best in writing to Mrs Norgaard about our meeting in Paris. I have understood that our business in Paris is to organize the European Baptist Federation and to adopt a constitution. As yet we have only the committee of seven and a tentative constitution. After we organize the council of the Federation we should probably plan a later meeting of all the members of the council to which we should invite representatives of the Young People and the Women. Perhaps I should have invited them to the meeting in Paris. But I still feel that we

[93] EBF Constitution adopted, Bilthoven, Holland, 6 September 1975, EBF Archive.
[94] Minutes of the EBF Council, 1983, Box 807, EBF Archive.
[95] Minutes of the EBF Council, 1950, Box 801, EBF Archive.

> should organize the Federation and adopt a constitution before we have Women and the Young People present.[96]

Lewis, struggling with whether he had done the right thing or not, was anxious to maintain the ecclesial integrity of the new organisation by only inviting *bona fide* representatives of Unions to the inaugural meeting, though the Youth and Women were to become key organisations within the developing life of the EBF and later, as we have seen, each came to have a place on the Executive Committee and voting rights within the Council. The problem was that key individuals could be excluded from the heart of the fellowship.

The suggestion from the Youth organisation about church planting was taken seriously and the minutes of the EBF Council of 1950 go on to say:

> In view of the importance of Strasbourg as headquarters of the Council of Europe, a serious effort should be made to establish a Baptist church in that city. It was felt that first of all a worker with a knowledge of French and German should be found and put to work on this field. The French and Swiss Baptists should take the lead in finding such a man, and the Baptists of Europe and America should be asked to provide funds for his support for the first few years.[97]

At this very first meeting of the Executive of the Council there is an apparent movement beyond fellowship to what might be called 'an episkopal function', with youth leaders making a suggestion to the Executive of the Council who then determine whether or not to act on the idea. This they apparently sought to do in what might be described as a thoroughly Baptist way by engaging the help of two member Unions, the French and the Swiss, and seeking the support of Baptists in two continents to fund the worker to be selected for the task.

The specific ways in which 'episkopal' functions have been worked out through the General Secretaries of the EBF is the subject of a later chapter. For the moment it is crucial to see that the desire came 'from below'. It was part of the wider desire to develop a strong sense of identity, community and united mission within the EBF. It seems that this, in turn, comes from the fact that, compared to the BWA, the EBF is more closely related to the local Unions and churches. As time has gone on there have been fresh initiatives that have been taken. By the beginning of the twenty-first century the EBF had several institutions and agencies, such as IBTS, Baptist-Response Europe (1991-2005), European Baptist Aid (2005-), the EBWU, the EBM and the European Baptist Youth and Children's Workers Conference,[98] all of which draw together a wide range of committed people from local churches in regular patterns of meetings.

---

[96] Letter from W.O. Lewis to Mabel Nisted, Stuttgart, 12 October 1950, BWA Correspondence Box 23, Angus Library, Regent's Park College, Oxford.

[97] Minutes of the EBF Council, 1950, p. 4, Box 801, EBF Archive.

[98] A full list of such organisations and committees appears in the *EBF Directory*, 2002.

This is not mirrored in the BWA quinquennium meetings style,[99] where many groups, such as the International Mission Secretaries, have been anxious to declare they are not in any way subject to the jurisdiction of the BWA Executive Committee and staff, but simply, for convenience, meet at the same time as the BWA General Council.[100] The explicit theological undergirding of this European position, not least in relation to leadership, has been constructed over a period of time.

The process has not, however, been without tension. In 1950 it was assumed that a mission worker for the EBF would be a man. An important development occurred in 1991 at the EBF Council in Varna, Bulgaria, when the Nomination Committee proposed that the Revd Birgit Karlsson, female General Secretary of the Swedish Baptists, be elected Vice- President. This Council meeting, held in the 'heady' days of the collapse of totalitarian regimes all across Eastern Europe and the consequent immediate sense of a new day of religious freedom, was an occasion for reflecting on Baptist identity with papers presented by Grenville Overton (a Baptist minister from England), and with a special session on a new Baptist vision for Europe. These issues were wrestled with for over a decade, but the election of Birgit had to be faced immediately and raised ecclesial questions. The initial nomination to the Vice-Presidency was suggested by a Nominations Committee including theologians Vasile Talpos from Romania and Wiard Popkes (chair) from Germany. The minutes record:

> Dr Popkes intimated the nomination of the Rev Birgit Karlsson of Sweden to serve as Vice-President for the following two years. This was received with acclamation and when the vote was taken it was carried unanimously.[101]

Several Baptist Unions in Europe have for some time ordained women to Christian ministry – Sweden, the Baptist Union of Great Britain, Italy and Denmark. However, to many Unions, especially in the east, this idea was contrary to scripture and certainly, in those Unions, no woman occupied a senior leadership role outside of the sphere of so-called 'women's work'. The subsequent debate about Birgit Karlsson clearly addressed the issue of the integrity of the member Unions. If the initial reception had been unanimous, the implications of Birgit Karlsson assuming the presidency began to become an

---

[99] A full description of the work of the EBF is contained within the Annual Reports presented to the EBF Council. The most recent is EBF General Council, Lisbon, Report Book, 2008, EBF Archive.

[100] Contrast this with the insistence of Hans Guderian that the EBM was formed by the EBF and that at least one member of the EBF Executive must be present for the annual meetings of the EBM Council and that reports from the EBM should be received and discussed at every meeting of the EBF Executive Committee. Minutes of EBF Executive, 17.1, p. 7, Switzerland, April 2002.

[101] Minutes of the EBF Council, Varna, 1991, p. 8, Box 801, EBF Archive.

issue in certain Unions such as Romania and Moldova.[102]

The issue was unity in diversity. Unions were accepted into the EBF even though they had differing practices in some areas, such as women in ministerial leadership. Was it then legitimate for senior officers of those member Unions to occupy offices within the EBF structures, if elected by a majority of the Council members? This reflection was to prove a milestone in the development of the EBF and would involve the officers of the BWA. The debate on these issues came to a critical point in 1993 when Birgit Karlsson was proposed for the presidency in line with the Constitution and the custom and practice of the EBF since its foundation. On 16 June 1993 the Council of the Baptist Union of Romania met and declared the ordination of women as pastors unbiblical and announced its intention not to be represented at the Chisinäu (Kishinev), Moldova, meeting in September 1993 when Birgit Karlsson would be installed as President. This move was seen to be strange, as a senior Romanian Baptist had been a member of the EBF Nomination Committee at the 1990 EBF General Council when Birgit Kalsson had been unanimously elected Vice-President, the records showing that Romania was represented by Vasile A. Talpos (President), Nikolia Gheorgita (General Secretary), Beniamin Poplacean and Iosif Stefanatui.[103]

Immediately, officers of the EBF, including Peter Barber, the EBF President at the time of the original vote, and John Merritt, the then current President, wrote appealing to the Romanian leadership to change its stance and attend the Council.[104] In a phone call to Peter Barber on 14 July 1993, General Secretary Gheorgita said they had thought the matter over and would attend the Kishinev Council. A letter followed, handed to the EBF officers at the BWA meetings in Harare in August 1993.[105] However, again the decision was reversed, despite a strong letter from the BWA General Secretary, Denton Lotz, saying that the position of President within Baptist bodies was functional and not sacramental.[106] So thought – at times anxious thought – was being given to the nature of the 'episkopal function' within the EBF.

The Minutes of the EBF Council meeting in Kishinev record that the transition to the Presidency of Birgit Karlsson was a moving occasion:[107]

---

[102] It should be noted that at this point there was no separate Baptist Union of Moldova in membership with the EBF. It was still part of the AUCECB. The Union was accepted in at the Council in 1992 after Birgit Karlsson had been elected.

[103] Register of Attendance, EBF Council, Varna, 1991, Box 801, EBF Archive.

[104] Copies of these letters in Box 811, EBF Archive.

[105] *Ibid.*

[106] Letter of BWA General Secretary Denton Lotz to the Romanian Union and EBF Officers, 12 July 1993, Box 811, EBF Archive.

[107] Minutes of the EBF Council, Kishinev, 1993, Box 811, EBF Archive.

> She [Birgit] was moved by the emotions of the event and shared some of her personal testimony. She became a Christian at the age of 15 due to the outreach of a Baptist youth group. Her parents were non believers. Her parents never followed her way of faith, and her home church became her family. She noted that now the EBF and its unions have become her family. She related her pilgrimage since approaching the moment when she would move into the President's role. She pleaded with all Baptists and unions to erect signs of peace and unity in these times of conflict, disunity and hate.

After this, the place of women within the EBF Council was consolidated, with Anna Maffei, President of the Italian Baptists, being appointed as Chair of the External Relations Division from 2004, and Ruth Gouldbourne, a British Baptist minister and theological tutor, being elected as Chair of the IBTS Board of Trustees at the EBF Council in 2006. Through the tensions around the election and installation of Birgit Karlsson as President of the EBF, the place of women within certain of the Unions came to be accepted as something which would not divide other Unions from fellowship even if women holding important posts within their own Unions were called to exercise leadership roles within the EBF structures.[108] The matters debated regarding the position of Birgit Karlsson turned out to be a real point of development for the EBF.

As the EBF grew into a diverse family, becoming fifty-two Baptist Unions by 2005,[109] there were great differences on many issues between the Unions, but the common heart of the evangelical 'gathering' or believers' church tradition appeared able to withstand the disagreements on many, if not all, issues. What began to emerge after this traumatic episode concerning leadership was that a real sense of *koinonia* was to hold the Baptist communities together through various important issues, notably the debate about the work of the jointly owned International Baptist Theological Seminary, relationships with North American mission agencies and other contentious issues.[110]

'Credible testimony': The Place of Mission

In the early meetings of the EBF Council and Executive there are to be found many mission-orientated discussions and examples of hopes regarding mission

[108] The exceptions to this are Kazakhstan and Kyrgystan, who cited the ministry of women in some EBF Unions as one of their reasons for withdrawal from the EBF in 2006. However, this was one of a whole list of reasons and there appeared to be much greater concern that they perceived that some Western Unions did not condemn homosexuality as strongly as they would wish.

[109] This number has reduced with the withdrawal of Kazakhstan and Kyrgystan.

[110] These issues will be examined in more detail in Chapter 5 dealing with the General Secretaryship of Karl Heinz Walter and Chapter 6 dealing with the influence of the North American mission agencies.

initiatives; for instance, at the 1950 Paris meeting the view was expressed that Spain was an open door for church planting and that Baptists in Hispanic America should be encouraged to engage in mission partnership with Spanish Baptists.[111]

At the Council meeting in Hamburg in 1951 prioritising took place on mission initiatives in Brussels, Iceland and Greece.[112] This emphasis on mission as a prime motive for local churches cooperating together nationally and internationally is the theme of the Confession of Faith drawn up by representatives of the Austrian, German and Swiss Unions between 1974 and 1977. Section 5, on Spiritual Gifts and Ministries (in translation), reads:[113]

> Each local congregation is understood as a manifestation of the one body of Christ and is responsible for ordering its own life and ministry. These local congregations are bound together, not primarily through organsational ties, but by the one Lord and the one Spirit. The congregations strengthen each other through fellowship in the faith, and by learning from each other, through intercession and by mutual aid. Such things as structure of the congregation and denominational organization, administration and finance, institutions and works, are not ends in themselves, but are instruments of the mission of the church in this world.

The authors, drawn from these different German-speaking Baptist communities, cite 1 Cor. 1:2; Eph. 4:3-6 and 1 Cor. 16:1-4 in support of this stand. Later, this relatively recent Confession of Faith, goes on to express something of the relationship which should exist, not only between churches of the same confession, but also across the diverse confessions, and stresses witness to the world:[114]

> Jesus Christ is building his community in the various churches and fellowships. Regardless of the diversities and regardless of error and fault on all sides, it cannot be God's will for denominational barriers to hinder the visible fellowship of all believers and thus their credible testimony to all the world.

This attitude of Baptists from the German-speaking part of Europe would find echoes amongst Baptists in England and Wales, Scandinavia and parts of Central Europe, including Hungary, Italy and Croatia, and the impact of that on the life and work of the EBF will be analysed.

It has been the view of Baptists in Europe that their mission involved more than witness to the gospel by word; it also involved witness in deeds and in a concern for a just society. Soon after the formation of the EBF Council and

---

[111] Minutes of the EBF Council, 1950, p. 4, Box 801, EBF Archive.

[112] Minutes of the EBF Council, 1951, p. 12, Box 801, EBF Archive.

[113] In G.K. Parker, *Baptists in Europe – History and Confessions of Faith* (Nashville, Tenn.: Broadman Press, 1982), p. 67.

[114] *Ibid.*, p. 69.

Executive, the issue of religious freedom was on the agenda. Inevitably, this grew in importance with the establishment of the socialist states of the Eastern European bloc and the work of many communist governments in the suppression of evangelical Christians.[115] This became an area that was to develop and become a significant feature of the work of the EBF Council and, later, of successive General Secretaries. This right of religious freedom had been a clarion call of most Anabaptist[116] and Baptist groups from the time of Balthasar Hubmaier and Thomas Helwys onwards. Helwys had published *A Short Declaration of the Mistery of Iniquity* in 1612. This was, as A.C. Underwood argues,[117] 'the first demand made in England for universal religious liberty – for freedom of conscience for all'. From the point of view of the EBF and its later involvement in the pursuit of human rights and religious liberty, no doubt this is the most telling point:

> Our lord the king is but an earthly king, and he hath no authority as a king but in earthly causes, and if the king's people be obedient and true subjects, obeying all human laws made by the king, our lord, our lord and king can require no more for men's religion to God is betwixt God and themselves; the king shall not answer for it, neither may the king be judge between God and Man. Let them be heretics, Turks, Jews or whatsoever, it appertains not to the earthly power to punish them in the least measure.[118]

This appeal, addressed to the King of England, Scotland and Wales, became something of a model for the later demand for human rights and religious liberty. Helwys dedicated the text to King James I. This vision was a continuing one in European Baptist life.

The leadership of the EBF followed very much in the spirit of Helwys. Soon the Executive of the EBF became involved in the pursuit of human rights and religious liberty, and its importance will be looked at in Chapter 7. However, it should be noted that it was not until 1994 that the EBF Council, meeting in Dorfweil, Germany, accepted a recommendation from a Task Force consisting

---

[115] For general introductions to this topic see T. Beeson, *Discretion and Valour* (London: Fontana Books, 1974) (Note: the 1984 edition embraces some major differences) and M. Bourdeaux, *Opium of the People: The Christian Religion in the USSR* (London: Faber and Faber, 1965). Keston Research (www.Keston.org), arising out of the work of Michael Bourdeaux, continues to provide updated information on issues of religious liberty in Eastern Europe.

[116] 'On Heretics and Those who Burn Them', in H.W. Pipkin and J.H. Yoder (eds.), *Balthasar Hubmaier: Theologian of Anabaptism* (ET from the German original, Scottdale, Pa.: Herald Press, 1989), pp. 59-63.

[117] A.C. Underwood, *A History of the English Baptists* (London: Carey Kingsgate Press, 1947).

[118] T. Helwys, *The Mistery of Iniquity*, Extant copy in Bodelian Library, University of Oxford.

of Thorwald Lorenzen (Chair, IBTS), Per Midteide (Norway), Ebbe Holm (Denmark), Anatoly Pchelincev (Russia) and Theo Angelov (Bulgaria) to:

> Collect material on human rights' violations in each country;
> Provide prayer information for the unions;
> Organise a consultation for a network of lawyers;
> Provide informational material for an annual EBF Human Rights' Day;
> Promote religious freedom for all people.[119]

At that meeting a continuing Human Rights Task Force was established to develop this as an important activity within the overall mission of the EBF.[120] The Task Force was to operate within the External Relations Division of the EBF who had their terms of reference unanimously amended as follows:

> Conducting the [EBF] human rights programme, prepare the human rights lawyers programme, participate in the BWA Commission on Human Rights, serve as the membership committee of the EBF, and look into the relationship with other churches.[121]

An early area of activity of this Human Rights Task Force was the production of a booklet by Thorwald Lorenzen of IBTS, Rüschlikon,[122] and the establishment of an EBF Human Rights Day to be observed each year. The then EBF General Secretary, Karl Heinz Walter, went to considerable lengths to produce promotional material, posters, information leaflets and worship material to promote the day.[123] The 1994 EBF Council Minutes record:

> The date is 11 December with 1 Timothy 2. 1-4 as the theme. A Human Rights poster will be provided, as well as a paper detailing situations in the various countries. A small brochure detailing the basic laws on human rights and religious liberty will also be provided.[124]

Successive Chairs of the External Relations Division of the EBF, Per Midteide, Ole Jørgenson, Sven Lindström, Tony Peck and Anna Maffei,[125] all

---

[119] Minutes of the EBF Council, 1994, p. 14, Item 21.1.3, Box 812, EBF Archive.
[120] *Ibid.,* p. 13, Item 19.5.
[121] *Ibid.*
[122] T. Lorenzen, *Freedom of Religion as a Human Right* (Hamburg: EBF, 1995).
[123] Examples of this promotional material in the mid 1990s exist in the EBF Archive.
[124] Minutes of the EBF Council, 1994, p. 12, Minute 19.5, EBF Archive.
[125] Tony Peck, then a Tutor at Bristol Baptist College, proceeded to develop the Thomas Helwys Centre for the Study of Religious Liberty at the College and delivered a paper, 'Grace and Law: Baptists and Religious Freedom: Historical Antecedents and Contemporary Context' to the British Baptist Assembly in 2002. The paper was subsequently printed in *BQ*, Vol. XXXIX, No. 7 (July 2002), pp. 315-27.

took especial interest in the work of the Human Rights group, which was initially convened by Ebbe Holm of Denmark, though as is recounted in Chapter 7, the group ceased to hold meetings after 2002. The Working Group was to advise the EBF General Secretary, organise conferences and monitor human rights issues within Europe and the Middle East. Member Unions offered the names of various legal specialists in the area of religious liberty to serve on the Task Force, including Malcolm Evans, Professor of International Law at Bristol University, who was recruited by the Council of Europe to monitor religious liberty laws in many countries in Eastern Europe.[126] So, it can be seen that by the 1990s religious liberty, as a key component of human rights from a Baptist perspective, had become a key part of the mission of the EBF.

'The rapidly changing situation': Responses to New Challenges

As the retirement of Knud Wümplemann[127] as General Secretary approached, a special EBF Search and Structure Review Committee was established to identify a new General Secretary and look at the structures of the EBF in the light of the changes in the structures of the BWA and of the then current needs in Europe. Karl Heinz Walter emerged as the new General Secretary and the Report of the Structures Committee was accepted in 1990 at the EBF Council in Holland. This proposed replacing the old committee system with a new system of Committees and Divisions and with Chairs of these Committees and Divisions serving on the EBF Executive Committee. The argument for this change was provided by the Structure Review Committee:

> The meetings of the Council tended to be retrospective, repetitive and passive. There was a need for greater participation, discussion of current major issues and shared forward-planning...the number of Committees and activities had increased without there being a strong linking mechanism...the Federation, as presently structured, was not geared to respond to the rapidly changing situation in East and West Europe in terms of political structures, social issues and mission opportunities....the full implications and obligations of taking over Rüschlikon did not seem to have registered on the Federation.[128]

This far-reaching report produced by the Structure Review Committee (SRC) (initially chaired by Bernard Green, then General Secretary of the Baptist Union of Great Britain, later by Peter Barber, General Secretary of the Baptist Union of Scotland), marked the most radical restructuring of the EBF in

---

[126] See M.D. Evans, *Religious Liberty and International Law in Europe* (Cambridge: Cambridge University Press, 1997).

[127] On Knud Wümplemann see Chapter 5, pp. 165-185.

[128] Report of the EBF Structure Review Committee, EBF Council, De Bron, 1990, Box 810, EBF Archive.

the forty years since its foundation. It was designed to spread the workload from the General Secretary to working members of the Executive Committee who chaired the new division structure. It also recognised a new dimension to the work of the EBF in the area of theological education, now that the Southern Baptist Convention FMB had handed over the Rüschlikon operation to the EBF. The desire of the SRC appears to have been greater involvement of more people in the work of the EBF, putting the Council back into the role of driving the agenda, as had been the original pattern, rather than listening to the reports of others, as had gradually become the pattern from the 1970ş onwards. The 'division' pattern was inaugurated at the Council meeting held in Varna, Bulgaria, in 1991 and served the EBF well during the time of post-communist transition and as the number of member Unions increased dramatically with the emergence of many new nation-states out of the collapse of the USSR and Yugoslavia.[129]

There were further changes in this period, some of them involving geographical consideration. The EBF was originally formed to embody member Unions and Conventions within the historic boundaries of Europe.[130] However, a request for membership of the EBF from the Association of Baptists in Israel was received in 1987 and, in the light of this, the Executive proposed an amendment of the Constitution to allow the Baptists in Israel to join. The new clause read: 'MEMBERSHIP: Any Baptist national body in Europe and the Middle East which desires to....'.[131] The Association of Baptists in Israel was received in during the EBF Council meeting in 1989. Later, Unions in Lebanon, Egypt, Jordan and Syria joined the EBF. With the break up of the old Soviet Empire in 1990-1991, the Unions of the newly independent countries which had been part of that Empire joined the EBF. It was not seen as unreasonable to suppose that Tajikistan, Uzbekistan and Turkmenistan could be counted as part of 'Baptist Europe' if not 'geographical Europe' and that on a similar basis it could be conceded that Georgia, Armenia and Azerbaijan were part of a south east tip of Europe.

The challenges for the EBF of operating in a post-communist world emerged clearly in the 1990 Council at De Bron, in the Netherlands, as it faced issues of Baptist identity (which would take up much of the time of the Council throughout the 1990s) and the challenge to adapt EBF life as many new Unions were created in Eastern Europe as the USSR imploded. The early atmosphere

---

[129] For instance, six new Unions were welcomed into the Council in 1991, seven in 1992, seven in 1993, four in 1994, two in 1995.

[130] By this should be understood a Europe bounded by the Mediterranean and North Seas, the Atlantic Ocean but including the whole territory of the former Russian Empire/Union of Soviet Socialist Republics (USSR), and thus stretching across North Asia to the Pacific Ocean.

[131] EBF Constitution amendment agreed by the EBF Council, 1987, Box 807, EBF Archive.

was euphoric, with much talk of a new era of religious freedom and evangelism, but as the decade progressed, the EBF and the Unions faced many challenges of post-modernism, post-communism and new laws constraining the rights of churches throughout the region.[132] As will be seen in subsequent chapters, the 'Division structure' had only a limited success and the interaction within the EBF Council appeared to remain dependent upon the President and the General Secretary creating an atmosphere, or giving permission for debate. Certainly, by the mid 1990s, it might reasonably be postulated that the EBF Council had relapsed into the essentially passive mode which the Structure Review Group had sought to challenge, and that not all of the Division meetings within the Council, designed to be places of debate and interaction, actually drew attendance and participation to achieve the ends envisaged.

It can be seen that the EBF has had a developmental model which took a dramatic leap forward following the collapse of the communist bloc and under the dynamic leadership of Karl Heinz Walter.[133] However, one area of difficulty that remained was the legal standing of the EBF, especially as the European Union developed. In the 1990s, when the office was based in Hamburg, the EBF was able to maintain bank accounts and enter contracts by having registration under the umbrella of the German Baptist Verein.[134] However, this was seen as less than satisfactory and Peter D. Deutsch, President of the Swiss Baptist Union, who was a lawyer and had been much involved in establishing a Swiss Verein to take ownership of the Rüschlikon property, looked at the situation and suggested that Swiss law had the most open and flexible laws for establishing a 'Verein' – a legal organisation which had a Germanic continental reality. This was the best way forward that could be hoped for in the absence of any European Union-wide legislation for the creation of charitable non-governmental organisations able to have a legal 'person' that had acceptance throughout, at least, the area of the European Union and the European Economic Area.[135]

Building on work done by Deutsch and a special sub-committee created from the EBF Executive, at a meeting of the EBF held in Prague on 27 September 2001, the then fifty-one member bodies of the EBF changed the

---

[132] These issues will be examined in Chapter 4 on the work of Karl Heinz Walter.

[133] Chapter 5 will examine the episkopal leadership of K.H. Walter who served as EBF General Secretary during the 1990s.

[134] A 'Verein' is an association registered for non-governmental charitable purposes. It is a structure common in German speaking countries and corresponds, in many aspects, to the concept of a charity in English law.

[135] The European Union continues to expand and, with the additional countries of the European Economic Area, will, within five years, have in excess of 50% of the countries which have a Baptist Union in membership with the EBF within the boundaries of the EU itself, or as accession countries.

legal structure of the EBF to establish a 'Verein' registered in the Swiss Canton of Zürich, giving the EBF a full and independent legal status and enabling it to engage in activities and to seek non-governmental organisation status at the Council of Europe and elsewhere. The purpose of the EBF was defined in the Statutes as follows:

> Article 2: Purpose
>
> The purpose of the association is to strengthen and draw together Baptists in Europe and the Middle East on the basis of their Christian witness and distinctive convictions, to encourage and inspire them in faith and fellowship and shared responsibility and to seek in all its endeavours to fulfill the will of Jesus Christ, Lord and Saviour.
>
> The association is a body affiliated to the 'Baptist World Alliance'. It seeks to share its concern and further its purposes.
>
> EBF owns and operates the 'International Baptist Theological Seminary of the European Baptist Federation', located in Prague.[136]

This 'statement of purpose' reflects the aims established at the beginning of the life of the EBF and commences with the same key emphasis on *koinonia* and mission. The new Statutes go on to define membership as was discussed in the 1950s, based upon ecclesial groupings of churches within Unions and not upon a membership by individuals, institutions or by the determination of some other apparently superior body. Article 3 states:

> Any Union, Convention or similar Baptist body in Europe and the Middle East which desires to cooperate in fellowship and work shall be eligible for membership subject to approval of the Council on the basis of a two-thirds majority of the votes cast.[137]

The EBF leadership worked hard, not only to ensure a very separate ecclesial identity for the EBF, built around a Council drawn from appointed delegates of member Unions, but also a legal entity. This legal entity was fully achieved in January 2002 with the establishment of a 'Verein' under Zürich cantonal law in Switzerland. At present the *EBF Handbook* declares there are 54 member bodies in 45 countries.[138] If we exclude the Middle East, and then redefine Europe as the islands and continental land mass including the European Union, countries of Western and Northern Europe, Central Europe,

---

[136] Article 2, Statutes of the EBF, 27 September 2001, EBF Office Archive.

[137] EBF Statutes as agreed 27 September 2001 at the EBF Council meeting in Prague and recorded in the Minutes, EBF Office Archive. The Statutes were ratified by the Officers of the EBF and submitted to the Zürich Cantonal Authorities Business Court on 5 April 2002.

[138] *EBF Directory 2006*, Prague.

and the countries which were formerly part of the USSR, the number of member Unions is adjusted to 46 and the countries to 39. At the EBF Council held in Lyon, France, in September 2006, there was a good representation from these member Unions.

When Tony Peck became EBF General Secretary in 2004, he sought to address the new challenges and the problem of passivity by having a theme to the EBF Council with a keynote address and discussion groups.[139] In 2005 the keynote address was on mission in Europe by Peter F. Penner, Director of the Institute for Mission and Evangelism at IBTS, Prague. In 2006 the keynote address was on theological education by Otniel Bunaceau, Dean of the Baptist Faculty of the University of Bucharest.[140] On both occasions the addresses provoked interaction and discussion in the General Council, but it remains to be seen if the outcome of the discussions will actually affect the life and work of the EBF and its member Unions. The hope certainly is to continue to engage in a meaningful way in an ecclesial reality beyond the local and even beyond what might be considered – certainly from a theological and missiological perspective – the artificial bounds of the nation state. This has been demonstrated as being, from the beginning, an intention within the EBF in the ways outlined above. The vision has been for *koinonia*, leadership, mission strategy and mutual support.

Conclusion

The ecclesial model which has been explored throughout this chapter sees the local gathering convictional community of believers as of core importance and the trans-local and trans-national being lesser ecclesial realities, though nevertheless theologically important. These relationships may be thought of as a web of interconnectedness which places the emphasis on the local gathering church, but makes it theologically essential for such a church to engage in associating with other baptistic groups within a nation. Through such associating (Union or Convention), the gathering community commits to those other wider organisms which are continental and transcontinental. These organisms have some ecclesial realities which are important, not least in relationship to the wider world of political and Christian life. I have sought to explore the underlying theological concern amongst European Baptists for an ecclesiology of the more-than-local, especially in relationship to the development of an ecclesial reality beyond the national and covering a geographical continent, though as we have seen, Baptist definitions of Europe are wider than those of geographers. The first fifty-seven years of the EBF have

---

[139] Themes have so far included mission, theological education, church-state relations and the theology of creation care.

[140] Unpublished papers, EBF Office Archive, Prague.

affirmed some key ecclesial insights. A root understanding has been that of *koinonia*, fellowship, sustained even through the dark days of the clash of West and East Europe with very different political ideologies.[141]

The basic Constitution of the EBF established certain clear points about the nature of the organisation and the historic ecclesial point that this was not a free society of individuals, churches and unions, but a structure based on Unions within Europe. However, it should be noted that, from the beginning, mission agencies working in Europe and others were invited to be present at EBF Council meetings and to participate in discussions, again reflecting Baptist ecclesiology which sees a principal responsibility of the gathering convictional community to be missional in character. However, although the mission agencies attended, they did so without full membership rights. The approach seen in the EBF might be regarded as in marked contrast to the NABF, which has a much simpler structure, does not have a formal council and normally is only able to gather representatives from the member bodies in North America when people meet at other events, such as the General Council of the BWA.[142] In Europe there has been a centripetal movement from the gathering community of believers in the local church. The local church chooses to enter into an interdependent relationship within an association, which then is part of a wider national body, or union, generally made up of local churches, associations of local churches and perhaps specific departments or agencies, such as missionary organisations or theological seminaries. These national unions or conventions then freely enter into continental relationships, which co-exist within the global family of the BWA. Within the European setting it is also important to compare Baptist ecclesiology and theology with the other main Christian World Communions, which have differing ecclesiological understandings. This will be explored in the next chapter.

---

[141] Some specific examples of this are found in subsequent chapters.

[142] So, for instance, a dinner was held for the North American Baptist Fellowship Executive at the BWA General Council meeting in Seville, Spain, July 2002. The previous Executive meeting had been held as an adjunct to the BWA Executive in Birmingham, England. Amongst items discussed was the plan to remodel the Executive more on the lines of the EBF Executive (established in the 1950s) and to consider the creation of an NABF Council to meet annually. See Report of the NABF in *BWA General Council Report Book, Seville Spain July 8-13, 2002.* BWA Archives, Falls Church, Virginia. USA. As noted elsewhere, former US Presidents Clinton and Carter have in mind the creation of a stronger North American Baptist (USA/Canada) community around a covenant and a meeting was held in 2008 to advance this idea.

CHAPTER 3

The Ecumenical Dimension

Following examination of the ecclesial nature of the European Baptist Federation (EBF), which was developed from its inception and strengthened through the work of such leaders as E.A. Payne and Henry Cook, I move on to consider how this European Baptist ecclesial structure compares with that of other Christian World Communions.[1] The chapter sets out the features of the main denominational groups with whom Baptists in Europe have had to deal and their current ecclesial structures in Europe, making comparisons with the EBF. I will not analyse those traditions that do not have a significant exposure in Europe nor those specific national and minority groups who have a larger ecumenical affiliation, but are confined to a specific locality.[2] The chapter also examines EBF relationships with the World Council of Churches (WCC), the Conference of European Churches (CEC), and evangelical bodies and other groupings such as the Community of Protestant Churches in Europe (CPCE – formerly known as Leuenberg Fellowship).

In analysing the relationship of the EBF to other Christians I will seek to show that the particular 'bottom-up' ecclesial reality of the EBF has strengthened its ability, on behalf of its member Unions, to engage in dialogue with other Christian traditions and to participate in various forms of activity with others of the traditions represented in what is often referred to today as the 'Christian World Communions'. It will also be noted that European ecumenical leadership has had a significant number of Baptists involved in national and

[1] For the sake of consistency and understanding I will use the phrases 'Christian World Communions', or 'Christian Communion' in this chapter, as in Chapter 2, rather than the word 'denomination', which might simply refer to a particular national group within a larger ecclesial communion. The Christian World Communions meet annually and were originally known as the World Confessional Families.

[2] An example of such a group might be the Czechoslovak Hussite Church, formed in the time of the first Republic in 1920 by liberal Catholics with the intention of creating an identity based on the teachings of Jan Hus and as part of the emergence of the first Czechoslovak Republic. This denomination still exists and is very involved ecumenically with about 230 congregations in the modern Czech and Slovak Republics. However, it does not exist beyond the boundaries of the Czechoslovak nation state created after the First World War.

pan-European ecumenical work. The section on the dialogue with the CPCE[3] will demonstrate the strength of the ecclesial reality within the EBF, which enabled it to enter dialogue with the CPCE in 2002 with the confidence of the member bodies, who affirmed both the ecclesial reality and ability of the EBF Council to do this, and their trust in the appointed group understanding whom they represented and to whom they were accountable.[4]

Christian World Communions

The twentieth century has been described as the 'ecumenical century',[5] with the development of the famous Edinburgh Missionary Conference of 1910 followed by the Life and Work and Faith and Order movements, the WCC and the World Evangelical Fellowship.[6] Alan Sell argues that ecumenism has been 'a concern of the Church from New Testament times onwards'.[7] Most of the major expansion in ecumenical work and relationships in Europe occurred after the Second World War, and the late 1940s and the early 1950s proved to be the time for major developments in the field of conciliar ecumenical and confessional organisations.[8] At the same time, denominational life has continued, and denominations have formed 'world bodies'. Most of the major Christian World Communions have a significant presence, and often their

---

[3] The Community of Protestant Churches in Europe [CPCE], formerly known as the Leuenberg Church Fellowship, consists of over 90 church denominations in Europe and Latin America drawn from the Lutheran, Reformed, Moravian, Waldensian and Methodist traditions.

[4] I will demonstrate this is in marked contrast to the Baptist World Alliance [BWA] where, for instance, the dialogue between the BWA and the Roman Catholic Church in the 1990s was disowned by Baptists in Latin America and parts of Europe, not least because the delegations had been put together by the BWA Officers with a North American dominance and also partly on the basis of who could pay to attend. These issues were exposed at a forum hosted by the Doctrine and Worship Commission of the BWA in Buenos Aires in July 1995 at which I was present. The BWA General Council did not appoint, or approve, the delegation, nor has it done so for the latest round of meetings 2005-2010 – in marked contrast to the approach of the EBF.

[5] For an overview of this reality see R. Rouse and S.C. Neill (eds. vol. 1), H.E. Fey (ed. Vol. 2) J.H.Y. Briggs, M.A. Oduyoye, G. Tsetsis (eds. Vol. 3), *The History of the Ecumenical Movement*, vols.1, 2 and 3 (Geneva: WCC, 1998 and 2005).

[6] On the development of the Evangelical Alliance, especially in Europe, which began much earlier in 1846, see I.M. Randall and D. Hilborn, *One Body in Christ: The History and Significance of the Evangelical Alliance* (Carlisle: Paternoster, 2001).

[7] A.P.F. Sell, 'Richard Baxter and the Unity of the Church', *Commemorations: Studies in Christian Thought and History* (Cardiff: University of Wales Press, 1993), p. 31.

[8] The World Council of Churches [WCC] was formed in the period 1938-1948, The Conference of European Churches [CEC] in 1959 and the European Baptist Federation [EBF] in 1950.

international base, in Europe. Christian World Communions, as a term, dates from the nineteenth century, but has only been in common use since 1979. The Baptist World Alliance (BWA), as one such World Communion, dates from 1905.[9] Richard V. Pierard argues that Christian World Communions are an important alternative to conciliar ecumenism.[10] According to the WCC there are twenty Christian World Communions,[11] many of which have their historical roots in Europe and are represented in several countries or regions of Europe.

Perhaps many would consider the World Alliance of Reformed Churches (WARC)[12] to be a communion closely related to Baptists, given that they describe their member bodies as coming out of the Reformed tradition arising from the work of Huldrych (Ulrych) Zwingli and Jean (John) Calvin and consisting of member bodies drawn from the Reformed, Presbyterian and Congregational traditions.[13] WARC was formed in 1970,[14] with its headquarters in Geneva. In Europe there are thirty-nine member bodies in twenty-seven

---

[9] For a definition and the importance of Christian World Communions see 'Christian World Communions', in A.J. van der Bent (ed.), *Historical Dictionary of Ecumenical Christianity (*Metuchen: Scarecrow Press, 1994), pp. 79-80.

[10] See H.E. Fey, *World Confessionalism and the Ecumenical Movement*, 1970. Mimeographed draft, IBTS Library, Prague. See also R.V. Pierard, 'The Christian World Communions – Ecumenism on a Global Scale' in *Ecumenism and History: studies in Honour of John H Y Briggs*, and H. Meyer 'Christian World Communions', in *A History of the Ecumenical Movement Volume 3, 1968-2000.* There is some doubt about the exact date of the first meeting and this is examined in E. Perret, *Twenty Years - The Conference of World Confessional Families 1957-1977*, World Confessional Families [WCF], Rome, 16 May 1977, Duplicated Paper, G. Claas Box 33, EBF Archive.

[11] WCC Statistics Office, April 2002, WCC website: *Church and Ecumenical Organizations, Christian World Communions* at http://wcc-coe.org/wcc/who, accessed 25 April 2002. A more recent source is H. van Beek (ed.) *Handbook of churches and councils: Profile of Ecumenical Relationships* (Geneva: WCC, 2006).

[12] It should be noted there is also a Reformed Ecumenical Council of 38 denominations formed in 1946, with offices in Grand Rapids, Michigan, based on a range of confessions including the Gallican Confession, Heidelburg Confession, Second Helvetic Confession, 39 Articles and the Westminster Confession. However, it only has three member bodies in Europe – The Reformed Synod of Denmark, the Greek Evangelical Church and the Evangelical Reformed Church of France.

[13] World Alliance of Reformed Churches [WARC] information published on their web site at http://warc.jalb.de, accessed 26 April 2002.

[14] WARC web site referring to the amalgamation of a group of Presbyterian and Reformed national churches with a group of Congregational denominations. The original group was 21 Presbyterian churches from Europe and North America who commenced working together in 1875. In 1970 the World Alliance of Congregational Churches joined with them, see www.warc.ch, accessed November 2006.

countries.[15] The constitution of WARC says (Article IX) that:

> to promote the closest possible community and cooperation among member churches in particular areas of the world and the effectiveness of the total work of the Alliance, the General Council may authorize the organization of an area by the member churches in any given area of the world.[16]

Reformed churches in Europe, such as the Church of Scotland, the Reformed Church in Switzerland, the United Reformed Church in the United Kingdom, the Reformed Church in Hungary and the Evangelical Church of the Czech Brethren, see themselves as ecclesial bodies belonging to a Christian World Communion to which they give the power and authority to determine regional areas and to organise and supervise the life of those areas. Each organised area meets in area council, provides for an administrative committee, and elects officers.[17] This, it will be immediately apparent, is a different model from the 'bottom-up' approach of Baptist life in Europe, where a local congregation joins an association of Baptist churches, formed into a Union or Convention which then, through its decision-making body or assembly, decides to join the EBF.

Another established Protestant Christian World Communion in Europe is the Lutheran World Federation (LWF). It has a strong Lutheran basis of faith which:

> sees in the three Ecumenical Creeds and in the Confessions of the Lutheran Church, especially in the unaltered Augsburg Confession and the Small Catechism of Martin Luther, a pure exposition of the Word of God.[18]

This organisation was founded in 1947 and now consists of 133 member bodies in seventy-three countries.[19] From the statistics of the LWF there are forty-five member bodies in Europe, but this includes the fourteen State, or regional Lutheran Churches in Germany.[20] Unlike the WARC, the LWF appears to have no regional structure, though in forming the Assembly and Council of the LWF

---

[15] WARC web site. I use the term member body, but the Reformed tradition refers to member churches by which they mean an ecclesial organisation of local churches formed into Synods and with a National Synod.

[16] Constitution of the WARC, Offices of the WARC, Geneva, Switzerland.

[17] *Ibid.*

[18] Constitution of The Lutheran World Federation [LWF] as adopted by the LWF Eighth Assembly, Curitiba, Brazil, 1990, including amendments adopted by the LWF Ninth Assembly, Hong Kong, 1997. See http://www.lutheranworld.org/Archives, accessed 25 January 2007.

[19] For the purpose of consistency I am using the term member body, but the Lutherans themselves speak of member churches such as the Lutheran Church of Great Britain.

[20] LWF Statistics 2002, at http://www.lutheranworld.org , accessed 23 January 2003.

due regard is given to the numerical size of member churches and their distributions by continents and countries.[21] The only structure developed between the member bodies and the LWF is a National Committee for those countries where there are several member bodies. However the Constitution makes clear that the 'right of direct communication between member churches and the LWF shall be retained'.[22] From the perspective of Lutheran ecclesial understanding there are national or state churches which can choose to join the LWF if they subscribe to the doctrinal basis. LWF officers come from LWF's seven geographical areas, which include Central Eastern Europe, the Nordic Countries and Central Western Europe.[23] But the Lutheran ecclesial communities have no definable European identity, and where others have wanted to relate to them, such as the Anglican churches of the Isles[24] and the Diocese of Europe, this has had to be done with a particular country, as in the Meissen Agreement.[25] As will be seen later, in seeking discussions with the EBF, the LWF had to resort to the vehicle of the CPCE.

The Anglican World Communion is also a major Christian World Communion arising out of the Protestant Reformation. Anglicanism was established as a state church with an eclectic theological basis aiming at a 'Christian comprehensiveness'.[26] This comprehensiveness was never complete and radical puritans (at one time classified as Dissenters) and Roman Catholics remained outside, with the continental Anabaptists being condemned in the Church's Thirty-Nine Articles. Today Anglican churches see themselves as those who '(u)phold and proclaim the Catholic and Apostolic faith, based on the Scriptures, interpreted in the light of tradition, scholarship and reason.'[27] The Church of England has become the 'mother church' of the Anglican World Communion. The Anglican presence in Europe is principally in the Church of England, the Episcopal Church of Scotland, the Church of Ireland and the Church in Wales. Additionally the Lusitanian Church of Portugal and the Spanish Reformed Episcopal Church are members of the Anglican

---

[21] LWF Constitution, Clause VII 3.at http://www.lutheranworld.org, accessed 23 January 2003.

[22] *Ibid.,* para. IX.

[23] LWF Constitution and Bye-Laws at http://www.lutheranworld.org, accessed 18 December 2006.

[24] Here I am using the Isles in reference to Europe as used in N. Davies, *The Isles* (London: Macmillan,1999).

[25] *The Meissen Agreement*, The Council for Christian Unity of the General Synod of the Church of England, 1992 (London: Church House Publications, 1992).

[26] P. Avis (ed.), *Pushing at the Boundaries of Unity: Anglicans and Baptists in Conversation* (London: Church House Publishing, 2006), p. 7.

[27] From *An Introduction to the Anglican Communion* (London: Anglican Consultative Council, 2002).

Communion.[28] Since 1980 one Diocese of the Church of England has been the Diocese in Europe. This might be thought a strange title as it seems to imply the other forty-three dioceses of the Church of England are not in Europe. The Diocese at present has 220 congregations in twenty-nine countries. Geoffrey Rowell, the Diocesan Bishop, describes the mission of his diocese as to:

> serve Anglican and English-speaking people throughout Europe, plus Morocco, Turkey and the whole of the former Soviet Union. Together with our sister Churches, we are also a kind of shop window for Anglicanism in countries where we are a small minority Church committed to ecumenism and playing our part in the mission of the one Church in Europe.[29]

The diocesan seat is Gibraltar, though the bishop lives in West Sussex.[30] A significant point is the strong accent on the ecumenical dimension of the ecclesial reality, which does not appear so obvious in the declared aims of WARC, LWF and the EBF. There are also some Anglican churches with different Episcopal discipline (American Episcopal for instance) but they do not represent a significant presence in Europe.

Formed out of the Anglican Church, the Methodist Church has a limited presence in Europe. Methodist missionary endeavours in mainland Europe have resulted in the creation of Methodist communities in other European countries.[31] The World Methodist Council (WMC), formed in 1881, reports that it has seventy-seven member churches with thirty-six million active adherents in over 130 countries. However, apart from the British Isles, Methodist presence across Europe is relatively weak.[32] Methodism operates in a very geographical/regional way, through Methodist Conferences, and the WMC acts

---

[28] The Lusitanian Church was organised as a Synod in 1880 and fully integrated into the Anglican Communion in 1980. It has one bishop and ten churches. The Spanish Episcopal Church was formed when the Anglican Bishop of Mexico visited Spain in 1880 and took under his care several congregations seeking to follow Anglican teaching and order. It currently has one bishop and thirteen congregations.

[29] Pastoral letter from the Bishop following his enthronement in November 2001, at www.europe.anglican.org/, accessed 18 July 2006. The other Anglican Churches referred to are the Lusitanian Church, Spanish Episcopal Church, Church in Wales, Church of Ireland and the Episcopal Church in Scotland.

[30] *Ibid.*, accessed 13 January 2007.

[31] For Methodist life in Europe see P.P. Streiff, *Methodism in Europe: 19th and 20th Century* (Tallinn, Estonia: Baltic Methodist Theological Seminary, 2003).

[32] *Ibid.* Principal Methodist Churches outside the British Isles are the United Methodist Church in Northern Europe, the United Methodist Church in Germany and the United Methodist Church in Central and Southern Europe. These churches historically originate from the North American United Methodist Church. It may be that there is some hesitancy amongst British Methodists to work closely with United Methodists.

in an advisory capacity.[33] By contrast with Baptists in Europe, Methodism has little or no concept of an ecclesial reality outside of a particular Methodist Conference. A clear illustration of this would be the election of the Central Committee of CEC in 2004 at its Assembly in Trondheim. The General Secretary of CEC was told it would be unacceptable to British Methodists to be represented on the CEC Central Committee by a Methodist from another European country in the WMC, confirming the view of many externally that the WMC has a limited profile in many Methodist Conferences.[34] However, there is a desire on the part of Methodism to develop a sense of regional ecclesiology. Linda Greene of the WMC, based in North Carolina comments:

> We are especially pleased with the re-establishment of Methodist churches in eastern Europe. Our organization operates on a five-year (quinquennial) cycle. The World Methodist Council is also represented in the Conference of Secretaries of Christian World Communions.[35]

Within the Protestant section of the Church most other groupings to be found in Europe do not have a significant and wider ecclesial reality beyond a national or sub-regional church grouping, with the possible exception of Pentecostals, who will be considered later. In ecclesial terms, it is Baptists, more than any other denominational grouping, who have sought to foster a pan-European ecclesial identity. It is also Baptists who appear to have the greatest spread of any Christian World Communion denominational group across the nations of Europe. This Baptist presence has often been unrecognised in studies of religion in Europe; for example Grace Davie, in *Religion in Modern Europe*, does not include any reference to Baptists.[36] Admittedly Baptists cannot claim anything approaching the numerical strength of the Catholic Church, the Orthodox Churches or the major Protestant traditions in Europe. Through the EBF, however, they have a European identity which is stronger than that of the other Protestant denominations.

Roman Catholic and Orthodox Presence in Europe

In terms of the most significant expressions of Christian life in Europe this leaves an examination of the two major historic Episkopal and territorial

---

[33] Statement of the World Methodist Council, International Offices, Lake Junaluska, North Carolina at www.worldmethodistcouncil.org, accessed 28 January 2007.

[34] This situation was reported to me by the EBF General Secretary after an interview with the CEC General Secretary at Dunblane in June 2005. The pressure from British Methodism to insist on their own place at the CEC Central Committee deprived any EBF Union of a place on the CEC Central Committee in the period 2005-2009.

[35] Letter from L. Greene of the World Methodist Council to me, 26 April 2002.

[36] G. Davie, *Religion in Modern Europe* (Oxford: Oxford University Press, 2000).

Churches, the Roman Catholic Church and the Orthodox Church. The main Protestant Christian communions or denominations have traditionally been closer to Baptists but the Catholic and Orthodox Churches have a position of dominance which means that Baptists in Europe inevitably relate to them in various ways. The Roman Catholic Church exists as a Christian World Communion with the ecclesial pattern assuming dioceses presided over by a bishop in communion with the see of Rome.[37] His Holiness, the Pope, appoints those bishops upon the advice of his Apostolic Nuncios and having consulted the appropriate authorities within the Vatican. In fact, in most countries or groups of countries the bishops cooperate together in some form of Conference of Bishops, and across Europe as a whole there is a Catholic organisation, the Council of European Bishops' Conferences (CCEE), with a secretariat based in Switzerland. The CCEE has few, if any, ecclesial functions, but in the last twenty years has worked to cooperate with the member churches of CEC.[38] Two specific initiatives have been the First and Second European Ecumenical Assemblies held in Basle, Switzerland and Graz, Austria.[39] More recently the CCEE has signed 'Guidelines for Cooperation'[40] and the Introduction states:

> At this time of transition to a new millennium in Christian history, CEC and CCEE are aware of their responsibility to serve the process of reconciliation among the churches towards visible unity, to join together in a witness of proclamation of the Gospel in Europe, and to seek ways of cooperation in social and cultural life.[41]

The accent of this ecumenical document is on *koinonia*, reconciliation and mission. Indeed, clause 2.2 of the Guidelines says:

> In pursuing and deepening their cooperation, CCEE and CEC respect the ecclesiological, historical and structural differences between their two organisations. This is in order to avoid misunderstandings and false expectations on both sides, but also to see our differences as mutually enriching.[42]

Clearly, the Roman Catholic Bishops, acting through their national conferences, wish to engage in some modest ecclesial life and functions at a pan-European level and the Second European Ecumenical Assembly had a message from Pope John Paul II which, *inter alia*, said:

---

[37] A complicating factor is the existence of the Uniate churches in some parts of Europe.

[38] The Conference of European Churches [CEC] is an organisation drawing together over 125 Orthodox and Protestant Churches in Europe.

[39] A third European Ecumenical Assembly took place in Sibiu, Romania in 2007.

[40] Guidelines for CEC/CCEE Cooperation adopted in Guernsey, March 1999 and signed in Prague, February 2000, CEC/CCEE, Geneva/St Gallen, May 2000.

[41] *Ibid.*

[42] *Ibid.*

> I express my good wishes to the participants in the Second European Ecumenical Assembly... convey the assurance of my prayerful closeness to the brothers and sisters of the Christian Churches and ecclesial communities of Europe, who in the name of the Lord and in the spirit of Reconciliation have gathered to hear the word of God calling us to reconciliation and communion.[43]

The Orthodox Church exists in a range of autocephalous churches in almost every part of Europe which are essentially territorial in character.[44] However, as the Ecumenical Patriarch of Constantinople[45] commented in 2002, he does have an exceptional authority:

> As the First Throne in the Orthodox Church, indissolubly connected with the content of Orthodox conciliar consciousness and acquires the fullness of its expression in the revitalization of the conciliar system, the operation of which reveals ecclesiastical structures and the canonical composition of the whole body of the Orthodox Church.[46]

This statement appears to mean that the Ecumenical Patriarch has his eye set upon a General Council of the Church, pointing back to encyclicals of 1902 and 1904 calling for preparatory work to the rekindling of 'the Orthodox conciliar self-consciousness'.[47] Work proceeded throughout the last century on pre-planning for a Holy and Great Council, with the Third Pre-Conciliar meeting taking place in Chambesy-Geneva in 1982. Preparatory work continues for a fourth Preconciliar Panorthodox Consultation which would concern the relations of local Orthodox Churches to each other and to the Ecumenical Patriarchate (Diaspora, Autocephaly, Autonomous and the Diptychs).[48] It is such a Holy and Great Council which would have a pan-European expression

---

[43] Message from Pope John Paul II, the Vatican, 20 June 1997, in 'Reconciliation gift of God and source of new life', *Documents from the Second European Ecumenical Assembly in Graz* (Switzerland: CCEE/CEC, 1998).

[44] The principal autocephalous churches being the Russian Orthodox Church, Romanian Orthodox Church, the Ecumenical Patriarchate, Serbian Orthodox Church, Greek Orthodox Church, Orthodox churches in Finland, Poland and Georgia and the Ukrainian Orthodox Church. In Western Europe there is generally a diocese owing allegiance to the Ecumenical Patriarch.

[45] I use this title which is his own official title and will use the forms declared by the Orthodox Church in their official publications.

[46] Statement on Conciliar Self-consciousness by the Ecumenical Patriarch, 2002 (Constantinople/Istanbul, 2004).

[47] Statement by the Ecumenical Patriarch on initiating the common search for convening a Panorthodox Holy and Great Council in which the entire ecclesiastical body of Orthodoxy would be represented, Constantinople 2000, at www.ecupatriarchate.org, accessed 28 January 2007.

[48] Information provided by the Office of the Ecumenical Patriarch, April 2002.

and would be able to address issues about the mission and ecclesiology of the Orthodox Church in Europe. Until such a Council is convened, essentially, there can only be a wider perspective beyond the national orthodox churches by consultation and some measure of dialogue between the Ecumenical Patriarch and his brother Metropolitans and Primates. There is also some agreement between the Ecumenical Patriarch and his brother Metropolitans and Primates to enter dialogue with other Christian World Communions, such as the World Alliance of Reformed Churches.[49]

Within the context of discussions that have taken place about matters of an ecumenical nature within the EBF family, the most potentially divisive issue has been about relationships between the EBF and the Catholic and Orthodox communities in Europe. On the whole the EBF, as a body, has not entertained serious dialogue and contact with the CCEE, not least because some Unions, such as the Italians and Belgians, who live in a situation where Catholicism (religious, social and political) is experienced in a very negative and threatening way, would be concerned about over much contact being made. In this context it is important to note that Baptists across Europe have had markedly different attitudes to various ecumenical and confessional traditions and these attitudes have been influenced by the ecclesial setting in the particular context, the attitude of partner missionary organisations and the nature of the relationship between the state and the Christian churches. Inevitably, given that Baptist thinking comes 'from below', the difference in outlook of the various member Unions has affected the attitude of the EBF as a whole. However, as will be seen, within the EBF there is active communal discussion of the issues, and at certain key points participation in ecumenical events as a European Baptist community in ways which have been much more significant than in other parts of the world Baptist community and more than has been possible for other Christian World Communions in a European context.

In terms of Baptist contact with the Roman Catholic Church, formal encounter on the part of European Baptists has generally been confined to settings of a more ecumenical nature. However, in 1991 the EBF General Secretary, Karl Heinz Walter, was invited as one of fourteen fraternal delegates to the special Synod of Catholic Bishops in Rome.[50] No other significant contact was made by the EBF, as such, until Tony Peck, as the new EBF General Secretary, attended the funeral of Pope John Paul II in 2005. He was

[49] Within the general family of Orthodoxy it should be noted there are also oriental churches such as the Armenian Apostolic Church, the Syrian and Coptic Orthodox churches which have a presence in the region.

[50] Of the fourteen Christian groupings invited, three Orthodox accepted, five declined. All the non-Orthodox – Anglican, Lutheran, Reformed, Baptist – accepted. CEC information document 91/33, 1991.

part of a Baptist delegation of three – the BWA General Secretary, Denton Lotz, the General Secretary of the Baptist Union of Great Britain (and President-elect of the BWA), David R. Coffey, and Tony Peck as BWA Regional Secretary for Europe and the Middle East. On the night prior to the funeral the delegation met with Anna Maffei, President of the Italian Baptist Union, who expressed some disquiet at the Baptists sending a delegation to the funeral in view of the negative experiences Italian Baptists had of this particular Pontiff and the general negative reality of being a Baptist in Catholic Italy.[51] The delegation listened to her with respect, understanding only too well the problems experienced by Baptists in countries which had a high proportion of Catholics and where the social order was dominated by a Catholic culture. Nevertheless, the approach of contact and dialogue has been a mark of the life and work of the EBF and the delegation attended the Papal funeral without any other significant opposition.

The World Council of Churches

At this point, examination needs to take place of certain specific ecumenical communities with which the EBF has had to engage. The first ecumenical challenge for European Baptists in the period under review came with the formation of the WCC in Amsterdam in 1948.[52] In post Second World War Europe there was a ferment of activity as churches sought to develop a new spirit of cooperation. As Baptists in Europe were discussing the formation of a European-wide dimension to their work at the 1948 BWA London meeting,[53] Baptist bodies were also discussing whether to identify with this new world body. Baptists in America were divided, with Northern (American) Baptists (ABC)[54] deciding to belong and sending a strong delegation to the Amsterdam meetings, but with Southern Baptists standing apart. The provisional WCC organisations were already involved with the BWA Relief Committee in assisting Baptists in working with displaced people in mainland Europe. But in Europe only the British Baptists, under the General Secretary, M.E. Aubrey, had shown a strong inclination to join the WCC, and this matter was of some concern to the ABC leadership. Edwin A. Bell, American Baptist Churches representative in Europe, was asked to provide some reflection on the situation

---

[51] Information provided by Tony Peck in a personal interview immediately after the funeral in Rome.

[52] For the history of ecumenism in general and the WCC in particular see the three volume, *A History of the Ecumenical Movement,* referred to earlier in this chapter at footnote 5.

[53] Minutes of the BWA Meeting, London, 1948, copy in possession of the author.

[54] On the various names of what is now American Baptist Churches (USA) see R.E. Schlosser, 'Chronology of the American Baptist Churches', *American Baptist Quarterly,* Vol. XIV, No. 2 (June 1995), pp. 167-76.

and wrote to Marlin Farnum that the attitude of European Baptists was:

> one of reserve because of the historic domination of the free churches by the official church groups, and the fact that uniformly in Europe ecumenical and reconstruction committees are made up almost entirely of people from the larger, 'official' church groups. ... Drs t'Hooft and Cockburn seem to have a sincere desire to achieve genuine ecumenicity and relationships in the various countries.[55]

However, Bell went on to note that by contrast with the helpfulness of the WCC leadership, most of the subordinate staff in Geneva were 'European Lutherans' and were not so helpful to those from the Baptist and Free Church streams of church life.

If the thought of active involvement in formal ecumenical ecclesial structures was not conducive to the EBF Executive in the 1950s, it should not be assumed this represented some general European Baptist isolationism. The 1958 Second European Congress of the EBF, held in West Berlin, had a welcome at the opening ceremony from Martin Niemöller, President of the German Evangelical Church (EKD) and of the Social Committee of the Christian Churches in Germany.[56] The issue appears at this stage to have been about how far the EBF, as a Federation, had the authority to represent member bodies in other discussions and how the diverse approaches of the member Unions to other Christian communions could be adequately reflected. This reticence did not extend to individuals participating in the wider Christian scene, nor to the EBF itself involving representatives of other traditions in the events staged by the EBF. The Executive Committee of the EBF discussed ecumenical relations when they met in 1959 at De Vinkenhof in Holland, when the issue was raised by Hans Luckey of Germany, who had just completed his term as EBF President. Luckey, Director of the Baptist Seminary in Hamburg, was a committed ecumenist and, in October 1961, was elected President of the National Council of Churches in Germany (Arbeitsgemeinschaft Christlicher Kirchen in Deutschland) in succession to Martin Niemöller.[57] The cautious attitude of the 1950s was to change and the 1960 EBF Council in Vienna welcomed Lutheran Superintendent George Trear, who brought a greeting from

---

[55] Letter from E.A. Bell to M.D. Farnum, 18 March 1948, ABFMS Archives, Box 395, American Baptist Historical Society, Valley Forge, Pa.

[56] Minutes of the EBF Executive Committee, Berlin, 24-25 September 1957, p. 49, Box 801, EBF Archive, International Baptist Theological Seminary [IBTS], Prague and B. Green, *Crossing the Boundaries: A History of the European Baptist Federation* (Didcot: Baptist Historical Society, 1999), p. 39.

[57] Reported in European Baptist Press Service [EBPS] Bulletin, November 1961, EBPS Bulletins for 1961, 61:39, EBPS Archive, IBTS, Prague.

the Lutheran Church of Austria.[58] Meanwhile, the attitude of Bell to the WCC was changing. When he came towards the end of his service, he wanted to induct his successor to the WCC and wrote to Erik Rudén suggesting a visit. He especially planned meetings with Baptists working for the WCC, including Glen Garfield Williams, Secretary for Interchurch Aid in Europe, Paul Abrecht in the Study Department, and Edwin Robertson, Secretary for Research in the Use of the Bible in the Churches.[59]

One problem with the WCC was that in some countries where Baptists might be sympathetic to the WCC, the national state church wanted to exercise control, even over the delegations sent to the WCC by other churches. The Danish Baptists wanted to join the WCC, but the state church persisted in saying that they must choose the people who represented Danish Baptists.[60] Such attitudes by national churches – Lutheran, Reformed and Anglican – did little to encourage European Baptists to join, though the leaders of ABC continued to encourage them.[61] Nevertheless, despite this initial reluctance, J.H.Y. Briggs notes that Baptist groups in Europe who are WCC members, include the Danes, the Hungarians, the Italians and the British, and that they amount to five-per-cent of the whole WCC membership, just one-per-cent behind the Reformed and Methodists.[62] The EBF itself remained, in a formal sense, apart from the WCC, though there were many informal contacts, especially through the relationship of the EBF General Secretary to the World Confessional Families. Some activities of the WCC did prove attractive to European Baptists, even when individuals were opposed to the idea of the WCC as such. One particular example was the summer programme run at Casa Locarno, the Ecumenical Conference Centre used often by the WCC. This programme of lectures and relaxation was especially popular with Baptists from Eastern Europe, the funding of which required assistance from American Baptists, Southern Baptists and the EBF. The then ABC Fraternal delegate in

---

[58] Minutes of the EBF Council, Vienna, September 1960, p. 78, Box 801, EBF Archive, IBTS.

[59] Letter from E.A. Bell to E. Rudén, 22 October 1959, Erik Rudén Papers, Box 1, Angus Library, Regent's Park College, Oxford.

[60] The Danish State Lutheran Church has been one of the most authoritative and repressive of state churches in regard to Baptists. At a meeting of Danish Baptist Pastors held at IBTS, Prague, 25-29 April 2005, a significant period of time was devoted to discussing the way Danish Baptists are illegitimised by the inability to have recognised confessional theological education, to have civil registration of births and to have any real access as an ecclesial community to government. My observations as a lecturer, panelist and participant in this conference. In conversation J.H.Y. Briggs confirmed my perceptions (23 February 2007).

[61] Report of E.A. Bell to ABFMS, March 1948, ABFMS Archives, Box 395.

[62] J.H.Y. Briggs, 'Baptists and the Ecumenical Movement', *Journal of European Baptist Studies* [JEBS], Vol. 6, No. 1 (September 2005), pp. 11-17.

Europe, Denton Lotz, wrote to EBF General Secretary, Gerhard Claas, in 1979:

> I have so many requests from Baptists in the USSR for Casa Locarno I am embarrassed. Now Franz Klem has told Lehotsky how nice it is and reluctantly I sent a recommendation to Meyhoffer [WCC] from Sudar! And Lehotsky all these years has been against the WCC. Then this past year we had four from Latvia and two more have been invited, and now an Estonian wants to come, in addition to the regular group of Baptists every year from Poland and Hungary![63]

Lotz's view was that the WCC Casa Locarno experience produced a very positive echo amongst Eastern European Baptists and developed a good ecumenical spirit, apparently even amongst some who had previously been opposed to the WCC and its work.

In another letter, to Carl Tiller at the BWA, Lotz, reflecting on his experience of serving as an ABC missionary in Europe, reported on attending the WCC Central Committee as the BWA observer and remarked, 'I enjoyed this opportunity to be an observer for the BWA. There is more flexibility and mobility [in the WCC] than many realise.'[64] This attitude might be said to sum up the experience of Baptists in Europe who came into contact with the WCC through countless special projects, bi-lateral study commissions and experiences such as Casa Locarno. However, European Baptist involvement in the WCC remained modest throughout the first fifty years of the life of the EBF. At the same time, certain individual Baptists, such as E.A. Payne,[65] and some Baptist Unions, such as the Danes, the Russians and the British, made significant contributions to the life of the WCC.[66] The level of EBF involvement in the WCC at the present time might be regarded as limited and focused, particularly on the relationship between the Baptist Union of Great Britain and the WCC, with Ruth A. Bottoms from Britain serving on the Central Committee of the WCC, and as Moderator of the Commission on World Mission and Evangelism. Another British Baptist, J.H.Y. Briggs, also served on the Central Committee and other committees of the WCC.[67]

One area of the life and work of the WCC where European Baptists have

---

[63] D. Lotz to G. Claas, 1 February 1979, G. Claas Correspondence, Box 33, EBF Archive, IBTS.

[64] D. Lotz to C. Tiller, 10 August 1977, G Claas Correspondence, Box 33, EBF Archive, IBTS.

[65] On the involvement of E.A. Payne see W.M.S. West, *To Be A Pilgrim: A memoir of Ernest A Payne* (Guildford: Lutterworth Press,1983).

[66] The involvement of key individuals has been charted by J.H.Y. Briggs in 'Baptists and the Ecumenical Movement', pp. 11-17.

[67] *Ibid.*

been consistently involved has been that of the Faith and Order Commission.[68] A succession of European Baptist theologians gave themselves to this group and ensured that the commission's work was regularly brought into the thinking arena of the EBF and its member Unions. Prominent amongst those engaged in these tasks throughout the history of the EBF have been Günter Wagner (IBTS, Rüschlikon), W.M.S. West (Bristol Baptist College), Keith W. Clements (Bristol Baptist College) and Christopher J. Ellis (Bristol Baptist College).[69] European Baptist interest was especially sparked by the publication, in 1982, of the Lima Document, *Baptism, Eucharist and Ministry* (BEM).[70] The then EBF General Secretary, Knud Wümplemann, encouraged all the Unions in Europe to study this report and to make their responses. In a circular letter of November 1984 he commented:

> The 'Lima-text' on 'Baptism, Eucharist and Ministry' is now being discussed in many countries. The EBF office shall be happy to distribute among the member unions the Baptist responses to this – not least to Baptists – very important document.[71]

By 18 November 1985 Wümplemann was able to report:

> The unions have already received copies of the responses of the 'Lima Document' on Baptism, Eucharist and Ministry, from the Baptist Unions in the Soviet Union, Great Britain and Scotland. We have also now received responses from Western Germany and from Denmark.[72]

Michael Kinnamon comments that:

> Faith and Order's major achievement of the last third of the century, however, was the document *Baptism, Eucharist and Ministry (BEM)*... Indeed BEM is widely regarded as the most influential theological text of modern ecumenism. It has been translated into nearly forty languages, used as an unofficial teaching

---

[68] W.M.S. West, 'Baptists in Faith and Order – A study in Baptismal Convergence', K.W. Clements (ed.) *Baptists in the Twentieth Century* (London: Baptist Historical Society, 1983), pp. 55-75.

[69] Whilst it might appear that there has been a disproportionate involvement by Bristol Baptist College, it should be noted that West began his involvement with Faith and Order whilst a local pastor at St Albans and after doing doctoral studies in Zürich, and Ellis whilst a local pastor in Sheffield.

[70] *Baptism, Eucharist and Ministry*, Faith and Order Paper 111, WCC, 1981, Geneva.

[71] Letter from the EBF General Secretary to all the member Unions, 8 November 1984, EBF Correspondence 1982-1986, Box 2, EBF Archive.

[72] Letter from the EBF General Secretary to all Unions, 18 November 1985. EBF Correspondence 1982-1986, Box 2, EBF Archive.

document in many churches, and has contributed to liturgical renewal amongst Protestants and served as a resource of numerous dialogues.[73]

This was certainly the experience amongst Baptists, and many Unions in Europe engaged with the issues it raised, not least how Baptists were to regard those baptised in infancy who went on to make an active profession of faith and to engage seriously in the life and work of their own churches and not a few of whom wanted at some point to be involved with Baptist churches. This became a key point in national ecumenical discussions in the British Isles and Scandinavia and would later be addressed in the various inter-confessional dialogues, and, as far as the EBF is concerned, would be at the heart of the dialogue with the CPCE churches (see later). Knud Wümplemann's positive assessment indicates how the EBF sought to assist in the process of the reception of BEM and to enable the Unions in Europe to see how other European Baptists were dealing with the issues raised and reacting to the contents of BEM. This kind of activity by the EBF is in marked contrast to the lack of such ecumenical involvement by the other regions of the BWA, especially the North American Baptist Fellowship (NABF).[74] Outside Europe the regional Baptist bodies do not seem to interact ecumenically within their continents. It is a commonplace remark of Baptists within NABF that 'being ecumenical' relates to conversation and inter-action with other Baptist denominations within the USA.[75]

The situation in Europe is mixed. There are active ecumenists among Baptists but the position of Baptist leaders in several European Baptist Unions might be called into question if they became involved in wider ecumenical dialogue through the WCC or other bodies. Whilst the EBF has generally sought not to take sides in any disputes, Officers of the EBF or the fraternal representatives of the mission agencies, working in partnership with the EBF, might sometimes assist in enabling constructive dialogue between those

---

[73] M. Kinnamon, 'Assessing the Ecumenical Movement' in *A History of the Modern Ecumenical Movement* Vol. 3, p. 56.

[74] This contrast was remarked upon by Tony Peck, EBF General Secretary, following a discussion between BWA General Secretary, Denton Lotz, and the BWA Regional Secretaries in their annual meetings in Falls Church, 1-3 March 2005. Peck says representatives from elsewhere in the world were excited to discover that the EBF had engaged in ecumenical dialogue with the Conference of Protestant Churches in Europe [CPCE] and participated in the life of CEC. Personal interview with Tony Peck, Friday, 4 March 2005.

[75] Alan Stanford, Baptist Regional Secretary for the Baptists of North America, confirmed this understanding to me in conversation at the BWA General Council in Mexico City, July 2006. An exception to this might be seen in the Progressive National Baptist Convention (Inc) and American Baptist Churches USA who are members of the American Council of Churches and of the WCC and participate in those bodies.

holding different points of view. So, for instance, in the Yugoslavia Baptist Union, the Executive Committee was divided in 1981 over the activities of Stepan Orcic, then President of the Seminary at Novi Sad, and Branco Lovrec,[76] editor of the Baptist Journal. Several pastors, including Orcic and Lovrec, had engaged with ecumenical developments in the country and this had created tension within the Union. Josef Horak, a leading figure in the Union, had demanded their removal from office. John David Hopper, at that time Southern Baptist Convention (SBC) fraternal delegate in the area, was asked to mediate in the dispute and agreed to meet with the Union Committee and the two men on 16 May 1981.[77] In the event, Lovrec went on to become the President of the Croatian Baptist Union and a Vice-President of the BWA,[78] and Orcic continued as the Seminary President for many years.

Arguably, the willingness of many European Baptists to be involved ecumenically has a great deal to do with the missiological dimension of the Baptist vision. William Burrows postulates that the discernment of what mission means locally is the major task of the particular congregations that exist in specific geographical and cultural settings, but he adds that 'nurturing international and cross-cultural bonds among families of Christians is the prime mission of organizations such as the Vatican, the World Council of Churches, and the Lausanne Committee for World Evangelization'.[79] This statement, from a major figure in the international mission studies world, is important. It specifically associates the WCC with local and wider mission in the world. It also focuses on one of the key ecclesial dimensions of the EBF, which, has as been seen, has a stronger ecclesial reality in the context of Europe than most other Christian World Communions – mission. The missional dimension holds a key to a principal reason for the 'bottom-up' approach to ecclesial life having a significant form and purpose – the purpose is that of the encouragement and sustaining of the missionary task. This will be examined further elsewhere, especially when looking at specific initiatives, such as the EBF Indigenous Missionary Project.

---

[76] B. Lovrec, a retired medical doctor, has remained prominently involved in Yugoslavian, then Croatian Baptist life and in ecumenical activities until today.

[77] Report of J.D. Hopper, April 1981, EBF General Secretary Files, Box 3, EBF Archive.

[78] B. Lovrec served as a BWA Vice-President from 2000-2005 and is now an elder statesman amongst the young leadership of the Baptist Union of Croatia. Croatia was a region within Yugoslavia, gaining freedom from the Federal Republic in the early 1990s.

[79] W.R. Burrows, 'Reconciling all in Christ: An old new paradigm for mission', *Journal of the International Association for Mission Studies*, Vol. XV,1998, p.85.

The Conference of European Churches (CEC/KEK)

The WCC is, by definition, global. CEC is, also by definition, European. CEC was formally established in 1959 with an assembly held at the Nyborg Strand Hotel in Denmark. The conference theme was 'European Christianity in the Secularised World of Today'.[80] From the beginning, CEC was seen principally as an organisation for Protestant and Orthodox denominations to belong to and the first assembly had forty-five denominations from twenty countries present.[81] However, there was hesitation in some parts of Europe about the development of this organisation, particularly amongst the Nordic countries and in the British Isles. Some ecumenical bodies, such as the British Council of Churches, were present at the early meetings, holding watching briefs for a range of denominations not yet willing to join but interested in what was happening. Inevitably most European Baptists were amongst those wary of a pan-European group, though from the beginning the EBF took a serious interest in the Nyborg Assemblies.[82] For the Lutheran and Reformed churches, the idea of a European ecumenical body was important and they pressed forward with their vision, despite the hesitancy in North and North West Europe and within specific Christian communions. Naturally, Baptists, seen by others to be part of the historic family of churches arising out of the Reformation,[83] were invited to participate. At the end of the debate on the question, the EBF Executive resolved that the Federation, as such, should take no action.[84] Few Baptist denominations in Europe joined the embryo CEC and even such committed ecumenists as the British Baptists did not join in their own right until the mid 1960s, preferring, with other British churches, to be represented through the British Council of Churches, rather than have direct membership. It was only after a Welsh Baptist, Glen Garfield Williams,[85] was appointed General Secretary of the CEC in 1962,[86] that Baptist involvement became more

---

80 R. Gurney (ed.), *CEC at 40: Celebrating the 40th anniversary of the Conference of European Churches 1959-1999* (Geneva: CEC, 1999), p. 12.

81 *Ibid.*, p. 13.

82 Details of Baptist participants have been noted elsewhere and EBF President, Baungaard Thomsen, was a keen advocate of the EBF having at least observer status at these gatherings.

83 Though many Baptist scholars, myself included, would argue we belong more to the gathering churches of the radical reformation (G.H. Williams *et al*)/believers church (Darnburgh, Estep, Garrett and others)/gathering church (Jones and Wright)/pneumatic church (Newbigin) stream of Christianity and not the magisterial reformation stream.

84 Minutes of the EBF Executive Meeting, 7-9 September 1959, De Vinkenhof, Holland, p. 67, Box 801, EBF Archive.

85 Two of the four General Secretaries of CEC to date have been Baptists: G.G. Williams, 1962-1986, and K.W. Clements, 1997-2005.

86 G.G. Williams served as General Secretary of CEC until his retirement in 1986.

pronounced.[87]

When the developing CEC held a series of conferences at Nyborg, Denmark, in 1959 and 1960,[88] the EBF Council, meeting in September 1959, in Vienna, agreed:

> That the Officers of the Federation should appoint an observer at the Conference (Nyborg II). As to future Conferences it was recommended that the invitations would go to the National unions as the Federation's representatives and not to the Federation as such.[89]

This view was echoed when the EBF Executive met the following year in Belgium. The decision of the Executive meeting in Brussels to appoint an observer was reported by the newly-formed European Baptist Press Service, which described events at the Executive:

> The committee.... approved the appointment of an observer to represent the European Baptist Federation at the third Conference of European Churches, an ecumenical gathering to be held in Nyborg, Denmark, next year. Several Baptist Unions are expected to send delegates.[90]

The presence of an observer from the EBF at both Nyborg I and Nyborg II had been noted when European members of the BWA had met at Oxford early in 1961. The Executive went on to reiterate the view expressed at the EBF Council in Vienna, noting that:

> Since the European Baptist Federation is not a church, but a federation for co-operation between the various European Baptist Unions, invitations to send delegates to the Ecumenical Conference at Nyborg should be given to the national Baptist Unions. At two of the previous conferences, the EBF had been represented by one or more observers and thus it was further recommended that the Federation would appreciate being able to send an observer to the next conference in Nyborg.[91]

By Nyborg VII, held in Engleberg, Switzerland, in September 1974, the Baptist

---

[87] For a brief history of CEC see Gurney, *CEC at 40*. The EBPS records that there were 12 Baptists from 9 European countries (6 West, 3 East) present, EBPS News Release 62: 277, EBPS Archive.

[88] These Conferences are often referred to as Nyborg I and Nyborg II. The first was an exploratory event, the second was on the theme, 'The service of the church in a changing world'. See Gurney, *CEC at 40*, pp. 13-15.

[89] Minutes of EBF Council, Vienna, 10-13 September 1960, p. 83, Box 801, EBF Archive.

[90] EBPS Bulletin 10, J.A. Moore (ed), Rüschlikon, 1961, EBPS Archive.

[91] Minutes of the EBF Executive Committee, Brussels, 4-5 September 1961, unnumbered page, EBF Archive.

Unions of Denmark, Germany (East and West), Great Britain, Italy, Poland, Sweden, Switzerland and USSR had all joined CEC.[92] It is worth noting that at this time Knud Wümplemann and Gerhard Claas were General Secretaries of their respective Unions and involved with Nyborg VII, and would go on to encourage greater EBF participation as they later occupied leadership roles within the EBF.

It could be argued that 1974 marked something of a turning point for CEC and several of those involved, including British Baptist, E.A. Payne, who had been in attendance at the Nyborg meetings in his role as a President of the WCC. Payne sent a letter to G.G. Williams advocating a greater emphasis on *koinonia* and worship in the assemblies and less on the actual programme work of CEC between Assemblies.[93] A decade later, in 1985, David Lagergren from Sweden, as EBF President, reported to the EBF Executive Committee on a Consultation he had attended at Sigtuna, Sweden, on the involvement of the Nordic churches with the agencies associated with CEC, in particular on the European Ecumenical Commission on Church and Society. During the Consultation, Lagergren had been challenged about why Baptists had so little involvement in these European Ecumenical structures. Lagergren responded:

> I underlined the main purpose of the European Baptist Federation had always been to be a bridge between East and West and that, in my opinion, it was very unlikely that the EBF or any of its member unions in the Nordic countries would engage in such a unilateral West European undertaking as the European Ecumenical Commission on Church and Society.[94]

Lagergren was being somewhat disingenuous. The founding fathers of the EBF envisaged, as has been seen, something far more than a 'bridge'. It was typical of officers of the EBF to be actively involved in the ecumenical machinery and to operate as if there was a representative function for EBF officers within the wider ecumenical constituency, whilst at the same time protesting, if ever challenged, that they simply had observer status or a listening ear. In fact, in Europe the EBF has had more of an ecclesial reality at European level than most other Christian World Communions and there is, amongst other groups, as

---

[92] 'Technical and Informatory Documentation', CEC, Nyborg IV, E.A. Payne Papers, Box 64, Angus Library.

[93] Letter from E.A. Payne and seven others to G.G. Williams, CEC, 13 October 1974. E.A. Payne Papers, Box 64, Angus Library.

[94] Report from D. Lagergren to the EBF Executive Committee, Lisbon, Portugal, 1985, Box, 6, EBF Archive. Note: the European Ecumenical Commission on Church and Society was amalgamated within CEC at Graz in 1997.

will be seen, a recognition of the representative role of EBF officers.[95]

The CEC Assembly in Stirling, Scotland, in 1986, had several Baptists present[96] and the EBF appointed a delegate, David S Russell (past EBF President and retired General Secretary of the Baptist Union of Great Britain). As became the norm at such CEC Assemblies, the Baptists present had met together as a denominational caucus and sent a request to the EBF regarding the EBF Congress planned for Budapest in 1989 proposing that there should be a strong programmatic emphasis on peace.[97] Discussing this theme in the context of the Stirling CEC Assembly they noted that:

> On the one hand there is a risk of some of our church people focusing their attention on peace and environmental issues while others appear only to be concerned with their inner and personal peace. Our concern is that these issues could polarize positions and widen the gap between Baptist people.
>
> In the light of these insights we suggest that the [EBF] Council take into consideration a theme for the 1989 Budapest Congress which deals with both the aspects of peace described in the concept of 'shalom', both reconciliation with God and reconciliation with humankind and creation.
>
> We feel that such a theme would not only bridge the gap between contrasting Baptist positions but could also be a service (diakonia) to our fellow Christians in Europe who face similar issues.[98]

This initiative was important: it came from people representing significant Unions within the EBF; it was a reflection on the CEC Conference theme of 'Glory to God and Peace on Earth'; and it was an attempt to make positive input into the planned EBF Congress to be held in 1989. Within the EBF Executive Committee there was a feeling that this theme would be addressed in the overall Congress theme.

Presenting a report to the EBF Executive Committee, the EBF representative at the CEC Assembly, David Russell, noted:

> Baptist voices were heard at the Assembly, both in plenary and in sections... Baptists have a significant role to play in the ongoing debate [on the nature and

---

[95] This has been most clear, for instance, in the role EBF has played in discussions with the CPCE in a series of meetings from 2002-2004 and in EBF representation on the CPCE Study Commissions.

[96] Representing ten Unions – Denmark, Germany (East and West), Hungary, Italy, Poland, Sweden, Switzerland, UK, USSR. Letter from 'Baptist delegates to the IX CEC Assembly', Box 806, EBF Archive.

[97] Minutes of the EBF Executive Committee, September 1986, Glasgow, Box 806, EBF Archive.

[98] Letter of 9 September 1986 from the Baptist delegates to the IX CEC Assembly. The group included Union Officers from several large EBF member bodies, Box 806, EBF Archive.

> mission of the church].... There is a need for Baptists to consider seriously their mission role in Europe alongside other churches....the issues from the WCC Faith and Order Lima Report should involve Baptists... two Baptists were elected to serve on the Advisory [now Central] Committee, Sergei Nikolaev and Paulo Spanu.[99]

This reflects a general concern of Baptist representatives serving within CEC that sometimes not enough attention was paid to evangelism and mission. Of course, within CEC this proved to be a difficult topic as what is seen as mission and evangelism within baptistic communities can be viewed by the Orthodox and certain national or state churches as proselytism. Nevertheless, at the Stirling Assembly in 1986, the CEC Policy Reference Committee proposed that:

> The churches' mission in a secularised Europe be given priority for the next period. The need for this theme was underlined in statements by several member churches, by President André Appel and by other speakers in the Assembly. The European churches owe this concentration on mission in their own continent to the churches of other continents, which they once evangelised. In the changing situation in Europe it is necessary to focus attention not only on studies but also on the practical exchange of information about ways in which the gospel can be proclaimed faithfully in different situations and about appropriate and effective forms of mission. Within our ecumenical fellowship proselytism has no place.[100]

This positive recommendation, with its acknowledgement of concerns about proselytism,[101] became firmly embedded in the programmatic work of CEC, much to the delight of Baptists involved. In November 1991 representatives of CEC participated in the fifth Encounter with European Roman Catholics at the famous Catholic shrine of Santiago de Compostela in Spain. Unfortunately, Nikolai Zverev from Russia was unable to participate, though Paulo Spanu, the other Baptist representative on the CEC Advisory Committee was there.[102] Here the theme of mission was once again addressed and the following points made:

---

[99] Report of D. S. Russell to the EBF Executive Committee, Glasgow, September 1986, Box 806, EBF Archive.

[100] Report of the Policy Reference Committee to the CEC Assembly, Assembly IX. Doc. No. 54, p. 3, Box 806, EBF Archive.

[101] Bishop Nifon, an Orthodox bishop from Romania, complained about the proselytising of Baptists and evangelicals at the CEC Advisory Committee in May 1990 in Italy. He felt this was the big ecumenical problem, not relationships between Orthodox and Catholics. CEC Central Committee Minutes 1 to 13, May 1990, Geneva.

[102] Zverev wrote to the CEC General Secretary explaining that the situation amongst Baptists in the former USSR had become very difficult. Replying, CEC General Secretary, J. Fischer, asked about the emerging Baptist Unions in the Baltic and the Ukraine, Box 106, EBF Archive.

> The churches of Europe have a right and a duty to evangelise whether they find themselves in a majority or a minority situation. It should be a golden rule that evangelism should be carried out with the cooperation of local churches and not against them. This thinking, however, did raise once again the question of how to evangelise, bring people to the Gospel and welcome new Christians into the community of the local church, without being accused of proselytism.[103]

Indeed, future CEC Assemblies were to endorse the themes of mission and the need to take action, though it was 2004 before the Anglican Church Missionary Society provided the bulk of the funding for a Baptist project worker to be appointed by CEC and to begin to map the ecumenical mission work and the prospects for further cooperation.[104]

CEC, the EBF and the Changing Face of Europe

Karl Heinz Walter, assuming the General Secretaryship of EBF in 1989, at a time of massive political change in Europe, sought to develop deeper contacts with CEC. In his own mind he believed the changing situation with regard to the collapse of communism and the attempt of some of the Orthodox churches to reassert themselves as national churches in countries such as Russia, Romania, Ukraine and Moldova, could either represent a threat or an opportunity for Baptist Unions, and so he began to encourage the External Relations Division of the EBF to explore the relationship of the EBF and its member Unions to CEC.[105] Jean Fischer, CEC General Secretary, also perceived it important to keep contact with the Baptist churches in the former USSR. The All-Union Council of Christian Baptists in the USSR had been a member of CEC, but as this communist-required institution changed shape into the Euro-Asiatic Federation of Baptist Unions and the one All-Union Council gradually became seventeen individual national Unions, the situation changed radically. It was this changing picture, indicated in a letter from CEC Advisory Committee member Nikolai Zverev, which prompted Jean Fischer to organise a special CEC delegation from Germany, Norway, Northern Ireland, Italy and France to visit specifically the Baptist congregations in Russia in May 1991.

---

[103] CEC/CCEE Final Communiqué from the 5th Encounter, Santiago de Compostela, November 1991 (Geneva: CEC).

[104] This was D.R. Jackson, a British Baptist, who had served on the Mission and Evangelism Core Group of the EBF from 2000. On joining the CEC staff he was asked to work from a base in a Reformed theological and mission institute in Budapest. Jackson was, at the same time, appointed an adjunct lecturer in evangelism at IBTS, Prague, and has regularly participated in IBTS conferences on mission, thus strengthening Baptist information and involvement in this important work of CEC.

[105] In particular he encouraged Robin Gurney, CEC Associate Secretary, to attend EBF Councils and network with members, explaining informally the work of CEC and sitting in on meetings of the EBF External Relations Division.

Two Baptists were included in the delegation, Luca Maria Negro (Italy) and Jean Figuerre (France). Diplomatically, no Orthodox representative was included, the remaining members being drawn from Anglican, Lutheran, Reformed and Methodist backgrounds.[106] The visit was primarily pastoral, seeking to stand with the Baptist community as it faced the realities of the transformation of its ecclesial life. To some of the Orthodox churches the emergence of autonomous Baptist Unions in their own canonical territories was unacceptable, even though Baptist churches were judged by the Moscow Patriarchate to be one of the traditional Christian churches of the Russian people.[107]

Inevitably, there were many on-going difficulties as the face of Europe changed. For instance, the Evangelical Christian-Baptists of Georgia applied to join CEC at the Central Committee in May 1994 and this provoked some opposition from the Orthodox, with a vote of sixteen members of the Central Committee for the proposition and three against. The French Baptist Union was accepted into membership unanimously at the same meeting. At the same meeting the BWA, and by implication the EBF, was accused of being 'imperialistic'.[108] This accusation was not well received and led to some Baptist Unions standing back from joining CEC, despite Karl Heinz Walter and Robin Gurney (CEC Communications Officer) setting up special sessions on CEC at EBF Council meetings. This experience and the hostility of the Orthodox Church to many Baptist Unions appears to have fostered a latent fear of the so-called ecumenical movement, despite the best efforts of the EBF General Secretary to point out the positive advantages. Despite the reluctance of some and the lack of a warm response from the Orthodox, several Baptist Unions, especially in Western Europe, were very active in CEC and, in 1990, the Italian Baptists hosted the CEC Presidium and Advisory [now Central] Committee at their 'Villagio della Gioventù' in Santa Severa.[109]

At the EBF Council in 1991 in Varna, Bulgaria, some discussion took place on the CEC Assembly to be held in Prague in 1992. Karl Heinz Walter intimated that Baptist Unions not in CEC who were members of the EBF would

---

[106] CEC document 91/08, 14 May 1991, CEC, Geneva.

[107] This point was made to me when attending a Russian Baptist Assembly in Moscow by the Ecumenical Representative of the Moscow Patriarchate, Father Vsevolod Chaplin.

[108] Notes on agenda document of the Central Committee – hand written by T. Lorenzen, who attended on behalf of the EBF as a Baptist observer, CEC 1992-1997, Box 806, EBF Archive.

[109] The Villagio was built for Italian Baptists in the early 1950s as a meeting place for youth and families. It was intended as a place for evangelical witness and inter-cultural gatherings. This was the first occasion it had been used as a venue for an ecumenical meeting. The CEC Central Committee was not to meet on Baptist premises again until meeting on the IBTS campus, Prague in September 2004.

be invited to send observers to Prague. At a later point in the Council, Knud Wümplemann, former General Secretary of the EBF and at that time President of the BWA, asked for permission to make a comment to the Council, referring to some remarks made by the Danish Ambassador, who had been present for part of the Council, that there were two main ways of influencing the future in Europe. The first of these was through the Council of Europe, which would deal essentially with legal matters affecting the status of churches. The second way was through CEC. Wümplemann commented on the need to 'deal with many human problems such as refugees, the rights of minorities and the use of the death penalty'.[110] The Tenth Assembly of CEC was held in Prague in 1992 and member Baptist bodies participated, but unfortunately EBF General Secretary, Walter, had to withdraw from participation at the last moment.[111] The theme of this Assembly was 'God Unites – in Christ a New Creation' and one of the contributory documents to the theme included what has proved to be a controversial ecumenical document on mutual recognition between the Waldensian, Methodist and Baptist churches in Italy.[112] The Document on Mutual Recognition from Italy was generally recognised as being one of the most progressive ecumenical concordats between Protestant denominations and hence it was used to stimulate discussion at the Prague Assembly. The core of the document declared:

> The joint Synod and Assembly joyfully affirm that the Baptist, Methodist, and Waldensian Churches mutually recognize each other as churches of Jesus Christ on the basis of a shared understanding of the Gospel, a shared vocation of witness and service in our country and a shared acceptance of the stance on faith expressed in the aforesaid document; therefore invite – Baptist churches to accept Methodists and Waldensians as full and equal members and Waldensian and Methodist churches to accept Baptists as full and equal members; each maintaining their own denominational distinctiveness...[113]

This document had been signed in Rome on, as it was put, the 473rd anniversary of the 'sixteenth-century Reformation'.[114] The Waldensians had asked for the document to be so described as they themselves looked back

---

[110] Minutes of the EBF Council, Varna, Bulgaria, September 1991, Minute 48, p. 12, EBF Archive.

[111] Fax from K.H. Walter to Czech Baptist General Secretary, Pavel Vychopen, 31 August 1992, Box 107(2), EBF Archive.

[112] CEC Official Study Document, Vol. 17, No. 3, June 1992, CEC, Geneva.

[113] Document of Mutual Recognition, The Baptist Union of Italy, the Waldensian Church of Italy, the Methodist Conference in Italy, Rome, 2-4 November 1990, Baptist Union of Italy, Rome.

[114] It is expressed in this way as the Waldensians and the Hussites both hold the view that they were part of earlier 'Reformations', though the Wyclif, Waldensian and Hussite events are often described by others as part of the Proto-Reformation.

beyond that date to a proto-reformation. This was another sign of significant changes in Europe – the language used was no longer being determined only by Western Europe. For other Baptist Unions in Europe the fact that the Italians took this step without reference to issues of believers' baptism, church order and the eucharist has never been a significant problem as the ecclesiology of baptistic groups is from the local church to the region to the continent, and the doctrine of subsidiarity would give full competence to the churches in a Union to determine such matters. However, the Waldensians, then later the Methodists, are signatories to the CPCE or Leuenberg Church Fellowship and through the succeeding years this has been a point of tension for the Leuenberg churches.[115] Nevertheless, in Prague the document was seen as significant, causing Hermann Goltz, CEC Study Secretary, to comment that it 'Represents a needed encouragement and example to us all, to be continually open in all our diversity to the gracious gift of committed fellowship in Christ'.[116] Baptists have, in certain areas, been ecumenical pioneers.

By the 1990s, Baptists had become a vociferous minority within CEC as the Baptist representatives developed confidence and gained more Unions in membership within CEC. For instance, at the Eleventh Assembly in Graz in 1997, Polish Baptist President Konstanty Wiazowski served on the Nominations Committee, British Baptist,[117] Keith G. Jones, on the Policy Reference Committee, and Russian Baptist, Nikolai Zverev was re-elected onto the Central Committee. Zverev had a remarkably long career representing Russian Baptists in the ecumenical arena, but with the development of the autonomous national Unions and the appointment of Pjotr Konovalchik, a pastor from St Petersburg, as President of the Russian Baptist Union, Zverev was given fewer opportunities to participate. Konovalchik took the key position at the 1997 Graz Assembly and more recently Zverev, though still involved in the international office of the Russian Baptists, did not participated in the CEC Central Committee after 2003, and he was not elected to serve on the Central Committee at the Twelfth Assembly in Trondheim in 2003.[118] It seems strange that a representative of one of the few growing Christian World Communions in Europe (at least in Eastern Europe) should be removed from the Central

---

[115] This agreement presented a stumbling block in the 2000-2004 conversations between CPCE (the new name for Leuenberg) and the EBF. The point will be returned to later.

[116] CEC Documentation Service, Vol. 17, No. 33, June 1992, p. 3.

[117] J.A. Newton, in his review of English nonconformists and ecumenism, generally seems to miss the significant involvement of English Baptists in the wider ecumenical scene in Europe. See his 'Protestant Nonconformists and Ecumenism', in A.P.F. Sell and A.R. Cross (eds.), *Protestant Nonconformity in the Twentieth Century* (Carlisle: Paternoster, 2003), pp. 357-80.

[118] At the 12th Assembly no Baptist was elected to serve on the CEC Central Committee and no-one else from within the baptistic grouping of churches. This must mark a disappointing development in the relationship between the EBF Unions and CEC.

Committee, when Baptists have played a key role since the earliest days. So far, the leadership of CEC has felt unable to comment on this,[119] though some speculate that again this might have elements of an Orthodox 'backlash' relating to the complex issue of proselytism.

However, though Baptists have ceased to have an elected representative on the CEC Central Committee, and in all circumstances this must be viewed as disappointing and regressive, it cannot be deduced that the EBF, as such, is, for its part, any the less involved or willing to be involved with CEC. Nor can it be asserted that the CEC officers and staff themselves are not keen to keep strong relationships with the EBF as an ecclesial body through whom Baptist communities in Europe can be contacted and with whom dialogue can take place. For the Twelfth Assembly, CEC appointed the new EBF General Secretary, Tony Peck, to be a member of the Church and Society Commission.[120] Darrell Jackson, a British Baptist minister, joined CEC staff as a researcher on Mission in Europe, based in Budapest, and the CEC Central Committee held its meeting in the European Baptist Centre in Prague from 27 September to 4 October 2004. When the EBF officially opened its Prague offices in March 2005, CEC sent a representative to the opening and dedication service.[121] At the EBF Council in Lyon, France, in September 2006, the new CEC General Secretary, the Anglican Colin Williams, attended for most of the Council and hosted a special breakfast event for the Baptist Unions in membership with CEC.[122]

Since 1989, CEC has also been involved in European Ecumenical Assemblies. The first three of these[123] were joint initiatives between CEC and CCEE, the Roman Catholic Bishop's Conference for Europe. Both events were designed to operate within and outside the established frame of ecumenical encounter, including both delegates of member churches and representatives of the wider Christian community and especially para-church organisations. The First Assembly was held in Basel, Switzerland, in 1989 and provoked little stir

---

[119] Though an exchange between the EBF General Secretary and the CEC General Secretary does point at least, in part, to manouverings by British Methodists to retain a seat on the Central Committee. This would be in addition to a seat for a 'mainland' European Methodist. This has the danger of working against Baptists and the desire to preserve the balance between Orthodox, state churches and gathering churches.

[120] The Commission was established in 1999 as a result of the integration of the European Ecumenical Commission for Church and Society [EECCS] and CEC. It is designed to encourage and sustain a Christian contribution to political, social and economic life in Europe. It has Secretariats based in Brussels and Strassbourg.

[121] Hana Tonserová, a Czech Hussite pastor working in the Patriarchal Offices in Prague.

[122] Agenda of EBF Council 2006, EBF Office Archive, Prague.

[123] The events have been Basel in Switzerland 1989, Graz in Austria 1997 and Sibiu, Romania, in September 2007.

or contact within the EBF. The Second Assembly, held in Graz, Austria, in 1997, had at least twenty-six Baptists from thirteen Baptist Unions.[124] Indeed, others were present, but not at the Baptist caucus meeting.[125] The EBF General Secretary was only able to attend the initial meetings of the Assembly. This Ecumenical Assembly seems, in a more engaging way, to have involved European Baptists. Indeed, Pjotr Konovalchik, President of the Russian Baptist Union, opted to attend the Second European Ecumenical Assembly in preference to the BWA General Council meetings held almost at the same time.[126] The EBF officers also worked hard to ensure Baptists participated fully in the Third European Ecumenical Assembly of 2007. The EBF General Secretary went so far as to have consultations with the General Secretary of the CEC and the Rector of IBTS to discuss the make-up and purpose of the EBF delegation.[127] The CEC General Secretary, recognising Baptists are under-represented in many national ecumenical delegations compared to their actual presence in Europe, actively sought to assist the EBF in securing a greater Baptist presence.[128] For Williams, there is a recognition of the importance of the EBF as being an ecclesial reality with whom he can relate and which has a Europe-wide focus reflecting the geographical area of CEC.

Ecumenical Roles Played by EBF General Secretaries

As noted earlier, the Christian World Communions were originally established in 1957 as the World Confessional Families (WCF), but more recently as the 'Christian World Communions' (CWC),[129] and have brought together the General Secretaries and other key representatives of the world denominational bodies.[130] The original use of the term 'Confession' in the title was recognised

---

[124] Information obtained from a letter to the BWA and EBF from Baptists at EEA2, Box 107, EBF Archive. The total attendance was over 10,000.

[125] My personal recollection.

[126] This caused much disturbance within the leadership of the BWA, though Konovalcik argued he could make a much more useful contribution to this event than to the standard format of a BWA General Council. Conversation with me at the time.

[127] Exchange of emails between Tony Peck and Keith Jones, May 2005, K.G. Jones personal files, IBTS, Prague.

[128] Comments made by C. Williams at the EBF Council, Lyon, France, September 2006.

[129] I use this version throughout as it is the general description within the circle of the BWA, though Meyer, and others, call them the World Christian Communions.

[130] The number of such bodies is constantly increasing, but includes the Anglican Consultative Council, the BWA, the Ecumenical Patriarchate of Constantinople, the Quakers, Seventh Day Adventists, Lutheran World Federation, Mennonite World Conference, Moscow Patriarchate, Roman Catholic Church, Salvation Army, World Alliance of Reformed Churches, World Convention of Churches of Christ, World Methodist Council, Disciples/Churches of Christ, World Evangelical Alliance, The Holiness Churches, the Moravians, Old Catholics, Oriental Orthodox, United/Uniting

to be ambiguous; Edmond Perret noted that Lesslie Newbigin, addressing the group in 1962, commented: 'Were the Churches to settle what they meant by confession, they would have settled the problem of Christian unity'.[131] However, the World Confessional General Secretaries formulated a working definition in the same year which spoke of the WCFs as 'organizations which represent families of churches'.[132] WCF meetings were intended to cover such matters as cooperation between the different confessional groups and matters of ecumenical interest.[133] By 1967 the following definition had been adopted for the WCF:

> Each World Confessional Family consists of churches belonging to the same tradition and held together by this common heritage; they are conscious of living in the same universal fellowship and give to this consciousness at least some structured expression.[134]

Originally seven world confessions were involved, though, as Meyer comments, 'from the beginning there was tension between confessionalism and ecumenism, which nevertheless did not mean that there were conflicts of principle.'[135] By 1976 the number had grown to fourteen[136] and to seventeen by 2000.[137] The unions formed out of the Reformation and post-Reformation churches were, as we have noted earlier, formal and developed federal structures. However, the Anglican Communion is obviously different in pattern, and the difference is even more pronounced among the Orthodox with, as Mayer comments, its 'conciliar structures', and the 'Catholic with its conciliar and primatial structures'.[138]

The CWC have been an important factor in the ecumenical scene and have been a setting for dialogue between the various significant Christian communities. Barriers have been broken down and, by their very meeting, have countered issues of isolationism within particular parts of the greater Christian family. Some have argued that the development of world communions mitigated against the development of effective regional movements. There is

---

Churches. Today the group is more generally known as the Christian World Communions. The WCC normally has observers present.

[131] Perret, *Twenty Years - The Conference of World Confessional Families 1957-1977*, p. 15.

[132] *Ibid.*, from 1962 Minutes, p.14.

[133] *Ibid.*, p. 11.

[134] 'The Place of World Confessional Families in the Ecumenical Movement', in *Study Encounter IV*, Geneva, WCC, 1968, p. 46.

[135] Meyer, 'Christian World Communions', p. 103.

[136] *Ibid.*

[137] *Ibid.*, p. 104.

[138] *Ibid.*, p. 105.

some truth in that statement in respect of certain of the Magisterial Reformation churches and post-Reformation churches. However, it certainly does not seem to have hindered the growth and development of the EBF as an ecclesial reality, not least because, with so many wider church bodies having their base in Europe, the EBF, principally through its General Secretary, has often been involved in the heart of discussions and issues. Nevertheless, issues of authority within the various CWC members obviously influence what can actually be achieved within the meetings.[139] CWC meetings have often been held in Europe, and thus the General Secretary of the EBF, together with, on occasions, a theologian from either the seminaries in Rüschlikon or Hamburg, represented the BWA or supported the BWA General Secretary or President in attendance a meetings of the CWC. The more developed structure of the EBF, and the fact that the EBF Council often considered ecumenical matters, might also be regarded as contributory factors to the successful involvement of representatives of the EBF in the arena of the CWC. Inevitably, such involvement gave the EBF General Secretary a vital point of contact with the ecumenical movement and insight into the major themes and debates amongst the other denominations.

When C. Roland Goulding – a British Baptist, who had been pastor of Haven Green Baptist Church, London, and involved in the life of the EBF (serving as President in the years 1960-1961) – became General Secretary of the EBF in the summer of 1965, he took a particular interest in ecumenical work. In 1972 the CWC (at that time WCF) meetings were held in Geneva. In the denominational report on that occasion, Goulding focused on the way Baptists struggled to be accepted by others in many European settings. The minutes record:

> The Baptist Church [sic] has reason to regret the hostile attitude towards it adopted by some dominant non-Baptist groups. Spain provides examples. Yet 'ecumenical' action was recently taken by Roman Catholic children in a Spanish town, who demonstrated in favour of the reopening of a Baptist school.[140]

At this same meeting, considerable discussion took place on the theme of religious liberty, which continued to be an important concern of Baptists attending this meeting and also CEC. Goulding soon began to play a more detailed role, serving as one of the five members of the Working Group of the WCF, which met between the full Conference gatherings. Here again Goulding returned to the theme of religious liberty commenting, 'The attitude and

---

[139] For an ecumenical reflection on hermeneutic boundaries and their implications for relationships between the CWCs see R.K. Downton, *Authority in the Church* (New York: University Press of America, 2006).

[140] Minutes of the Conference of Secretaries of WCF, 27-29 November 1972, Geneva, p. 6, item K, C.R. Goulding Papers, London Box 31, EBF Archive.

performance of the R.C. Church had so changed in the last ten years that minorities in some places had no more difficulties and in some cases the cooperation received was almost embarrassing!' Goulding pointed out the difficulties experienced were far more pronounced in dealings with the Orthodox Churches and the very strict application of rules concerning 'Proselytism'. The Orthodox agreed with the basis of the WCC Document on Proselytism, but very little ever happened. Goulding argued that he would like to see some constructive approach in such countries as Bulgaria and Romania.[141]

From this plea, Bishop John Howe (Anglican Consultative Council) proposed a WCF Consultation with appropriate representatives of the Orthodox Churches. This, to Goulding and his successors, represented the achievements possible through the quiet diplomatic role the EBF General Secretary, acting in the place of the BWA General Secretary. By using the ecumenical structures and involving other traditions, the cause of the free dissenting churches could be argued outwith the national majority churches. This was more effective than by Baptists alone making protests and complaints within a particular nation. Goulding also saw his brief as taking back into the Baptist structures of the EBF and BWA the debates and discussions within the ecumenical world. Such an approach has always had the possibility of tension, but Goulding and his successors, Claas, Wümplemann and Walter, have all shared that conviction. From the WCF, Goulding introduced to the Commission on Cooperative Christianity of the BWA the need to have adequate documentation and exchange of information on bilateral conversations, and to take care when planning dialogues to have more adequate representation of the total constituency of a world confessional body, especially 'the churches of the third World'.[142] He also participated in some of the information-gathering and commented on the pre-publication text of *Confessions in Dialogue.*[143]

Participation in the meetings of the CWC was always an opportunity for an EBF General Secretary to make contact with local Baptist groups, and during the communist era this sometimes gave access to people whom it would otherwise be difficult to talk with. So, in October 1983, the CWC meetings were held in Sophia, Bulgaria, and the Baptist delegation was BWA General Secretary, Gerhard Claas; EBF General Secretary Knud Wümplemann and the EBPS Officer, John Wilkes. Knud Wümplemann reported: 'We had the

[141] Minutes of a meeting of the Working Group of the Conference of Confessional Families, April 1973, p. 2. C.R. Goulding Papers, London Box 31, EBF Archive.

[142] Document presented by C.R. Goulding to the Commission on Cooperative Christianity of the BWA, July 1973, BWA Archives, Valley Forge.

[143] N. Ehrenström and G. Gassmann, *Confessions in Dialogue* (Geneva: WCC, 1975).

opportunity to worship on three occasions with the Baptists in Sofia'.[144] In this way, though the EBF did not formally participate in either CEC or the WCC, and only a minority of the Unions (principally the Russians, British and Nordic) belonged to these organisations in their own right, the General Secretary of the EBF became known in Geneva and in the circles of those engaged especially in Faith and Order work. In this, and other more formal ways, the EBF has been committed to ecumenical endeavour in and beyond Europe.

Evangelicals and Pentecostals

As previously shown, the original purpose of the EBF, when it was established in 1949, did not include any reference to relationships with other Christian communions, nor with any of the emerging or existing ecumenical structures. The first recorded minute referring to ecumenism is, significantly, not to the wider ecumenical bodies but to the Evangelical Alliance:

> Dr Petersen spoke of a plan to form a World Evangelical Fellowship which would embrace Continental branches of the World's Evangelical Alliance and certain Evangelicals in America. He feared this might tend to introduce American controversies into Europe.[145]

It is significant that the British Evangelical Alliance was hesitant about joining the world body, the World Evangelical Fellowship (WEF), which was formed in July 1952, but they subsequently did so. There was a concern that the world body, under American influence, might be stridently anti-ecumenical. Most European Evangelical Alliances did not join WEF at this point, and formed their own grouping.[146] In the Baptist context, Petersen was sounding a note which was to be echoed and reinforced down through the years, that denominational and theological difficulties amongst Baptists in the USA would be transported to the generally harmonious Baptist community in Europe through missionaries or by contact with various para-church and denominational organisations based in the USA.[147] Here, however, the point is related to the general evangelical community and not simply to the Baptist

---

[144] Report to the April 1984 EBF Executive Committee by the EBF General Secretary, Box 806, EBF Archive.

[145] Minutes of the EBF Council, Copenhagen, 29-31 July 1952, p. 18, Box 801, EBF Archive.

[146] Randall and Hilborn, *One Body in Christ*, pp. 237-41. For the history of the World Evangelical Fellowship [WEF] see D.M. Howard, *The Dream that would not Die* (Exeter: Paternoster, 1986).

[147] As is demonstrated throughout this book, the fears of F.B. Petersen have been justified.

denominations in the USA.[148] This point was taken up in a letter from W.O. Lewis to E.A. Payne in September 1952:

> It looked for a while as if the various branches of the Evangelical Alliance on the Continent would join this American Fundamentalist organization.... But there was serious opposition to such an arrangement. Our Dr Petersen was the leader of the opposition. Under his leadership a European Evangelical Alliance has been set up and plans have been made to continue the work of the Evangelical Alliance independent of any American organization.[149]

Though Baptists from Britain, America and Germany, in particular, were involved in the founding of the Evangelical Alliance in London in 1846,[150] the Alliance, as such, has hardly figured at all in relationship to the EBF. It was always intended to be more than a national organisation,[151] and as the Evangelical Alliance developed in Britain, contacts with other evangelicals in Europe were seen as important. By the twentieth century many other countries had formed their own Evangelical Alliances and Baptist leaders featured prominently in many of these groups. J.H. Rushbrooke was involved in cooperative efforts with the Evangelical Alliance leadership during the 1920s when he was representing wider Baptist interests in the European mainland,[152] but at no point after the early period of the EBF was there any significant structural contact between the national Evangelical Alliances in Europe and the EBF or its officers. This does not imply any difficulties; indeed one EBF General Secretary, Theo Angelov, was prominent in the work of the Bulgarian Evangelical Alliance. Rather, it represents the fact that the EBF developed in a way which made public and formal contact with other Christian World Communions and ecclesial and structural groupings in Europe more straightforward than with the para-church Evangelical Alliances. In many ways the Evangelical Alliance has to be seen as a para-church body which lacks, therefore, a clear ecclesial structure – in contrast to the EBF. Also, there was the lack of any effective European Evangelical Alliance until recently and that organisation, understandably, has largely worked with national evangelical groupings, rather than with European-wide ecclesial realities such as the EBF. The Bulgarian Evangelical Alliance, for example, became active in the 1990s

---

148 North American Baptists and the BWA generally speak and write of the various conventions of Baptists in the USA as if each is a 'denomination', unlike the more common Western European usage which tends to use the word denomination as referring to all groups or bodies within a particular ecclesial and theological community.

149 Letter from W.O. Lewis to E.A. Payne, 16 September 1952, BWA/EBF Correspondence, Box 26, Angus Library.

150 Randall and Hilborn, *One Body in Christ*.

151 *Ibid.*, p. 159. At the inauguration in 1846 there were representatives from Europe.

152 *Ibid.*, p. 172.

and Bulgarian Baptist Pastor, Nikolai Nedelchev, served a term as European Evangelical Alliance (EEA) President. But these relationships are personal rather than ecclesial.[153]

Similarly, engagement between Baptists and Pentecostals has largely been at a personal level. There is a Pentecostal World Fellowship[154] which draws together a variety of Pentecostal believers from across the world for the purpose of:

> …mutual edification, ways and means of world evangelization and the promulgation of the Pentecostal message and experience. Expression is given to the inherent principles of spiritual unity and fellowship of Pentecostal believers, leaving inviolate the existing forms of church government followed by its members. Recognition is given to every freedom and privilege enjoyed by any group of churches as their undisturbed possession.[155]

It might be reasonable to conclude from this statement that Pentecostals take no note of Europe as a specific area, and do not see any form of *koinonia* between the Pentecostal communities in Europe that might be taken as expressing an ecclesial reality. However, from a Baptist perspective, the interface with Pentecostalism in Europe has been very significant.[156] In some countries the communist authorities forced 'marriages' of denominational structures between Baptists and Pentecostals, especially in the former USSR. In some countries these connections continue, while in others they have broken down.[157] However, Pentecostals have not operated in Europe as European Pentecostals,

---

[153] For these Evangelical Alliance-Baptist relationships see I.M. Randall, 'Evangelicals and European Integration', *European Journal of Theology*, Vol. XIV, No. 1 (2005), pp. 17-26.

[154] On Pentecostals see A.H. Anderson and W.J. Hollenweger, *Pentecostals after a Century: Global Perspectives on a Movement in Transition* (Sheffield: Sheffield Academic Press, 1999).

[155] Official Statement of Mission and Purpose of the Pentecostal World Fellowship at http://www.pctii.org/pwf/, accessed 28 January 2007.

[156] See I.M. Randall, '"Days of Pentecostal Overflowing": Baptists and the Shaping of Pentecostalism', in D.W. Bebbington, ed., *The Gospel in the World: Studies in Baptist History and Thought*, Vol. 1 (Carlisle: Paternoster, 2002), pp. 80-104.

[157] As in the Ukraine, where Baptist Union President, Gregory Kommandant, informed me, at the EBF Council in Radosc, Poland in 2003, that Baptists and Pentecostals have good relationships, though with the collapse of communism they did create separate ecclesial structures. The same is not true in Russia where, with the collapse of the old All Union Council of Evangelical Christian Baptists [AUCECB] there is a distrust by Baptists of those exercising charismatic or Pentecostal gifts such as glossolalia. For the context see T. Pilli, 'Baptist Identities in Eastern Europe' in I.M. Randall, T. Pilli and A.R. Cross (eds.), *Baptist Identities: International studies from the Seventeenth to the Twentieth Centuries* (Milton Keynes: Paternoster, 2006), pp. 92-108.

though they often participate in wider para-church groupings such as national Evangelical Alliances, and to a certain extent in the EEA.

There have been suggestions that European Baptists should more intentionally form links with Pentecostals. In his September 1977 report the EBF General Secretary, Gerhard Claas, wrote:

> I would like to recommend to the EBF Council to reconsider bilateral talks with other churches and church groups. There is, for instance, the new charismatic movement – not only among all the Evangelicals in Europe, but also within the Catholic church. Many of our Baptist churches are ready to receive and to practise the various gifts of the Holy Spirit.[158] However, there are also charismatic circles outside the so-called established churches. These circles are more or less ecumenical, and in some cases take the role of a local church.
>
> At the same time we cannot ignore that the Pentecostal churches are the strongest growing churches in Europe. As the Pentecostals in many places really have changed and are no longer that exclusive as they were in history the time might have come that Baptists seek bilateral talks with the Pentecostals.[159]

This has not, however, happened as yet, although what Claas wrote in 1977 about the significant growth of Pentecostals in Europe is even more true three decades later.[160]

The EBF and the Leuenberg Fellowship (now CPCE)

From the point of view of the development of the EBF as a body able, willing and trusted to engage in the ecumenical arena on behalf of its member bodies, the exchanges with the Community of Protestant Churches in Europe (CPCE), previously called the Leuenberg Church Fellowship, marks a whole new era and is without parallel in the other continental regions of the BWA. To this significant development I now turn. The Leuenberg Concordat[161] represents an attempt of the principal magisterial reformation churches in Europe to achieve a measure of unity through what is often termed ‘reconciled diversity’. This

---

[158] Though Gerhard Claas could not have known this, Russian and some Ukrainian Baptists have remained very opposed to the charismatic movement. Particular concern was expressed when Grenville Overton, a British Baptist, then later N.G. Wright, spoke positively about the modern charismatic movement at EBF Council meetings in the 1980s and 1990s.

[159] Report of the EBF General Secretary, G. Claas, to the EBF Council, September 1977, Box 803, EBF Archive.

[160] Anderson and Hollenweger (eds.), *Pentecostals after a Century*.

[161] *Agreement between the Reformation Churches in Europe* (Leuenberg Concordat) (Frankfurt am Main: Verlag Otto Lembeck, 1973). Hereafter, The Leuenberg Concordat, using the official English translation, copyright the United Reformed Church in the United Kingdom.

model assumes confessional families can move beyond the excommunications and condemnations of earlier centuries and accept one another as 'sister churches' without having to repudiate their own history. The principal groups concerned with the original Leuenberg Concordat were the Reformed and Lutheran Churches in Europe.

The Concordat was completed in 1973 and initially drew together the Lutheran and Reformed Churches and the related pre-Reformation churches, the Waldensian Church (Italy) and the Czech Evangelical Brethren. It affirms that the Church is founded upon Jesus Christ alone; and:

> It is he who gathers the Church and sends it forth, by the bestowal of his salvation in preaching and sacraments. In the view of the Reformation it follows that agreement in the right teaching of the Gospel and in the right administration of the sacraments is the necessary and sufficient prerequisite for the true unity of the Church. It is from these Reformation criteria that the participating churches derive their view of church fellowship.[162]

There then followed an explanation of a common understanding of the gospel and of the place and theological understanding of preaching, Baptism and the Lord's Supper. The issues of the mutual condemnations between the Lutherans and Reformed on these topics were then addressed. In respect of the Lord's Supper the point is made that:

> We cannot separate communion with Jesus Christ in his body and blood from the act of eating and drinking. To be concerned about the manner of Christ's presence in the Lord's Supper in abstraction from this act is to run the risk of obscuring the meaning of the Lord's Supper.[163]

In such circumstances and where such consensus exists between the churches, the condemnations pronounced by the Reformation confessions were seen to be inapplicable to Reformation family churches and their doctrinal positions. The issues of christology and predestination are also examined in the agreement, and the conclusion arrived at by the signatory churches was that the condemnations of the Reformation fathers are irrelevant and no longer an obstacle to church fellowship. The idea of church fellowship in Leuenberg was to be understood as relating to witness and service, the continuing theological task and making possible pulpit and table fellowship and the mutual recognition of ordination.[164]

It can immediately be seen that Baptists did not easily identify with the Leuenberg Concordat, for both Lutheran and Reformed had condemned the

---

[162] The Leuenberg Concordat, Clause 2, p. 36.

[163] *Ibid.,* Clause III.1, para. 19, p. 40.

[164] *Ibid.,* Clause IV.3, para. 35-45, pp. 42-43.

Anabaptists. The original signatories all practised infant baptism. Meanwhile, in theological circles the idea of the distinctiveness of the churches of the Radical Reformation was gaining credence over against the simplistic view that Baptists belong to the Magisterial Reformation. Now, there were those who wanted to argue a more distinctive position for the gathering believers churches. In any event, it was essentially the Reformed and Lutheran confessional families, together with the proto-Reformation Chiesa Evangelica Valdese (Waldensian), Církev Bratrská (Czech Brethren) and the Českobratrská Církev Evangeliká (Czech Evangelical Brethren) churches who signed the Concordat between 1973 and 1976. Baptists only began conversations with the Leuenberg Church Fellowship thirty years later.

One of the developments arising out of Leuenberg was the setting up of a 'continuing doctrinal conversations' group. There then continued a process of individual Lutheran and Reformed Churches in Europe exploring the issues raised and considering whether to become signatories. In August 1975 Lukas Vischer of the Faith and Order Commission of the WCC wrote to EBF General Secretary, Ronald Goulding:

> The adoption of the agreement (Leuenberg) does not mean that the Lutheran and Reformed churches will form a block in the ecumenical movement. On the contrary, it is the declared intention of the agreement to strengthen the ecumenical commitment of the two traditions. Therefore, the continuation committee has decided to invite ecumenical guests to the continuing doctrinal conversations. Would it be possible for you to name a Baptist participant?[165]

David Lagergen of Sweden was nominated to attend the meetings in Billinghus, Sweden, and thus began a fitful relationship between the Leuenberg Church Fellowship and the EBF. The WCC sought to assist the conversations by providing administrative support and in March 1976 they wrote to Goulding:

> The first doctrinal conversations after the passing of the Leuenberg Agreement between the Lutheran and Reformed Churches in Europe will be held in Sigtuna (Sweden) from June 10-16 1976.[166]

The letter went on to say they hoped Baptists would be represented as observers and that the Methodists, Anglican, Roman Catholic and Ecumenical Patriarch (Orthodox) had already appointed observers.

As time progressed more churches in Europe of the proto-Reformation and the Magisterial and post Magisterial Reformation joined the Leuenberg Church

---

[165] Letter from L. Vischer, WCC, to C.R. Goulding, EBF, 18 August 1975, C.R. Goulding Archive, Box 32, EBF Archive.

[166] Letter from R. Sbeghen, WCC, to C.R. Goulding, 18 March 1976, EBF Archive, London Box 22, EBF Archive.

Fellowship, which attempted to address the Council of Europe and the European Union as the Protestant voice in Europe. The Baptists, true to their Radical Reformation heritage, were sceptical of this development and remained very conscious of the past condemnations of Anabaptists and Baptists, though from time to time observers did attend events as invited.[167] In 2000 the Leuenberg Church Fellowship which, by this time, incorporated other groups such as the Methodists (who joined CPCE in 1994), contemplated a further approach to the EBF, recognising that there was a large and significant non-Catholic or Orthodox church or family of churches, still outside their vision of a Protestant Church Fellowship in Europe.[168] This was, from their perspective, a hindrance to their claim to represent all the non-Catholic and non-Orthodox, or, as CPCE termed it, 'Protestant' churches in Europe. In certain countries which lacked the comprehensive ecumenical framework of the United Kingdom and some of the Scandinavian countries, and where a CPCE member body or member bodies were the national, or folk church(es), national Baptist unions could also feel disadvantaged in their relationships by the attitude of the state, folk or national church. This was especially seen to be the case by the German Baptist Union. In November 1996 the Union of Free Evangelical Churches in Germany (the German Baptists) asked the Executive of the Leuenberg Church Fellowship to launch a dialogue with a view to possible cooperation.[169] The EBF and CPCE agreed it would be helpful to have a meeting between German Baptist representatives and CPCE, but in the end only limited work could be done as it was really just a meeting of German theologians. The final report from these meetings commented on the German Baptist perspective that Baptists should:

> not remain apart in an integrating Europe but to give a sign of reconciliation through a deepened communion with the Protestant churches joined together in the Leuenberg Church Fellowship.[170]

Following the meetings with the German Baptist Union, the CPCE representatives felt it was not significant enough to dialogue with one national

---

[167] This included a joint Baptist/Leuenberg Church Fellowship meeting at Bensheim in 1993.

[168] The cornerstone of CPCE is the definition of 'Church Fellowship' which is based on a consensus in understanding the gospel and that churches with different confessional positions accord each other fellowship in word and sacrament and strive for fullest possible cooperation in witness and service to the world.

[169] 'The Beginning of the Christian Life and the Nature of the Church', results of the dialogue between the CPCE and the EBF. EBF documents, Prague, July 2004, p. 1, EBF Office Archive, Prague.

[170] Final Report of the Leuenberg-German Baptist Conversations, The Leuenberg Concordat, pp. 9-10.

Baptist Union and indicated that their preference was to dialogue with all the Baptists in Europe by engaging in conversations with representatives of the EBF. This is a further testimony to the understanding of other Christian communions that the EBF was more than a simple annual gathering for information exchange, but had an ecclesial reality and was an appropriate organisation to engage with in theological dialogue. The German Baptist Union, therefore, approached the EBF Executive Committee and General Council requesting them to engage in dialogue with CPCE. This matter came onto the agenda of the EBF Executive Committee at their meeting in Dorfweil, Germany, in April 2000, when Stefan Stiegler commented on the proposals made to plan out the work of the Theology and Education Division of the EBF for the next three years at the 1999 Council.[171] Stiegler commented that he rejected the general proposals of his predecessor as Chair of the Division[172] and thought more attention should be given to theological reflection, especially in dialogue with the Leuenberg churches. Theo Angelov responded to the suggestion of Stiegler that the EBF should have a dialogue with the Leuenberg churches saying:

> the Executive should give full support. The discussion began on the level of theology. External Relations (another EBF division) could be included as well. It is very important how we present the whole situation to the Council – as a special consultation with the Protestant churches. In some unions ecumenism is a dangerous word. EBF has such dialogues on several levels.[173]

In the debate which followed, Polish Baptist youth leader, Leszek Wakula, asked what results EBF expected from the dialogue and would it be Unions or the EBF with whom the dialogue was conducted. Stefan Stiegler was anxious to maintain German Baptist critical involvement and argued the case for the EBF to facilitate a group of Unions to dialogue with Leuenberg, but Theo Angelov said the EBF, as itself, 'cannot be excluded altogether'.[174] As it happened, once EBF Council approval was obtained and certain Unions had indicated their desire for EBF to act on their behalf, and no Union opposed the plan,[175] the EBF became the body which acted. In the end the reality went much further than Theo Angelov had suggested. Far from the EBF not being excluded and

---

[171] Minutes of the EBF Council, 1999, Report of D. Peterlin to the EBF Council in Hamburg, September 1999, p. 11, Box 822, EBF Archive.

[172] This had been for the Division to do work on the theology of the child and the differing practices and liturgy for services of infant thanksgiving.

[173] Minutes of the EBF Executive Committee, April 2000, Dorfweil, Germany, p. 6, EBF Office Archive.

[174] *Ibid.*

[175] Minutes of the EBF Council, September 2000, Riga, Latvia, p. 9, EBF Office Archive.

the matter being handled by the Unions, the general view of the Unions (with the exception of the President of the Romanian Baptists, Paul Negrut) was that the EBF Executive Committee had the task of establishing the group and overseeing the work, and the EBF budget funded all the Baptist costs involved in the consultations. The EBF Executive decided to recommend to the Council 'participation in the conversations'.[176]

When the matter came to the EBF Council in September 2000 in Riga, Stefan Stiegler and Uwe Swarat, who had been part of the meeting between CPCE and the German Baptists, reported on the meeting between German Baptists and German theologians representing CPCE. During the discussion which followed 'members of Council expressed the importance of Baptists being involved in these consultations and encouraged the General Secretary to act on behalf of the EBF Council'.[177] This represented a significant move forward from the rather cautious initial view of the EBF Executive and the German Baptists, who thought the EBF might simply serve as a vehicle for gathering together the names of member Unions interested in the possibility of sharing in dialogue with CPCE. However, the Council agreed that the Executive Committee should invite member unions to suggest people who might serve on the group, but the Executive, itself, would put together the group to represent EBF Baptists.[178] At the same time CPCE invited the EBF to appoint 'observers' to sit on two doctrinal conversation groups in CPCE; one on mission to which the EBF Executive appointed Peter F. Penner of IBTS, and the other on ecclesiology to which the Executive appointed Eric Geldbach of Bochum.[179]

The decision to actually commence the formal dialogue awaited a General Assembly of CPCE in Belfast in 2001. The final report of the Baptist/CPCE group says:

> The LCF General Assembly 2001 in Belfast agreed that the representatives of the Baptist Unions in Europe should be involved in a theological dialogue on baptism, and besides on other issues which are perceived on either side to stand in the way of mutual church fellowship.[180]

---

[176] Minutes of the EBF Executive Committee, April 2000, p. 7, EBF Office Archive.

[177] Minutes of the EBF Council, September 2000, p. 9, EBF Office Archive.

[178] In fact, no Baptist Union objected to this approach, though later the President of the Romanian Union, P. Negrut, did write to EBF General Secretary, T. Angelov objecting to the conversations. Minutes of the EBF Executive, April 2001, Scotland, p. 3, EBF Office Archive.

[179] In fact they became, de facto, full participants and P.F. Penner was certainly involved in the mission group as one of the drafters of their report, in other words moving from observation to participation in the core group. Interview with P.F. Penner, March 2005.

[180] Leuenberg Concordat, pp. 10-11.

The EBF Executive consulted the Unions, but most were content to leave the choice of the Baptist team to the Executive, again, a sign of confidence in the EBF structures and an implicit lack of desire to limit the EBF team to a handful of Unions who were ecumenically engaged at European level. At the April 2002 Executive Committee at Maennedorf, Switzerland, the Executive agreed to appoint a team of eight to participate in the talks. The Baptist group would be led by the General Secretary, Theo Angelov, and include the Rector of IBTS, the Chairs of the External Relations and Theological Education Divisions of EBF, Uwe Swarat (Elstal, Germany), Sergei Sannikov (Ukrainian Baptist theological consultant), Andrea Strübind (Germany) and Johnny Jonsson (Sweden).[181] As it turned out, Uwe Swarat, Stefan Stiegler (Chair of the Theology and Education Division) and Andrea Strübind, all of whom had been suggested through contact with the German Baptist Union, declined to serve, which was rather strange, given that the German Union had originally pressed for the dialogue and Stiegler had expressed views at EBF Executive meetings that the German Baptists must be intimately involved in the process. However, at this time the German Baptist Union was going through a leadership and financial crisis, so it may be that the pressures on individuals and the thought that some might have to withdraw from posts within the Union and Seminary, affected their personal situations, thus prompting their refusal to serve.

Nonetheless, the EBF Executive, emboldened by the display of trust shown by the Unions generally, agreed to ask Paul S. Fiddes (Oxford, England), Wiard Popkes (Lüneburg, Germany), Kim Strübind (München, Germany) and F. Emanuel Wieser (Vienna, Austria) to complete the delegation.[182] Thus, the delegation was composed of nominees of the EBF Executive Committee exclusively as the member Unions had, in majority, given the task to the Executive, and the one Union which did not, the German Union, nominated people who declined to serve. The CPCE delegation was led by Martin Hein (EKD, Kassel) and included André Birmelé (Reformed, Strasbourg), Fulvio Ferrario (Waldensian, Rome), Eberhard Jüngel (EKD, Tübingen), Miloš Klátik (Reformed, Bratislava), Ernst Baasland (Lutheran, Stavanger), Martin Friedrich (EKD, Berlin), William Hüffmeier (CPCE Secretary, Berlin), Manfred Marquardt (Reutlingen), and J. Cecil McCullough (Presbyterian, Belfast).[183] The conversations extended over eighteen months, with the first meeting being hosted by Baptists at the Albertinen-Diakoniewerk in Hamburg, on the suggestion of Karl Heinz Walter, the second main session by the CPCE at Hofgeismar hosted by the Evangelical Church of Kurhessen-Waldeck, and the

---

[181] Minutes of the EBF Executive Committee, Switzerland, April 2002, p. 3, EBF Office Archive.

[182] Final list of EBF participants as recorded in The Leuenberg Concordat, p. 15.

[183] *Ibid.*

third and final meetings at IBTS, Prague, in January 2004.

The CPCE churches wished to explain clearly to the Baptists the nature and purpose of their 'Church Fellowship' model of ecumenism, which delivered, in theory, for the churches in Europe and South America,[184] who are signatories, 'unity in reconciled diversity',[185] and that this was found in the right preaching of the gospel and the right celebration of the sacraments, leading to pulpit fellowship, mutual recognition of ordination, table fellowship at the eucharist and mutual recognition of members.[186] In fact, though existing in theory, it cannot be argued that it exists in practice amongst the ninety-nine member churches.[187] However, the continuing work of the CPCE is to turn the agreement into a practical reality.

The joint conversations soon established that the Baptist delegates, and later the EBF Council, had no difficulty in affirming the CPCE mutual understanding of the gospel, which had been a critical point of convergence for Lutherans, Reformed, Czech Brethren, Waldensians, Moravians and Methodists. The joint report, 'The Beginning of the Christian Life and the Nature of the Church' says:

> We affirm the statement on the Gospel in the Leuenberg Agreement as the mutually accepted understanding of the Gospel.... the true understanding of the Gospel was expressed by the fathers of the Reformation in the doctrine of justification.[188]

As the section on the background to the dialogue process makes clear, it was relatively easy to assert 'we have found agreement in the most important themes of Christian doctrine, especially in the understanding of God's act of salvation in Christ and of gospel, faith and church'.[189] It was also possible for the Baptists to ask the CPCE churches to consider whether the anathema against the Anabaptists from the 1500s applied to them. This matter was not capable of being addressed fully in the dialogue, nor was the matter addressed by resolution when the CPCE Sixth Assembly was held in Budapest in 2006,[190] despite it being requested in the text:

---

[184] What might be thought of as an anomaly of the CPCE group of 99 member churches is that they have member churches in Argentina, Paraguay and Uruguay. These are what might be described as diaspora communities of Germans of Lutheran and Methodist background.

[185] The Leuenberg Concordat, p. 23.

[186] *Ibid.,* p. 43.

[187] In that there is no effective inter-changability of ordained ministry.

[188] The Leuenberg Concordat, p. 16.

[189] *Ibid.,* p. 26.

[190] For the CPCE Assembly materials see http://lkg.jalb.de, accessed 28 January 2007.

> We ask Lutheran and united churches of the CPCE, to clarify the meaning of the condemnations of the 'Anabaptists' contained in the Lutheran confessions. In this regard, we thankfully accept the results of the Baptist-Lutheran dialogue on the world level, recognising that, with the exception of the one expressed in CA 9[191] the condemnations do not apply to Baptists today.[192]

Beyond this historical issue, baptism remained the stumbling block. As with the earlier *Baptism, Eucharist and Ministry* document of the WCC, it proved possible to express clear theological views which were capable of being accepted by both sides. However, the difficulties were apparent in the detail of application, and the discussion concerning the important topic of who – and in what circumstances – should be the subject of baptism and how baptism is administered.[193] In a remarkable contribution to the whole process, Paul Fiddes, from the Baptist delegation, sought to return to discussion of the conversion-initiation journey and to look at different aspects of infant baptism and disciples baptism, reaching out and arguing the case for accepting alternative journeys of initiation[194] and commenting that:

> the image has been developed of Christian initiation as a process or journey. If this were to be accepted as a point of convergence between different traditions of baptism, then this paragraph (IV.11)[195] about the blessing of infants would need to be reviewed, seeing such blessing as having a significant place on the journey. Baptists, as well as those who baptize infants, would need to reflect upon the true meaning of infant blessing.[196]

This move by Fiddes, incorporated into the final printed book, no doubt raises many questions both for CPCE and for the EBF Unions, but it is noteworthy that, through this EBF dialogue, a line of thinking has been promulgated which the editors, one of whom is now the EBF General Secretary, thought it important to include. Indeed, this very point perhaps illustrates the role assumed by EBF General Secretaries at other moments in the past of providing

---

[191] They condemn the Anabaptists, who reject the baptism of children, and say that children are saved without baptism.

[192] J. Gros, H. Meyer and W. Rusch (eds.), 'Baptists and Lutherans in Conversation: A Message to our Churches (1990)' in *Growth in Agreement II: Reports and Agreed Statements of Ecumenical Conversations on a World Level 1982-1998* (Geneva: WCC, 2000), p. 174.

[193] *Ibid.*, p. 26.

[194] W. Hüffmeier and T. Peck (eds.), 'Baptists and the Leuenberg Agreement on Baptism' in *Dialogue between the Community of Protestant Churches in Europe (CPCE) and the European Baptist Federation (EBF) on the Doctrine and Practice of Baptism* (Frankfurt am Main: Verlag Otto Lembeck, 2005), p. 189.

[195] *Ibid.*, p. 28.

[196] *Ibid.*, p. 197.

leadership in the matter of ecumenical development beyond the safe territory of formal exchange of positions (an approach generally adopted by the BWA).[197] It remains to be seen if the EBF Council, in further discussion of the report with its member Unions, will seize on this proposal of Fiddes and incorporate it into further discussions with CPCE.

Though these ideas were discussed by the group as a whole, the formal text had to recognise the current status quo that the vast majority of Baptist churches in Europe would not easily accept any restraint on the baptism of believers of those from the CPCE traditions who asked for it, and the CPCE churches, though divided in their views about infant baptism,[198] nevertheless, intended to maintain a united stance, even though agreements which differ from this have been reached amongst some Baptists and some CPCE members.[199] So, in the final report the CPCE delegation affirmed:

> CPCE churches can recognize that the Baptist practice only to baptize believers who are asking for baptism and who have made a confession before baptism, is a proper practice of baptism according to the gospel [sic]. But the churches of the CPCE also claim for themselves that the baptism of infants of Christian parents is a possibility which is in accord with the Gospel.[200]

The group had gelled very well together, but it was clear that full 'church fellowship', as understood by the churches of CPCE, could not be obtained at this time. Baptism appeared to be the only insurmountable issue as the report went on to declare:

> the acknowledgement of each other's integrity self-evidently also includes the question of ordained ministers. For as long as we do not have a full recognition of ministry in a doctrinal sense, we nevertheless encourage the ensuring, the

---

[197] This can be observed in the various BWA dialogues, which certainly do not seem to assume any possibility of increased ecumenical relationship, but normally argue that greater understanding of the other tradition could be useful.

[198] For instance, the Presbyterian Church of Ireland practices a very strict form of household baptism, whereas many of the national and state Lutheran churches practice what Baptists call indescriminate infant baptism.

[199] For example, between the URC and the Methodist Churches in Britain and the Baptist Union of Great Britain. A variant exists in the relations between Italian Baptists and the Waldensians. On the British scene see A.R. Cross, *Baptism and the Baptists: Theology and Practice in Twentieth-Century Britain* (Carlisle: Paternoster, 2000).

[200] *Ibid.,* p. 26. It might be assumed that the reference to gospel with a lower case 'g' in the section on believers baptism over against Gospel with a capital 'G' in relation to infant baptism is simply a typographical error.

> enabling and the widening of a reciprocal acceptance of ministry in practical and pastoral ways at local, national or trans-national levels.[201]

As the editors noted in the Preface:

> the initial reception in ecumenical and theological circles was very encouraging. Most of all, the common statements on baptism, which in some respects go beyond the scope of existing convergences and may open a way to the overcoming of the controversies, have met with keen interest.[202]

If this is so, this will mark a major move forward in the application of the ecclesial reality of the EBF as it will demonstrate the ability to act on behalf of the member Unions in matters of sensitive doctrine, and clearly demonstrates an independence and depth of reflection outside the normal scope of the dialogues typical within the BWA family.

Conclusion

The EBF was born in the same era as many of the current ecumenical organisations and before several of the Christian World Communions were formed. From the outset, there have been certain questions as to how far the EBF, as the EBF, could be a participant in the world of structured and informal ecumenism. These issues have been debated, but more recently, and certainly in the dialogue with CPCE, the Baptists of Europe have entrusted to the EBF the role of lead player, and the Council has operated with a measure of ecclesial reality which is without parallel in Europe amongst the other CWCs. This has occurred and not caused any significant problems within the EBF, even though some member bodies have not sought to be engaged with the ecumenical movement or in dialogue with other Christian churches.

The member bodies have included committed Unions to the ecumenical endeavour, such as Great Britain, Sweden and Denmark; those who have engaged with national councils of churches and the like such as the Czech Republic, France and Hungary; those who have been indifferent, or connected only to the Protestant world, such as Italy; and those who have been openly hostile, such as the Scottish and Belarussian Baptists, being fearful of guilt by association. Whatever the stance, all appear to have been perfectly willing for the EBF Council, Executive and Officers to participate in dialogue with other traditions, in European ecumenical structures and within denominations, such as the Catholics or Orthodox, which might have presented a real challenge to their own self-understanding as national Unions.

Thus, the EBF has been, at a minimum, a conduit of contact and of dialogue

201 *Ibid.*, p. 28.
202 *Ibid.*, p. 5.

with other Christian World Communions. Most recently with CPCE, the EBF engaged in a serious ecumenical dialogue with a significant Christian grouping. The EBF was given ecclesial authority to represent even those not formally committed to the ecumenical community and certainly was able to offer real representation on behalf of many Baptist Unions who might have struggled to engage in such activity themselves. In all of this, the personal authority and standing of the EBF General Secretary was crucial, in terms of the ecclesial authority and status, and to the place of the EBF General Secretary, and to this we will turn in Chapter 5.

CHAPTER 4

The International Baptist Theological Seminary

This chapter examines the pre-history and formation of the Baptist Seminary in Rüschlikon,[1] Switzerland, which was established in 1949. It also analyses the subsequent history of the Seminary, focusing particularly on the way its history highlights different views about the outworking of Baptist ecclesiology. In this context there is an exploration of the relationship between European Baptists and Baptists in North America, particularly the Foreign Mission Board (FMB), subsequently the International Mission Board – (IMB) of the Southern Baptist Convention (SBC). These relationships were of crucial importance at various stages: when the Seminary was founded, at the time of the handing over of the Seminary to the European Baptist Federation (EBF) in 1988, and when the defunding of the Seminary by the SBC took place in 1989. The chapter examines these issues in detail, looking especially at the way in which thinking about decision-making in relation to church and mission is illustrated by these pivotal events. Attention is then paid to the thinking that led to the relocation of the Seminary from Rüschlikon to Prague, Czech Republic, in the mid-1990s – a move which was followed in 1997 by the refocusing of its academic work. All these changes raise important ecclesiological issues.

'To establish, without delay, a training school'

Carol Woodfin, in her thesis on the early years of the Rüschlikon Seminary, argues:

> that although the seminary was begun by the Foreign Mission Board without adequate consideration of European Baptists' needs and was, therefore, viewed by

---

[1] In German, Rüschlikon, Zürich. English transliteration Rueschlikon, Zuerich. There are some quotes 'Ruschlikon', but these are simply errors by the original author and have been left, for accuracy, as the original quote. The European Baptist Seminary has had a range of titles during the years since it was founded by the Foreign Mission Board of the Southern Baptist Convention in 1949. For the sake of convenience in this chapter I shall consistently refer to it by the current title, International Baptist Theological Seminary [IBTS]. It assumed this title on being passed into the ownership of the EBF in 1988.

many with scepticism, it earned a respected position in European Baptist life in its first decade.[2]

Baptists had, for a long time, been reflecting on the possibility of founding a theological institution in the heart of Europe. As early as 1908 there was public mention of an international school for theological training. When European Baptists gathered in Congress in Berlin in that year a resolution was passed unanimously urging the establishment of 'an international European Baptist College (Hochschule) in a central place'.[3] As part of the resolution there was a reminder to Baptists to continue supporting the existing institutions in Europe,[4] to encourage the founding of others, if needed, and to establish a fund to provide scholarships to 'allow especially gifted young men' who had completed studies in their own nation's seminaries to study further elsewhere. The resolution was aimed at the Baptist World Alliance (BWA) as there was no European Baptist body to which the resolution could be forwarded.[5] Speaking at the same Congress, C.E. Benander, Director of Bethel Baptist Seminary in Stockholm, called for 'a great European Baptist University' and opened up the idea that, whilst initial ministerial formation and theological education might be acquired in the home country of the student, there was a case for a Europe-wide institution to which the more able could go.[6] European Baptists were seeking to express their ecclesiology in a pan-European way in the area of theological education.

Between the 1908 Congress in Berlin and the next BWA Congress in 1911, there was, indeed, reflection on and discussion about the possibility of establishing a Europe-wide theological institution. In 1910 J.H. Rushbrooke,[7] later to be BWA Commissioner for Europe and someone who had a broad vision for Baptist life in Europe, wrote to Hungarian Baptists regarding the possibility of founding a College in Hungary.[8] Various other venues were

---

[2] C.G. Woodfin, 'Rueschlikon: The Establishment and Early Development of an International Baptist Theological Seminary in the Heart of Post-War Europe', MA Thesis, Wake Forest University, 1987.

[3] F.W. Simoleit (ed.), *Offizieller Bericht ueber den 1. Kongress der europaeischen Baptisten* (Kassel: Oncjen Verlag, 1908), p. 330. The German word 'Hochschule' refers to an institute of higher learning which is not part of the state university system. There is also a report of this event in the Angus Library, Regent's Park College, Oxford.

[4] These were principally in West and Northern Europe. In 1908 there were nine Baptist seminaries in the United Kingdom, one in Germany and one in Sweden.

[5] Simoleit, *Offizieller Bericht ueber den 1*, pp. 330- 331.

[6] *Ibid.*, p. 107.

[7] On J.H. Rushbrooke see B. Green, *Tomorrow's Man: A Biography of James Henry Rushbrooke* (Didcot: Baptist Historical Society, 1997).

[8] Baptist World Alliance [BWA] Continental Committee Minutes, December 1910, BWA Archive, Falls Church, Virginia.

discussed within the BWA, including Bulgaria and Berlin, but at the BWA Congress in Philadelphia in 1911 the proposed site was changed to St Petersburg.[9] This change of possible venue resulted from there being about twenty-five delegates from Russia present at the Congress who spoke about their struggles as believers. Immediately following their presentation, A.J. Vining addressed the Congress on the topic 'A Baptist Training School for Europe'. In the course of this address he highlighted the need for training to equip the many Baptists in Europe who currently had no access to trained ministry. Describing the people as 'patient veterans of Jesus Christ', he said that there were millions of them waiting for the coming of trained evangelists, and the pastor who is 'apt to teach'. He continued:

> Must these men call in vain? Shall we not gladly answer their appeal? There is one way that their pleadings may be answered – a way in which every man here may make himself heard. Establish a great cosmopolitan theological seminary in the heart of Europe! Make it possible for the young Baptist men of the different countries of Europe to receive a training that will qualify them.... Give the peoples, whose representatives these men are, a training school, in which Baptist ministers may receive help that will fit them for leadership, and in this hall are hundreds who will live to see Europe a great Protestant, Christian continent and Russia the mightiest Baptist stronghold on earth.[10]

It is not surprising that such rhetoric moved the congregation. The experience of Russian Baptists and other Baptists in Eastern Europe in the twentieth century was not to correspond to the powerful vision presented, but in 1911 Vining could not have anticipated two world wars, the Russian Revolution and the development of the communist bloc, all of which were to have a negative impact on the advance of Baptist life. Vining continued with his powerful delivery:

> ... Let these men sleep tonight, with their poor, tired aching heads resting on the downy, gold embroidered pillow of Baptist pledges! .... Send the good news to millions of waiting, watching, people, that we have this day decided to establish without delay, a training school for the Baptists of Europe.[11]

By early afternoon the same day US$ 66,000 had been pledged for erecting such a school for European Baptists.[12] This fund grew slowly with capital of some US$ 100,000 by the time of a BWA Conference on Europe, held in

---

[9] BWA Executive Committee Minutes, 21 June 1911, BWA Archive.

[10] BWA, *Record of Proceedings, Second Baptist World Congress, Philadelphia, June 19-25,1911*, (Philadelphia: BWA, 1911), pp. 240-1.

[11] *Ibid.*, p. 241.

[12] *Ibid.*, p. 242. F.B. Meyer is reported to have played a crucial part in securing these pledges.

Baptist Church House, London, 13-17 August 1948.[13] The original 1908 proposal had been for a European Baptist school 'in the heart of Europe', a school which was to be international. However, from 1911 the US$ 66,000 was raised for the establishment of a seminary in Russia, and the pan-European element was lost. At various points during the rest of the century reference was made to this fund within the BWA, but it was still linked to a national seminary for Russia. With the collapse of communism, a seminary was ultimately started in Odessa in the Crimea in 1989; then later the BWA money was used to purchase a building which now houses the offices of the Russian Baptist Union and, for a time, also housed the Moscow Theological Seminary. However, a new fund with different donors provided the means to finally purchase a site which was developed for the Moscow Seminary and officially opened in September 2002.[14]

Thus the plea for a European seminary, though it excited great interest and enthusiasm for a time, appears to have gradually been transmuted in BWA circles into the idea of a seminary for the Russian peoples. Woodfin argues that by the time the 1948 BWA Conference on Europe was held in London, the link between a European seminary and the BWA Fund for a seminary had been broken.[15] However, although the calls made in 1911 were diverted in another direction, nevertheless they were important in bringing to life the idea that there might be a European Baptist Seminary to which students could go for higher theological studies after initial formation in a national seminary.[16] This vision came to the fore when, in preparation for the 1920 BWA Meeting on Mission in Europe, C.A. Brooks, New York, and J.H. Rushbrooke were despatched on a tour of enquiry. They were sent on their way at a special service in Hampstead Garden Free Church on Sunday, 9th May, when J.H. Shakespeare,[17] Eastern

---

[13] This figure has been disputed at different points of history, but is given here based on the BWA Executive Committee Minutes and E.A. Payne, *Out of Great Tribulation: Baptists in the USSR* (London: Baptist Union of Great Britain [BUGB], 1974), pp. 29-30. See also BWA Proceedings of the Third and Fourth Baptist World Congresses (1923 and 1934),

[14] A completely separate initiative led to the development of the St Petersburg Christian University (Baptist) during the 1990s, which has a School of Theology. This development, in the city originally chosen in 1911, received no help from the BWA, nor did the school which was developed as the European Seminary, IBTS.

[15] Minutes of the BWA Conference on Europe, London, 13-17 August 1948, BWA Archive, and Woodfin, 'Rueschlikon', pp. 7-9.

[16] Other historians such as J.D. Hughey, E.C. Routh, W. Kahl and G.W. Sadler have chosen to see, possibly erroneously, the formulation of what was to become Rüschlikon in these earlier discussions about a European Seminary, see Woodfin, 'Rueschlikon', p. 8.

[17] For the work of Shakespeare in the BWA and in Europe see P. Shepherd, *The Making of a Modern Denomination* (Carlisle: Paternoster, 2002).

Secretary of the BWA, thanked the church for releasing their pastor, Rushbrooke, to undertake the enquiry. He informed the church that Brooks and Rushbrooke went with a letter of commendation from the British Prime Minister, David Lloyd George.[18] This journey of enquiry, once again, raised the issue of a European Seminary. Bernard Green comments:

> The most significant issue for Rushbrooke was that Prague had great potential as the centre of a new Baptist seminary for the Slav lands of Europe. With prophetic insight he saw the promise of widespread evangelical growth among Slav populations and wished to make the training of preachers, pastors, evangelists and teachers for this work a main thrust of the Baptist World Alliance's reconstruction programme. This would include facilities for all grades of education, including the most advanced university training which Baptists were capable of receiving.[19]

However, it is important to note that at this stage there was little thought of European leadership. Rather any possible seminary was seen as the result of a BWA initiative.

The report of the two Commissioners to the BWA London Conference in 1920 was received, and in the official Conference Minutes it was noted:

> The section regarding Czecho-slovakia [sic] is of peculiar interest. Here the Commissioners conferred with President Masaryk and with the Dean of the Protestant Theological Faculty. They find that of all Slav University centres Prague offers the largest opportunity for Baptist students.[20]

The report was positive in echoing the need for a Central European seminary, but the matter was not pursued in the decades that followed. At the BWA Conference on Europe in 1948, which was timed to coincide with meetings of the Executive Committee of the BWA, the SBC took a unilateral initiative reporting: 'The Southern Convention of the USA has voted US$ 200,000 for a seminary in Switzerland intended to serve the needs of South and Central Europe.'[21] On the day after the main presentations the Committee on Theological Education reported, and the minutes record:

---

[18] Green, *Tomorrow's Man*, p. 73.

[19] *Ibid.*, p. 76.

[20] BWA London Conference Minutes, 19-23 July 1920, p. 17 BWA Library, Falls Church, Virginia. Czecho-slovakia was created as a Republic in 1918. The first President of the Republic was Thomas G. Masaryk, a renowned scholar and former University Professor with a deep interest in Christianity. The country was divided into two separate democratic republics, the Czech Republic and Slovakia, in 1993.

[21] BWA European Conference Minutes, 13-17 August 1948, Baptist Church House, London, p. 5, BWA Library.

> The Committee stress the need for seminaries where national groups can teach their own ministers in the languages in which they will preach the Gospel to their people and with special reference to the problems of their own nation. It was agreed, however, that beside these, and in no way replacing them, there is a need of a seminary in Europe which shall be more than a national institution, a seminary which may satisfy the educational needs of several countries and which may be more of a graduate school than some of the smaller seminaries.
>
> The Committee recognise with gratitude the generosity of the brothers of the Southern Baptist Convention of the United States in their plans to establish a seminary in Switzerland which will serve wider than national interests. The Committee recommend that the exchange of students and professors between America and Britain and continental European lands be considerably extended and that special reference be made to the present facilities for the exchange of students into Germany.[22]

It is noteworthy that the minutes, whilst expressing gratitude for the initiative of the Southern Baptists, also quickly point out the importance of national contextual theological education. There is also a desire for partnership – 'exchange of students and professors'. There was, as will be seen, hesitancy amongst the Europeans present in 1948 about the establishment by an American mission agency of an institution in Europe that would be owned, managed and led by non-Europeans.

The decision to allocate SBC resources to a seminary owed much to W.O. Carver, a leading Southern Baptist missiologist of that era, and George W. Sadler, Area Secretary for Europe for the Southern Baptist Foreign Mission Board (SBC-FMB). Woodfin notes:

> W.O. Carver wrote to George W. Sadler in 1949 that he and Everett Gill Snr had discussed the idea of an international theological school in Zuerich more than forty years prior to its opening. Their reasons for choosing Zuerich were partly the same as the founders who later voted for the site: its centrality and Anabaptist heritage.[23]

Gill and Carver had conducted an active correspondence when Gill was a missionary in Italy and Carver was Professor of Missions at Southern (Baptist) Seminary in Louisville, Kentucky, USA. Woodfin posits that the discussion may have taken place when both families spent a summer at Grindelwald, Switzerland, in 1907.[24] It is clear that in the first half of the century several people had advocated a pan-European theological seminary, not to replace national seminaries, but to be a graduate school (in North American

---

[22] BWA European Conference Minutes, pp. 6-7, BWA Library.

[23] Woodfin, 'Rueschlikon', p. 9. See also the Baptist Theological Seminary, Trustees Minutes 1950, p. 1, IBTS Archive, Prague.

[24] Woodfin, 'Rueschlikon', p. 10.

nomenclature) or a post-graduate (using European terminology) institution at the heart of Europe. However, though many people had talked, including Edwin Bell of American Baptist Churches (ABC), nothing had happened. It was M. Theron Rankin, appointed Executive Secretary of the SBC-FMB in 1945, who conducted a thorough study of the possibilities before the Board and prepared a paper, 'Advance', which took up the idea of Sadler that an international seminary should be established.[25] Sadler and W.O. Lewis, then General Secretary[26] of the BWA, had both been advocates of such a plan, but it was Rankin who mobilised the resources. His hugely ambitious 'Advance' programme envisaged a SBC-FMB budget increase of 250 per cent per annum.[27] The fact that the seminary was to be American-led and American-funded made it difficult for it to be fully integrated into European Baptist life.

'A high grade seminary'

A number of possibilities for the location of the seminary were discussed, including Rome.[28] Indeed, a FMB poster was produced in 1948 showing several future projects and the statement about the future seminary came under a drawing of St Peter's and the Coliseum in Rome:

> For years European Baptists have been praying for a high-grade seminary to train the young Baptist university graduates whom God calls to be preachers, teachers, musicians and preachers' wives [sic]. The small national Baptist seminaries can train those of meagre educational advantages.[29] A seminary using the English language would attract the best qualified young people from the Baptist churches of the entire continent.[30]

---

[25] J.B. Weatherspoon, *M Theron Rankin: Apostle of Advance* (Nashville, Tenn.: Broadman, 1958), pp. 112, 129-30.

[26] W.O. Lewis was General Secretary of the BWA from 1939-1948. From 1948-1955 he served as Associate General Secretary for Europe involved especially in reconstruction of European Baptist life. See E. Geldbach, 'The Years of Anxiety and World War II', in R.V. Pierard (ed.), *Baptists Together in Christ 1905-2005* (Birmingham AL: Samford University Press, 2005), p. 94.

[27] M.T. Rankin, 'We plan to advance', *The Commission*, March, 1948, pp. 3-4 and 24.

[28] Woodfin notes that Rome and Jerusalem were among the locations discussed, 'Rueschlikon', p. 21.

[29] It is perhaps as well that this poster was for domestic consumption in the southern states of the USA as no doubt the Colleges in the British Isles, together with the German Seminary in Hamburg, would have taken exception to the idea they only trained those of 'meagre educational advantages'.

[30] Poster 'Southern Baptists Can Make These Dreams Come True! You and the Future of Missions'. These proposed projects were also reported in the FMB Report to the SBC, *Proceedings of the Annual Convention*, 1948, p. 88.

It is worth noting that the poster does not talk about South and Central Europe, the area discussed at the London meeting, but makes a bold play for the whole of the Continent and for the seminary to be established as a graduate school. Jesse D. Franks, a Southern Baptist Missionary based in Switzerland and responsible for their relief and development work, argued the case for Switzerland and had in mind Geneva.[31] On 6 April 1948, the FMB Trustees agreed, on the advice of Rankin, that:

> The secretaries be authorized to purchase property in Geneva, Switzerland, for a seminary for Europe and that a sum not to exceed US$ 200,000 be appropriated from rehabilitation funds for the purchase and development of the seminary.[32]

George Sadler was present when the FMB Trustees discussed the proposal and commented 'it is generally agreed that at the top of European needs, as they are related to Southern Baptists, is a fully-fledged first class theological seminary'.[33]

There are questions, however, about the extent to which 'European needs', or certainly European wishes, were taken into account. The importance of Sadler, Franks and Rankin in bringing the seminary into being cannot be in doubt. But earlier discussions had seen such a seminary as a joint venture by Europeans and Americans. The unilateral action of the FMB, simply announcing their intention to the Europeans at the 1948 London meeting, was to create difficulties in future relationships between Europeans and the FMB. The motives of the FMB were to be of assistance to Europeans and to the cause of theological education, but the approach might reasonably be viewed as paternalistic. Clearly, in central Europe, the Baptist situation was bleak, with the Hamburg Seminary destroyed. But intellectual capacity and a feeling for what was needed in Europe did exist within the European Baptist community. These insights were not taken into account as Rankin set out his bold plans. Sadler noted that some Europeans present in London responded to the FMB plan with 'anything but enthusiasm'.[34] Writing later on his recollections of what was said, but was not minuted, at the London Conference, J.D. Hughey recalled that:

> Strong opposition was expressed. Many people thought that if an international seminary were established it should be under the auspices of the Baptist World

[31] J.D.W. Watts, 'Rueschlikon/Zuerich – Baptist Training Center', *The Commission*, January 1949, p. 5.

[32] FMB Minutes, 6 April 1948, FMB Archive, Richmond, VA., p. 18.

[33] G.W. Sadler, 'Report to the Board', FMB Minutes, 6 April 1948, p. 16, FMB Archive.

[34] G.W. Sadler, 'Historical sketch of the Baptist Theological Seminary, Rueschlikon-Zuerich, Switzerland', Unpublished notes, 1960, IBTS Library, Prague.

> Alliance, or at least an international committee. They were suspicious of the motives and distrustful of the ability of Southern Baptists.[35]

Woodfin argues for another contributory factor to the lack of enthusiasm. An article by J.D. Franks in the June 1948 *The Commission*,[36] spoke of the need for Americans to save Europe from its 'spiritual desolation' and stated that 'the spiritual liberation of Europe was a responsibility that must be assumed largely by forces outside of Europe, chiefly by American Christianity'.[37] Baptist communities in Europe were apparently being discounted.

Thus, the seminary, long desired by Europeans, got off to a poor start, with a feeling among many European Baptist leaders that Southern Baptists had acted without consulting other Baptist groups. The German Baptists made the strongest objections to the plan, believing a seminary in Switzerland could affect their work in Hamburg.[38] Günter Wagner, a student and later lecturer at Rüschlikon, also argued that many German Baptists had little respect for American theology.[39] Johannes Norgaard, then Principal of the Danish Baptist Seminary, pressed the FMB to change the site to Copenhagen, making the point that Switzerland would prove to be too expensive, which, indeed, turned out to be correct.[40] However, in a post-war context, Switzerland had the advantage of being neutral and it was not involved in war reconstruction. Franks identified possible sites in Switzerland – five in Geneva, which he favoured as the 'most beautiful city in the world, the most neutral and also a wonderful place to live',[41] two in Basel and five in Zürich. These sites were visited by Mrs R. George Martin, President of the Southern Baptist Woman's Missionary Union, Theron Rankin and George W. Sadler. The group was most attracted by the Bodmer estate at Rüschlikon, Zürich. Franks was later to write, 'it was rather amusing how everybody at first sight fell for this location... everything was just right and seemed to the committee to fit perfectly into the needs, plans and

---

[35] J.D. Hughey, 'The Baptist Theological Seminary of Rueschlikon, Retrospect and Prospect', *Quarterly Review*, April-June 1963, p. 4.

[36] *The Commission,* magazine of the Southern Baptist Convention Foreign Mission Board.

[37] J.D. Franks, 'Europe Must have a Baptist Seminary', *The Commission,* June 1948, p. 4.

[38] It is interesting to note that German Baptists argued strongly in the 1990s for IBTS to move to their new campus at Elstal, Berlin, whereas most other Unions in Europe favoured Prague.

[39] Woodfin – interview with G. Wagner in Switzerland, 5 March 1987. Written copy in possession of Carol Woodfin.

[40] For full details of all those who opposed the FMB plan see Woodfin, 'Rueschlikon', pp. 37-39.

[41] J.D. Franks, 'Our Seven Years in post war Europe', 1954, duplicated Report, Box 21, IBTS Archive.

hopes we had for the institution'.[42] Several were mindful of the Anabaptist heritage in Zürich and that the German-speaking area of Switzerland had more Baptist churches than the French- speaking cantons. The purchase from the Bodmer family took place and the Swiss Baptists held a surprise tea party for the representatives of the FMB at the Belvoir Hotel.[43] The nature of this contribution from Europeans is perhaps indicative of how limited the European Baptist involvement was at this stage.

The FMB moved quickly to establish an initial faculty academic team, which consisted exclusively of Southern Baptist missionaries – J.D. Franks, John Allen Moore and John D.W. Watts. Franks was asked by the FMB to chair a Seminary Committee and the first meeting was held on 27 November 1948, when Franks explained that the selection of other faculty, the President (the American term for Principal or Rector) and others, would be by the FMB in Richmond, Virginia.[44] From the beginning it was clear that no European element was to be included in the decision-making process. Later, there was to be a Board of European advisors but, in essence, the Seminary was a Southern Baptist institution. The wives of Franks, Moore and Watts were appointed by the FMB alongside their husbands as missionaries, and served as members of the Administrative Committee in typical FMB fashion. The Committee began to design the curriculum and alter the buildings. At this point a European Baptist, Arthur B. Crabtree, was added to the academic staff in April 1949, though paid by the Southern Baptists. An English Baptist who had gained his doctorate at Zürich under Emil Brunner, the famous Reformed theologian, Crabtree was appointed to teach theology, and he and his wife were designated 'special contract workers' by the FMB. The Administrative Committee took the view that two further teachers were required and hoped that one might be a European. Ultimately, Claus Meister, the son of the President of the German Baptist Union, Jakub Meister, was selected. Claus Meister was finishing his doctorate at the University of Basel. Alexander Haraszti, a medical doctor from Hungary preparing for missionary service in Africa, was also recruited. No-one was appointed to teach New Testament, and Franks later commented, 'imagine beginning a Baptist theological seminary with no New Testament professor!'[45] However, serious attempts had been made to include Europeans on the teaching staff.

The Seminary, inaugurated on 4 September 1949, was launched onto the European Baptist world as work was commencing to form the EBF. Critics felt

---

[42] J.D. Franks, 'Baptist Theological Seminary', commentary for slide presentation, undated duplicate, IBTS Library.

[43] J.D. Franks, letter to *The Commission,* January 1949, p. 25.

[44] Minutes of the Baptist Theological Seminary Administrative Committee, 1948, IBTS Closed Archive, Bs016, Prague.

[45] Franks, 'Our Seven Years', p. 11.

the institution had been rather imposed on European Baptists, but George Sadler, appointed to be the first President on an interim basis, was determined to make the institution useful within the European Baptist community. The inaugural service in the Salemskapelle in Zürich saw W.O. Lewis, now Associate General Secretary of the BWA and soon to be General Secretary of the EBF, preach in German. Emil Brunner, of the University of Zürich, was present and wished the Seminary well.[46] Others participating in the inauguration weekend included Arnold T. Ohrn, General Secretary of the BWA, Edwin A. Bell, ABC Mission representative in Europe, and Johannes Norgaard from Copenhagen. In his inaugural address as the first President, George W. Sadler described the Seminary as 'something new under the sun',[47] presumably on account of the fact that it was intended to be, from the beginning, strongly multi-national. Sadler was familiar with SBC seminaries in other countries, having been Principal of the Baptist College and Seminary at Ogbomosho, Nigeria, from 1921 to 1931.[48] Sadler's hopes appeared to be fulfilled when, despite the criticisms that had been made of the Seminary, twenty-eight students, representing sixteen nationalities, were enrolled.[49] It seemed that, at the grassroots level, European Baptists responded to the opportunities that were being presented for study within the context of a wider European community.

The largest group – six students – was from Germany, and the first student to be enrolled was Walter Füllbrandt, the son of a pastor from eastern Germany who had resettled in southern Germany.[50] The realities of post-war Europe could have led to an explosive situation within the student community but, in fact, it appears that a vision of shared faith in Christ produced something of a special character that transcended the boundaries of nationality. Writing in the British *Baptist Times*, Arthur Crabtree observed:

> [Students] who during the war stood on different sides of the barricades now mingle in Christian courtesy and friendship. To look into their faces is to see a cross-section of contemporary history and to realize how much their training

---

[46] Programme of the Inauguration Ceremony and Dedication, Box E21, IBTS Archive.

[47] Rueschlikon Reports, November 1949, p. 1, IBTS Archive, Bs016.

[48] Information about G.W. Sadler from the 'Missionary Family Album', 1948, SBC-IMB Archives, Richmond, and from H.E. Sadler, 'My Father - as I see him', *The Commission*, January, 1958, p. 2-4.

[49] Minutes of the IBTS Trustees, 1950, p. 3, Box E1, IBTS Archive.

[50] W. Füllbrandt recalled to me his apprehension at being part of a community including those from neighbouring countries which had been under Nazi oppression, in a discussion, November 1996. In the mid 1990s he served on the IBTS Board of Trustees, being Chairman of the Board, 1996/1997.

> means for the future. They are like a mirror reflecting the spiritual face of Europe.[51]

Günter Wagner, a German student of that period, who was to go on to become Professor of New Testament at IBTS, recalls:

> It would happen that a German would share a room with a Dutchman who had spent many years in a forced labour camp. And we came together here as young Christians from very different political backgrounds, even from nations that had been enemies and fought wars against each other.[52]

Wagner went on to recall one incident in particular when he came to know an American fellow student and discovered that he had been a pilot of an American plane in 1944, during the bombardment of Berlin. Wagner had, at that time, been stationed in an anti-aircraft battery in Berlin. Said Wagner, 'I probably fired on his plane'.[53] This original community of students, drawn from very different Baptist environments, saw that the Seminary had the potential to be a place of genuinely communal learning.

During the first year of the Seminary's life, however, the student body became concerned about the teaching style. As most members of the faculty were American, the approach to educational methods that was employed was unfamiliar to the Europeans. The system, basically American, consisted of daily assignments, 'pop' tests, reading assignments and semester papers. Many students found this system strange compared to the relative independence of students in European universities. At the end of the academic year six students, including Wagner, wrote a letter to the Administration expressing their dissatisfaction with this system, which they felt was 'harmful to.... personal initiative' and 'an oppression'.[54] Whilst the students acknowledged the willingness of the American teaching team to collect experiences and useful insights, they felt that:

> the obligatory character of practically all the student's work took away joy and personal initiative. The joy was also considerably diminished because the professor did not presuppose that the student felt himself the responsibility to prepare seriously for the vocation he had received from God.[55]

---

[51] A.B. Crabtree, 'Helping to Train Europe's Ministers', *The Baptist Times*, 1 December 1949, p. 9.

[52] Interview in film 'Rüschlikon – Bridge for the Future', SBC-FMB film, 1985, IBTS Library Treasure Room.

[53] *Ibid.*

[54] Letter addressed to 'The Administration', 30 April 1950, IBTS Archive, Bs016, Prague.

[55] *Ibid.*

This was undoubtedly a call for more academic freedom and represented the clash of educational theories; however there does not seem to have been a breakdown in relationships between the faculty and the students and some attempt was made to address the concerns of the students, though the teaching method was to be maintained for some time.[56]

There was also a desire to listen to European Baptist leaders' views about the development of the Seminary. J.D. Franks advocated a more local Board of Trustees for the Seminary, a move that proved very helpful in changing perspectives. Franks wrote to all the European Baptist Unions inviting them to nominate two people to serve on the Board. Most replied naming one, but as Franks commented later:

> When the list was finally completed, I realized that European Baptists had chosen men [sic] of their best, most outstanding leadership to represent them on our Board… The willingness of such men to identify themselves so intimately with this project indicated their belief in its worthwhileness.[57]

The use of the word 'trustee' in this instance was somewhat misleading, as no real power could be placed in their hands. Rather, the role was to liaise between the Seminary and the key European Baptist Unions and provide some advice to the Seminary on the needs and realities in different parts of Europe. The first Annual Trustees' Meeting was held at the Seminary in March 1950. Present were Johannes Norgaard of Denmark; Percy W. Evans and M.E. Aubrey from England; Alfons Sundqvist from the Swedish-speaking Union in Finland; Hans Luckey and Jakub Meister, from Germany; A.A. Hardenberg of the Netherlands; Manfredi Ronchi of Italy; Yngvar Vold of Norway; Gunnar Westin of Sweden; Kaspar Schneiter and Emil Pfister from Switzerland; Richard Rabenau of Austria and Henri Vincent of France.[58] All of these were leading figures in their Unions, who were used to forming policies, but the reality, as Sadler told them at the first Trustees' meeting, was that ultimate authority rested with the FMB. In fact there were no determining lines of responsibility: it was unclear what matters rested with FMB staff, FMB Trustees, FMB missionaries at the school, or European 'Trustees'.[59] Sadler's

[56] Baptist Theological Seminary Rüschlikon, Faculty Minute Book, IBTS confidential records, Prague.
[57] Franks, 'Our Seven Years', p. 13.
[58] IBTS Board of Trustees Minutes, 1950, p. 1, Box E1, IBTS Archive. Those appointed were principally either Union Officers (M.E. Aubrey, J. Meister, M. Ronchi, G. Westin, R. Rabenau, H. Vincent), or Seminary Presidents (P.W. Evans, J. Norgaard, Hans Luckey).
[59] Decades later, the consequences of this were to be dramatic. I refer to the case of Glenn Hinson, a distinguished Professor at Southern Baptist Seminary; I deal with the actual incident later in this chapter.

personal hope, which he expressed, was that in the much longer term the direction of the Seminary might be centred in Europe.[60]

A European President

George Sadler's appointment as President was an interim one. He was approaching the end of his distinguished career and the need was for someone younger. The person identified was a European, the 47-year-old Josef Nordenhaug, a Norwegian with a science degree from the University of Oslo, who had felt a call to ministry and studied at the Southern Baptist Theological Seminary in Kentucky where he had gained a Master of Theology degree and later a doctorate in New Testament and Greek. He had served as an assistant pastor in Oslo, then held pastorates in Kentucky and Virginia. He became an America citizen in 1937. Since 1948 he had been editor of the SBC-FMB magazine, *The Commission.*[61] There is a story that Sadler thought of Nordenhaug one morning whilst shaving and immediately telephoned Theron Rankin.[62] Whatever the veracity of this story, Rankin sent for Nordenhaug and said he should consider becoming the President of the Seminary. Nordenhaug was cautious. He knew that many Europeans were sceptical about the way the Seminary had been created and about the strong SBC involvement. The Board therefore agreed that Nordenhaug could travel to Europe and visit various Unions to discover how well the Seminary was being received. Between 28 January and 11 March 1950 Nordenhaug visited Switzerland, Italy, Germany, Sweden, Norway, Denmark, Holland and Great Britain. The purpose of his visit was not made public, though many guessed. In his report to the FMB in March 1950 he commented: 'The imagination of Baptists in Europe has been stirred by the establishment of the seminary in Zürich.'[63] Given Nordenhaug's initial caution, this verdict augured well for the future of the Seminary as a genuine part of European Baptist life.

After further reflection, Nordenhaug indicated his willingness to accept the challenge, and the FMB elected him President at their meeting on 4 May 1950. Interestingly, he was not asked to become a missionary of the FMB, but was assigned to the post as a Richmond-based Board employee.[64] This may have given him a slightly higher status within the FMB; certainly Theron Rankin had

---

[60] IBTS Board of Trustees Minutes, 1950, p. 11, IBTS Archive, Bs016.

[61] Biographical information on Nordenhaug drawn from *The Baptist World*, September 1960, p. 7, a biography compiled on the announcement of his election as General Secretary of the BWA.

[62] Carol Woodfin offers this in her dissertation based on an interview with Karin Nordenhaug Ciholas, daughter of Josef Nordenhaug, in Switzerland, in July 1985, Woodfin, 'Rueschlikon', p. 76.

[63] Josef Nordenhaug, Report to the FMB, 15 March 1950, p. 1, SBC-IMB Archive.

[64] FMB Minutes, 4 May 1950, p. 4, SBC-FMB Archive.

great confidence in him and appeared to leave him to run the Seminary as he felt best. He was inducted in September 1950. Nordenhaug had, in fact, been an advocate of an international Baptist university in Europe. Whilst serving as a local church pastor in Virginia he was invited to speak at the annual meetings of the Woman's Missionary Union of Virginia, held in March 1948. His topic was 'Christ's Reign Challenged in Europe'. During his address he stated:

> The students of Spinoza and Kant demand of us a Baptist University for our mission emphasis. The Baptist faculty are there, a few in each country; but they have not the means to create a Baptist European University. It is the greatest tragedy to become conscious of a crisis without at the same time becoming conscious of a commission.[65]

This does not mean that Nordenhaug completely shared the vision of the FMB. He believed a European institution should have a faculty selected largely from among European leaders and that the Seminary should be primarily a post-graduate institution, in his mind, to offer advanced training to European Baptist ministers.[66] Therefore, when he arrived at the Seminary he sought to develop and upgrade the academic programmes to offer, not only initial ministerial formation, but also a post-graduate degree. The seminary was being shaped according to European perspectives.

The years which followed were arguably the best years during the period the FMB owned and controlled the Seminary. Nordenhaug was a staff member of the FMB and was trusted by the senior officers of the Board. At the same time, his European background gave him a keen sense of the possible dangers of European Baptist leaders reacting against perceived American 'imperialism'. His own Norwegian birth and upbringing were highly valuable in this regard: those who remember him say he never lost his slight, lilting Norwegian accent.[67] Nordenhaug, who had a 'natural authority',[68] stamped his personality on the Seminary during his ten-year presidency, from 1950 to 1960. To take a relatively minor example, although European Baptists take different views on the ethical issues of games on a Sunday, use of tobacco and consumption of alcohol, he was against all three and imposed that regime.[69] He was concerned

---

[65] Quotation from the speech of Nordenhaug from the *Religious Herald*, Virginia, 25 March 1948, p. 23.

[66] Letter from J. Nordenhaug to G.W. Sadler, 8 April 1948, Meister Papers, IBTS Archive.

[67] F.H. North, 'A Leader Passes', *The Commission*, December 1969, p. 20.

[68] Woodfin, in interviews with Norgaard, Wagner and Crabtree, notes they all commented on this feature of the man, Woodfin, 'Rueschlikon', p. 85.

[69] Though the influence of Nordenhaug has not been constant throughout the whole life of the institution, it should be noted that his puritan Nordic style still has influence at IBTS where there is a no smoking rule and consumption of alcohol in public places is

about the image of the Seminary in the conservative Reformed Parish of Rüschlikon, where Baptists were relatively unknown. Amongst other impositions to help present the Seminary in a positive light he banned the wearing of beards by students.[70] More substantially, Nordenhaug's strong desire seems to have been to work for the integration of the various nationalities in the Seminary; recognising that part of the purpose of the Seminary was to turn students from many nations into one community in Christ, with a wider vision of a peaceful community in Europe. Students from different nationalities were assigned to the same dormitory and Nordenhaug refused to allow slighting references to other nationalities.[71] Here was a pan-European Baptist outlook at its best.

Nordenhaug understood the Seminary to have two main goals – the achievement of high academic standards and preparation for active ministry. He constantly reminded faculty, students and trustees of both aims. He warned: 'The ministry can become only a profession, with men trained like skilled surgeons, who know how to reason skilfully and are theologically wise, but who are spiritually handicapped'.[72] Later the Seminary was to be accused of having an over-riding interest in scholarship and of failing in the preparation of women and men for active service, but this accusation, whether true or not, belongs to a later period. Certainly, under Nordenhaug and J.D.W. Watts (who was Academic Dean, and then President from 1964-1970) the approach was to make clear that theology was being studied within a believing community and with the accent on understanding and interpreting scripture for congregations of believers. This was seen to be in contrast to the approach to theology within State Universities. Yet both Swiss and German Baptists had deep concerns about the Seminary. As Carol Woodfin notes: 'There was sometimes the suspicion that Rueschlikon stood in danger of producing *allzu intellektuellen Prediger*'.[73] The German Baptist Union continued to view the Seminary with suspicion and scepticism, feeling it to be in competition with their own Hamburg Seminary. The German Union demanded that students who had taken the full course at Rüschlikon should still go to the Hamburg Seminary for a further period of training. This requirement was not imposed by the Swedish, British, Danish, Norwegian or Yugoslavian Unions, all of whom had national

forbidden, despite a wide variety of practices in these areas within the European Baptist community.

[70] Woodfin interview with K. Nordenhaug Ciholas, Switzerland, 1 July 1985. Woodfin personal papers.

[71] Recollections to me by Walter Füllbrandt in discussion, Prague, April 1997.

[72] Faculty Minutes, 29 August 1950, p. 12, IBTS Archive.

[73] Woodfin, 'Rueschlikon', p. 134, based on a comment by Kaspar Schneiter 'Neus aus Rueschlikon' *Gemeindebote,* 1 June 1951, pp. 82-83. In a German context the concern was the image of the intellectual Lutheran university-trained pastor who was too remote from his congregation.

seminaries of their own and all of whom were willing to admit Rüschlikon graduates to their lists of accredited pastors.[74] To this extent the Seminary had become part of European Baptist ecclesial life.

No doubt because of his intimate involvement with the staff at FMB headquarters and his status as a staff member, rather than a missionary, Nordenhaug was given great power to carry forward the work of the Seminary. One task was to expand the number of buildings available to house students and staff and another was the erection of a Chapel. The funding of the chapel building demonstrates the importance of Southern Baptist ownership and possibly something of the earlier connections of Nordenhaug with the Woman's Missionary Union (WMU). At their annual meetings in 1955 the WMU voted to pay for the chapel out of their Lottie Moon Christmas offering, in honour of Mrs George R. Martin, WMU President 1945-1956 and chairperson of the BWA Women's Department.[75] The chapel design represented an expression of the ecclesiology of Nordenhaug. He wrote about the building in a leaflet published on its completion.[76] The architect was a local person, Hans von Meyenburg, but Nordenhaug and the Faculty had considerable say in the modern octagonal design of the chapel, with a central lantern, seeking both to express the notion of the gathered church meeting around Word and Table. Daylight shone down on the table, symbolising the light of God's revelation. Not surprisingly, local residents objected to such a modern design and a certain Swiss xenophobia emerged. Nordenhaug met this challenge head on. One local resident, Emma Luise Haab-Escher, objected that the building was too conspicuous, did not blend in with the local landscape and was too American in design. The architect retorted that the style, drawing on Anabaptist insights, was much more European Protestant than North American. Von Meyenburg noted it was not the only chapel building in the canton of Zürich of modern design.[77] The design was ultimately accepted, and in itself it was a sign of how the Seminary had absorbed European Baptist ecclesiology.

---

[74] BUGB had serious discussions within the Ministry Department during the 1980s as to whether a Rüschlikon degree could be printed after the name of a minister in the official list of accredited ministers. The ruling on such matters implied that a degree must be recognised by the Universities of Cambridge, Oxford or London. Eventually, R.E. Clements of Cambridge University indicated that the Rüschlikon MTh could be seen as equivalent to a Masters from a British University. See Minutes of the Ministerial Recognition Committee of BUGB, 1981-1983, Angus Library.

[75] Mrs Martin had been on the group from the FMB who selected the site for the Seminary in 1948.

[76] Leaflet on the new Rüschlikon Chapel, Miscellaneous Papers, IBTS Archive, Bs016.

[77] Von Meyenburg letter to W. Schneider, lawyer for Mrs Haab-Escher, 21 January 1958. An article in *Neue Zujercher Zeitung* by Rudolf Schilling on 8 December 1963 described five modern chapel buildings in the area including that of the Seminary, IBTS Archive, Bs016.

More broadly, Nordenhaug plunged himself into strengthening the links between the Seminary and the Baptist Unions in Europe. He realised the importance of the Seminary being accepted by European Baptists and though he and the majority of the faculty were staff members or missionaries of the SBC-FMB, he travelled widely throughout Europe seeking to build bridges between the Seminary and the Unions. During his presidency he spoke at the EBF Congresses in 1952 and 1958 and at the 1955 BWA Congress in London. Whilst the Seminary had no direct representation on the Executive of the EBF, throughout his tenure as President he attended the EBF Executive as representative of the SBC-FMB. His own clear commitment was to see the Seminary play a pivotal role in stimulating fellowship amongst European Baptists.[78] Woodfin argues:

> While Rueschlikon was certainly not the only factor leading to growth in European co-operation, it did parallel some European developments towards greater unity. The European Baptist Federation grew out of the same London Conference where the seminary was announced...The European Baptist Women's Union was formed in London in 1948 and met on the seminary campus next fall....The European Baptist Mission was founded in 1954 in Zuerich.[79]

The Seminary soon became established as an important conference venue for European Baptists. At one conference in 1950 fifty pastors from thirteen countries participated, and it was noted that a:

> new and mutual understanding to an extent otherwise unobtainable has been made possible for men [sic] ordinarily separated by distance, language, and traditions. Here we have seen and experienced truth of words which are often only a mere cliché such as 'all are one in Jesus Christ'.[80]

Thus the Seminary, under the direction of Nordenhaug, clarified its life and mission and became a settled institution within the work of the FMB and the EBF during the 1950s, and initial concern about the unilateral action of the FMB gradually subsided. Within the constraints of the Seminary's position as part of the mission of FMB, Nordenhaug did all that he could to connect the Seminary with the European Baptist ecclesial context.

---

[78] Nordenhaug made this point in his notes 'Retrospect and Prospect'.

[79] Woodfin, 'Rueschlikon', p. 101.

[80] J.D. Franks, 'European Baptist Pastors Hold First Conference', *Alabama Baptist*, 20 July 1950. Similar positive reports appeared in *The Baptist Times* (Great Britain), *De Gemeinde* (Germany), *Bannaret* (Norway), and *Veckposten* (Denmark).

Strained Relationships

Fundamentally, however, the position remained that the Seminary was funded and operated principally by the FMB. All the important decisions were made by the President, acting within the policies of the FMB staff and Board of Trustees in Richmond, Virginia. This position continued throughout the period 1960-1985. The Presidents who followed Josef Nordenhaug were all FMB missionaries and most of them served for only three or four years. For several of them the presidency at Rüschlikon was a phase in their missionary, seminary or ministerial career. For some others circumstances intervened to cut short their service.[81] During this period a reaction against a moderate theological position within Southern Baptists became increasingly dominant and several people who represented this conservative reaction joined the Board of Trustees of the FMB. One key leader in this movement was Judge Paul Pressler of Houston, Texas, who was to play a crucial role in the attitude of Southern Baptists to other groups within the world Baptist family.[82] He describes a visit to Rüschlikon in 1984:

> When we arrived at our hotel from the airport (in Zürich), the seminary president, Altus Newell, was waiting at the registration desk. We quickly put our bags in the room and went with him to the village of Rüschlikon, where the seminary was located. We were extremely surprised to find very few people on campus. Our tour was quite restricted. In the cafeteria were students who sat at the far end. I asked whether I could meet them and was quickly told that it could not be allowed in our schedule. We had tea with one of the staff members and the president and received an excellent tour of the physical facilities. We were completely isolated from contact with anyone except the president and this particular staff member.
> I heard later that students who had not already left for Christmas were told to leave the campus for the day and that everyone was instructed not to have contact with us. My desire to see the seminary evidently was taken as a threat and as an investigatory tour.[83]

It is clear that in the mid-1980s the relationship between the missionaries running the Seminary and those serving as Trustees with the FMB became

[81] For instance, Clyde Fant and his wife left suddenly in 1983 having been appointed only a year before. He was followed by Altus J. Newell, who left equally suddenly three years after his appointment when an opportunity for service opened in the USA.

[82] P. Pressler, *A Hill on Which to Die: One Southern Baptist's Journey* (Nashville, Tenn.: Broadman and Holman, 1999). Judge Paul Pressler was later to serve as a member of the Southern Baptist Study Commission which, in October 2003, recommended that the SBC should withdraw from membership of the BWA, a decision enacted by the Messengers at their June 2004 Convention meeting. One specific charge was of the 'liberalism' of Eric Geldbach of Bochum, Germany, a prominent Baptist theologian and scholar within the EBF.

[83] *Ibid.*, pp. 231-2.

strained, as the ethos of the SBC began to shift in a more conservative direction. By contrast with European Baptist approaches to ecclesial responsibility, the approach of Southern Baptists represented a top-down managerial style, with the FMB in Richmond, and behind them the Trustees, wanting to engage in the micro-management of the Seminary. As will be analysed in Chapter 6, the missionary arms of the SBC and of American Baptist Churches (ABC-IM) were generally understood to be the main American partners with European Baptists. However, the nature of the two partnerships was very different. ABC had, for many years, sought the views of European Baptists about the most appropriate ways to assist with mission in Europe. The partnership was marked by small scale, but consistent work with European Unions.[84] In contrast, the FMB had often engaged in mission tasks without consulting partners, as in the establishment of Rüschlikon, and had operated particular mission enterprises with little effective liaison with European partners.[85] Individual FMB missionaries often had excellent personal relationships with European Baptists and offered good models of personal partnership, but the style of leadership from Richmond appears to have been that the FMB Trustees and senior staff knew best and carried through policies on a global scale.[86]

In the late 1980s a sea-change took place with regard to Rüschlikon which, in retrospect, occurred at the right time. It brought a new sense of cohesiveness to the EBF and, as can also be seen in retrospect, was an important preparatory move before the collapse of communism in Europe in 1989-1990. The sea-change focused around a series of inter-related events. The first was the appointment of John David Hopper as President. In Hopper was a historian and linguist with a fine pedigree of service with the FMB, especially relating to Baptists in south-east Europe, including Yugoslavia. It is not clear from the available records who argued for Hopper's appointment, but it is interesting to note that some of the conservative (increasingly termed 'fundamentalist') FMB Trustees had begun to argue the case for appointing a like-minded missionary to the position. Two FMB missionaries working in Europe had been highly critical of aspects of Rüschlikon to certain members of the Europe Committee of the FMB Trustees, especially to Ron Wilson, of First Southern Baptist Church, Thousand Oaks, California, who was to play a prominent role in the

[84] See Chapter 6.

[85] Again, see Chapter 6, and the difficult relationships between the SBC-FMB and, for instance, Belgian Baptists, over many years.

[86] In the Richmond offices there was, during this period, a global planning room where the FMB President (the CEO) and Vice-Presidents for the region would meet regularly to look at a large map and plan their work. I experienced this room and the 'war room' planning atmosphere on a visit to Richmond in 1991.

subsequent dissemination of critical attitudes to Rüschlikon.[87] The two missionaries were Phil Roberts,[88] who worked for the FMB in Belgium and then became Professor of Missions and Evangelism at Southeastern Baptist Seminary, and William L. Wagner,[89] a missiologist who served as an FMB missionary, firstly, (from 1965) in Austria and then as FMB Regional Consultant for Evangelism and Church Growth, based in Belgium. Roberts and Wagner promoted the view that the Seminary should be moved from 'liberal' and expensive Switzerland to Belgium, where both were adjunct teaching staff at the Evangelical Faculty at Heverlee, Belgium. An FMB Task Force studied the issue and a group of Trustees visited both Belgium and Rüschlikon; the outcome was that the Seminary would not move to Belgium. Because of their critical stance towards Rüschlikon, any move to appoint either Roberts or Wagner as President would certainly have been opposed by the existing Seminary Faculty.

What seemed to be needed was someone as Seminary President who could hold together the existing faculty, could keep a proper relationship with the EBF, and could also satisfy the increasing pressure from some of the FMB Trustees to have a more conservative seminary leadership. John David Hopper was a popular missionary with the nationals and was conservative in scholarship and nature. The European FMB staff team, G. Keith Parker and Isam Ballenger (who had himself been the Seminary President from 1978-1981), 'felt that we needed someone in whom the Easterners had confidence'.[90] Nevertheless, Isam Ballenger realised 'the faculty would not be pleased'[91] at this appointment as they queried both Hopper's scholarship and his leadership potential. Nevertheless, the President of the FMB, R. Keith Parks, and the European Regional staff of the FMB, pressed the case for Hopper and the existing Faculty came to accept the situation as the least upsetting option. At this juncture the appointment of Hopper went ahead. He had, at some point in the process, met with leading Trustees and had given them assurances that he

---

[87] R. Wilson from California served as an FMB Trustee throughout this period. Paul Pressler comments: 'It was Ron's keen analysis of the situation that caused tremendous changes at the FMB. When an effort was made to draw attention of FMB members away from the real issues, Ron was always perceptive in identifying problems and communicating to other members of the board. The IMB would not be the same today without the contribution of Ron Wilson', quoted in Pressler, *A Hill on Which to Die*, p. 283.

[88] R.P. Roberts was highly disruptive within the Belgium Baptist Union and was ultimately asked to leave the country by the Belgium leadership. Since January 2001 he has served as President of Midwestern Baptist Theological Seminary, Kansas City.

[89] W.L. (Bill) Wagner is now E. Herman Westmoreland Professor of Evangelism at Golden Gate Seminary, California.

[90] Personal letter to me from Isam Ballenger, 11 December 2003.

[91] *Ibid.*

would move the Seminary in a more conservative direction.[92] It does not appear, from the Minutes of the EBF or from the Minutes of the Rüschlikon Executive Committee, that these assurances were ever formally reported to the Europeans, but the FMB Trustees decided to let the appointment proceed. This happened despite clamour from others to pursue an approach more in keeping with the increasingly-influential fundamentalist agenda within the Southern Baptist community.[93]

At the first meeting of the Rüschlikon Executive Committee which John David Hopper attended, in February 1988, he indicated he was not 'pessimistic about the future'.[94] One of the issues to be addressed was financial. In noting that he was coming to the Seminary at a time of financial crisis, he suggested that this 'presents us all with a challenge – a challenge to rise to the occasion'.[95] Among the ideas discussed in the Administrative Committee, with Hopper and H.W. Wayne Pipkin present, was a proposal to sell the whole campus and relocate to a cheaper and more compact base.[96] At this point it was not clear how the FMB would react to such a proposal, especially as those on the Rüschlikon campus had so effectively argued against moving to Belgium and for maintenance of the work in Switzerland. Another proposal at this meeting was to establish an International Baptist Lay Academy (IBLA) of the Seminary, to be based in Budapest at the Hungarian Baptist Seminary, but controlled by the Rüschlikon operation and funded by the FMB. JoAnn Hopper had first suggested this idea.[97] This envisaged the President and the Director of the Institute for Mission and Evangelism (FMB) serving on the Board of the Lay Academy and lecturers from the seminary doing much of the teaching.[98] The

---

[92] *Ibid.*

[93] On this whole development over a space of 20 years see, for instance, G.C. Cothen, *The New SBC: Fundamentalism's Impact on the Southern Baptist Convention* (Macon, Ga.: Smythe and Helwys, 1995); J.F. Baugh, *The Battle for Baptist Integrity* (Austin, Tx.: Battle for Baptist Integrity Inc. 1997); P. Pressler, *A Hill on Which to Die*; J.W. Merritt, *The Betrayal of Southern Baptist Missionaries by Southern Baptist Leaders 1979 –2004* (Ashville, North Ca.: Published by the author, 2004), later reprinted as Merritt, *The Betrayal: The hostile takeover of the Southern Baptist Convention and a missionary's fight for Freedom in Christ* (Ashville, North Ca.: R. Brent and Co, 2005).

[94] Personal comment to the author, San Antonio, Texas, 18 February 2007.

[95] President's Report to the February 1988 Executive Committee, Box 808, EBF Archive.

[96] Administrative Committee, 1 February 1988, Agenda item 5, p. 2, IBTS Archive, Bs016.

[97] Interview with JoAnn and John David Hopper, San Antonio, Texas, 18 February 2007.

[98] 'Proposed International Baptist Lay Academy (IBLA), Budapest Hungary, East Branch, Rüschlikon Seminary', document submitted to the Seminary Executive Committee, February 1988, IBTS Archive Bs016.

title of the document refers to Budapest as being the 'East Branch, Rüschlikon Seminary'. This initiative aimed to provide: training for lay pastors and preachers; training for other local church leaders; preparation for Eastern Europeans for further study where desired; a venue for literature production and curriculum development; a forum for the exchange of knowledge, skills, methods; leadership and impulse for the development of national lay training programmes.[99] The FMB took this work forward from 1990, funding a Director, leasing premises, and providing scholarships for students, until the first missionary Director, Errol Simmons, retired in 2000. It proved to be important in the development of a number of younger Baptist leaders from Eastern Europe.

Meanwhile, Isam Ballenger, a missiologist and Europhile, had been appointed Vice-President of the FMB for Europe and the Middle East. His Area Director, Keith Parker, was a former lecturer at the Seminary and had his office on the Rüschlikon campus. Ballenger became convinced that the way to secure a useful future for the Seminary in Europe was to take forward the established missiological principle of transferring to 'nationals' the assets of missionary societies when it was deemed that 'nationals' were capable of using the assets properly. This principle had been in operation in other mission agencies for several years.[100] Ballenger visited several key European leaders, including the German Baptist leadership in Bad Homburg, the British Baptist leadership and, most crucially, the EBF General Secretary, Knud Wümplemann, in Denmark. Ballenger told the EBF General Secretary he believed the EBF should ask the FMB for the property when the anticipated FMB Task Force visited Europe. Ballenger commented: 'With the task force's coming to Europe, knowing they would be impressed with European leadership, it was a moment which probably would never return. That was the case.'[101]

---

[99] *Ibid.*, pp. 3-4.

[100] Since the Second World Missionary Conference organised by the International Mission Council in Jerusalem in 1928 the emphasis had been on the indigenisation of mission. For instance, the Serampore College was transferred to Indian Christians in 1949 from BMS control. See, S. Neill, *A History of Christian Missions* (London: Penguin, 1986).

[101] Letter to me from I. Ballenger, 11 December 2003.

The 'Key of Ownership'

The FMB Trustee Task Force did, indeed, return to the USA and recommended to the Board that the property be transferred to the EBF.[102] The proposal was agreed by the FMB Trustees. In Ballenger's words:

> The task force supported the transfer of property, the Europeans were ready to receive it, and the *kairos* came. Immediately thereafter, the Trustees began lamenting losing this valuable property.[103]

Ron Wilson took a very different view of the decision when, as he put it, 'we gave away Ruschlikon [sic] seminary to the European Baptist Federation (EBF)'. He continued:

> ... this vote finally happened after much chess playing by the staff and the Europeans with our board. Remember that originally we were examining the possibility of selling Ruschlikon Seminary, changing its emphasis and relocating the property we could buy and renovate in Brussels, Belgium.... A committee was formed to go over and examine this possibility, but liberal European leadership was ready for them. Trustees were presented with a scenario of doom and destruction if Ruschlikon were to be sold and a different kind of ministry developed.[104]

For Wilson and others the main issue was what they perceived as 'liberal European leadership' (a phrase not defined), but there were also those who considered that the European Baptists would not have the financial resources to maintain the Seminary in Switzerland. Wilson commented that, amongst those present during the discussions, was L. Paige Patterson,[105] a leading fundamentalist and protégé of Judge Pressler in the fundamentalist resurgence amongst Southern Baptists.[106] Patterson had been President of Criswell Bible College in Dallas, then later President of Southeastern Seminary and, more recently, Southwestern Seminary in the USA. Wilson noted Patterson gave

---

[102] Letter from I. Ballenger to J.D. Hopper, IBTS Archive. In reality, the EBF was not a substantial legal body at that time and so a Swiss Verein had to be established, consisting initially of Swiss citizens, to receive the property and assets. The Verein legally founded the Czech o.p.s., which manages IBTS in Prague. The legal complexities of all of this are worthy of further study and research in their own right and remain complex as long as there is no EU-wide legal approach to founding non-profit organisations.

[103] Letter to me from I. Ballenger, 11 December 2003.

[104] Pressler, *A Hill on Which to Die*, pp. 237-40, gives the full text of the letter.

[105] L.P. Patterson is generally acknowledged, with Judge P. Pressler, to be a principal architect of the fundamentalist resurgence within the Southern Baptist Convention.

[106] L.P. Patterson, *Anatomy of a Reformation: The Southern Baptist Convention 1978-2004* (Fort Worth: Southwestern Seminary Publications, 2006).

clear arguments for selling the Swiss property and moving. Wilson cited these as:

1. The opportunity would be lost with the Brussels property.
2. If we gave the property to the Europeans they would not support the institution to the degree that it would be able to stay in Rüschlikon.
3. Declaring that its success was tied to its location was an empty argument because he predicted that they would be forced to sell that property and be forced to move elsewhere in Europe.
4. At that point, when the institution would be moved, there would be an endowment created that would help perpetuate theological liberalism in Europe for decades.[107]

Although Patterson and Wilson argued their case, FMB President, Keith Parks and Vice-President for Europe, Isam Ballenger, argued that Switzerland remained the right place to be and they considered that under J.D. Hopper the institution would operate in a way which would give greater confidence to Europeans and would also be seen as more conservative theologically. Mark Corts, Chair of the Trustees, led the meeting with the view that handing the property to the EBF was right, and a resolution was passed to transfer the formal ownership of the Seminary to a Swiss Verein. The legal situation in Switzerland meant that the Seminary could not technically be owned by a Europe-wide organisation (the EBF) that did not itself have full legal status.[108] Thus a Swiss 'Verein' was created: The Baptistische Theologische Hochschule, Rüschlikon. This consisted of Swiss residents, approved by the EBF Council, who signed letters with the EBF Officers to say they would only act in accordance with the decisions of the EBF Council, or its appropriate committees, providing such actions were legal within Swiss law. This hugely significant change of ownership took place in 1988. There was a promise from the FMB to continue funding a significant part of the work of the Seminary for a fourteen-year period, with gradual reduction in the FMB share. The European Baptist Convention[109] paper, *Highlights*, recorded the handing over of the property by the FMB in the following way:

---

[107] Letter from R. Wilson to the FMB Trustees quoted in Pressler, *A Hill on Which to Die*, pp. 238-240.

[108] Peter D. Deutsch, Swiss Baptist President and a lawyer in Berne used to comment that the EBF was legally 'nothing'. In fact a *de minimus* legal standing existed for the EBF as a 'committee' of the German Baptist Union until a Swiss Association for the EBF was created in 2001.

[109] The European Baptist Convention (now International Baptist Convention) consists of English-speaking Baptist churches in capital cities and in areas where the US Army and Air Force have been based throughout Europe and the Middle East. Most churches were originally Southern Baptist in ethos, often founded by US service personnel and pastored by FMB missionaries.

> The Key of Ownership of the property of the Baptist Theological Seminary in Rüschlikon was given by FMB president R. Keith Parks to EBF General Secretary Knud Wumplemann on May 28. The gift of the property represented a further step in the rich 40-year partnership in theological education between European Baptists and Southern Baptists.
>
> … At the ceremony Dr Parks emphasized that the partnership between the Foreign Mission Board and European Baptists would not end with the passing of the key. He assured his hearers that the contributions will continue at the present level until 1992, when, by prior agreement, a gradual curtailment of funds will begin. Nevertheless, Rüschlikon Seminary needs increased giving from European Baptists at once to maintain the work.[110]

The indications were that the Seminary, having been for four decades under the control of the FMB, would be embedded in European Baptist life.

The idea in the statement by Parks of an FMB-EBF 'partnership' was, however, open to interpretation. The FMB soon made several suggestions to the EBF about how the EBF might operate and take care of the Seminary. One such request was that the EBF draw up a 'written statement of European Baptist principles common to all European Baptists… which would give expression to the Seminary's Baptist, biblical commitment and to which seminary teachers would subscribe'.[111] At the EBF Executive Committee in De Bron, Netherlands, on 27 September 1990, it was agreed to reply to the request pointing out the somewhat different perception of Baptist ecclesial polity in Europe to that pertaining in the southern states of America. The Scottish Baptist Union General Secretary, Peter Barber (as EBF President), Wiard Popkes, an alumnus of Rüschlikon and Professor of New Testament at Hamburg University and in the German Baptist Seminary (IBTS Board of Trustees), and Karl Heinz Walter (EBF General Secretary) commented:

> We as European Baptists recognize our diversity which flows from the differences in our national cultures and religious backgrounds, in the various influences which contributed to the origins of our national Baptist movements, and in our own historical developments. We accept and welcome this diversity which in our view enriches us. We feel that though we are diverse, we are members of one Baptist family, having one Lord, one faith, one baptism.
>
> Because we accept only the Bible as our sole authority and guide, it is not common for Baptists in Europe to sign a confession or creed. Therefore it is also not common for us to ask Baptist teachers to subscribe to a statement of faith. We do affirm, however, that the Board of Trustees of the Seminary carefully examines

---

[110] *Highlights,* news journal of the European Baptist Convention, Wiesbaden, Germany, July 1989 edition.

[111] Quoted in a reply from the President and General Secretary of the EBF and the Chairman of the IBTS Board of Trustees, 27 September 1990, Letter in the IBTS Archive, Bs016.

> the prospective teachers of the BTS with regard to their integration in the life and witness of their unions and with regard to their conformity to basic Baptist beliefs and biblical authority.[112]

This is a crucial statement. European Baptists recognised their diverse traditions, while affirming that, in the midst of their diversity, they were 'members of one Baptist family, having one Lord, one faith, one baptism', and it was this which they wanted to see expressed in the Seminary. This letter noted the momentous changes going on in Europe with the collapse of communism and that they had asked the Board of Trustees to initiate a process of examination of the core of the Baptist principles which European Baptists hold in common.[113]

The response from the EBF Executive was far from satisfactory from the point of view of the fundamentalist members of the FMB Trustee body. Ron Wilson, as one of the leaders in this group, wrote to William Hancock, the FMB Trustees Chairman, on 3 May 1991, and this letter was later 'leaked' from the FMB. It offers a unique insight into the approach of the fundamentalist members of the FMB Trustees. Wilson stated:

> If we are going to make changes we are going to have to do it in the next 24 months… In my way of thinking, the obvious place to start is Europe and in particular, Rüschlikon Seminary. I laid the groundwork to approach this problem at the last meeting when I questioned the teaching on the virgin birth. Now you and I know that there are many other questions to be raised to that teaching faculty but I felt that the virgin birth is so fundamental and would be a safe controversy in the SBC because even among liberal circles of Southern Baptists, there are few who openly question or deny the virgin birth…. I finally have found the nerve on which to approach Rüschlikon and that is alluded to earlier about the virgin birth. I talked to Phil Roberts on the 11th April and he reminded me of a copy of a letter signed by three of the teachers at Rüschlikon which gives insight to their belief concerning the virgin birth. Paige Patterson has a translation of that letter and as soon as he can find it, he will send me a copy.[114]

Wilson and Hancock took the view that they had a 'window of opportunity' to turn the FMB to their agenda. The nerve point was to be Rüschlikon and help was being sought from Phil Roberts, a missionary in Belgium, who was

---

[112] Letter from EBF Officers to I. Ballenger, SBC-FMB, 27 September 1990, Box 91, EBF Archive.

[113] *Ibid.*

[114] R. Wilson to W. Hancock, 3 May 1991. This letter was leaked from the FMB and circulated widely amongst EBF leaders. The full text is reproduced in Merritt, *The Betrayal of Southern Baptist Missionaries by Southern Baptist Leaders 1979–2004* (2004), pp. 63-8.

embroiled in disputes with the Belgian Baptist Union.[115] John W. Merritt, himself an FMB Missionary, notes the way certain FMB Trustees now launched a sustained attack on the Seminary. He comments:

> In the spring of 1991 some FMB Trustees contended that the seminary in Rüschlikon was liberal, and questioned whether European professors at the seminary believed in the virgin birth of Christ. Isam Ballenger informed John D Hopper… that accusations had surfaced again among FMB Trustees…. Hopper called the professors together to discuss the accusations. They decided that a letter clarifying their beliefs should be sent to Ballenger.[116]

The letter replying to the FMB Trustees' charges was constructed by the three people whose theology was of concern to some within the FMB – Thorwald Lorenzen, Professor of Theology; Hans Harald Mallau, the Old Testament specialist; and Günter Wagner, the New Testament Professor.[117] The basis of the attack by the FMB was the defence in 1985 by these three of Eduard Schuetz, a German Baptist scholar, who had been accused falsely of denying the truth of the doctrine of the Virgin Birth. They had sought to defend the integrity of Schuetz. The matter had been discussed when the FMB team visited the Seminary and the three professors expressed surprise that the matter had surfaced again. The three commented in their letter, which was addressed to Isam Ballenger:

> Our statement relating to Dr Schuetz was formulated in response to the false charges that Dr Schuetz had denied the truth of the doctrine of the Virgin Birth… If further clarification is needed, we would like to emphasize that the Virgin Birth belongs to the doctrines in the New Testament which affirm that Jesus Christ is truly God and truly human. Neither in our statement written in 1985, nor in our teaching activities have we ever denied the truth of the infancy narratives in the

---

[115] R.P. Roberts objected to the fact that Baptist property in Belgium was all technically owned by the Union, and the President, Samuel Verhagaehe, and R.P. Roberts were engaged in conflict over the property of the International Baptist Church in Brussels.

[116] Merritt, *The Betrayal of Southern Baptist Missionaries by Southern Baptist Leaders 1979–2004*, p. 57-8.

[117] On the theology of Lorenzen see T. Lorenzen, *Resurrection and Discipleship: Interpretive Models, Biblical Reflections, Theological Consequences* (Maryknoll, NY: Orbis Books, 1995). Lorenzen served as senior pastor of Canberra Baptist Church, Australia, until 2005 when he retired. Mallau died in 2005. Wagner is in retirement. All three were of German background and were long-term members of the Rüschlikon staff. Wagner had been a student, doctoral student, assistant and then Professor at the Seminary.

> Gospels of Matthew and Luke. Hoping this clarifies that matter somewhat, we remain...[118]

This was a carefully crafted response by these three senior Faculty members, one of whom, Wagner, was a serving member of the Faith and Order Commission of the World Council of Churches. It was, however, far from the end of the story.

While the theological debates continued, important administrative changes were put into effect. At the 1989 EBF Council in Budapest the General Secretary, Knud Wümplemann, referred to the hand-over of the property to the EBF, and the Council was asked to adopt a Charter and Bye-Laws and to elect the first group of Trustees.[119] John David Hopper presented a report outlining the developments at the time of the hand-over. In this report he noted:

> Last year at the EBF Council you requested the Seminary property from the Foreign Mission Board, SBC. In the October, 1988 meeting of the Board, FMB Trustees agreed to the transfer of the property.... At the request of the Executive Board, between January and June this year we drafted a charter and bye-laws for the seminary... As far as possible we tried to obtain a consensus which is quite difficult in such a document in an international setting.[120]

The reports were received with thanks to John David Hopper, the Rüschlikon Executive Board and to Isam Ballenger and Keith Parker for their hard work.[121] The Trustees appointed included the incoming EBF General Secretary, Karl Heinz Walter, representatives from different parts of Europe, two representatives of the Foreign Mission Board – Isam Ballenger and Keith Parker – a representative of American Baptist Churches Board of International Ministries, Alice Findlay, and a local Swiss Baptist, Gabi Marinello, who was a businessman. Marinello was made President of the Verein and devoted himself with great energy to the legal and financial affairs of this now wholly-owned child of the EBF.[122] In line with Baptist ecclesial thinking, the responsibility for this aspect of theological training in Europe was assumed by the European Baptist communities.

In 1989, with the Seminary owned by the Europeans, the EBF Officers and Board began to seek to develop the Seminary in line with the wishes of the EBF

---

118 Letter of 21 June 1991 from T. Lorenzen, H.H. Mallau and G. Wagner to I. Ballenger in response to a criticism from FMB Trustees, IBTS Archive, Bs016.

119 EBF Council Meeting, 26-27 July 1989, Budapest, pp. 5, 6 and 8, Box 807, EBF Archive.

120 Report of J.D. Hopper to the EBF Council, 1989, contained in the papers of the Council, Box 807, EBF Archive.

121 Minutes of the EBF Council Meeting, 26-27 July 1989, Budapest, p. 6, Box 807, EBF Archive.

122 *Ibid.*, p. 8.

member Unions. But the Seminary was still essentially staffed by SBC Missionaries – John David and JoAnn Hopper, Kent Blevins and Deborah Crone-Blevins, Earl and Jane Martin, Dixon and Kandy Queen-Sutherland, and Mr and Mrs Murphy Terry (Administration) – and the FMB was still providing a high level of institutional funding.[123] Also, the FMB regional office was on the campus. Given these circumstances, it was clear that the FMB Board of Trustees would maintain a keen interest in the work of IBTS. Herein appears to lie a continuing problem for mission agencies: even when they hand over ownership of real estate and look to nationals to operate an institution, if their own personnel remain involved and if there is some level of institutional support from the missionary body, it is difficult to 'let go'. In the specific case of Rüschlikon, conservative members of the Trustees of the FMB believed they still had a legitimate interest in the future life of the Seminary, in that they understood Hopper had been appointed as President to steer the Seminary in a theologically more conservative direction in line with the general move in this direction within the leadership of the SBC. They were determined to ensure that this happened or if it did not to end their involvement in the Seminary.

'To discontinue financial support'

The decisive point for the Trustees of the SBC-FMB came in 1991 when Hopper recruited E. Glenn Hinson, of Southern Baptist Seminary, to serve as an adjunct staff member at Rüschlikon and to deliver the first in what was to be a series of lectures named in honour of J.D. Hughey, a former Rüschlikon President (following Nordenhaug, 1960-64) and a distinguished Southern Baptist missionary. Hinson chose the topic of religious liberty.[124] Although Hinson was in a tenured professorship post at a Southern Baptist seminary, members of the FMB Board of Trustees reacted negatively to his appointment at Rüschlikon, based on a reading of some of his earlier published works. They now acted decisively. At a meeting of the FMB Board of Trustees on 9 October 1991 in Richmond, Virginia, they voted to defund IBTS by US$ 365,000 per annum. Leading this campaign was R. Wilson. Reporting on the decision to the EBF Council in the following year, Hopper commented:

> In October 1991, the Foreign Mission Board Trustees voted to discontinue financial support of the Seminary effective the end of December, within two months. The vote to defund Rüschlikon was taken without any consultation with either the European Baptist Federation leadership or the BTS/Rüschlikon

---

[123] In 1988 they provided 42.3% of the total income and in 1989 49.7%. These figures are from the Presidential Report to the EBF Council, 24 August 1990, p. 2, Box 809, EBF Archive.

[124] Report of the President, J.D. Hopper, to the EBF Council, Varna, Bulgaria, September 1991, Box 809, EBF Archive.

> president. The vote to remove the subsidy was reviewed and reaffirmed in a meeting of the FMB in December 1991 in which the EBF executive secretary Karl Heinz Walter, the BTS/R chairperson, Dr Wiard Popkes, and the seminary president, Dr Hopper, participated.... The reason given for defunding was that Dr Glenn Hinson, a guest professor from the Southern Baptist Seminary in Louisville Kentucky, was chosen to teach a four month course including Christian spirituality, medieval church history and Latin during the fall semester of 1991. The FMB trustees considered Dr Hinson not conservative enough to teach at Rüschlikon.[125]

With this single action the whole future of the seminary had become critical and the 'partnership' relationship between Southern Baptists and European Baptists placed in jeopardy.

It might be thought strange that the focus should be the use of a Southern Baptist scholar who taught spirituality and history. However, the deeper issue was about control.[126] Thus, Ron Wilson believed that defunding the Seminary would show the authority of the Trustees over the staff, especially Keith Parks.[127] John W. Merritt, who followed the developments from his standpoint as an FMB missionary, comments:

> The action came as a complete shock to European Baptist leaders; to administrators and trustees of the seminary and to the entire seminary family of faculty, students and staff. None of the above had any idea that such an action was being contemplated, or that it would actually be taken without any consultation with European Baptist leaders. In reality, the action was also against the FMB staff, against Southern Baptist missionaries, and against many Southern Baptists who were not submissive to the Convention's fundamentalist leaders.[128]

The European Baptist leadership saw this not primarily as a breach of trust with the Seminary at Rüschlikon, but with the EBF and the then thirty-two Baptist Unions in membership with the EBF. Reaction came from the Unions themselves who believed they had been betrayed, and they wondered about the quality of partnership from that time forward between the FMB and the

---

[125] Report of the President, J.D. Hopper, to the EBF Council in Hoddesdon, England, September 1992, Box 810, EBF Archive.

[126] With changes in leadership at Southern, Southwestern, Southeastern and New Orleans, fundamentalist trustees were able to appoint presidents and senior staff in tune with their theological and political preferences over succeeding years.

[127] This point is brought out in the argument of J.W. Merritt in *The Betrayal*. Pressler in *A Hill on Which to Die* makes much of the fact that Ron Wilson believed the FMB staff had misled the Trustees over the issue of the original gift to the EBF.

[128] Merritt, *The Betrayal*, p. 58.

individual Unions.[129] Baptist leaders who expressed concern included Peter Barber (General Secretary, Baptist Union of Scotland) and David R. Coffey (General Secretary, Baptist Union of Great Britain), both of whom had positive relations with the SBC leadership.[130] Both had been engaged in expanding FMB involvement in their own Unions using short term volunteers, two-year Journeypersons and career missionaries.[131] Little was provided by way of explanation from the FMB Trustees and perhaps the defunding had not been part of the pre-planned strategy. The decision certainly shocked many serving FMB missionaries in Europe, who were well integrated into the programmes of the national Unions with whom they served.[132]

On behalf of the Seminary Trustees, Wiard Popkes, from Germany, who was Chairman of the Trustees, wrote to the FMB on 10 October 1991:

> The decision of the FMB to cut off all funds for the BTS as of December 31 1991, is a veritable shock for the Board of Trustees. It is difficult to find appropriate words of response. The decision was made altogether unexpectedly, without any consultation with the Board of Trustees or the BTS.... The sudden change of mind of the FMB cannot be regarded by us other than an unfriendly action and a break of trust.... The cooperation between SBC and Baptists in Europe has been long, fruitful and trustful....We do not really know the underlying motivations of the FMB's decision. It seems, though, that they were not aware of the repercussions of such a step for the credibility of future activities of the FMB/SBC in Europe. We hope the Lord will prevent even greater damage and that the trustful, fraternal cooperation with FMB missionaries, as we know and appreciate them in Europe, will be maintained.[133]

The EBF Executive Committee also decided to plead with the FMB that they think again, reinstate the grant and honour their commitment 'otherwise we fear irreparable damage will be done to the honour in which the Foreign Mission Board is held in Europe and confidence eroded in any future dealings European

---

[129] See European Baptist Press Service 'Newsflash' of 1 October 1991, EBPS Archive, IBTS, Prague.

[130] In a comment to me on 3 December 2006, D.R. Coffey, now BWA President, reported that he had always had a good relationship with Morris Chapman, Executive Secretary-Treasurer of the SBC.

[131] The relationship on a wider level is explored more fully in Chapter 6. Here it is worth noting the interconnectedness between the FMB and IBTS/EBF and the FMB and the member bodies of EBF.

[132] See elsewhere for the effect upon missionaries, many of whom subsequently left the service of the FMB.

[133] Letter from Wiard Popkes to the FMB Board Chairman, 10 October 1991, Popkes Archive, IBTS.

Baptist leaders may have with the Board.'[134] The chairman of the FMB Board of Trustees, William Hancock was, apparently, overwhelmed with negative responses from Europe.[135] On 2 November 1991, Popkes wrote to him again drawing attention to the moral aspect of the issue; the FMB was reneging on an agreement without offering the BTS Trustees the possibility of responding.[136] Hancock made arrangements for the EBF General Secretary (Walter), the Chair of the IBTS Board of Trustees (Popkes) and the EBF President (Merritt) to attend the FMB Europe Area Committee on 5-6 December 1991 to discuss the situation.

Keith Parker explained to the IBTS Board of Trustees, when they met in November 1991, what had taken place within the FMB Board:

> The regional committee for Europe [of the SBC-FMB Trustees] worked through and voted on and made a proposal in June [1991] for a three-year reduction after 1992. But this proposal was not presented to the full Board in the subsequent meeting. It was the chairperson's decision to present it to the full Board in October. There was intensive pressure to change the vote to no funding after 1992. The following day at a personnel meeting somebody noticed on a list that Dr Glenn Hinson was teaching at Rüschlikon. This became the major discussion. Drs Ballenger and Parker were called in and reprimanded... In the plenum on October 9 the agenda was changed, the entire budget was accepted, except Rüschlikon, and Rüschlikon was defunded.[137]

Isam Ballenger, FMB Vice-President for Europe, also met with the EBF Trustees to report on the apparent sudden decision to defund. He expressed regret at his unsuccessful representation on behalf of European Baptists in the October FMB discussion. However, he indicated some hope that the defunding would be rescinded in December, thanks to a good case being put forward, which included suggesting that the FMB Trustees needed to act ethically and with integrity. Ballenger went on to express the view that there was little hope of funding beyond 1992.[138] In itself this time-table, if it had been followed, could be seen as a way of placing responsibility for the Seminary firmly in the hands of the Europeans.

However, there was also pressure from those who did not wish the decision in favour of the immediate defunding of the Seminary to be rescinded. On 27

---

[134] EBF Executive Committee to the FMB Chairman, October 1991, Box 820, EBF Archive.

[135] IBTS Board of Trustees [BOT] Minutes, 1-2 November 1991, p. 4, Box E4, IBTS Archive.

[136] W. Popkes to W. Hancock. Letter in Popkes Archive, IBTS. The letter is reproduced in Merritt, *The Betrayal*, pp. 61-3.

[137] Report by G.K. Parker, IBTS BOT Minutes, 1-2 November 1991, p. 4, para. 06, IBTS Archive.

[138] *Ibid.*, p. 5.

November 1991 an unsigned letter on the stationery of the First Southern Baptist Church of Thousand Oaks, California, was written to FMB Trustees. Ron Wilson was the pastor of this church and a member of the FMB Board of Trustees.[139] This long letter was designed to stiffen the resolve of the FMB Trustees at the forthcoming December meeting. It referred to the many letters of protest that had been received about the defunding and suggested that:

> the great majority of letters come from folks of liberal, or at best, moderate bent... upon reading the letters, you obviously noticed the similarity of wording and phrasing. One wonders if a model letter was used... How in the world could any sane person say we are missing the door of opportunity in Eastern Europe when we are giving the $365,000 to train hundreds of students instead of the 38-48 at Rüschlikon?
>
> Our action in October is not controversial with mainstream Southern Baptists. The concerns over Rüschlikon by knowledgeable Baptists have always been centered in Scripture and the seeming lack of respect for the Scriptures at that institution. This concern is not of recent vintage but goes back many years. Glen Hinson is not the issue at Rüschlikon. He simply proves the point.... A college professor described Rüschlikon as 'being the toxic waste dump for liberalism in Europe'. The staff, both home in Richmond and on the field, has allowed modern liberalism to continue to be taught at that school. How do I know this to be true? ... Glen Hinson![140]

The letter met the charge that the defunding was unethical by a counter-accusation that the staff of the FMB, J.D. Hopper, and European Baptist leaders had broken promises made at the handing over of Rüschlikon in 1988, and it claimed that Hopper, as an FMB employee, was working against the policy of the Board and was lacking in integrity. It was a tour de force.

In the event, Wilson's view prevailed. The December meeting in Virginia was as much for show as anything. The EBF team met with the FMB Europe, Middle East and North Africa Committee, the officers of the FMB and some FMB staff. William Hancock did not, however, allow the European delegation to meet with the full Board, or to address the Board about the charges of 'liberalism' at the Seminary. As Merritt comments:

> Capable representatives had travelled at considerable expense in time and money from Europe to Richmond to engage in serious discussions concerning partnership in missions and theological education, but no such serious discussions were allowed or conducted.[141]

---

[139] Copies of this letter circulated in Europe as early as January 1992. The letter is reprinted in full in Merritt, *The Betrayal*, pp. 70-2.

[140] *Ibid.*, pp. 70-9.

[141] *Ibid.*, p. 79.

Hopper and his wife decided to resign as FMB Missionaries in 1992, after twenty-seven years of service. The defunding had already claimed two other casualties, Isam Ballenger and Keith Parker, both of whom had come to the conclusion that they could no longer, with integrity, represent the SBC-FMB in Europe and both had resigned after the reaffirmation of the defunding decision in December.[142] This series of events, and the refusal to allow the appointed representatives of European Baptists to speak to the FMB Board of Trustees, marked a very low point in the relationship of Southern Baptists and European Baptists. Whilst the way of acting of the FMB had often been in contrast to the partnership model of ABC-IM, nevertheless, until this point, even when actions had been announced rather than agreed by consultation, there had generally been mutual cooperation and discussion. Now, the FMB Trustee leadership, especially Ron Wilson, had created a situation in which even a direct approach by senior leaders of the EBF could be ignored. There had been a clash between two different views about Baptist ecclesiology; one which allowed local communities to take decisions and one which imposed an agenda on the churches without consultation and may not be regarded as truly baptistic.

A New Chapter

From this moment on, the SBC-FMB withdrew from active involvement with IBTS. More widely, the Mission's policy moved from working with existing Baptist groups to more independent missionary operations relating to specific people groups.[143] The FMB defended its actions over IBTS and never apologised for reneging on a promise made at the time of the handover of the property.[144] Another effect of the FMB defunding and the continuing attacks upon the Seminary was that the missionaries serving there from the FMB resigned as career missionaries. There had been discontent within Southern Baptist life about the fundamentalist resurgence, and the defunding became a key spark for many 'moderate' Southern Baptists to come together and form the Cooperative Baptist Fellowship (CBF), with a missions agency, the first missionaries appointed being the Hoppers, followed by other missionaries serving in Europe.[145] This was the start of a very constructive relationship

[142] Report of J.D. Hopper to the Board of Trustees, 24 April 1992, Box E5, IBTS Archive.

[143] This whole philosophical adaptation is well chronicled in Keith E. Eitel, *Paradigm Wars: The Southern Baptist International Mission Board Faces the Third Millennium* (Oxford: Regnum Books International, 2000). In particular, see Chapter 4, 'Gospel Missionism's Lingering Legacy and Post-Modern Trends in The SBC's Foreign Mission Board (1910–1997)'.

[144] See Merritt, *The Betrayal*, pp. 85-87.

[145] See Cothen, *The New SBC: Fundamentalism's Impact on the Southern Baptist Convention*. Also, Merritt, *The Betrayal*, especially Chapter 4.

between the EBF and CBF. With the appointment of the Hoppers and also the Blevins as missionaries of the CBF,[146] the EBF Council decided that the place of the SBC on the IBTS Board of Trustees should be taken by a representative of CBF.[147] CBF took up the mantle of the SBC, connecting mainstream Baptists in the Southern States of the USA with IBTS, which had been such an important enterprise of the old FMB. They committed to ensuring that the funding which had been taken away by the FMB would be provided by their own mission agency and though, by 1998, no career missionaries from CBF were on the staff at IBTS, the close relationship has continued. At the tenth anniversary of the founding of CBF, in their Annual Assembly in the Omni Center, Atlanta, Clarissa Strickland, a founder employee and senior CBF staff member, told the Assembly that IBTS was one of the key reasons for CBF coming into being.[148] In 2006 IBTS was named as the first Global Partner of CBF in the area of theological education.

The new chapter in the history of IBTS in the 1990s included the selling of Rüschlikon and the relocation of the Seminary to Prague, Czech Republic, in 1995. The defunding ultimately made it impossible for the Seminary to continue in Switzerland. Despite the emergence of the CBF and their decision to seek to replace the funding lost from the FMB, it proved impossible to produce a financial plan drawing sufficient support from the EBF Unions and the USA to keep the Swiss base viable. The new IBTS Board of Trustees, led by Wiard Popkes, began to examine all the options for the future. Three possible venues emerged – Berlin, Budapest and Prague. J.D. Hopper, speaking to the EBF Council in England in 1992, referred to all the difficulties faced in continuing in Switzerland – financial, visa problems, and maintenance of the property – but went on to say, 'nevertheless the question of moving is primarily one of strategy. The object would be to make the seminary an even more effective and influential institution and more closely related to the EBF.'[149] The German Union, now reunited East and West, was looking for a new central base for their Union offices and Seminary in Berlin and longed for the Seminary and the EBF offices to be moved there. Speaking to the 1993 Council, Hopper presented the following criteria for relocation:

---

[146] Following on the resignations of I. Ballenger and G.K. Parker, John David and JoAnn Hopper and Kent Blevins and Deborah Crone-Blevins resigned as FMB missionaries.

[147] From this moment in 1990 until 2008 CBF representative in Europe, J.A. Smith, based in Berlin, has been the CBF Board member on the IBTS Board of Trustees.

[148] Clarissa Strickland speaking at the 'A Decade of Promise' Banquet, Omni Centre, Atlanta, 27 June 2001. Personal recollection of the author. See also *Fellowship*, Vol 11, No 6 (August 2001).

[149] Minutes of the Baptist Theological Seminary, Rüschlikon Association (Verein), forming part of the EBF Council Minutes, High Leigh, Hertfordshire, 1 October 1992, p. 9, Box 810, EBF Archive.

1. Good access (here Berlin is better than Prague).
2. It must be a place where BTS would be financially viable.
3. It must be politically stable, and allow visas for students.
4. It should be near an established university and good library system.
5. The location must also appeal to various donors being asked to contribute.[150]

An extended discussion on the report then took place, which included what sort of teaching programme would be followed.[151] The Council agreed to give the EBF Executive Committee power to proceed to purchase a property if one became available before the next Council meeting, provided that 'all unions of the Federation are kept informed and consulted with before any decision is taken (consultation does not imply a called meeting, and does allow for telephone and/or fax consultation)'.[152]

The November 1993 meeting of the Seminary Board of Trustees proved crucial in the decision-making process.[153] Here options for Prague and Berlin were discussed.[154] Sites were commented on and it was finally agreed that Prague represented the future option: cooperation could be assured with the historic Charles University; it was a cultural meeting point between the Slavic and Latin worlds; it would show commitment to the totality of Europe;[155] costs would be lower than Berlin; and opportunity to purchase a good site was at hand, whereas the planned Berlin complex was not at a similar stage. A six-month process of consultation began, with the Unions being asked for their

---

[150] Minutes of the EBF Council, Kishinev, Moldova, 23 September 1993, p. 9, Box 811, EBF Archive.

[151] *Ibid.,* pp. 9-12. The EBF Council Minutes contain details of most of the significant contributions.

[152] *Ibid.*

[153] Task forces had visited Berlin, Budapest and Prague. Locations in Italy, Switzerland and Belgium had been ruled out at an earlier stage on cost-of-living and other grounds. Letter from John Biggs to J.D. Hopper, 14 October 1991, IBTS Relocation Archive, IBTS.

[154] CBF Missionary, Paul Thibadeaux, prepared a comprehensive and confidential report at the request of Karl Heinz Walter on the options of Berlin and Prague. This report appears not to have been archived by the EBF, but I am in possession of a copy left at Baptist House, Didcot, by a member of the EBF Executive Committee at a special meeting held on 30 November 1993.

[155] Defining Europe is notably difficult. Generally accepted both culturally and geographically, it is from the Atlantic to the Urals, from the North Cape to the Mediterranean and Bosphorus. A central point is some way north of Vilnius, Lithuania, but Prague sits geographically firmly half way between West and East and, in 1994, 50% of Baptists lived to the West of the city and 50% to the East. On this see P. Rietbergen, *Europe: A Cultural History* (London: Routledge, Second Edition, 2006), pp. xvii-xxxv.

views on the venue and the package. Partners in the USA were also consulted, but generally they felt, in line with the ecclesial outlook that had developed over a long period of time, that the Europeans must decide. Karl Heinz Walter wrote to all forty-six member Unions and twenty-five replied.[156] Not all were in favour of Prague, but the consensus pointed that way, resulting in the EBF Executive Committee resolving, in May 1994, that property should be purchased in Prague, the Jenerálka site having already been identified as suitable by a joint Board of Trustees and EBF Executive Committee search group.[157] The process of reconstruction of the Prague site, with an authorisation committee of EBF Officers chaired by Birgit Karlsson, as President, and a Relocation Committee, chaired by Board of Trustees member John Biggs from England, proved a monumental task.[158] The involvement of the EBF officers, though leading sometimes to delay in decision-making, nevertheless ensured the EBF was fully involved in the actual development of the facilities. The first students moved onto the site in September 1994. The first meetings of the Board of Trustees to be held in Prague took place on 2-4 November 1995. The Seminary was officially opened as complete in April 1997.[159]

J.D. Hopper retired as President at the opening ceremonies. The whole experience from the handover in 1988, through the defunding and then the relocation, had been a heavy burden to bear and it was mutually agreed he should retire as a missionary. The academic model and academic programmes for the Seminary had proved difficult to agree. With the change in climate in Europe, and national Unions in the East now able to have their own seminaries, the role of IBTS had to change. A statement on the role of IBTS had been worked out by the Theological and Education Division of the EBF, chaired by Paul Fiddes of Oxford, in a process lasting from a meeting in February 1993 in Hamburg through to the IBTS Board of Trustees meeting of September 1994.[160] The search now commenced to find a European to serve as President. The Search Committee was led by Brian Haymes, a Board member and Principal of Bristol Baptist College. The Search Committee invited Stefan Stiegler, Old Testament lecturer at Elstal, to succeed J.D. Hopper and, by postal ballot of the Board of Trustees and then the member Unions of the EBF, he was appointed.[161] However, a disagreement between Stiegler and the existing Faculty, about the nomination for a New Testament lecturer, meant Stiegler

[156] IBTS BOT Minutes, April 1994, p. 3, Minute 7, IBTS Archive.

[157] IBTS BOT Minutes, November 1993, pp. 9-11, and April 1994, pp. 11-13, IBTS Archive. EBF Executive Committee Minutes, May 1994, Box 812, EBF Archive.

[158] Minutes of EBF Authorisation and Relocation Committees, IBTS Archive, Bs016.

[159] IBTS Opening Celebrations Programme, 19 April 1997, IBTS Archive.

[160] The Hamburg-Lillehammer text is presented as Appendix 3.3 to the EBF Executive Committee, Sofia, March 1996, Box 813, EBF Archive.

[161] S. Stiegler, later to be Rector of the Elstal Seminary, Berlin. IBTS BOT Minutes, Hotel Fushbau, 12-14 September 1997. Box E11, IBTS Archive.

withdrew from office before he was installed and this threw the Seminary into crisis, with several Unions in Eastern Europe and the German Union demanding the Seminary be closed and the assets divided amongst emerging new seminaries, with Faculty members involved in the incident being dismissed.[162]

The IBTS Board of Trustees met in emergency session in Hamburg before the EBF Council in September 1994. Keith Jones, incoming chair of the Board of Trustees, presented a position paper to the meeting outlining the current crisis and offering six options for the future.[163] The Board considered all the options and worked hard over their weekend together to prepare a paper to present to the Council entitled 'The Prague Vision'.[164] This dramatically different way forward, in which the concentration would be on post-graduate study, was ultimately accepted by the EBF Council at Novi Vinodolski, Croatia, in 1997: sixty-six votes in favour, none against and six abstentions.[165] This restructuring caused consternation among the existing student body and academic staff.[166] The Seminary was further Europeanised, with a Rector and small Academic Team concentrating on specialist areas at post-graduate level. Many students doing undergraduate studies had to relocate. Most of the existing academic staff did not wish to work with the new model or did not fit into the lecturing needs of the Seminary.[167] The only missionary staff retained were ABC missionaries, David and Ellen Brown, who fully supported the actions of the EBF Council and committed themselves to work with the new Rector and Pro-Rector.[168]

In this period there was also uncertainty over the role of the International Baptist Lay Academy (IBLA) near Budapest, a development established by the Board of Trustees of IBTS. Initially, Errol Simmons, an SBC missionary who directed IBLA, was allowed by the FMB to attend IBTS Board meetings to present his reports.[169] Then his FMB superiors approached the EBF General

---

[162] Letters and telephone conversations with K.H. Walter and IBTS BOT Minutes, Hotel Fushbau, 12-14 September 1997. Box E11, IBTS Archive.

[163] K.G. Jones, 'Situation Report and Options Document for the Board of Trustees, August 1997'. Copy in my personal archive.

[164] 'Forward from Tallinn' and then 'The Prague Vision', IBTS Archive. The Prague Vision, IBTS BOT Archive, September 1994.

[165] Minutes of the EBF Council, Croatia, 1997, pp. 9-11, Box 817, EBF Archive.

[166] See EBF Minutes, Box 817, EBF Archive.

[167] IBTS BOT Minutes, 12-14 September 1997, 25 September 1997 and 6-8 November 1997, Box E11, IBTS Archive.

[168] D.M. Brown served as a Director until 2001. He then served as an ABC staff person in Valley Forge and continues as an Adjunct Lecturer at IBTS.

[169] Indeed, IBLA Executive Committees were held during IBTS BOT meetings at Rüschlikon, as in April 1993. See IBTS BOT Minutes, Meeting No. 8, 29 April-1 May 1993, IBTS Archive.

Secretary, Karl Heinz Walter, requesting that the structural arrangements for IBLA be changed so that IBTS, as founder, was removed out of the arrangement and the EBF Executive Committee be the body to whom Simmons reported. Walter presented these concerns to an IBTS Board meeting in April 1997 and, after considerable discussion, it was agreed that 'IBLA will in future report directly to the EBF and the IBTS BOT [Board of Trustees] will receive the IBLA report through the General Secretary of the EBF, Karl Heinz Walter.'[170] For his own part, Errol Simmons was reluctant to leave the meetings of the Board of Trustees,[171] but this represented direct contact between the FMB and IBTS and the leaders of the FMB in Richmond, Virginia, were anxious it should not continue. The FMB ceased supporting and funding IBLA with the retirement of Simmons in 2000 and the EBF Executive agreed that IBLA should be re-incorporated into IBTS. Thus, an initiative of the Europe-based FMB missionaries and Rüschlikon faculty became a growing-point in the development of the ministries of the EBF. Based in Prague, the IBLA courses, suitably revised to deal with changing needs in Europe, continued as the 'Certificate in Applied Theology'.[172] This lay certificate programme, aimed at university level one standards, continues as a highly successful part of the portfolio of activities offered by IBTS. It received no FMB funding, but two Southern Baptist State Conventions, Texas and Virginia, have regularly supported the programme.

The new 'Prague Vision' model envisaged ministerial formation taking place in national seminaries, with IBTS serving as a Europe-wide postgraduate institution acting as a resource for all the Unions and Seminaries. In fact this model was not 'new' in terms of concept. It had first been articulated by C.E. Benander in the early years of the twentieth century, and had been re-emphasised in 1948. It can be argued that in the 1990s European Baptists finally made theological education at IBTS their own. From this point onwards there began a ten-year development of IBTS.[173] Master in Theology degrees awarded by the University of Wales were validated for IBTS in Baptist and Anabaptist Studies, Biblical Studies, Applied Theology and Contextual Missiology. IBTS was also given rights to supervise Master of Philosophy and Doctor of Philosophy degrees and this was renewed with strong affirmation by

[170] IBTS BOT Minutes, 17-19 April 1997, Item 13.2.1, p. 7, IBTS Archive.

[171] Personal conversation with me, April 1997.

[172] D.M. Brown handled the transfer of assets to Prague and as a member of the then IBTS Directorate did the initial design of the revised Certificate in Applied Theology programme, which continues very successfully as a full part of the work of IBTS.

[173] The early years from 1997 are set out in K.G. Jones, 'The International Baptist Theological Seminary of the European Baptist Federation', *American Baptist Quarterly*, Vol. XVIII, No. 2, June 1999, pp. 191-200.

the University of Wales Validation Board in 2004.[174] The Czech Ministry of Education also granted IBTS higher education institution status in 2002, based on the fact that IBTS had validation by the University of Wales, with the right to teach and award a European Union Bologna-standard Magister in Theology. The Czech Government Accreditation Commission renewed this right in 2006 until 2014.[175]

Publication of a theological journal, *The Journal of European Baptist Studies,* also began in 2000. Two Research Institutes founded in Rüschlikon, in Baptist and Anabaptist Studies (1982) and Mission and Evangelism (1988), have been joined by a further three institutes – Biblical Studies (2004), Contextual Studies in Systematic Theology (2004) and the Thomas Helwys Research Centre for Religious Freedom and Human Rights (2006). From this research work IBTS is now publishing between three and five books a year.[176] What Rüschlikon could never quite obtain from the Swiss Government and Universities (formal recognition of the BD and ThM degrees), has now been obtained in two ways by the EBF-owned institution in Prague with degrees validated by the University of Wales and with IBTS being an accredited degree-awarding institution in the Czech Republic. With over 140 students, IBTS refocusing has proved to be right for the circumstances of Baptists in the new Europe.[177]

This Europeanised IBTS still has partnerships with North American agencies. The ABC representative in Europe was always closely associated with the work of IBTS. Personnel for the SITE (Summer Institute of Theological Education) programme came from ABC-IM: the first full-time appointment was of a young missionary, Denton Lotz.[178] From his appointment in 1971 until 2000, the post has been held by an ABC-IM missionary, and the agency continued to have serving mission staff in the full-time academic team of IBTS from that date until 2004.[179] There have been similarly constructive

---

[174] IBTS Submission and Quinquennial Review Report, University of Wales, 2004, IBTS Archive.

[175] IBTS Magister Degree Submission, Czech Ministry of Education Accreditation Commission 2001 and 2006, IBTS Archive.

[176] The full publications list can be accessed at www.ibts.eu.

[177] The story of the building work at Prague and the development of the educational programmes is set out in Petra Veselá, *Fit for a King* (Prague: IBTS, 2004).

[178] Denton Lotz went on to service as Director of Youth with the Baptist World Alliance under General Secretary Gerhard Claas and, following the untimely death of Gerhard Claas in a road accident, he became interim General Secretary, then was appointed General Secretary in 1988 and continued to serve in this role until December 2007.

[179] The last person to serve was Cheryl A. Brown, ABC-IM missionary, who had to retire as Director of Biblical Studies at IBTS because of ill health from 31 August 2004, thus bringing to an end a 33-year period of ABC-IM career missionary involvement on the campus.

relationships in recent years with the CBF. There were, however, tensions over the move to Prague and the restructuring. It was suggested, for example, that the Blevins, a CBF missionary couple,[180] were not acting properly in the work of IBTS.[181] They had reacted against the proposals regarding restructuring. However, the IBTS Board itself asked Kent Blevins to serve as Seminary Co-President for the 1997-1998 academic year and he affirmed his willingness to do so.[182] Painful differences of opinion over policy continued, but it became clear in this period that European leadership was setting the direction for the Seminary, and both ABC-IM and CBF affirmed this policy. The work of IBTS, by contrast, found no affirmation within the ranks of the FMB-IMB leadership. In 2000 the FMB established its Central and East Europe office in Prague, but personnel based there seemed to be advised not to have contact with IBTS. Apologies were made to European Baptists by various FMB emissaries to Europe,[183] but the fracture between the FMB and IBTS was complete.[184] Ron Wilson suggested that the appointed leaders of the Baptist Unions were not the 'real leaders' and that the FMB should only work with the 'non compromised leadership of Eastern Europe'.[185] Wilson chose Emanuel Bible College (later University), Oradea, Romania, as an alternative place to fund.[186] The issue of who are the 'real leaders' is an ecclesiological one: can local Baptist communities – including continent-wide bodies – elect their own leaders and direct their own seminaries, or do they have to bow to the pressure of powerful forces from outside their context?

Conclusion

In this study of IBTS, a model of ecclesial/missional cooperation has been analysed. The initial commitment of SBC to theological education within the

---

[180] Some Europeans objected to Kent Blevins and Deborah Crone-Blevins for their role in criticising Stefan Stiegler and undermining the attitude of students to the refocusing of IBTS by the EBF Council.

[181] Concerns expressed by K.H. Walter at a special meeting of the BOT in Hamburg, September 1997, and explored in a disciplinary meeting with Kent Blevins later that month, BOT Minutes, IBTS Archive.

[182] IBTS BOT Minutes, November 1997, p. 3. Kent Blevins obtained an appointment at Gardner-Webb University in the USA and returned to work there in July 1998.

[183] See Chapter 6 and the general account of relationships between Europeans and North Americans.

[184] In the mid 1990s the FMB defunded the Arab Baptist Theological Seminary in Beirut.

[185] Merritt, *The Betrayal of Southern Baptist Missionaries by Southern Baptist Leaders 1979–2004*, p. 69.

[186] See Chapter 6.

EBF area was substantial, from the point of view of resources and personnel[187] but, as has been observed, from the beginning a somewhat intrusive pattern was used, both in terms of the control of the work of the missionaries and in the design of the theological programmes. Fortunately for European Baptists, in the 1980s the key regional personnel of SBC-FMB were former faculty members of IBTS and, during the time of R. Keith Parks as FMB Chief Executive Officer, a progressive attitude to partnership between SBC-FMB and Baptist regional and national bodies was pursued. With the emergence of a more conservative leadership of the SBC, a directive pattern of mission leadership was re-imposed, leading to the defunding of IBTS and the withdrawal of SBC-FMB from involvement in theological education.[188] The refusal of the FMB Trustees to meet the EBF delegation to discuss this issue, and the decision of the FMB Trustees to reconfirm their decision to completely defund IBTS, almost immediately sparked off a chain of reactions which reverberated around the world and might be considered to have reached a terminal point some years later, on 1 October 2004, when the SBC completed the procedure to withdraw fully from the BWA, which it had been instrumental in founding in 1905.[189] In contrast to the ideological isolationism of SBC, the path mapped out by European Baptists, in which there is an acknowledgement of the need to find unity within diversity, is illustrated in the way in which IBTS began to function from the 1990s onwards under the direction of the diverse Unions that make up the EBF.

---

[187] In addition to IBTS, both mission boards were involved in support of national seminaries, in funding and personnel, but reflecting on such national involvement falls outside of the scope of this present work.

[188] It is to be noted that following the 1989 defunding of IBTS, SBC-FMB pulled back from similar arrangements elsewhere in the world, including the Arab Baptist Theological Seminary in Beirut, and since the resignation of R. Keith Parks, the SBC-IMB President, Jerry Rankin, has indicated the SBC-IMB will have no further involvement in theological education.

[189] The wider chapter on the SBC indicates the route by which, in reaction to the Cooperative Baptist Fellowship being formed and joining the BWA in 2003, the SBC accused the BWA of liberalism and funding what they regarded as doubtful projects through Baptist World Aid.

CHAPTER 5

A Focus of Unity – General Secretaries

From the moment of the inception of the European Baptist Federation (EBF) the role of its officers has been crucial. The Baptist World Alliance (BWA), from its formation in 1905, had a senior staff figure responsible for Europe. In the immediate years after the Second World War, this was Walter O. Lewis. When the first formation meeting of the EBF was held in Paris in 1950 Lewis was asked to serve as temporary chairman and it was he who welcomed everyone to the meeting and briefed them:

> At a Conference called by the Alliance in London in 1948, a Committee of Seven was appointed to launch a scheme for the closer integration of European Baptists. This Committee met in Rüschlikon-Zürich on 8 October 1949 and drew up a Constitution and plan for a European Baptist Federation. This plan had been submitted to as many of the Baptist unions of Europe as could be reached. General approval of the plan had been expressed by Great Britain, Denmark, Norway, Sweden, Germany, Holland, France, Switzerland and Italy.[1]

It was Lewis who, having made the introductory speech and obtained agreement of the delegates from the Unions for the constitution, declared that the EBF was now formed, and called for the election of officers. The principal officers of the Federation, in keeping with much Baptist polity, were to be a President, Vice-President and Secretary. Lewis was elected, pro-tem, to the office of Secretary.[2]

Thus began the development of the office of the General Secretary of the EBF, which has successively been filled as follows:

Walter O. Lewis	American	1950 – 1955
Henry Cook	English	1955 – 1959
Erik Rudén	Swedish	1959 – 1965
Ronald Goulding	English	1965 – 1976
Gerhard Claas	German	1976 – 1980
Knud Wümplemann	Danish	1980 – 1989

---

[1] Minutes of the inaugural meeting of the Council of the EBF, Rue de Ville, Paris 7, Friday, 20 October 1950, pp. 1-2, Box 801, EBF Archive, IBTS, Prague.

[2] Minutes of the EBF Council, Paris, October 1950, p. 3, Box 801, EBF Archive.

Karl Heinz Walter	German	1989 – 1999
Theodor Angelov	Bulgarian	1999 – 2004[3]
Anthony A. Peck	English	2004 –

Lewis was already an Associate General Secretary of the BWA. The others were to become Regional Secretaries for Europe of the BWA, in each case following the decision of the EBF to appoint them its General Secretary.[4] Gerhaard Claas went on from the EBF to become General Secretary of the BWA, though his tenure of office at the BWA was cut short by a fatal car accident. Knud Wümplemann served a term as President of the BWA, 1990-1995.

Whilst the office of President of the EBF carries with it the clear general leadership of the EBF, and the President chairs meetings of the Council and oversees Congresses, it is an honorary and essentially part-time post held for a maximum of two years. Most of the Presidents in the history of the EBF have been senior officers within their own Unions or seminary rectors and unable to devote much time between meetings to the affairs of the EBF.[5] Therefore, the office of General Secretary has had a major role within the work of the EBF, because the holders of this office have been much more than administrators and letter writers, but 'living letters'[6] developing the policies of the EBF and moving between the Unions strengthening the ties that bind together European Baptists. Indeed, this is consistent with how General Secretaries[7] in the member bodies, especially in the West, have been viewed as, for instance, 'being a focus of unity for the Union in so far as they are transmitters and interpreters of the word of God in scripture... [having a] personal episcope... offered in the

---

[3] This list is contained in the Editorial, K.G. Jones, *The Journal of European Baptist Studies*, Vol. 2, No. 3, 2002, pp. 3-4.

[4] From Eric Rudén onwards it has been customary for the General Secretary of the BWA to serve as part of the EBF Search Committee so that the appointment can proceed in parallel.

[5] A list and pictures of EBF Presidents can be found in B. Green, *Crossing the Boundaries: A History of the European Baptist Federation* (Didcot: The Baptist Historical Society, 1999), pp. 214-218.

[6] This phrase is used by Bent Hylleberg in his portrayal of Knud Wümplemann in 'Knud Wümplemann: General Secretary of the European Baptist Federation and President of the Baptist World Alliance' in *Journal of European Baptist Studies*, Vol. 2, No. 3, 2002, pp. 5-20. It is an apt way of describing these eight men who, over fifty-three years, have played a pivotal role in the shaping of European Baptist life.

[7] See, for instance, S. Murray (ed.), *Translocal Ministry: Equipping the Churches for Mission* (Didcot: Baptist Union of Great Britain, 2004) and I.M. Randall, *The English Baptists of the 20th Century* (Didcot: Baptist Historical Society, 2005) especially chap. 11, pp. 471-90.

context of Assembly and Council.'[8] Some Presidents have initiated new policies or had a crucial role at the time of major change in the European Baptist community, but an analysis of the life and work of the EBF demonstrates that the General Secretaries have been the key people in the work of the EBF.

EBF General Secretaries, as ordained pastors, have exercised real personal episkope[9] and been a focus of unity for the EBF.[10] Given that the General Secretaries have served, on average, 6.75 years (three times as long as the presidency), the opportunity for greater impact on the Baptist family in Europe is obvious. This chapter seeks to place two key General Secretaries in the context of the development of the EBF, to examine the main foci of their periods of service and to reflect on the appropriateness of differing styles of leadership within a loose ecclesial organisation such as the EBF. The two chosen, Knud Wümplemann and Karl Heinz Walter, were among the longest-serving General Secretaries. They have been chosen because of the formative periods in which they served. Ronald Goulding also served a considerable period of time, but the particular era during which he served, constrained by the divide of the 'iron curtain', means that this was a period of only modest development within the ecclesial life of the EBF.[11] It is because of the significant impact in different ways of Wümplemann and Walter that they provide illuminating case studies.

The EBF General Secretaryship and the BWA

When W.O. Lewis retired in 1955, an opportunity was afforded to establish the relationship between the EBF General Secretary and the BWA Associate Secretary for Europe. Lewis had come to Europe as an American Baptist Churches (ABC) missionary, serving as ABC representative for Europe and then as Associate Secretary of the BWA and as Director of BWA Relief work in Europe. He had been present at the 1948 and 1949 meetings which had planned the EBF, served as Chairman at the 1949 foundation meeting in Paris and thence as Secretary. He had been one of the initiators of the European Baptist Mission and was at the heart of most of the post-war Baptist

---

[8] The Faith and Unity Executive Committee, the Baptist Union of Great Britain, 'Spiritual Leadership in the Baptist Union', *The Nature of the Assembly and the Council of the Baptist Union of Great Britain* (Didcot: Baptist Union Publications, 1994), pp. 30-4.

[9] For a recent collection of essays on episkope, or trans-local ministry see Murray, *Translocal Ministry*.

[10] The personal dimension of oversight is reflected on in N.G. Wright, 'The Petrine Ministry: Baptist Reflections, *Pro Ecclesia*, Vol. XIII, No. 4 (Fall 2004), pp. 451-65.

[11] On C.R. Goulding see Green, *Crossing the Boundaries*, pp. 58-110.

developments in Europe.[12] At the 1954 EBF Council meeting, held in Munich, it was agreed that Ruben Swedberg (Sweden), Josef Nordenhaug (Baptist Theological Seminary) and Joel Sorenson (EBF Youth Committee)[13] should write to the BWA General Secretary, Arnold Ohrn, with a view to consultation on the successor to W.O. Lewis. In Langesund, in September 1956, Ohrn was present and gave assurance to the EBF that whilst any BWA Associate Secretary must be appointed by the Alliance, it was the intention of the BWA to appoint someone who would be acceptable to Europe, and discussions were taking place on this matter with representative people in Europe.[14] At this stage an initiative by the EBF, as an ecclesial body wishing to choose its own leadership, was not in the minds of the officers of the BWA.

Edwin Bell, the European representative of ABC, reported on the exchanges in Norway and was somewhat critical of the attitude of the BWA officers. Writing to his colleagues in New York, especially Dana Albaugh, the ABC-IMB Chief Executive, he said:

> No action was taken concerning a Secretary for the Federation at the meeting in Norway. There was a proposal submitted by the Council of the EBF to combine the office of Associate Secretary of the BWA and the Secretaryship of the Federation. The reply of the BWA this year was that it was not considered feasible to divide responsibility for one man between the two organizations. The Secretary would, therefore, have to be appointed, paid and be responsible to the Administrative Committee of the BWA, though he could function as the Secretary of the EBF.[15]

He noted that the BWA Executive Committee had not been able to make a choice and Edwin Bell himself thought that J.D. Hughey, then an SBC missionary on the staff at Rüschlikon, should be appointed, since he knew Europe well and had a facility with languages. But Bell went on to say that 'Dr Hughey will probably not get serious consideration because of his denominational affiliation'.[16] More tellingly, Bell added that he had talked the matter over with Arnold T. Ohrn, BWA General Secretary, who had, so Bell commented:

---

[12] This was summarised by Henry Cook in paying tribute to W.O. Lewis at the EBF Council in Langesund, Norway, 1956. EBF Minutes, p. 30, Box 801, EBF Archive.

[13] Minutes of the EBF Council, Munich, September 1954, p. 27, Box 801, EBF Archive.

[14] Minutes of the EBF Council Langesund, Norway, 1956, p. 31, Box 801, EBF Archive.

[15] Letter from E.A. Bell to J.L. Spriggs, 13 October 1956, ABFMS Archives, Box 476, American Baptist Historical Society, Valley Forge, Pa.

[16] In 1969 E.A. Payne wrote to Theodore Adams, BWA President, asking if Hughey should not be considered to succeed Nordenhaug. Letter of E.A. Payne, 16 February 1969, BWA Europe Box 2, Angus Library, Regent's Park College, Oxford.

> rather naively disclosed his plan – or at least his hope – to have Dr Nordenhaug succeed him as General Secretary of the BWA in 1960 and of course the whole staff of the BWA could not be from one denomination.[17]

Edwin Bell reported to his colleagues that he was not fully able to understand the insistence of some in the BWA that the EBF should remain so completely an auxiliary of the BWA itself. This matter had been contested by the Dutch. E.A. Payne and the EBF Constitution Committee had also been careful to keep the distinction, in line with Baptist polity. In fact, Bell indicated he had a mind to encourage the EBF to name their own Secretary, but he realised that would raise issues of funding.[18] Bell was premature, but prophetic, in his thinking.

Arnold T. Ohrn and his colleagues in the BWA had wanted to approach George Beasley-Murray, then a tutor at Spurgeon's College in London, to take the post of BWA Associate Secretary for Europe, but as they were considering Beasley-Murray, Joseph Nordenhaug offered him a position at Rüschlikon, which he accepted.[19] Accordingly, the BWA Executive Committee decided to postpone the search for a permanent Associate Secretary until 1957 and invited Henry Cook to continue as Acting Associate Secretary. The EBF Executive meeting in Hamburg in January 1957 noted this sequence of events and the discussions that had taken place in Washington D.C. regarding the search for a replacement to Lewis. Hans Luckey, EBF President, suggested that a further letter be sent to the President and General Secretary of the BWA about the nominating process in which they:

> would welcome consultation, particularly with regard to the kind of work the new secretary will be called upon to do. There are many problems peculiar to Europe that must be considered in making an appointment.... The Executive Committee has been discussing among other things the question of the evangelisation of Europe, and this, we feel, is an area of service that must not be forgotten.[20]

Given the overall remit of the BWA, it is highly unlikely that the issue of the evangelisation of Europe would be forgotten, especially by Ohrn, himself a European, but what the letter betrays is a certain anxiety that, though prominent Europeans served on the BWA Council, Executive and Committees, there was not yet any clear linkage between the BWA and EBF officers. There was also a concern that the Administrative Committee of the BWA, which was composed

---

[17] Letter from E.A. Bell to J.L. Sprigg, 13 October 1956, ABFMS Archives Box 476.
[18] *Ibid.*
[19] Report from A.T. Ohrn to the BWA Executive Committee, Washington DC, 22-23 May 1956, Minutes p. 7, item 25, BWA Archives, American Baptist Historical Society, Valley Forge, Pa.
[20] Letter from the President and Secretary of the EBF to the President and General Secretary of the BWA, Hamburg, January 1957, Box 22, EBF Archive.

entirely of people from the USA, had too much influence. This concern lasted for quite a period of time as evidenced in a letter in 1965 from Josef Nordenhaug to Ronald Goulding, replying to a letter[21] requesting that the EBF General Secretary should serve on the BWA Administrative Committee. Nordenhaug said this was not possible and that only North Americans able to pay their own travel served:

> I am very sorry that there is a misunderstanding abroad concerning the work of this Committee [the Administrative Committee]. I can testify that these men are in no wise given to promote the influence of their own conventions... It is, of course, quite fashionable around the world to be anti-American and to say that everything is controlled from America. Some of this may slip over in the area of the Alliance as well.... No action of the Administrative Committee is valid until the Executive Committee passes on it. If it is the will of the Executive Committee members in certain European countries to change the procedure.... they can of course do so.[22]

At this point, in the search for an EBF Secretary, there was no easy assumption, as would later be the case, that the Associate Secretary for Europe of the BWA and the EBF General Secretary should be the same person. It might, in hindsight, be thought extremely inadvisable to have had this dual functioning within the one person, but the BWA, with a history of fifty-years of work in Europe without a formal European structure, was not fully cognisant of the attitudes and desires of the EBF. Nevertheless, the letter concluded that 'the Committee shares with you a concern that this appointment may be a source of blessing to Europe, and will be glad to cooperate with the Nominating Committee in any way that is desired.'[23] Against this background, Ohrn had the difficult task of bringing the BWA Executive into the discussions when he reported to them in Hamilton, Ontario, in August. Firstly, he reported the great debt everyone owed Henry Cook for his work as EBF General Secretary and BWA Acting Associate Secretary in Europe.[24] There had been delay in getting the key players on the Search Committee together, but Ohrn reported he had been in correspondence with them all. He went on to say, recognising the delicacy of the situation: 'As a result of such consultations and correspondence as had hitherto taken place, it was deemed advisable to postpone the matter for

[21] Letter from C.R. Goulding to J. Nordenhaug, 12 February 1965, BWA Europe, Box 3, Angus Library.

[22] Letter from BWA General Secretary J. Nordenhaug to C.R. Goulding, 17 February 1965, BWA Europe Box 3, Angus Library.

[23] Letter from the President and General Secretary of the EBF to the President and General Secretary of the BWA, January 1957, Box 22, EBF Archive.

[24] Minutes of the BWA Executive Committee, 29-30 August 1957, Hamilton, Ontario, p. 14, item 44, BWA Library, Falls Church, Virginia.

another year, so that the decision could be made in Europe in 1958.'[25] In the discussion which followed the report from Arnold Ohrn, others also spoke, including E.A. Payne, a member of the BWA Executive. Increased support for the London office was thought desirable and these concerns led to a motion being adopted:

> The matter of an Associate Secretary in Europe be referred to the Administrative Committee; that the Administrative Committee report to the Executive Committee at Rüschlikon next year; that Dr Henry Cook be asked to continue to serve as Associate Secretary in Europe until the Executive Committee meets next year.[26]

The whole situation was to have a certain tension within it as the BWA Search Committee struggled to identify a candidate. The EBF continued to press its point, as did constituent Unions. The Dutch Baptist Union sent the EBF a letter about the appointment of EBF officers stating:

> that the election of the Secretary or Secretary-Treasurer is the prerogative of the General Council of the Federation, and that, in case the Baptist World Alliance wants to combine with that position the Associate Secretaryship of the BWA in Europe, the BWA should consult the Federation.[27]

Ernest Payne, General Secretary of the British Baptists, Chairman of the EBF Constitution Committee, and a noted constitutionalist, remarked:

> The question does not arise in the Constitution [of the EBF] itself, which makes it plain that the Secretary of the Federation must be appointed by the General Council. In practice he may also be a secretary of the Baptist World Alliance, but again he may not, and that is a matter for consultation.[28]

Prior to the EBF meetings in Berlin in September 1958, Arnold Ohrn made a full statement on the appointment, explaining the problems encountered along the way and the efforts made to consult with the EBF and representatives from Europe.[29] A new ecclesial outlook was emerging amongst European Baptists.

On 26 November 1957, at the BWA Administrative Committee, it was reported that preparations were being made to nominate Erik Rudén, General Secretary of the Swedish Baptist Union and Vice-President of the EBF, to the

---

[25] *Ibid.*

[26] *Ibid.*

[27] Letter from the Baptist Union of the Netherlands to the EBF Executive Committee. Discussed by the EBF Executive Committee in Berlin, September 1957, EBF Minute Book, p. 48, Box 801, EBF Archive.

[28] Minutes of the EBF Executive Committee in Berlin, 24-26 September 1957, p. 48, Box 801, EBF Archive.

[29] Minutes of the EBF Council, Berlin, September 1957, p. 47, Box 801, EBF Archive.

post, but that this matter could only be advanced when the BWA Executive Committee met in Europe the following August.[30] Ohrn reported this to the EBF Executive.[31] Swedish Baptist leaders were unhappy at the thought of losing their General Secretary and wrote to the President and General Secretary of the BWA to voice their objections to the move, but the BWA Administrative Committee had remained firm, confirming their desire to nominate Rudén at their May 1958 meeting. However, they did write to the Swedish Baptists expressing:

> the concern of the Administration Committee for the problems faced by the Swedish Baptists in the light of this decision, agreeing to talk over the matter with Swedish leaders as to the time when Dr Rudén, in case he accepted the call, should assume the new position, attempting to find a satisfactory solution for both parties.[32]

This did not satisfy the Swedish Baptists, and two of their leaders, Gunnar Westin and Joel Sorenson, both present at the BWA Executive, abstained in the vote that: 'Dr Erik Rudén be elected the BWA Associate Secretary in Europe and that the Administrative Committee be authorized to settle the necessary details if Dr Rudén felt led to accept.'[33] Erik Rudén responded by thanking the Executive Committee for the confidence expressed in this call and stating he hoped to be able to give his answer within a few weeks.[34]

The EBF's 'right to choose its own Secretary'

At the time, several people took the view that the approach of the BWA in this matter did not augur well for relationships between the BWA and the EBF. However, a way forward was found. When the EBF Council met on 25 July 1958, a Nominating Committee was appointed with Ernest Payne in the chair and with Arnold Ohrn as a member. Here a complicated resolution was devised to assure Eric Rudén that the EBF Council and Executive had every confidence in him, but also to assert the rights of the EBF in appointing their Secretary. Eventually, the Nominating Committee was able to recommend unanimously and the EBF Council to accept without dissent that:

---

[30] BWA Executive Committee Minutes, Rüschlikon, 6-8 August 1958, p. 6, item 26, BWA Library.

[31] Minutes of the EBF Executive Committee, Berlin, 24 July 1958, p. 52, Box 801, EBF Archive.

[32] BWA Executive Committee Minutes, Rüschlikon, 6-8 August 1958, p. 7, item 26, BWA Library.

[33] *Ibid.*

[34] Eric Rudén did respond positively by telegram on 1 October 1958.

1. The Council of the EBF express to the Executive of the BWA the satisfaction with which it has heard of the proposal that Dr Erik Rudén be appointed Associate Secretary of the BWA.
2. The Council express the hope that Dr Rudén will accept the invitation, if it is extended to him, and invites him from the time he takes up his appointment to be Secretary of the EBF until the next meeting of the Council.
3. On the assumption that Dr Rudén will accept and until he can take up his work or alternative arrangements be made the Council expresses the hope that it will prove possible for Dr Cook to continue as the Secretary of the EBF, with thanks for his services.
4. Dr Rudén be elected President of the EBF until such time as he becomes Secretary.
5. Brother Huizinga be elected Vice-President, and if and when Dr Rudén becomes Secretary, Acting-President of the EBF.[35]

This complicated formula preserved the rights of the EBF. As Bernard Green comments, the Nominations Committee 'intended to make it crystal clear that the EBF claimed the right to choose its own Secretary'.[36]

Eric Rudén accepted the will of the BWA and the EBF and was appointed BWA Associate Secretary for Europe at a BWA Executive Committee held in Rochester, New York State, in the summer of 1959 and assumed his duties as Secretary of the EBF at the close of the EBF Executive Committee in De Vinkenhof, Holland, on 8 September 1959.[37] On 1 May 1959, at a meeting between BWA President, Theodore Adams, and British Baptists involved with the Alliance, the question was raised as to whether other areas of the world should now have their own agent or honorary Associate Secretary, 'e.g. the Far East, Australia etc' as 'clearly the post-1960 period would offer great opportunities for expansion'.[38]

A special EBF meeting was held in Baptist Church House, London, for the installation of Erik Rudén. It is interesting to note who was involved in the service as this indicates the importance of various institutions in the life of EBF. Arnold Ohrn spoke on behalf of the BWA and Ernest Payne, as Chairman of the Nomination Committee of the EBF, also spoke. Greetings were brought by Joseph Nordenhaug (President of the Rüschlikon Seminary), Edwin A. Bell (as ABC representative in Europe) and George W. Sadler (as SBC

[35] Minutes of the EBF Council, Berlin-Charlottenburg, 25 July 1958, p. 54, Box 801, EBF Archive.

[36] Green, *Crossing the Boundaries*, p. 41.

[37] BWA Executive Minutes, BWA Archive, Valley Forge, and EBF Executive Committee Minutes, De Vinkenhof, p. 68, Box 801, EBF Archive.

[38] 'The Future Programme of the Alliance'. Typescript note of a meeting of 1 May 1959 in Baptist Church House presided over by T. Adams, BWA President, Erik Rudén Papers, Box 1, Angus Library.

representative in Europe). Rudén and his wife were expected to relocate from Stockholm to London as the BWA had an office there and the EBF agreed the two offices should be in the same place.[39]

The issue of the site of the office for Rudén had been a matter of discussion during the whole process, with Ohrn being very concerned 'not to antagonize our British brethren',[40] and a meeting was held in London on 1 May 1959 under the title 'The Future Programme of the Alliance' which addressed this issue. The meeting drew together British Baptists involved with the BWA and Theodore Adams, the President.[41] Those present expressed satisfaction at the appointment of Erik Rudén, but several queried if there was need to uproot him from Stockholm, Ohrn informing Erik Rudén that 'Dr Payne, speaking on behalf of British Baptists, said he found no objection to your conducting most of the business of the Alliance from Stockholm, if that would be more convenient to you.'[42] In such an event, Adams and Payne agreed that some of the space occupied by the BWA in Baptist Church House, London, could be returned to the Baptist Union and that further thought should be given to the final location of the European Secretary. Geneva, Zürich, Stockholm and London were mentioned.[43] There was further discussion of the topic during the BWA Congress in Rio de Janeiro in June 1960. The BWA President, Theodor Adams, had asked Joel Sorenson, Ernest Payne, Henri Vincent, Mrs Edgar Bates, J.T. Ayorinde, Josef Nordenhaug, Erik Rudén and Arnold T. Ohrn to discuss the matter. However, it was felt all the European Baptists on the BWA Executive Committee should have opportunity to talk about the issues involved before the BWA itself made a commitment, so a meeting of these people was convened by Joel Sorensen on 25 June.[44] In the event, the decision was to

---

[39] J.H. Clifford established the BWA offices in Baptist Church House, 4 Southampton Row, shortly after the inaugural meeting in 1905. The office was moved to Washington DC at the time of the Second World War, but an Eastern Hemisphere Office was maintained in London until the retirement of C.R. Goulding, when the London base was demoted to simply being a postal address for donations to the BWA with a part-time administrator, Barbara Askew.

[40] Letter from A.T. Ohrn to E. Rudén, 14 April 1959, Erik Rudén Papers, Box 1, Angus Library.

[41] Typescript document 'The Future Programme of the Baptist World Alliance', Erik Rudén Papers, Box 1, Angus Library.

[42] Letter from A.T. Ohrn to E. Rudén, 11 May 1959, Erik Rudén Papers, Box 1, Angus Library.

[43] Notes of the meeting 'The Future Programme of the Alliance', item 2, Erik Rudén Papers, Box 1, Angus Library.

[44] Report to BWA Executive Committee, Rio de Janeiro, 25 June 1960, BWA Executive Committee Minutes, p. 6, item 23, BWA Library.

continue with the office in London.[45] To some extent this reflected the importance of the British Baptist community within Europe.

This geographical arrangement remained in place throughout the General Secretaryship of Rudén (1959–1965) and of Ronald Goulding, who succeeded him, and who served from 1965 to 1976. Goulding was, in any case, a British Baptist and so an office in London suited his needs. Events surrounding the appointment of Gerhard Claas from Germany as General Secretary, in 1976, led to what would prove to be an itinerant pattern developing for the EBF over a 28-year period, with the office moving to the country of origin of the General Secretary (in succession Germany–Denmark–Germany–Bulgaria) over the period 1976 to 2004. This led to a number of problems, such as a failure to build up expertise in support staff, the loss of records and documents in the moves, and confusion amongst the member unions and outside bodies about the location of the office, especially in the years surrounding a change of secretary. After much discussion within EBF circles about this issue, at the EBF Council held in Oslo in September 2002, the decision was taken that the EBF office, like the office of the BWA and the offices of most of the national unions, should be permanently located in one place and any subsequent General Secretary appointed would be expected to relocate to this EBF base.[46] The permanent base chosen was the EBF-owned International Baptist Theological Seminary (IBTS) complex in Prague.

Erik Rudén, following his appointment and inauguration, went on to render sterling service to the EBF, and his General Secretaryship saw many policies and programmes of the EBF developed. These were to prove the mainstay of the life of the Federation through the difficult post-war and cold-war years until the implosion of communism in Eastern Europe in 1989 when many features of the EBF had to change. He had a great concern to communicate with the constituency and he soon launched the magazine, *The European Baptist.* He was assisted in the development of better communications by the growing importance of the European Baptist Press Service (EBPS), which Southern Baptist Missionary, John Allen Moore, had launched in 1961 on a part-time basis, but which improved in quality and effectiveness with the passing years and with the appointment of full-time Southern Baptist Convention (SBC) missionaries with journalistic skills.[47] EBPS continued to serve the EBF even

---

[45] This was initially for a five-year period, but extended in a decision taken on recommendation of J.B. Middlebrook at the BWA Executive Committee in Hamburg in 1964, BWA Executive Minutes 1964, p. 24 item 38, BWA Library.

[46] Minutes of the EBF Council, Oslo, September 2002, EBF Office Archive.

[47] The Southern Baptist Convention - Foreign Mission Board [SBC-FMB] sought out and appointed a succession of US citizens with such skills – Theo Sommerkamp, John Wilkes, Stanley Crabbe, Martha Skelton, Todd Dickerson. From 2003 the SBC-IMB declined to assist in further ways, and the EBPS is now operated for EBF on a

beyond the 1990s when the policy of the SBC-Foreign Mission Board (SBC-FMB) changed and generally missionaries were appointed to evangelistic and church-planting tasks.[48] This is one example of a foundation laid by Rudén in the early 1960s which had on-going European-wide significance for Baptists. However, the Swedish Union continued to seek the advice of Rudén and as early as 1963 he wrote to the BWA Administrative Committee offering his resignation from the BWA and the EBF saying:

> I have been asked to take up my new position in Sweden in 1965. My suggestion is that I do that on a limited scale during the first part of the year. Already plans make it necessary for me to continue serving as European Secretary until the World Congress in 1965. Thus I shall terminate my present work on 1 July 1965.[49]

By contrast with Rudén's appointment, care was taken with the appointment of his successor. Joseph Nordenhaug, as BWA General Secretary, had early consultation with the EBF officers. Out of this consultation, the name of Ronald Goulding, then Pastor of Haven Green Baptist Church, Ealing, West London, emerged. Goulding was recognised as the clear favourite to succeed Rudén.[50] European Baptists now had the major say in who would serve them in a representative and leadership capacity.

In the 1960s and 1970s, under Rudén and his successors, Goulding and Gerhard Claas, the role of the EBF General Secretary increased in importance and the 'living letter' concept grew. Rudén himself visited nineteen of the twenty-three member unions within the EBF in the first two years of his secretaryship.[51] There was also a growing concern that the EBF should reach out and give assistance to those in need in Europe. Goulding was given responsibilities within the BWA for relief work and this emphasis became more marked under Class. The experience Class brought to the post was as a pastor, youth secretary and General Secretary of the Baptist Union of the Federal Republic of Germany. He was known as an evangelist, a campaigner for human rights, a skilled negotiator with governments and someone who could associate with church leaders of many traditions. In 1980 he was appointed as BWA General Secretary, and there was an expansion of the work of the Alliance, with

---

contractual basis by a journalist of the German Baptist Publishing House, Oncken Verlag.

48 See Chapter 6 for an analysis of the changing role of the SBC-FMB within Europe at this time.

49 Letter from E. Rudén to J. Nordenhaug, reported in the BWA Executive Committee, 17-21 August 1964, in Hamburg, p. 23, item 37, BWA Library.

50 *Ibid.*

51 Report of the General Secretary to the EBF Executive Committee, Brussels, September 1961, Box 801, EBF Archive.

a shift from concern about fellowship to more active programme work. A Scottish born Canadian Baptist, Archie Goldie, was appointed Director of Baptist World Aid in 1983.[52] This was to have implications for European Baptist work. In the 1980s, Gerhard Claas kept the European situation, especially that in Eastern Europe, to the fore within the wider Baptist community. Reporting to the BWA General Council in 1981, he spoke of his delight at being able to baptise seventeen newly converted believers at one church in Eastern Europe.[53] The death of Claas on 21 March 1988, from injuries sustained in a car accident near Lodi, California, USA, was a severe loss to the Alliance and also to European Baptist life.

During all this period there were questions about how the work of the EBF was to be financed, especially in relation to new projects. For certain specific work in Europe there was funding from the BWA. Thus the European Baptist Women's Union (EBWU) and the European Baptist Youth Committee (EBYC), both of which had emerged out of BWA work among women and youth,[54] became increasingly recognised within the EBF. As the work of the EBF Executive developed the EBWU and the EBYC were given places on the Executive. In the post-war years special attention was being paid to European youth.[55] But EBF General Secretaries recognised that the Federation had very little funds with which to support such enterprises. In the early period, Ruth Pepper, President of the EBWU, was financially supported by women in the USA.[56] Henry Cook hoped for oversight of the EBWU by the EBF.[57]

The financial side of the EBF gave Secretaries, from Cook onwards, cause for anxiety.[58] Edwin Bell was able to confirm that the ABC Women's organisation was helping to support Mrs Pepper's travels.[59] However, he went on to venture the opinion that the EBWU, the EBYC and the EBF should seek to develop a coordinated budget and put together a single request for funding

---

[52] Job Description of the Director of Baptist World Aid, BWA Executive Committee Report Book 1981, section 23a, p. 8, BWA Library.

[53] BWA General Secretary's Report, General Council Report, 1981, item 10, BWA Archive.

[54] The BWA Youth Committee grew out of the appointment of Joel Sorensen as Associate Secretary for Youth Work at the BWA Congress in Cleveland, Ohio, in 1950, *Eighth BWA World Congress Official Report*, BWA, Washington DC, 1950.

[55] R.S. Denny Report to BWA Executive Committee, Hamilton, Ontario, 29-30 August 1957, Minutes p. 4, item 22, BWA Library.

[56] Letter from H. Cook to E.A. Bell, 25 November 1951, EBF/BWA Correspondence Box 27, Angus Library.

[57] *Ibid.*

[58] Letter from H. Cook to A.T. Ohrn, 21 November 1955, BWA/EBF Correspondence Box 27, Angus Library.

[59] Letter from E.A. Bell to H. Cook, 13 December 1955, BWA/EBF Correspondence Box 27, Angus Library.

from the North American mission agencies, in 'the effort to secure the underwriting of reasonable resources for the work of the Federation.'[60] This suggestion was never taken up. During the Secretaryship of Ronald Goulding, the Baptist Unions in Europe were expected to meet one-third of the costs of the London office.[61] Gradually, as will be seen, the EBF took more and more responsibility for the support of its principal officers.

'New things are really happening in Europe'

Knud Wümplemann was appointed General Secretary in succession to Gerhard Claas and served the EBF for ten years, two five-year terms, during the latter days of the cold-war when, as he put it, new things were happening in Europe.[62] Wümplemann, a Danish Baptist pastor, was brought up as a young child in the Evangelical-Lutheran Church.[63] However, new spiritual influences impacted on the family. His father suffered from tuberculosis, thought to be incurable, and the family asked a Pentecostal pastor for prayer. Healing took place, and Knud's parents were then baptised by the Pentecostal pastor, using the local Baptist church. Knud was baptised on Easter Day 1936 at the age of 13.[64] His parents ran a home for the elderly, and visiting preachers and pastors often stayed there. Through these visits, Knud became acquainted with pastors and foreign missionaries. He trained for service in the Danish Post and Telegraph service. Writing at the time of his nomination as President of the EBF, the Danish newspaper *Berlingske Tidende* said:

> From the beginning Knud Wümplemann considered a career with the Post and Telegraph Service. If he had continued there he certainly would have become General Secretary. And the Danes wouldn't have had so many problems with the Department as we have today.[65]

Thanks to the influence of his pastor in Aarhus, Kjell Kyrø-Rasmussen,

---

[60] *Ibid.*

[61] Letter from J. Nordenhaug to C.R. Goulding, 17 February 1965, BWA Ronald Goulding Files, Angus Library.

[62] Report of the EBF General Secretary to the EBF Executive in Budapest, April 1987, EBF Archive Box 1, David S. Russell Papers, Angus Library.

[63] For the early biographical material on Knud Wümplemann I was able to benefit from access to his personal papers, an article on him prepared by Bent Hylleberg and on personal conversations with Knud and his wife Karen at BWA meetings and in his home in Tølløse, Denmark.

[64] *Ibid.*

[65] *Berlingske Tidende*, 7 August 1989, when Knud Wümplemann had been nominated at the BWA General Council meeting in Zagreb to be the next President of the BWA. I am indebted to Bent Hylleberg for this translation, which he also quotes in 'Knud Wümplemann' *Journal of European Baptist Studies*, p. 6.

Wümplemann was challenged to consider Christian ministry and studied from 1944 to 1947 at the Baptist Theological Seminary in Tølløse. The buildings were commandeered by the German army of occupation in Spring 1945 and the students were hosted in a home belonging to the local bank manager. It was here that Wümplemann met his future wife, Karen, one of the daughters of the bank manager. They married in 1947. In the same year Wümplemann participated in the BWA Congress in Copenhagen. At a conference of theological students held in the Köbnerkirkchen, presided over by Principal Arthur Dakin of Bristol Baptist College, Knud Wümplemann was called on to welcome the students from outside Denmark.[66] Wider links were developing.

On completing seminary training Wümplemann became assistant pastor in Pandrup to Laurits Jørgensen, where Knud learnt much from Jørgensen's gentle, but firm style of ministry. The Wümplemanns then moved to Copenhagen where he assisted Bredhal Petersen, one of the founders and first President of the EBF. This further opened the eyes of Knud Wümplemann to a wider world. Two years of further study followed, at Central Baptist Seminary, Kansas City. He then returned to the Copenhagen church as senior pastor. He was the first full-time General Secretary of the Danish Union from 1964 until 1980. From 1965 he served on the BWA Executive Committee and this proved important in preparing him for his subsequent ministry.[67] He was also on the EBF Council from 1967 and served as President of the EBF (1977-1979). At the EBF Executive meeting held in Brighton in July 1979, the Executive, under David S. Russell.[68] as the new President,[69] noting the call of Gerhard Claas to the BWA, established a Nominating Committee to search for a successor. It is significant that now the EBF took the lead. The members of the Committee were Russell, David Lagargren (Sweden), Michael Zhidkov (USSR), together with the BWA General Secretary and another representative of the BWA.[70] Wümplemann was called, and accepted the call, to serve the EBF as General Secretary/Treasurer.

A priority for Knud Wümplemann in his time as General Secretary was the

---

[66] W.O. Lewis (ed.), *Seventh Baptist World Congress*, Denmark 1947, p. 60, Conference of Theological Students, Minute 94.

[67] Knud Wümplemann commenced serving on the Executive in the light of the new Bye-Laws and attended his first meeting on 30 June 1965 at Miami Beach, USA. BWA Executive Committee Minutes, 30 June 1965, BWA Library.

[68] D.S. Russell described some of his adventures whilst President in D.S. Russell, *In Journeyings Often* (London: BUGB, 1981), pp. 44-72.

[69] D.S. Russell, General Secretary of the British Baptists, had succeeded Knud Wümplemann as President at the EBF 1979 Brighton Congress. Knud Wümplemann, therefore, was not present at the Executive as the immediate ex-President is not an EBF officer and does not serve on the Executive.

[70] Minutes of the EBF Executive Committee, Brighton, 25 June and 5 July 1979, Box 803, EBF Archive.

building of fellowship between Baptists in Western and Eastern Europe. For him there was one Baptist community in Europe, East and West. In 1970, as a member of the EBF Council, he had been asked to make contacts in the Soviet Union and to try to strengthen links with the *Initsiativniki* (the Reform Baptists),[71] who refused to register their church buildings and suffered persecution from the state. From this beginning Knud Wümplemann was to make twenty visits to the USSR over the next twenty years, attempting to reach a clearer understanding of both the registered and unregistered Baptists.[72] At the same time he sought to strengthen western Unions. Reporting to the EBF Executive Committee in May 1985, Wümplemann, inevitably, concentrated on the events of the EBF Conference in Hamburg of the previous year. He expressed delight that as the German language had been used more than at previous conferences, a greater number of people had been able to participate more fully. His whole emphasis throughout this time was on the importance of deeper fellowship amongst European Baptists.[73] Wümplemann rejoiced towards the end of his secretaryship that relationships with churches in the East became easier. Writing to the EBF Executive in April 1987 he commented:

> New things are really happening in Europe these days: signs of spring are obvious: new life is breaking through; this sometimes means struggle, but it certainly also – and first of all – means renewal and new expectations and hope. The breakthrough of new hope which has caused the greatest interest all over the world is the democratization process going on in the Soviet Union. This process is felt also in the churches.[74]

Theological education was the second of Knud Wümplemann's great concerns. Though he had not been involved in this work himself, he had benefited from his various periods of study and he regarded as extremely important his involvement with the Seminary at Rüschlikon. He welcomed, and was intimately involved in the transfer of ownership from the Southern Baptists to the EBF. Typically, when reporting to the 1983 BWA Executive Committee meeting at Columbia Baptist Church, Falls Church, Virginia, he concentrated

---

[71] A contemporary article by a communist author, I. Braznik, of Moscow University, was printed in *Science and Religion*, December 1969, pp. 54-57, and labelled this group obscurantist. The article appears as an appendix in the book M. Bourdeaux, *Faith on Trial in Russia* (London: Hodder and Stoughton, 1971), pp. 182-9.

[72] Wümplemann's interest at this time is recorded in 'European Baptists and Baptists in the USSR', in D. Lotz (ed.) *Baptist Witness in the USSR* (Valley Forge: ABC, 1987), pp. 49-52.

[73] Report of the General Secretary to the EBF Executive, Lisbon, May 1985, EBF Archive Box 1, D.S. Russell Papers, Angus Library.

[74] Report of the EBF General Secretary to the EBF Executive in Budapest, April 1987, EBF Archive Box 1, D.S. Russell Papers, Angus Library.

on theological education and especially proposals from the European Baptist Theological Teachers' Conference[75] held the previous year in Denia, Spain. The concern was that the way the BWA operated did not permit adequate participation by the regions and there were calls for some re-structuring of the BWA Commission on Study and Research.[76] In the same report he pointed out that the Rüschlikon Seminary had come into being about the same time as the EBF and 'it has during the years in different ways meant a great deal to European Baptists.... The student body has never been larger than it is today'.[77] He remained completely committed to the vision of Rüschlikon as vital to the life of the EBF and emphasised the importance of close relationships between the EBF Unions and the Seminary. In May 1985 he reported to the EBF Executive meeting in Lisbon:

> In January the new President of the Rüschlikon Seminary, Dr Altus J. Newell, was inaugurated. We are grateful to the Foreign Mission Board of SBC for effective cooperation in finding such a well qualified leader of this, to European Baptists so important, institution. Dr Newell hopes to visit the unions and its seminaries in the near future to build up closer relations between the unions and the seminary.[78]

The concern for theological education in Europe meant an interest in all the seminaries serving the Unions. In 1986 Wümplemann started his report to the EBF Executive by saying: 'One of the most encouraging developments within our European Baptist Federation right now is the fact that no less than four theological seminary projects are under way in eastern Europe.'[79] These projects were the new seminaries in Radosc, Poland; in Bucharest, in Romania; and in Moscow, and the redevelopment of the Budapest seminary buildings.[80] His report also detailed the fact that twenty new European students had been admitted to Rüschlikon, but the financial difficulties of the institution were increasing as the dollar declined against the Swiss franc. He returned to the

---

[75] Meetings of European Theological educators had begun early in the life of the EBF arising in conjunction with the Seminary at Rüschlikon. Later, these were mirrored with the establishment of the BWA Conferences on Theological Education (BICTE) the first being held at Ridgecrest, North Carolina, in 1982.

[76] Report of the EBF General Secretary to the BWA Executive Committee 1983, item 20d, BWA Executive Report Book, BWA Library.

[77] *Ibid.*

[78] Report of the EBF General Secretary to the EBF Executive Committee, Lisbon, May 1985, EBF Archive Box 1, D.S. Russell Papers, Angus Library. In fact, Dr Newell only remained at the seminary two years before returning to the USA.

[79] Report of the EBF General Secretary to the EBF Executive Committee, Novi Sad, May 1986, EBF Archive Box 1, D.S. Russell Papers, Angus Library.

[80] The Moscow building also became home to the Union offices and it was not until September 2002 that the Moscow Seminary finally had a purpose-built campus of its own.

theme of the strategic position of Rüschlikon at the March 1989 meeting, stating that the Seminary had:

> ... during the years been the one most important tool binding Baptist Unions of widely different background, view points and conditions together in growing fellowship. The greatest event happening to the EBF last year was, therefore, the generous decision of the Foreign Mission Board of the SBC to hand over the seminary property to the EBF and at the same time under the dynamic leadership of the new seminary president, Dr John David Hopper, to continue the long term partnership between the FMB and EBF in Rüschlikon.[81]

As Secretary/Treasurer Wümplemann also took seriously the need for European Baptists to finance their own work. For him this was an expression of the fellowship to which he was committed. At the EBF Council in September 1983 a resolution was passed to reduce the grant assistance from the BWA by US$4,000 and to seek to do that in subsequent years.[82] This programme was adhered to and by the early 1990s the core budget of the EBF was being provided by the member bodies.[83] The march towards self-sufficiency accelerated during the 1980s, as the pattern of income and budgeting shows in a report Wümplemann presented to the 1986 EBF Executive in May:[84]

Contributions (in Deutsch Marks)	**1984/85**	**1985/86**	**1986/87**	**(1990/91)**
Member bodies	60,000	83,059	120,000	(216,750)
BWA	64,315	60,000	37,000	(20,000)

He was also committed to finding funds for helping needy parts of Europe. This, too, was an expression of fellowship. In his 1988 Report to the BWA Executive Committee he stated that:

> US$ 154,000 was channeled to projects in Belgium, DDR, Hungary, Poland, Romania and Spain. For victims of the earthquake in Armenia US$25,000 has been sent through the EBF. New great challenges have come from the USSR to support literature-projects which have just recently been permitted by the State.[85]

---

[81] Report of the EBF General Secretary to the BWA Executive Committee, March 1989, BWA Library.
[82] Minutes of the EBF Council, Stockholm, 29 September-1 October 1983, Box 807, EBF Archive.
[83] BWA Report Book, March 1984, BWA Library.
[84] EBF Executive Committee May 1986, Novi Sad. EBF Archive Box 1, D.S. Russell Papers, Angus Library.
[85] Report of the EBF General Secretary to the BWA Executive Committee, March 1989. BWA Report Book 14d, p. 2, BWA Library.

The development of the new Division of the BWA, Baptist World Aid, from 1983 onwards, brought a new focus in channelling aid. Knud Wümplemann, while very aware of global issues, was seen as 'aggressive in seeking to have the many needs of Europe met'.[86] He advanced certain key projects, especially a major translation of the William Barclay Commentaries into Russian, which required a significant cooperative effort between EBF, Baptist World Aid and the British charity 'Feed the Minds'.[87] An EBF Eurolit Committee was created to oversee the project, which was agreed as being appropriate for Russian pastors, many of whom only had basic education. In the early 1990s this initiative was criticised by Southern Baptist representative, Dorothy Patterson, wife of leading fundamentalist Southern Baptist Paige Patterson, at the Baptist World Aid Executive. She denounced Professor William Barclay as being too liberal and stated that Baptist World Aid should have used a more conservative scholar. This view was rebutted by the Director of Baptist World Aid, Paul Montacute, who pointed out that the original policy negotiated by the EBF Secretary was based on the requirements of Russian Baptists and not the attitudes of the financial donors.[88] This desire to support the recipients and to argue the case for maximum assistance for Europe was in line with the whole pattern of how Knud Wümplemann developed his secretaryship. Indeed he began to use the term EBF-Aid. From his BWA perspective Archie Goldie comments that 'though he was a strong advocate of the needs of Europe, he was also someone who desired cooperative and team working and throughout his secretaryship we kept each other informed of what we were doing and there was no tension between us.'[89]

Karl Heinz Walter and 'Europeanisation'

Knud Wümplemann was succeeded by Karl Heinz Walter, a German pastor who had trained at the Hamburg Seminary. His first introduction to the life of the EBF was when he was the German Baptist Youth Secretary, in which connection he joined the EBF Youth Committee in the 1960s. He also served a quinquennium as Chair of the BWA Youth Department (1970-1975). From his involvement in youth work he went to be pastor of the church at Bremerhaven and, after a successful pastorate, the EBF Search Committee approached him

---

[86] Interview with Archie Goldie at BWA Offices, Falls Church, Virginia, 3 March 2003.

[87] Archie Goldie recalls this as a major endeavour which used the diplomatic skills of the EBF General Secretary to the full and recognised the integrity of the Russian requirements supported by EBF. Interview with Archie Goldie at Falls Church, Virginia, 3 March 2003.

[88] Baptist World Aid Executive Committee, Montreal, July 1991, BWAid, BWA, Falls Church, Virginia and my recollection as a member of the BWAid Executive Committee at the time.

[89] Interview with A. Goldie at BWA Offices, Falls Church, Virginia, 3 March 2003.

with a view to him becoming General Secretary. By now BWA involvement in this process was not significant, being limited to the BWA General Secretary serving on the Search Committee. His induction to office took place in the final session of the momentous EBF Congress in Budapest in 1989 when it was already apparent that very significant change in the political realities of Central and Eastern Europe would affect the EBF. Indeed, it might not be unreasonable to regard the history of the EBF to the present time as being 'Before Budapest' and 'After Budapest'. As has been demonstrated, the mark of the General Secretaryship of Knud Wümplemann was 'fellowship' and 'theological education'. The accent of the ten years of the ministry of Walter might be characterised by 're-shaping' and 'reaching out'. There was an expansion in the number of member bodies of the EBF and there were significant attempts to provide support and relief for the newly-freed communities of Central and Eastern Europe.

Immediately after the Budapest Congress in the summer of 1989, political change began to gather pace in Central and Eastern Europe. At the same time Karl Heinz Walter established the office of General Secretary in the Albertinien Hospital complex in Hamburg by invitation of the hospital director, Walter Füllbrandt.[90] Wider circumstances, especially the collapse of Soviet hegemony and the changing of the geopolitical realities of Central and Eastern Europe, inevitably dictated some elements of the secretaryship of Walter, but his character, interests and leadership style also had a major effect. He took stock of the huge upheavals of the time when he presented his report to the EBF Council at De Bron, Netherlands, in September 1990.[91] As well as taking up concerns about Eastern Europe and encouraging the formation of Baptist Response-Europe (BRE, see below) and also addressing the defunding of the Seminary at Rüschlikon[92], he turned to the possibilities which might occur for the 're-evangelisation of Europe'. This became a theme to which Karl Heinz Walter would return again and again. In his Report to the Council he commented:

> These new developments give an important role to the EBF as a bridge builder and a central focus of unification. It is easy to understand that after so many years of no national identity many people look for it. But it is also more than evident that our future chances lie in a 'Europeanisation'. We have to think of 'European

---

[90] Walter Füllbrandt was the first registered student of Rüschlikon in 1949 and served as Chairman of the IBTS Board of Trustees in the mid 1990s. His own ministry represents the classical way that IBTS graduates have gone on to exercise key roles within the EBF community.

[91] EBF Council, De Bron, Netherlands, 1990, Report Book for the Council Meeting, p. 2-3. Box 809, EBF Archive.

[92] See Chapter 4.

> Nation' and of 'European Baptist Unions' even if today nobody knows all the implications this will have in the future.[93]

Two years later, in his Report to the EBF Council held in High Leigh, England, Walter quoted, with strong approval, an address by the then Czechoslovak President, the former dissident, Vaclav Havel:

> The new democratic regimes have to struggle with problems which have slept before under the glacier of the cold war. The citizens are happy in the new freedom but at the same time they are perplexed and puzzled. They have difficulties to become worthy citizens with their own full rights, and they struggle to get rid of the old bad attitudes which Communism had rooted so deeply in their minds... All the old conflicts, injustices and hostilities have returned. Nothing was forgotten and nothing forgiven.[94]

Karl Heinz Walter suggested to the Council that the analysis offered by Havel was one that should be affirmed. The communist world had collapsed. Now the nations that had composed that world were drifting apart as new democracies, but Europe was 'like a large kettle filled with a highly explosive mixture'.[95] Havel, said Walter, had proposed that there were two options: to wait and see if the kettle exploded or to get engaged in creatively helping chart the future of Europe. Walter believed these options, in revised form, faced European Baptists, either to 'sit and wait the second coming of the Lord.... or to influence this new world in the direction of peace and for the better of all people in the name of our Lord Jesus Christ. I understand my ministry in the latter sense.'[96] Here was someone offering leadership to European Baptists.

At this and other points, Walter affirmed his intention to be an activist and to meet what he, echoing Havel, perceived to be a particular *kairos* moment in Europe, with nations and the peoples of those nations searching for a way ahead. Not for him the 'quietist' approach, advocating that Christians should be subservient to authorities – a view which was articulated in certain Unions within the former communist empire. Rather, he saw European Baptists being engaged with civil and international society. Hence he was an advocate of the EBF seeking representation at the Council of Europe and the European Parliament as a non-governmental organisation, anticipating, rightly, that many of the new and emerging governments of Central and Eastern Europe would not

---

[93] Report of the General Secretary, EBF Council Book, De Bron, September 1990, p. 5, Box 809, EBF Archive.

[94] Speech of Vaclav Havel to Summit of the OSCE Helsinki Conference in July 1992, quoted in the report of the General Secretary of the EBF to the High Leigh Council meeting of the EBF, September 1992, Box 810, EBF Archive.

[95] *Ibid.*

[96] Report of the General Secretary, EBF Council Report Book, High Leigh, England, September 1992, pp. 1-2, Box 810, EBF Archive.

automatically grant full freedom of religion to all groups, especially to some of the smaller evangelical communities. He drew attention to this danger in his Report to the EBF Council at Varna in 1991 when he noted:

> Former laws are not automatically valid in the new republics. Therefore it is very important that our brethren will have a legal position for their churches and to influence the preparation of new laws. Just one example: the new and good law on religious freedom in the USSR will not be automatically valid in the new republics. This is of great concern for us and wherever it was possible I intervened with the respective political leadership like in Georgia or with the majority churches.[97]

This concern for the wider involvement of the EBF in European affairs, both ecumenical and political, was a recurrent theme, but one which was not always accepted, especially in some of the ex-communist countries.[98]

This raised issues of Baptist identity. Here, for Walter, was the focus of theological reflection. In some ways this might appear understandable. During the General Secretaryship of Knud Wümplemann, Baptists in Western Europe had been reasonably stable in their theological and ecclesial outlook. Baptists in the East had operated with what Karl Heinz Walter described as a 'survival theology', which certainly did not involve much exploration of wider theological concerns. The life of the churches was locked in a time-warp, not least politically. But from 1990 onwards the opportunities for West and East to interact grew. This was at a time of ferment within Western, as well as Eastern, Baptist life. In post-communist, post-Christendom, post-modern Europe, Baptists soon found many of the old certainties questioned, and a lively debate began on Baptist identity and theology. It was against this background that the EBF held a special Consultation in 1992 on 'The Role of Baptists in Europe'. This experience was to teach Karl Heinz Walter and the Union leaderships in Europe that they had not yet developed a confident way of dialoguing together. He said of the meeting:

> Those who took part experienced intensive talks and brotherly[99] listening to each other. We felt very happy about the atmosphere. The conference decided that the first results should be sent to participants and the unions for further comments to be sent back to the EBF office. Out of the confidential and open discussion it was

---

[97] Report of the General Secretary, EBF Council Report Book, Varna, Bulgaria, September 1991, p. 2, Box 809, EBF Archive.

[98] Such exclusion had not been universal. The All-Union Council had participated in the World Council of Churches and, of course, in the peace conference issues discussed in Chapter 7.

[99] Some 'sisters' were present, but the use of inclusive language was not at that time common within EBF circles, though it became more common after the Swedish Baptist Union General Secretary, Birgit Karlsson, was appointed President of the EBF.

> also added to 13 statements what was content of the very diverse discussion. It was a mistake from my side to send it out. *But we were disappointed that some had taken this as if this was a confession of faith, which was never intended* and even gave it to the press. The intention was very clear and sad at the same time. I am very grateful for all the help to overcome this unchristian attack.[100]

This experience was a cruel blow for Karl Heinz Walter. He had hoped to begin a friendly debate on issues of Baptist identity to strengthen the bonds within the EBF across Europe. This was to prove difficult, although not ultimately impossible.

Reaching Out

Karl Heinz Walter encouraged the EBF to reach out ecumenically and also in social concern. Before the 1991 Council, Walter had been one of a delegation of three people from the EBF, which included the President, Peter Barber (Scotland), and Jakob Dukhonchenko from Kiev to a gathering of Protestant churches in Basel. Walter commented to the Council:

> While the Roman Catholic Church has very early stated that they are intending to work in the direction of a Christian Europe, all other churches are still in the process of discussion. What will be the Christian church in a more and more secularized world? The ecumenical movement is also in tremendous change. In the past years the membership or guest status (for Baptists) within the ecumenical movement was just the means to have an open door to the rest of the world. The ecumenical movement is experiencing a real crisis and no one is able to predict the future. The Protestant churches are just starting with the discussion of their future role.[101]

In fact, Walter was not completely fair in thinking that Baptists in the communist block (he was particularly thinking of the countries in the USSR) had belonged to the BWA and CEC simply to have an open door to the rest of the world. This assumption of a very pragmatic approach by some Unions in the East may have been typical of the time, but subsequent events have demonstrated that at least some had – and have – a greater commitment to the ecumenical encounter. Several Unions, such as Russia and Georgia, continued in membership with these bodies and at points could be more committed to the ecumenical meetings than to Baptist gatherings. So, in 1998, the Russian Baptist President, Petr Konovalchik, with a delegation, participated fully in the Second European Ecumenical Assembly and in the Assembly of the

---

[100] Report of the General Secretary to the EBF Council, High Leigh, September 1992, Report Book, p. 3, Box 810, EBF Archive.

[101] Report of the General Secretary, EBF Council, Varna, Bulgaria, September 1991, Report Book, p. 3, Box 809, EBF Archive.

Conference of European Churches at the expense of attending the BWA General Council in Vancouver, Canada.[102]

For his own part, Karl Heinz Walter saw it as fundamentally necessary to seek to present to others a clear description of the Baptist community in Europe, especially as new national Unions came into being following the collapse of the USSR. So, at the Varna Council of 1991, he sought the approval of the Council to respond positively to an invitation from the Vatican to be present at a special Assembly of Roman Catholic Bishops of Europe in Rome in October/November 1991. He was one of a number of ecumenical representatives invited to address the Pope in Synod, and during the course of his address he commented:

> For the Baptist churches in Europe the opening of the East, therefore, is a continuing challenge for evangelisation. After communism has failed, we meet people with a big inner vacuum. These people have no relation whatsoever to churches and traditions.... I appeal to you to exercise your influence in order that in all places not only all religions are treated equal and fair [sic] but also all Christian churches. This is the only way to have real evangelisation of Europe and a reformation in ecumenical cooperation. In this context I would like to expressively [sic] thank His Eminence Cardinal Luistiger for his remarks on Saturday. This has given me a lot of hope personally.[103]

Here is a continuation of his main concerns – the need to address the missionary question in Europe, the desire to have equal rights for all faith traditions and the commitment to demonstrating that Baptists were part of the main stream of international Christian life. Although Baptist communities in various countries of Europe might be quite small, the overall community of Baptists in the world made them significant players in the Christian world family.[104]

Another form of outreach was social. Facing the rapidly changing situation in Eastern Europe, Karl Heinz Walter called together leaders from Eastern Europe and a range of mission agencies, in January 1990, at the German Free Church Conference Centre, Dorfweil, to gain first-hand information about the changing situation and to consider starting a programme for immediate aid. The outcome of this meeting was that:

---

[102] My observation. The BWA General Secretary, D. Lotz, was critical of this decision by the Russian leadership.

[103] From text of address of K.H. Walter to the Extraordinary Synod of Bishops, Rome, 27 November-4 December 1991. Full text in EBF Council Report Book, High Leigh, England, 1992, Box 810, EBF Archive.

[104] *Ibid.* The beginning of his address focused on statistics, suggesting the Baptist community in Europe was approximately 2.5 million people.

> a large part of the time of the EBF office and myself had to give [sic] to the relief programme – BRE... This large programme was a heavy burden on the office. We had the help from some students, but the main work had to be done by my secretary, Karen Schaffrik, and by my wife, who is helping in the office.[105]

Through the initiative of Walter a coordination committee was formed, bringing together the Director of Baptist World Aid, the EBF General Secretary, the European representative of ABC International Ministries, the Europe Area Secretary of the SBC-FMB, the Europe Area Secretary of the British Baptist Missionary Society (BMS), the International Secretary of the Baptist Union of Great Britain and, within a short space of time, the Europe Liaison of the Cooperative Baptist Fellowship (CBF).[106] This in itself might be viewed as a most significant development of his General Secretaryship. Under W.O. Lewis there had been a measure of cooperation between ABC and Southern Baptists, but the development of a committee structure and the deliberate attempt to organise addressing the major challenges by cooperation between the donor bodies marked a new era.

Tension could have arisen between Baptist World Aid and BRE, but initially Archie Goldie and later, and more significantly, Paul Montacute, successive Directors of Baptist World Aid, sought to engage in constructive dialogue with the Hamburg office and worked hard at presenting Baptist World Aid and BRE as part of one international Baptist aid and development agency.[107] Indeed, if tensions existed, they were at their most noticeable in Britain. Baptist World Aid and the International Desk of the Baptist Union cooperated happily in raising funds, but in this period the BMS became more aggressive in fundraising for aid and development. This led to a series of meetings convened under the auspices of the Fellowship of British Baptists to develop a protocol to avoid direct competition and advertising with misleading information.[108] There was also an internal EBF point of tension in regard to the administrative costs of BRE. It was agreed by the EBF Executive[109] that no aid money would be used for EBF administration costs. The BWA, by contrast, has always taken 10% for administration in respect of Baptist World Aid. As Baptist World Aid

---

105 Report of K.H. Walter to the BWA Executive Committee, March 1991, Report Book, p. 84, BWA Library.

106 *Ibid.*, p. 85. See Chapter 6 for details of the emergence of the CBF arising out of the Southern Baptist defunding of the Rüschlikon Seminary in 1989.

107 Paul Montacute had been Youth Officer of the British Baptist Union until 1990 and shared an understanding of European Baptist life with Walter, making the possibility of cooperation much more achievable.

108 Minutes of the Council of Fellowship of British Baptists, Protocol on Relationships between the aid and development agencies, 1994, Angus Library.

109 Reported in the EBF Baptist Response-Europe [BRE] Report to the BWA Executive Committee, March 1991, Report Book, p. 86, BWA Library.

had the expertise and was generally the conduit for significant sums of money from America, inevitably there was some debate about the contradictory nature of the two policies. This was combined with a tendency for Karl Heinz Walter to engage in cross-subsidy at critical points in the financial year. For him, the importance of seeing projects advance, and a deep concern that others understand the moment of opportunity, were paramount. He anticipated, rightly, that after a few years the eyes of the Western world would turn elsewhere and the former communist states would slip into modern developing capitalist economies, and the opportunity to present the holistic message of the gospel in a fresh and open way would pass.

One area of struggle for Walter was to have healthy cooperation with recipient Unions, many of which were only just beginning to be formed in the wake of the disintegration of the USSR and the break up of Yugoslavia. He noted this problem and showed his determination to bring a measure of oversight in his Report to the BWA Executive:

> Only very few Baptist Unions in east and west have named a person or a committee in their countries to partner BRE. While we are trying to coordinate our efforts we are confronted with uncountable private initiatives which made it almost impossible to influence in a good way [sic]. For this year we will not be able to work without such committees for responsible leaders. Some countries have done this and the results are remarkable.[110]

By the time of the EBF Council in Varna in September 1991, BRE had become a very time-consuming activity. Walter reported that income in 1990 had been 1.75 million Deutschmarks, of which 1.48 million was distributed during the year. The focus of the work was in purchasing and distributing Bibles and children's Bibles for Romania, USSR, Bulgaria and the Ukraine; providing support to build seminaries in Poland, Romania, Estonia; assisting in social work in the former German Democratic Republic and providing medical assistance.[111]

Changes and Challenges for the EBF

The model of the EBF inherited by Karl Heinz Walter was virtually unchanged from that developed in the mid 1950s by the Constitution Committee under the chairmanship of E.A. Payne. This model had worked well with a total of around twenty member bodies, but during the 1990s, with the break-up of the large socialist republics of Eastern Europe and the commencing of Baptist work

---

[110] Report of EBF BRE to the BWA Executive Committee March 1991, Report Book, p. 86, BWA Library.

[111] BRE Report, EBF Council Report Book, Varna, Bulgaria, September 1991, pp. 3-5, Box 810, EBF Archive.

in countries like Albania, membership of the EBF grew until, in 2002, it numbered fifty-one. The BWA had been modestly restructured in 1990 and now Karl Heinz Walter believed some remodelling of the EBF was necessary. Proposals were discussed which would lead to the creation of four Divisions – Theology and Education; Mission and Evangelism; Communication, Promotion and Fellowship; and External Relations.[112] Walter advocated this new model as being more appropriate for the time, saying to the BWA Executive Committee, 'we are looking forward to it with great expectation'.[113] He drove the proposals forward in a thoroughly Germanic way, and Council accepted the development of the four-division structure, mirroring, in some way, the structures Walter had encountered in the BWA. Throughout his General Secretaryship he remained a strong advocate of the divisional format, though, in truth, some divisions, such as Communications, could not really function effectively as most Unions sent their Officers to the Council and not their magazine and newspaper editors.[114]

Another initiative was missional. The remit of the EBF has never really included cross-cultural mission. The EBF was the arena for the founding of the European Baptist Mission, which became the cross-cultural mission agency for most Western European Baptist Unions after its foundation in 1952. It now includes many Central and Eastern European Unions. Again, however, Walter, in his proactive leadership, expanded the understanding of what the EBF should and could do by seeking to develop an EBF mission in Albania. Albania was the one ex-communist country without any Baptist work because of the very repressive communist regime there. With the collapse of this regime, missionaries from the West were able to enter the country, and Walter took the initiative to try to develop a coordinated Baptist response, creating an Albania Committee to coordinate the involvement of missionaries from the BMS, CBF and SBC-IMB. The cooperation lasted only part of the decade, with the withdrawal of SBC to work independently in 1997, and the conclusion of the EBF Albania Committee that the work properly belonged to mission agencies. This led to the creation of International Baptist Cooperation in Albania.[115] In

---

[112] EBF Bye-Laws agreed by the EBF Council, De Bron, Netherlands, September 1990, and accepted by the BWA Executive, McLean, Virginia, March 1991. BWA Executive Report Book, p. 88-9. It should be noted that when the EBF Constitution was completely revised in 2002 the matter was not even reported to the BWA Executive Committee meeting in Falls Church, March, 2003, though D. Lotz was present and took part in the decision made.

[113] Report of the EBF General Secretary to the BWA Executive Committee, March 1991, BWA Report Book, p. 84, BWA Library.

[114] The exceptions were the editors of the British *Baptist Times* and the German *De Gemeinde.*

[115] On the creation of International Baptist Cooperation in Albania, see the Report of the EBF General Secretary to the BWA Executive Committee, Report Book 1998, p. 30, BWA Library.

1996 Walter reported that the EBF cooperative venture had established two churches with a combined membership of 120. A further two churches had been started by Baptist missionaries from Brazil. To the BWA he reported discussions about forming a 'Union of Baptist Churches in Albania.'[116] This venture might be regarded as a unique initiative by a regional Baptist body; some people were always critical of Walter for initiating this, but in the light of the situation in many parts of the world,[117] where different Baptist mission agencies created their own Unions, Conventions or Associations, it might be judged that Karl Heinz Walter saved Albania from the establishment of more than one Baptist association.[118]

If the General Secretaryship of Knud Wümplemann might be said to have been marked by an accent on maintaining contact with the East, consolidating the sense of fellowship, or *koinonia* within the EBF, and arguing the case for theological education, that of Karl Heinz Walter might be seen as an era of profound change, with a strong desire on the part of the General Secretary to see the EBF take on challenges and develop several significant programme initiatives. It was clouded by the deteriorating relationship with the SBC-FMB[119] and by the failure of the Prefabricated Church Project and the mixed success of the Lillehammer Conference. The Prefabricated Church Project was a dream of Walter to provide a system-built factory-produced building which could be mass produced to be erected in many parts of Central and Eastern Europe. Working with the General Secretary of the Bulgarian Union, Theo Angelov,[120] a Bulgarian architect was commissioned to design a structure to create a worship room with gallery and basic facilities which would be pre-fabricated at an assembly plant to be built in Bulgaria and could then be transported by heavy trucks, purchased second hand from the USA army, by German Baptists.[121] Though Karl Heinz Walter put much energy into this

---

[116] Report of the EBF General Secretary, BWA Executive, March 1996, Report Book, p. 76, BWA Library.

[117] For instance, Zimbabwe, where there are four Baptist organisations in membership with the BWA, each with origins in a different mission agency. This type of arrangement had been largely avoided in Europe because of a comity agreement dating back to the early part of the century, though this had been abandoned in 1948.

[118] In view of the fact that SBC-IMB would not join International Baptist Cooperation in Albania in 1998, it remains to be seen whether a rival body to the Baptist Union of Albania will now be established.

[119] See Chapter 6.

[120] Theo Angelov was to serve as EBF President 1995-1997 and as EBF General Secretary 1999-2004.

[121] As the USA redeployed troops from West Germany during the 1990s much surplus military equipment was sold cheaply or given away. Eckhard Schaeffer, German Baptist Union leader, became adept at obtaining these surplus resources to assist Baptist work in the East.

project,[122] only two buildings were ever erected. Whilst the plan had been to undertake construction in Bulgaria, in 1996 an attempt was made to relocate construction to Croatia, where economic conditions were seen to be better.[123] The concept was effectively abandoned when Walter retired as General Secretary in 1999.[124]

Another event which loomed large in his General Secretaryship was the 1994 Congress in Lillehammer, Norway. This Congress was designed to celebrate the new freedoms. The previous Congress in Budapest had been held at the dawn of the collapse of communism. All concerned in the EBF hoped the 1994 Congress would be the celebration of the reality of a new free Europe. The desire to hold the Congress in Norway had been the strong wish of Asbjorn Bakkevoll, a rising young leader of Norwegian Baptists, who already played a significant role on the world stage, leading the forward-planning group of the BWA. However, his premature death removed a key player in the arrangements. The original intention had been to hold the event in Oslo, but costs in one of the most expensive cities in Europe made that option impossible. The move was made to a cheaper venue, the Winter Olympics resort of Lillehammer, but there was a lack of financial control and the Event Group planned and obtained expensive technical equipment to provide exciting evening meetings. Then, many people from Eastern Europe, now free to travel, arrived at Lillehammer with no funds and no resources for housing and feeding, and emergency provision had to be made.

Technically and in terms of fellowship, the EBF leadership judged this Congress to be a great success, but financially it crippled the EBF. It proved very difficult to reconcile the financial accounts of the Congress and Karl Heinz Walter was driven to exchanging intense correspondence with the local Norwegian committee. Finally, one year later, in December 1995, the full deficit of US $358,000 was agreed. It was reported to the BWA Executive as, 'The still unbelievable deficit of DM 519,000. This deficit was covered by a loan from the sale of the property at Rüschlikon.'[125] As Secretary/Treasurer of the EBF, Karl Heinz Walter felt responsible for this, but also felt let down by the local arrangements committee and by the EBF Congress Programme Committee who had incurred much additional expenditure on technical equipment late in the day. It was to mar his relationship with leaders of Norwegian Baptists and with some members of the Board of Trustees of IBTS,

[122] Walter continued to feature the concept in his reports to both the BWA and the EBF.

[123] Report of K.H. Walter to BWA Executive Committee, March 1996, BWA Report Book, p. 77, BWA Library.

[124] In fact, no mention of this initiative was being made by March 1998. See EBF Report to the BWA Executive Committee, March 1998, BWA Report Book, p. 30- 32, BWA Library.

[125] Report of the EBF General Secretary to the BWA Executive Committee, March 1996, BWA Report Book, p. 77, BWA Library.

who discovered he had made an arrangement with the retiring President of IBTS, John David Hopper, to cover the deficit from the sale of the Rüschlikon property. This was the right of the EBF as the ultimate owner of IBTS, but was done without proper consultation with the Board of Trustees. It was a case of the General Secretary assuming to himself personal ecclesial powers not appropriate to the balance of power between the corporate (the EBF Council) and the personal (the appointed General Secretary). The longer term effect on EBF life was to create an atmosphere of caution with regard to Congresses. It has not proved possible to arrange a further Congress,[126] which has been judged by many within the leadership of EBF, to have been a weakening of *koinonia* between the churches.[127] The EBF Council has however, developed a plan for a weekend gathering in Amsterdam in 2009 as part of the commemoration of the founding of the first Baptist church in Europe in 1609.[128]

Representative Role in Ordination of Pastors

As seen in Chapter 2, the ecclesial nature of the EBF owed something to the initiative and theological understanding of British Baptists who were influential in establishing the constitutional and ecclesial nature of the EBF and looked very much to European traditions of emphasised interdependency.[129] J.H. Rushbrooke, in his travels in Europe after the First World War, might be regarded as a type of 'messenger' or overseer in the way understood by some Anabaptist groups and by the General Baptists.[130] As the EBF built upon the Oncken tradition, it is also clear that the importance of carrying forward certain traditions and order was seen to be a good thing. This is in marked contrast to the much more pragmatic and localised approach of the dominant traditions in the USA. Amongst European Baptists there are a variety of opinions about the meaning and practice of ordination amongst Baptists, but generally most Unions set aside and ordain specific people to the office of pastor or minister.

---

126 A Congress planned for Wroclau, Poland, in the late 1990s was cancelled because of concern about financial viability.

127 Prior to 1994 EBF Congresses had been held every five years either one or two years before a BWA Congress. These meetings preceded the formation of the EBF and their demise is much regretted in many parts of Europe.

128 For details, see Chapter 2.

129 H. Cook and E.A. Payne were influenced by the strong associational life of British Baptists and the messengers of the General Baptists. The German tradition of Oncken also strongly emphasised relationships between the churches as his Hamburg Centre expanded throughout Central and South Eastern Europe.

130 J.F.V. Nicholson, 'The Office of Messenger amongst British Baptists in the Seventeenth and Eighteenth Centuries', *BQ*, Vol. XVII, No. 5 (January 1958), pp. 206-23, and 'Towards a Theology of Episcope Amongst Baptists', *BQ*, Vol. XXX, No. 6 (April 1984), pp. 265-81.

As the 1993 document 'What are Baptists?' expresses it:

> Baptists also believe, however, that Christ calls some to exercise ministry of spiritual leadership with particular responsibilities for preaching, teaching and pastoral care. Among Baptists there has generally been a two-fold office of 'minister' and 'deacons'..... Within this accepted pattern, Baptist churches show some differences in their understanding of spiritual leadership. Most ordain their ministers by laying on of hands after they have completed their theological education. Some recognise the call of both men and women to be ministers whilst others recognise only men. Each Baptist church has the freedom to invite someone to serve it as minister, but some Baptist Unions will only designate as 'ministers' those who have had their vocation tested and approved by a wider group of churches than a single local church, thus recognising them as ministers of the Church Universal.... Within some Unions of churches, senior ministers are appointed to have pastoral care over a whole association of churches, though their authority [generally – KGJ] lies in the giving of counsel to a local church and its minister rather than exercising executive power over them.[131]

This statement reveals a general trend amongst European Baptists in taking the issue of ordination to the pastoral office very seriously. In the United Kingdom, Germany, Russia, Sweden, Czech Republic and many other Unions, the authorisation and supervision of ordination is closely bound up with the life of the Union itself. In Albania (a new Union) much debate is taking place about the steps necessary to ordain the first pastor, and the first Albanian Baptist to receive higher theological education made this the subject of his dissertation.[132]

Several Unions take, as their standpoint, the position adopted by the Baptist Union of Great Britain in 1948:

> Ordination is the act, wherein the Church, under the guidance of the Holy Spirit, publicly recognises and confirms that a Christian believer has been gifted, called

---

[131] 'What are Baptists? On the Way to Expressing Baptist Identity in a Changing Europe', EBF Division of Theology and Education, 1993. This paper was prepared following a Consultation on Mission of the EBF at Dorfweil in 1992 and arises out of the discussion there. It was circulated to EBF Unions for debate and further discussed at the European Baptist Theological Teachers' Conference in July 1992, with a revised draft being received at a meeting of the Theology and Education Division of the EBF Council in 1992, and further revisions incorporated at the EBF Council in 1993. It was commended for use amongst the EBF Unions by the EBF Council in 1992, Box 809, EBF Archive.

[132] A. Golloshi, 'Leadership in the Albanian Evangelical Community: A Theological Assessment of Paradigms, Practices and Vision', MTh Dissertation, IBTS, Prague, 2003.

> and set apart by God [with prayer] for the work of ministry and in the name of Christ commissions him [sic] for this work.[133]

This same report also sets out who should be involved in ordinations representing the wider church, stating: 'It seems proper that in the Service of Ordination there should be represented the Baptist Union, the Association, the College and neighbouring Baptist churches. The whole Baptist community is thus acting through its members.'[134] In a brief survey of patterns elsewhere, it was noted that ordination is regularly practised in a wide range of Unions, though in some cases, such as Germany, a period of probationary service is required before ordination.[135] This clear emphasis and intended involvement of the wider community, especially the translocal bodies, such as the Union, is less clear in other parts of the world, especially the USA. For instance, the SBC in 'Baptist Faith and Message', makes little reference to pastors, noted as follows:

> **Faith and Message 1925**
> **XII Gospel Church** – Its Scriptural officers are bishops, or elders and deacons.
>
> **Faith and Message 1963**
> **VI The Church** – Its Scriptural officers are pastors and deacons.
>
> **Faith and Message 2000**
> **VI The Church** – Its scriptural officers are pastors and deacons. While both men and women are gifted for service in the church, the office of pastor is limited to men as qualified by Scripture.[136]

At no point does the SBC suggest a trans-local or personal episkope role in ordination and at every point talks about the autonomy of the local church. However, in 1999 the BWA went so far as to declare:

> … early Baptists insisted that a local church was only a complete church when it had appointed its necessary spiritual leaders. These were the pastor, sometimes known as the elder or bishop, and deacons.... No one was ordained hastily… Most churches ordain pastors by the laying on of hands. In some conventions and unions, this occurs only after theological education has been completed. Although a local church is always free to call any person to serve as pastor, some Baptist

133 'The Meaning and Practice of Ordination Among Baptists', Report to the Council of the Baptist Union of Great Britain, 1957, BUGB Archives, Angus Library.
134 *Ibid.*, para. 50.
135 *Ibid.*, para. 46.
136 Baptist Faith and Message 1925, 1963, 2000. Comparison chart at www.sbc.net/bfm/bfmcomparison, accessed 7 December 2004.

> bodies will only accredit those ministers whose calling and gifts have been recognized by a wider representative body of churches. [137]

I have set out what might be regarded as a general position and sought to emphasise the greater importance of ordination in the majority European Oncken/English Baptist tradition – over against the more pragmatic, local church autonomy of the SBC – to explore a clear ecclesial issue, setting out the more-than-local role of the EBF General Secretary and the element of personal episkope which is recognised and often used. During the ministry of Karl Heinz Walter, as has been seen, the EBF underwent dramatic changes because of the collapse of communist regimes and the disintegration of the USSR. In certain Unions, especially those emerging as national Unions out of the All-Union Council of Evangelical Christian-Baptists, a major issue was to establish pastoral leadership in the churches and the Unions. In Bulgaria, where Baptists had undergone special persecution, there was a dearth of active pastors. For instance, in Sofia, Theodor Angelov, a biochemist, was, in effect, pastor of the central church in Sofia. He succeeded his father who had been imprisoned under the communists. It was unclear how an ordained pastoral succession was to be established in the Union, so Theo Angelov, and the Bulgarian Baptist Union, turned to Karl Heinz Walter, who journeyed to Sofia and performed the act of ordination of Theo Angelov in company with representatives of the local Baptist Union.[138] In the same way, in the Republic of Georgia the last ordained pastor and President of the Union, Guram Kumelashvili, was unwilling to make any move to continue the ordination of pastors. In the light of this the Union, together with the church in Tblisi, appealed to the EBF for help in ordaining Malkhaz Songulashvili.[139] Walter, participated in the ceremony with leaders of the Georgian Baptists and wide ecumenical representation.[140] Walter noted that, in an earlier generation, EBF General Secretary, Gerhard Claas, had also participated in an ordination in Georgia.

This approach of Unions, seeking to establish a sense of the wider trans-local and trans-national associating in ordination, appears to be a feature of European Baptist life, rather than a general Baptist understanding. The ministry of Karl Heinz Walter, who was always viewed as a skilled Bible teacher and spiritual mentor, appears to have been significant during the early to mid 1990s. The care taken by the Bulgarians and the Georgians may be seen as being in

---

[137] BWA Study and Research Division, *We Baptists* (Franklin, Tenn.: Providence House Publishers, 1999), pp. 29-30.

[138] Theo Angelov made specific reference to this act when he retired as EBF General Secretary in September 2004, Beirut, Lebanon. The facts are confirmed in a document to me from K.H. Walter dated 19 November 2004.

[139] Archbishop Malkhaz Songulashvili is currently the Presiding Bishop of the Baptist Union of Georgia and Pastor of Cathedral Baptist Church, Tblisi.

[140] Letter to the author from K.H. Walter, 19 November 2004.

marked contrast to somewhat irregular patterns of ordination that occurred in some Unions following the collapse of communism. Whilst it is not possible, nor appropriate within the scope of this chapter, to review less regular occurrences, it should be noted that the All-Union Council had maintained a proper spiritual role in approving and participating in ordinations of pastors during the communist years, often sending people considerable distances to ensure there was trans-local and ordained presence and participation in services of ordination. For example, Janis Turvits journeyed from Latvia to Klaipeda to ordain Albertis Latuzis as a pastor on behalf of the All-Union Council.[141] However, this function of providing oversight and valediction of ordination does not appear to have passed simply to the Euro-Asiatic Federation, a rather weak successor body. As we have demonstrated, some Unions preferred the more regularised and disciplined offices of the EBF, especially the on-going officer, the General Secretary, rather than the President, so, for instance, with the first ordination in the independent country of Macedonia in September 2006. EBF General Secretary, Tony Peck, preached and participated in the laying on of hands at the ordination of Marko Grozdanov in Macedonia, together with the Rector of IBTS and officers of the Baptist Union of Serbia. This trans-local personal episkopal role can be seen to be no passing issue, but carried forward through four decades of EBF life.

Conclusion

From the formation of the EBF it was seen to be important to have a stated office holder who had some permanency. The office of President was seen as giving status and honour to leading European Baptists and in the structure of a two-year term, to ensuring that the presidency could be moved around amongst the different regions and ethnic groups from the Atlantic to the Pacific and from the Barents sea to the source of the Nile.[142] The episkopal, or personal function in terms of time and service, has clearly been placed in the office of General Secretary. This title is connected with the development of baptistic denominations which marked out the role of an ordained pastor set aside for a period of years to provide oversight through service in a more-than-local ecclesial construct – an association, Union or Federation. Nevertheless, it is clear a personal episkopal element belongs to the office. In contrast to the EBF having over twenty-seven Presidents to date, it has only had nine General Secretaries, and each one has clearly been an important individual in the development of the work of the EBF, so that the period of their General Secretaryship can be seen to have marked the accent of the life of the

[141] Information supplied by the daughter of Alberis Latuzis, Lina Andronovienė, in a conversation on 7 December 2004.

[142] A list of Presidents of the EBF, with their country of domicile from 1950 until today, is provided in the Appendix.

Federation during that period.

Since W.O. Lewis, a North American working for the BWA, tentatively combined the new role of EBF General Secretary with that of BWA Associate Secretary, certain key issues have come to the fore and been hammered out on the anvil of experience as the EBF has developed a life in community which has been recognised and increasingly affirmed as an ecclesial community over against a societal or simply pragmatic movement. The first key development was the affirmation that the General Secretary belonged to and was appointed by the EBF and was answerable to the Council of the EBF, and although there was a close tie-in and relationship with the role of being BWA Regional Secretary, it has been shown in this chapter that, from Eric Rudén onwards, the EBF played the lead and major role in the appointment. In this process, the BWA is represented on the nominating group, but not with power to appoint someone to the EBF, nor the ability to veto an appointment agreed by the EBF. It is also clear that though the word 'Secretary' has been used, the leadership, ambassadorial (to other Christian World Communions and governments), episkopal, pastoral and representative (to the BWA, from the EBF to the member Unions etc) roles have developed and been affirmed by the European Baptist family.

As has been indicated, each individual Secretary has brought a particular strength to the post. The two we have examined most carefully each made a profound contribution to the development of the EBF in the key period of the 1980s and 1990s. Both served significant terms of service amounting to almost two decades. For Wümplemann, the pastoral nature of his calling and the deep convictions about the importance of theological education, seemed to enable the EBF family to develop a sense of true *koinonia* within the continent of Europe and, later, to include the communities in the Middle East and North Africa, from very different cultural and traditional backgrounds, without any noticeable or prolonged tension. The whole style of Wümplemann, in affirming and caring for people and situations, established a deep sense of family which has not even been strained too seriously by the attempts at division from fundamentalist elements within the SBC. At this point the EBF has been enabled to withstand the inevitable dangers of being pulled apart by varying theological traditions and by the attempts of some mission agencies from outside the continent to create their own following. In respect of Walter, we see the dynamism of the shift from pastoral and theological priorities to those of applied theology in the development of BRE, the creation of a structure of departments specialising in communication, mission, relationships with others and in theological reflection and education. This development was continued by his successor, Theo Angelov, who moved the mission agenda from discussion to hands-on involvement with the Indigenous Mission Programme begun in the twenty-first century.[143] So, the EBF not only exhibits a corporal sense of ecclesial reality involving the member bodies meeting and acting together in council, but there is also an important and respected personal element of episkope most clearly seen in the office of the 'General Secretary'.

---

[143] For analysis of this development see Chapter 7 on Mission in the World.

CHAPTER 6

Partnership in Mission: Inter-Continental Mission Work from the USA

Although Baptist life began in a recognisable form in Europe,[1] it became clear that the United States of America would prove to be the power-house of Baptist development. In 2004 about 75%[2] of people registered as baptised believers in membership with Baptist churches linked to the Baptist World Alliance (BWA) lived in the USA. This proportion may well change in coming years as Baptist communities in Asia and Africa expand. What has been most striking is that, though modern cross-cultural mission work by Baptists began in England with the Northamptonshire Association and the work of William Carey and the Baptist Missionary Society (formed in 1792),[3] it has been the North American Baptist mission thrust which has come to predominate in the world, with Europeans trailing far behind in calling, equipping and training missionaries who go to other countries to proclaim the Christian faith.[4] This cross-cultural mission thrust has been one of the prominent features of Baptist ecclesiology, and the development of specialist cross-cultural mission agencies – such as the Southern Baptist Convention-Foreign Mission Board (SBC-FMB) and the American Baptist Churches USA International Mission Department (ABC-IM), (formed as one body in 1814 as the General Missionary Convention of the

---

[1] All standard Baptist histories make this point, for example, H.L. McBeth, *The Baptist Heritage* (Nashville, Tenn.: Broadman Press, 1987), pp. 21-24, and W.H. Brackney, *The Baptists* (NewYork: Greenwood Press, 1988), pp. xvii - xix.

[2] Baptist World Alliance [BWA] *General Council Report Book*, Seville, Spain, 2002, pp. 197ff. BWA Library, Falls Church, VA. Of 44 million Baptist members, 33,300,000 belong to US Conventions. In 2004 the Southern Baptist Convention [SBC] withdrew from the BWA, but had been an active member from 1905 and many SBC churches are duly aligned to more than one convention. The SBC State Conventions of Texas and Virginia joined the BWA in their own right in 2005.

[3] See B. Stanley, *The History of the Baptist Missionary Society 1792-1992* (Edinburgh: T & T Clark, 1992), pp. 1-5.

[4] It is the claim of the SBC International Mission Board [SBC-IMB] that it is the world's largest Protestant cross-cultural mission agency with over 5,380 (2003) missionaries. Source www.imb.org, accessed 18 January 2003.

Baptist Denomination in the United States of America for Foreign Missions)[5] more shortly known as the Triennial General Missionary Convention[6] – have been major players in shaping Baptist life and thought. The Triennial Convention divided in 1843 over the appointment of slave owners as foreign missionaries.[7]

British and American agencies have worked cross-culturally in Europe in various ways. This chapter will seek to examine the role they played in the establishment of the European Baptist Federation (EBF) and the subsequent influence they have had both in shaping the EBF directly and by their influence on the member bodies of the EBF with whom they work. In particular we will look at the role played by mission agencies in the founding of the EBF, the development of what is now the International Baptist Theological Seminary (IBTS) of the EBF and the European Baptist Press Service (EBPS). The American and British Baptist communities became engaged in cross-cultural mission work in Europe long before the formation of the EBF, and it is important to indicate some of the situations in which this happened as it would be misleading to examine the role of the agencies in the formation and life of the EBF post 1949 without having at least an outline of their prior work. This chapter will seek to explore 'comity' agreements and the spheres of influence of the different mission agencies operating in Europe. What is the ecclesiological significance of their work? Who controls whom? How was influence used in shaping the life of the local churches and the unions? It will look at the attitudes to partnership amongst the differing agencies and their influence, notably in the changing missiological practice of the then SBC-FMB.

Mission Agencies in Europe

American involvement in European Baptist life came about in a variety of ways. One example is of the predecessor organisation[8] of ABC-IM which took

---

[5] The division of Baptists in the USA into the Northern and Southern Conventions, which developed very different cultures and missiological styles, is explained in B.J. Leonard, *Baptists in America* (New York: Columbia University Press, 2005), and McBeth, *The Baptist Heritage*. For the Triennial Convention and the various titles and dates of the mission agencies associated with what is now known as American Baptist Churches USA, see R.E. Schlosser, 'Chronological History of the Board of International Ministries', *American Baptist Quarterly*, Vol. XIV, June 1995, No. 2, pp. 108-21. Also, forthcoming, D. Van Broekhoeven, *The Baptist River* (Macon, Ga: Mercer University Press).

[6] The first meeting was held in 1817 with a 21-member Board of Commissioners, noted in Schlosser, 'Chronological History of the Board of International Ministries', p. 110.

[7] *Ibid.*, p.111.

[8] The American Baptist Missionary Union, now integral to American Baptist Churches USA International Mission Department [ABC-IM].

on mission work in Sweden, originally under the auspices of the American Baptist Publication Society. This Society had supported a former Lutheran Church priest, Anders Wiberg, who, after believer's baptism in the USA, became pastor of the Baptist Church in Stockholm in 1855.[9] By 1866, the American Baptist Missionary Union[10] had agreed to the establishment of a Swedish Seminary, the Betelseminariet, in Stockholm, about which J.H. Rushbrooke commented:

> Sweden possesses the oldest Baptist seminary on the continent. The wisdom of the American Baptist Mission Society in taking early steps to assist the training of ministers has been abundantly vindicated. In no European country – Britain not excepted – do Baptists form so large a percentage of the people; in none have they a stronger hold upon the educated classes, and in none do they enjoy more fully the respect of the entire Christian and non-Christian public. The lesson is easy to read, and it is confirmed by experience elsewhere. The trained evangelist and preacher is everywhere a necessity.[11]

Rushbrooke was writing in the 1920s, and the situation has changed much since then, but his point about the willingness of American Baptist Churches to establish and work with seminaries is an important one. The place of mission agencies in forming future generations of national and continental leaders is one that we shall return to.

Mention here should be made of Canadian Baptists, whom Rushbrooke encouraged to participate in European work in the early part of the century, particularly assisting Sunday Schools in Estonia and Latvia. The Canadians withdrew in the late 1920s because of lack of interest amongst Baptists in the Canadian provinces, only re-entering in the latter part of the century. The reasons for the withdrawal are set out in a letter from H.E. Stillwell to J.H. Rushbrooke[12] stating that it was impossible to get Canadian Baptists interested in European missions. Stillwell, himself anxious to help, summed up his frustration as follows:

> The result is we do not seem able to create interest. Now, the sum of all this is you had better make arrangements to provide for European Baptist Missions apart from Canadian assistance. I have just come from Western Canada where the Baptist body declined, in present circumstances, to undertake anything for

---

[9] A.W. Wardin (ed.), *Baptists Around the World* (Nashville, Tenn.: Broadman and Holman, 1995), p. 251.

[10] This name was adopted in 1846 by the Baptists in the northern states, in Schlosser, 'Chronological History of the Board of International Ministries', p. 111.

[11] J.H. Rushbrooke, *Some Chapters of European Baptist History* (London: Kingsgate Press,1929), p. 21.

[12] Letter from H.E. Stillwell to J.H. Rushbrooke, 2 February 1926, ABFMS Archive Box 254, American Baptist Historical Society, Valley Forge, Pa.

> Europe. The Maritime Baptists have undertaken nothing and I am unable to get them to do so. So it comes back to Ontario and Quebec and the result of our general appeal was less than $200. This being so, you should just count Canadian Baptists out.[13]

Rushbrooke was disappointed and pleaded with the Canadians to consider working with the Americans and British as possibilities opened up in Russia, but to no avail. The Canadians did enter the European scene later in the century in connection with francophone communities and in the development of youth leadership training.

Baptists from the USA were influential in supporting work in Catholic areas of Europe. An American Baptist Pastor, Howard Malcolm, having toured France in 1831 for health reasons, encouraged the American Baptist Missionary Society[14] to begin work there and, in 1832, John Casimir Rostan was appointed.[15] The influential founding-father missionary, Adoniram Judson, had been a prisoner in France and supported this development. He even offered to have support for his work in Burma reduced to enable this new development to commence. So, in 1832, Rostan, a native of Marseilles living in the USA, was sent to Paris. Despite his death from cholera thirteen months after arriving, the Board persevered in the desire to place missionaries in France.[16] The active participation of missionaries appointed by American Baptist Churches continued for a prolonged period.

In Italy, Southern Baptists began mission work in 1872. George B. Taylor from Virginia was appointed, and for thirty-four years, until his death in 1907, he was the director and inspirer of this enterprise.[17] Over the years, activities were developed in many places and, by 1915, there were over forty mission stations employing about thirty-eight Italian nationals.[18] Here is a feature which would become contentious and divisive in missiological theory later: the development of a major mission with a handful of cross-cultural full-time missionaries directing a work consisting mainly of local nationals. Again, the SBC-FMB, like its American Baptist Foreign Mission Society[19] counterpart, saw the need to establish theological training, and this was developed in Rome early in the twentieth century.

---

[13] *Ibid.*

[14] Now various bodies are amalgamated into ABC-IM.

[15] Schlosser, 'Chronological History of the Board of International Ministries', p. 110.

[16] See Pastor Robert Dubarry in J.H. Rushbrooke (ed.), *The Baptist Movement in the Continent of Europe* (London: Kingsgate Press, 1915), pp. 114-16.

[17] W. Kemme Landels in Rushbrooke, *The Baptist Movement on the Continent of Europe*, p. 126-127.

[18] *Ibid.*

[19] Name adopted in 1910, noted in Schlosser, 'Chronological History of the Board of International Ministries', p. 115.

The Triennial Conference of American Baptists also began supporting work in Germany, receiving a report on the remarkable Johann Gerhard Oncken from Barnas Sears, who went to Hamburg and baptised Oncken and six others on 22 April 1834.[20] The American Baptist Foreign Mission Board reported to their members in 1835:

> The Board immediately adopted measures to secure the services of Mr Oncken as a missionary and they placed, in the meanwhile, at the disposal of Professor Sears, a moderate sum, to be expended at his discretion, in promoting the cause of religion, in connection with the Baptist churches in Germany.... the Board have not yet been able to complete an arrangement with Mr Oncken, but they hope that he will soon be engaged in their service as a missionary. His piety, prudence, experience and zeal, justify a strong hope that he will be extensively useful.[21]

German Baptist influence was to spread across Europe. The American Baptist Churches took the view that they should support these indigenous German missionaries, rather than training and sending missionaries from the USA.[22] Southern Baptists, however, took a different view. Thus, SBC missionaries began to work in Hungary, for example, as part of the comity agreement of the London Conference in the 1920s and, in the same way as with Sweden, an early initiative was to help found a seminary in Budapest in 1920. A spacious building was acquired through the gift of a Southern Baptist laywoman, Varina Brown.[23] But, in some places, the role of Southern Baptist missionaries was resented, not least amongst German-speaking people in Hungary, and the German-speaking Baptists in the USA sent their own missionaries to work in the country in the earlier part of the century.[24]

The British Baptist Missionary Society (BMS) was more committed to cross-cultural mission work in Asia, Africa and the Caribbean, especially in countries which were part of the British Empire (later Commonwealth), than to Europe. However, inevitably, colporteurs and pastors from the British Isles travelled in Europe and some began evangelistic enterprises. From time to time

---

[20] See I.M. Randall, 'The Blessing of An Enlightened Christianity: North American Involvement in European Baptist Origins, *American Baptist Quarterly*, Vol. XX, March 2001, No. 1, p. 11.

[21] Report of the Board of the American Baptist Foreign Mission in the *American Baptist Magazine 1835*, pp. 229-33, American Baptist Historical Society, Valley Forge, Pa.

[22] This view was expounded by Ira Chase from Newton Theological Institute, following travels in France, and became known as the 'Chase Doctrine', see Randall, 'The Blessings of Enlightened Christianity, p. 7. Also S. Slade and R.S. Trulson in 'Planning and Partnering at American Baptist International Ministries' *American Baptist Quarterly*, Vol. XX, March 2001, pp. 51-7.

[23] See Rushbrooke, *The Baptist Movement in the Continent of Europe*, pp. 99-112.

[24] See Wardin, *Baptists Around the World*, p 263.

the BMS accepted involvement in Europe.[25] In 1870 the Minutes of the BMS record a £100 grant in aid being made to James Wall, who had gone from Calne in Wiltshire to undertake evangelism in Bologna.[26] In November of the same year the Treasurer of the BMS was empowered to receive contributions for the work in Italy, and a note later in the minutes records that Sir Samuel Morton Peto[27] praised the work of Wall, which he had personally observed over a seven-week period. In September 1871, Wall became a missionary of the BMS, and others were invited to join him. The General Baptist Missionary Society[28] also became involved, in supporting N.H. Shaw of Dewsbury who went to Rome, taking charge of the church at Via Urbana, which had been erected through the generosity of the Baptist holiday travel pioneer, Thomas Cook.[29] In various ways cross-cultural mission had an impact on Baptist life in Europe.

Developments to 1949

As can be seen, the two main North American Baptist mission societies – American Baptist Foreign Mission Society (ABC-FMS)[30] and the SBC-FMB[31] have had considerable involvement in European Baptist activity. Both had a natural interest in Europe, where many members of their supporting churches

---

[25] Whilst generally in the twentieth century there was a reluctance from the BMS to be involved in cross-cultural mission in Europe, possibly seeing it as less attractive to supporters than work in Africa and South America, this posture took a sharp change of direction in the 1980s with increasing contacts between British Baptists and Baptists in other parts of Europe. Under General Director, Reg G.S. Harvey and his successor, Alistair J. Brown, BMS became involved, from 1989 to the present, in Belgium, France, Italy, Croatia, Bulgaria, Czech Republic, Poland, Albania, Bosnia-Heregovina, Kosova and Kazakhstan.

[26] BMS Committee Minutes for 1870, BMS Archive, Angus Library, Regent's Park College, Oxford.

[27] Sir Samuel Morton Peto was a prominent Baptist layman and developed Bloomsbury Central Baptist Church, London. On Peto see Faith Bowers, *A Bold Experiment: Bloomsbury Central Baptist Church* (London: Bloomsbury Central Baptist Church, 1999), pp. 21-128.

[28] The General Baptist Missionary Society was the mission agency of the General Baptists of the New Connexion. It amalgamated with the Particular Baptist Missionary Society in 1891.

[29] See Landels, who was himself a British Baptist missionary in Italy, in Rushbrooke, *The Baptist Movement in the Continent of Europe*, p. 124.

[30] This title was adopted in 1910, see Schlosser, 'Chronological History of the Board of International Ministries', p. 115.

[31] In the rest of this chapter I will use the current titles of these two organisations. As has already become apparent, both organisations are products of a common history in the Triennial Conference and have developed by addition, absorption and name change over a period of a century.

had roots and looked to Europe as their ancestral home. The majority had become Baptists upon arriving in the USA and being confronted with the pioneer missionary spirit of the Baptist churches in the USA. This, in turn, led them to have an interest in seeing Baptist churches and ideas transplanted from the USA to the mainland of Europe. What has proved to be significant is the classic dilemma of how much each agency and their missionaries sought to engage with and support indigenous mission and how far what was offered, and supported, was a version of Baptist life and work shaped within the North American context. This has been reflected on extensively by missiologists[32] exploring the issue of how mission agencies of the global 'north' have succeeded or failed, to varying degrees, to engage in indigenisation in the global 'south', but nowhere near as much attention has been given to the 'new' world sending missionaries to the 'old'.[33]

In 1920 the BWA facilitated a meeting in London,[34] when various Baptist leaders gathered together and allocated specific countries to specific mission agencies. This allocation was based on a survey made by Charles A. Brooks, ABC representative in Europe, and J.H. Rushbrooke of England. Much information had been gathered through the assistance of diplomatic, consular and military representatives of Great Britain and the USA.[35] Whilst, as Rushbrooke often commented, 'The London Conference had no authoritative or executive character and its decisions were merely recommendations to a number of autonomous administrative bodies,'[36] nevertheless, the outcomes were taken with the utmost seriousness by the bodies involved and addressed three main topics: cooperative relief programmes in post-war Europe, coordinated mission policy (the comity agreements) and the appointment of Rushbrooke as Baptist Commissioner for Europe. Later he also became BWA

---

[32] For instance David Bosch, J. Andrew Kirk, Andrew F. Walls, Vincent J. Donovan and historians of mission such as Brian Stanley.

[33] I use these terms as they are generally understood: 'North' meaning developed nations in Europe, USA and Australasia; 'South' implying the regions of Africa, Asia and, to a lesser extent, Latin America; 'New' meaning the USA and Canada; 'old' generally implying West and Central Europe. They are not finite and academic definitions, but essentially populist terms which do have a wide currency in the media, amongst NGOs and in some non-specialist academic writing.

[34] C.A. Brooks and J.H. Rushbrooke, *Report of the Commissioners of the Baptist World Alliance*, presented at the Conference in London (London: Baptist Union Publications, 1920).

[35] British diplomatic and military assistance had been assisted by a letter from Prime Minister David Lloyd George to J.H. Shakespeare, expressing interest in the fact-finding visit by Rushbrooke.

[36] J.H. Rushbrooke, 'The Present Situation in Europe: Significant and Hopeful Developments, 1920-1927', 24 April 1928, p. 1, Typescript, ABFMS Archive Box 254.

Secretary for the Eastern Hemisphere, when J.H. Shakespeare[37] resigned in 1925.[38] In terms of the comity proposals, the SBC were given responsibility for Italy, Hungary, Rumania, Yugoslavia, parts of Russia and Spain,[39] ABC were given responsibility for France, Belgium, French-speaking Switzerland, Norway, Denmark, Poland, Czechoslovakia (also with Great Britain), Austria and the low countries, and Great Britain was given responsibility for Finland (with Sweden), Latvia, Lithuania, Estonia, Northern Russia (all jointly with ABC and the Canadians, if willing), Holland (with Australia). Some countries not represented in London accepted allocations made by the Conference: Australia for Holland, Brazil for Portugal, Canada for Estonia and Latvia, and the German-Americans for German-speaking churches in many lands and mission work in Bulgaria.[40] Throughout the 1920s and into the 1930s there was a common desire, in both North America and Europe, to work together at strengthening European Baptist life and work.

During the 1930s, with the growth of National Socialism in Germany, tensions began to arise in European Baptist relationships. The BWA established a commission on 'Nationalism' to explore the phenomenon and, in 1934, the report was published under the leadership of Nils Johan Nordström, Vice-President of the Swedish Baptists, who commented:

> We Baptists are convinced that the Church of Jesus Christ can never be a tool for nationalistic endeavours without losing her power and denying her mission to the world; that any sort of dependency on the State, which restricts her freedom to exercise love in the world, represents a real danger for the church and reduces her opportunities to carry the gospel to the ends of the world.[41]

German Baptists had always lived in a situation of difficulty because of the dictum of the Lutheran Church that the 'faith of the prince determines the faith of the people', and thus gathering free churches were always in an invidious

---

[37] On Shakespeare see P. Shepherd, *The Making of a Modern Denomination: John Howard Shakespeare and The English Baptists 1898-1924* (Carlisle: Paternoster, 2001). This is based on Shepherd's University of Durham doctoral dissertation.

[38] J.H. Rushbrooke served in this dual capacity from 1925 until the BWA Congress in Toronto in 1928, when he became General Secretary of the BWA, and the post of Commissioner for Europe was abolished.

[39] Spain had previously been the responsibility of ABC. In 1939 Dr Maddry of SBC had been reported as saying SBC was 'returning Spain to the Alliance'. However, the BWA Executive Committee noted this was not possible as the work in Spain had never been the responsibility of the BWA. BWA Executive Minutes, 21 July 1939, Atlanta, BWA Executive Committee Archives, American Baptist Historical Society, Valley Forge, Pa.

[40] Minutes of the London Conference 1920, pp. 18-19. Abstract in ABFMS Archive Box 254.

[41] N.J. Nordström, Report from the BWA Commission on 'Nationalism', BWA Fifth World Congress, BWA Archive, Valley Forge, Pa.

position. They had initially welcomed the Weimar Republic because, for the first time, the constitution guaranteed the demand of the separation of church and state, but this was not realised.[42] Nonetheless, many German Baptists were carried along by enthusiasm for the new order, as a bulwark against the perceived threat of communism and because of the talk about 'positive Christianity', which came from many of the leaders around Adolf Hitler. Inevitably, such attitudes placed them at odds with some other Unions in Europe and with the general attitudes of the mission agencies. The German Baptists themselves recognised that, after the controversial election of a Reichsbishop, there was pressure for them to be incorporated into this ecclesiastical structure. To resist was to be 'not German'. The Baptists' foreign and international links also contributed to this impression.[43] In this climate difficulties ensued about relationships. The venue of the BWA Congress, which was postponed until 1934, when it was still held in Berlin, caused problems. Erich Geldbach believes that, in the end, German Baptists and the BWA engaged in a massive self-deception.[44] J.H.Y. Briggs comments that German Baptists saw Hitler and the National Socialists providing them with powerful patronage, which they thought they could deploy against the Lutheran Church.[45]

The Second World War meant a severing of contacts between mission agencies in the USA and Britain and the continent of Europe. During these years some in Germany imagined a world in which German Baptist interests would be supreme. They considered an alternative organisation to the BWA and being freed from the influence of North Americans. One such was Paul Schmidt who was 'taken in by the Nazis and believed that they would be victorious'.[46] Schmidt was a delegate to the Oxford Conference in 1937 and opposed the message of sympathy to the Confessing Church.[47] Apparently, during the war, Schmidt[48] 'journeyed into Denmark, Norway and Holland, or at any rate wrote to Baptists in these occupied lands assuring them that Germany

[42] A. Strübind, 'German Baptists and National Socialism', *JEBS*, Vol 8, No. 3, May 2008.

[43] See A. Strübind, *Die unfreie Freikirche, Der Bund der Baptistengemeinden im, Dritten Reich* (Wuppertal/Zürich: Neukirchen-Vluyn, 1991), pp. 80-86.

[44] E. Geldbach, 'The Years of Anxiety and World War II', in R.V. Pierard (ed.), *Baptists Together in Christ 1905-2005* (Birmingham, Al.: Samford University Press, 2005), p. 74-99.

[45] Note to the author, 22 February 2007.

[46] Letter from E.A. Payne to D.T. Priestley, 4 June 1971, BWA Europe Papers Box 2, Angus Library.

[47] Bernard Green, forthcoming book on Baptists and the Second World War.

[48] Schmidt sought to defend his position on the basis of Romans 13 in a paper 'Unser Weg' (Our Road) given at the German Baptist Union Council, 24-26 May 1946, in Velbert. Translation copy in BWA Europe Box 2, Angus Library.

would win and suggesting a new organization to replace the BWA'.[49] Others had a very different outlook. In the midst of the war, W.O. Lewis, BWA General Secretary, was already beginning to anticipate the need to have a specific post-war plan for the North American mission agencies to address the situation in Europe. On 6 January 1943 he sent his proposals to Dana Albaugh at the American Baptist Foreign Mission Society.[50] Lewis set out three areas where he believed help could be provided, recognising:

> It is impossible at the beginning of 1943 to see the shape of things to come. But whatever the boundaries or form of government may be, we can be sure there will be great distress everywhere on the Continent and there will be hatred and bitterness that it will take many decades to overcome.[51]

His first priority was relief work. He advocated a joint investigative group from ABC and SBC to visit Europe as soon as hostilities were over. Then he argued for the importance of the mission societies making a serious contribution to the evangelization of Europe. He warned against uncertainty and vacillation. Lewis went on to review the 1920 decisions and reflect on them in the light of the political situation, arguing that 'emphasis should be laid on the education of leaders. Seminaries should be strengthened.' Lewis also argued that at least one person should be placed in the heart of Europe to keep in touch with the Unions.[52] Here was a vision of authentic Baptist community in Europe.

These concerns for commitment to renewal were echoed by British Baptist General Secretary, M.E. Aubrey. In August 1944 he wrote to W.O. Lewis describing the various agencies established involving Baptists.[53] Aubrey also said that an appeal for £150,000 was being launched by British Baptists for reconstruction work, and £50,000 of this would be earmarked for work in Europe. After the war there was a general desire, particularly in BWA circles, to restore friendly relations as soon as possible. Rushbrooke and Lewis gave themselves at once to planning the 1947 BWA Copenhagen Congress.

---

[49] Letter from E.A. Payne to D.T. Priestley, 9 August 1969. Payne had been given details of this by J.H. Rushbrooke 'who was in a position to know', BWA Europe Box 2, Angus Library.

[50] W.O. Lewis, 'Northern Baptists and Post War Europe', 5 January 1943, 15 pp. typescript, BWA, Washington DC, Box I 2.1, BWA Archive.

[51] *Ibid.*

[52] This recommendation was acted upon, with Edwin A. Bell appointed, who began his work in 1945.

[53] Letter from M.E. Aubrey to W.O. Lewis, 11 August 1944. One important point was that the United Nations organisation established for Reconstruction in Europe had, as Chairman, the prominent Baptist layman, the Rt Hon Ernest Brown MP, Chancellor of the Duchy of Lancaster, and Aubrey noted he would be sympathetic to Baptist concerns, Box I 2.2, BWA Archive.

However, there was uncertainty. Ernest Payne later recorded:

> M.E. Aubrey was in favour of waiting. Paul Schmidt and one or two other German Baptist leaders kept in the background for some years. They never altogether escaped from the cloud that hung over them in the eyes of many for their failure to stand with the Confessing Church leaders in the 1930s, their ultra nationalist attitudes and their refusal to join in the reconciling work of the ecumenical movement. ... Many of us tried hard to get Dr Lewis to set down what he knew, but we could never bring him to the point of doing so.[54]

Despite the caution of some, at the end of the Second World War the BWA called another conference in London, held in 1948. Some planning for this event took place in Oslo on 27 February 1948, when European members of the BWA Relief Committee met with incoming BWA General Secretary, Arnold T. Ohrn, to engage in preparing for the event. It took place in Baptist Church House, London, on 13-14 August 1948.[55]

The group of Baptist leaders present, which included W.O. Lewis, Erik Rudén, Johannes Norgaard and Edwin Bell,[56] agreed to ask all the Unions to submit in advance 'a complete a picture as possible of conditions and needs, spiritual and otherwise: number of members, churches, trained preachers, educational institutions, staff, students and buildings'.[57] It was also agreed that cooperating Mission Boards should make submissions indicating what had been done since the previous conference in 1920. The minutes of that meeting would be made available to delegates.[58] The intention of the 1948 Conference was described by Edwin Bell as being to look at:

> 1. The mandate system (for want of a better term);
> 2. Theological education on the continent;
> 3. Relief;
> 4. Reconstruction.[59]

Lewis seemed hesitant about this meeting, appearing to be concerned about the deteriorating conditions in Europe and possibly mindful of the ambivalent

---

[54] Letter from E.A. Payne to D. T. Priestley, 4 June 1971, BWA Europe Box 2, Angus Library.

[55] Minutes of the BWA Relief Committee Executive, Oslo, February 1948, ABFMS Archive Box 395, and London Conference File, Box 3.23H, BWA Archive.

[56] Unfortunately, the Chairman of the European Section of the BWA Relief Committee, B. Grey Griffith, was not present, but it was agreed he should be fully informed by W.O. Lewis about all the issues discussed to avoid any bottleneck in action.

[57] Minutes of the BWA Relief Committee Executive, Oslo, February 1948, ABFMS Archive Box 395.

[58] *Ibid.*

[59] Letter from E.A. Bell to M.D. Farnum, 4 March 1948, ABFMS Archive Box 395.

role of certain German Baptist leaders during the war and fearing tensions in the gathering. Nevertheless, the mission agencies and Europeans were convinced there was real value in such a round table in the pattern of the 1920 meeting. Bell wanted the preparatory work done to enable the agenda to be addressed, and wrote to Marlin Farnum in New York on 14 April 1948 saying:

> If the plans discussed there are carried through with a fair degree of thoroughness they should produce satisfactory preparation for the Conference. The only thing I am afraid of is that some of these things may go by default in the hesitation and uncertainty which Dr Lewis has manifested about having the Conference as such, and substituting a meeting of the BWA Executive Committee instead.[60]

This crucial meeting did go ahead as intended and, amongst the many decisions taken, one was to end the comity agreement which gave certain societies a mandate for certain areas. J.D. Hughey commented later: 'Leave each Baptist body in Europe free to receive aid from any other group in the Baptist World Alliance as might be agreed by all involved'.[61] Hughey, and his immediate colleagues in SBC and ABC took this as a signal, not only to develop mission work in many European countries, but also to engage in pan-European developments which initially involved both mission agencies in institution-building. Foremost in these capacity-building moves was the EBF itself and the establishment of the Rüschlikon Seminary. Amongst the institutions marked out for help was the German Baptist Seminary in Hamburg. The Principal, Hans Luckey, prepared, in 1949, a paper reflecting on the parlous state of his institution.[62] He described the difficult circumstances of both pastors and students 'occupied with finding a place to live and with getting enough to live on that they have had little time for spiritual things', but he went on to refer to the wider support being received and:

> recent visits of Baptist professors from England have greatly strengthened and inspired us. We have in mind especially recent visits of Prof. E.A. Payne of Regent's Park, of Prof E.C. Rust of Rawdon, and of Prof. G.H. Davies of Bristol.[63]

Reporting to the BWA Executive Committee in Cleveland, Ohio, on 20 July 1950, W.O. Lewis, in retrospect, said that the 1948 Conference 'marks one of

---

[60] Letter from E.A. Bell to M.D. Farnum, 14 April 1948, ABFMS Archive Box 395.
[61] J.D. Hughey, *Baptist Partnership in Europe: The HOW of Christian Missions in Europe today* (Nashville, Tenn.: Broadman Press, 1982), p. 15.
[62] Hans Luckey, 'Our Seminary and German Baptists since the war', 1949, BWA Europe Box 2, Angus Library.
[63] *Ibid.*, p. 3.

the turning points in the history of the Baptist World Alliance'.[64]

SBC, ABC and EBF: Laying Foundations

In conjunction with the 1952 BWA Executive Committee held in Tølløse, Denmark, two years after the founding of the EBF, a special 'Committee on Cooperation in Europe' met to review what had happened since the 1948 meeting in London. Theodore F. Adams, pastor of First Baptist Church, Richmond, Virginia, presided at this meeting and the report made to the BWA Executive rejoiced: 'in the progress made in work in Europe since the London Conference in 1948 and recommends that we reaffirm the principles adopted at that time, with such changes in wording as are called for by the formation of the European Baptist Federation'.[65]

Adams went on to report closer cooperation between the various national bodies and the European, Scandinavian and American mission boards and societies. Certainly, the early years of the EBF seemed to mark a high point in cooperation, greatly assisted by the friendship between W.O. Lewis, E.A. Bell and George Sadler. This conference, however, posed a challenge for ABC. Edwin Bell had been based in Paris since his arrival in Europe in 1946. Now plans were afoot to create a seminary in Switzerland and J.D. Franks of the SBC-FMB, who was responsible for relief coordination, had been located there. American Baptists, however, were involved with the World Council of Churches (WCC), which had located to Geneva. The European context was changing.

Dana Albaugh, Chairman of the Europe Department of ABC, rehearsed the arguments for and against relocating the office to Zürich:

1. There is value in keeping as close as possible to SBC;
2. The office would be near enough to the WCC in Geneva;
3. Might enable the strengthening of the relationship between BWA (in which Southern Baptists will be strong) and WCC.

However, Albaugh also recognised some negative issues in relocating. One was that an uncooperative attitude from the Southern Baptists might hamper action by ABC. Another issue was that some in the ABC leadership felt the right way forward was close contact with the WCC and to be based in Geneva might be more useful given the wider Protestant and world contacts.[66] In the event,

---

[64] BWA Executive Committee Minutes, Cleveland Ohio, July 1950, item 10, p. 5, BWA Archive.

[65] BWA Executive Committee, Denmark, 4-8 August 1952, item 46, p. 1, BWA Archive.

[66] Letter from D.M. Albaugh to E.A. Bell, 27 September 1948, ABFMS Archive Box 395.

Edwin Bell did relocate to Zürich, making it possible for ABC to become involved with the Rüschlikon Seminary and to maintain a reasonable working relationship with the SBC representatives in Europe until the events of 1989 and 1990 led to a change in personnel and approach by the SBC.[67]

When the EBF was founded, one development was that W.O. Lewis, a missionary of ABC, became the first General Secretary, whilst continuing as BWA Associate General Secretary for Europe and Director of the BWA Relief Programme. Lewis, though past European retirement age, continued to be supported by the Foreign Mission Board of ABC, and the member bodies of EBF provided modest contributions for the office and related costs of the EBF. The appointment of Henry Cook in 1955 was seen as temporary and he was taken care of financially by his home (British) Union. All the office costs for the EBF were born by the member bodies. In 1959, with the appointment of Erik Rudén, the needs of the EBF became greater. EBF work increased and the role of regional representative of the BWA began to decrease. In 1958 the budget of the EBF was US$500, but the proposed budget for 1959 was lifted to US$ 19,000.[68] In late 1958 the EBF Finance Committee met and George Sadler of SBC suggested that the two mission boards assume responsibility for US$ 15,000 of the US$ 19,000 EBF budget for 1959. The proportions proposed did cause concern as Erik Rudén wrote to Edwin Bell, 'I know that some SBC people have raised objections to American support of the European Baptist Federation because this organisation is and must be a European and not an American affair'.[69] George Sadler's view, expressed to Erik Rudén, was, 'I believe an appropriate amount [of money] could be found for any deficit which might accrue because of the failure of the European Unions to play worthy parts in the programme of the European Baptist Federation'.[70] This was comforting, but perhaps undermined to some extent European responsibility.

George Sadler had expressed caution about the willingness of the European Unions to address the enlarged mission budget of EBF. However, Edwin Bell took a more positive view of the action and interest of the larger western Unions, writing to Rudén:

> I am happy indeed for the interest which the leaders in Germany and England are manifesting in the work of the Federation and the prospect of the implementation of this interest by financial support. This is very encouraging and I believe that the

---

[67] 1989 saw the defunding of IBTS leading to the resignation of the Area Vice-President for Europe, Isam Ballenger and the Area Director for Europe, G. Keith Parker.

[68] Letter from E. Rudén to G.W. Sadler, 5 February 1959, Erik Rudén Papers, Box 1, Angus Library.

[69] Letter from E. Rudén to E.A. Bell, 20 January 1959, Erik Rudén Papers, Box 1, Angus Library.

[70] Letter from G.W. Sadler to E. Rudén, 10 February 1959, Erik Rudén Papers, Box 1, Angus Library.

> generous action by the Baptist groups in these two countries along with Sweden, as the three leading countries of Baptist life in Europe, will stimulate the other groups to respond in similar manner.[71]

Certainly development of pan-European structures was aided by the spirit of post-war cooperation which existed amongst leading European Baptists such as Henry Cook, Rudolf Thaut, Hans Luckey and Henri Vincent. However, at this early stage in the development of these pan-European bodies, the cooperation between Joseph Nordenhaug, George Sadler of the SBC-FMB and Edwin A. Bell of ABC cannot be over-emphasised, for it was the financial resources of SBC and ABC which provided the buildings and staffing for the Seminary at Rüschlikon and, in the first years of the EBF, 'the Federation was still dependent upon the help of the American Conventions'.[72]

The Seminary and the EBF were, in fact, often linked together. George W. Sadler, first President of IBTS, Rüschlikon and later special representative of the SBC-FMB in Europe, writing in the *European Baptist* on his time in Europe commented:[73]

> The EBF and the Baptist Theological Seminary of Rüschlikon are almost twins. Both have grown vigorously during the past eleven years and together, they have accomplished the unbelievable. Never before in the history of European Baptists has such unity and forward-lookingness been accomplished. Indeed, it could not have been said prior to 1948 that there was such an entity as 'European Baptists'..... Since that time, there has developed a spirit of oneness which has resulted in the organization of a women's missionary group,[74] a home missions program and a foreign mission board.[75]

Sadler went on to comment that the change of circumstance which allowed for these pan-European developments was the BWA-sponsored meeting held in London in 1948 when the old comity agreement gave way to the principle that 'any national Baptist organization is free to cooperate with any other Baptist

---

[71] Letter from E.A. Bell to E. Rudén, 15 January 1959, Erik Rudén Papers, Box 1, Angus Library.

[72] Treasurers' Report to the EBF Council, Hamburg, Germany, 1968, Box 801, EBF Archive. In 1967 the EBF member Unions had given £674 to the work of the EBF and ABC, alone, had given £1571!

[73] G.A. Sadler was writing in the *European Baptist*, April 1960, shortly after being presented with the Rüschlikon Scroll of Honor for service to European Baptist and IBTS life.

[74] The formation of the European Baptist Women's Union [EBWU], to which Sadler refers, predates that of the EBF. See Y. Pusey, *European Baptist Women's Union: Our Story 1948-1998* (Oakham, Rutland: EBWU, 1998).

[75] The European Baptist Mission (EBM), formed in 1952, and representing many of the Baptist Unions in Western and Central Europe.

bodies or mission boards within the fellowship of the BWA' and that the 'various mission boards be asked to consult each other and to cooperate with the European Baptist Committee'[76] to avoid duplication or neglect of any area.[77]

Although there was freedom, there also needed to be focus. The development of the Seminary at Rüschlikon was crucial: it became a resource in the shaping of the EBF. Though ownership of the Seminary only formally passed to the EBF from the SBC-FMB in 1988, from the beginning, Sadler, then Nordenhaug, saw the role such an international institution, training pastors and leaders from across Europe, could have in creating a climate of cooperation amongst Baptists in Europe. The Seminary, developing in parallel with the EBF itself and acting as a venue for many key EBF meetings and conferences, became a natural focus of European Baptist life. ABC saw the important strategic role of the Seminary and so based Lahrson in Zürich and later provided missionary personnel to serve on the faculty. Amongst these was Denton Lotz, later to become General Secretary of the BWA.[78] The vision of some, such as Charles A. Brooks and Rushbrooke, had been for a European-wide institution that had the strongest possible academic standing. They wrote in 1920:

> The centre chosen for such an institution must offer ample facilities for every grade of education, including the most advanced university training which Baptist students may be capable of receiving. It is needful that long views should be taken, and that in shaping a policy for the evangelization of Europe, the BWA should have in view the preparation of competent theological tutors, apologists and writers, as well as itinerant evangelists and local pastors. The proximity of a university is therefore essential, and this university must be one in which Baptist students would be placed under no disadvantage and in which Baptist tutors could find a place among the members of staff.[79]

Not all of this was achieved, but the importance of Rüschlikon was apparent when European Baptist leaders and North American mission agency representatives met in Denmark at the time of the BWA Executive Committee in 1952. Under the chairmanship of Theodore Adams (ABC), the special Committee on Cooperation in Europe singled out the 'need for more and better trained pastors and leaders', remarking on the requirement to strengthen

---

[76] A Committee of the BWA, which preceded the formation of the EBF and which consisted of members of the BWA Executive Committee resident in Europe.

[77] Minutes of the 1948 London Meeting quoted in *The European Baptist*, April 1960, p. 5, EBF Archive, IBTS, Prague.

[78] D. Lotz, ABC missionary in Europe, based at Rüschlikon 1971-1982, BWA General Secretary 1986-2007. Josef Nordenhaug, SBC missionary in Europe, President of Rüschlikon 1950-1960, BWA General Secretary 1960-1970.

[79] Brooks and Rushbrooke, *Report of Commissioners of the BWA*, pp. 35-36.

national seminaries but also advocating '(t)he further expansion and strengthening of the excellent work already so well begun at the Seminary in Rüschlikon'.[80]

During this foundational period, the BWA Associate Secretary for Europe, W.O. Lewis was an ABC pastor, and the founder and first President of the Rüschlikon Seminary, George A. Sadler, was a Southern Baptist missionary responsible, as Area Director, for work in Europe. Edwin A. Bell served as ABC representative in Europe.[81] Each of these made an important contribution to developing European Baptist life. There was a general belief that the Southern Baptists were the more argumentative of the two main North American groups and theologically more conservative. But there was a relaxed attitude. On the eve of founding the EBF, W.O. Lewis was writing to Jessie R. Ford, Secretary to Arnold T. Ohrn, BWA General Secretary, about his plans to be in the BWA offices in Washington DC and said:

> I am almost dying to hear you tell about the meeting of the Southern Baptist Convention. A letter from R. Paul Caudhill[82] says everything went off very well. It would be a great joke if the Southern Baptists were better behaved in Chicago than the Northern Baptists in Boston.[83]

Ford replied:

> The Convention in Chicago was interesting. It was the most peaceful thing I have attended. It hardly seemed like a Baptist meeting without some argument or discussion.... My personal opinion is that probably a good deal went on behind the scenes, and also that being in a 'furrin' country had something to do with it.... Maybe we are really getting 'religion' both north and south.[84]

The spirit of cooperation seemed to be evident.

As already noted in Chapter 4, the idea of having a seminary covering a significant part of Europe had been set out in the Commissioners Report to the 1920 Conference,[85] where they argued 'this Bohemian city (Prague) might be

---

[80] BWA Executive Committee Minutes, August 1952, p. 13, item 46, BWA Archive.

[81] Edwin A Bell served in a distinguished way as ABC Missions representative in Europe. Papers connected with his ministry are found in ABFMS Archive Box 395.

[82] R.P. Caudhill was a Southern Baptist Pastor and Chairman of the BWA Relief Committee.

[83] Letter from W.O. Lewis to J.R. Ford, 25 May 1950, BWA Correspondence Box 22, Angus Library.

[84] Letter from J.R. Ford to W.O. Lewis, 29 May 1950, BWA Correspondence Box 22, Angus Library. The reference to 'furrin' (foreign) country is because Chicago is not in a southern state and out of the traditional venue area for SBC Conventions.

[85] Brooks and Rushbrooke, *Report of the Commissioners of the Baptist World Alliance*, p. 35.

chosen as the home of a preachers' training college, having in view the preparation of pastors and evangelists'.[86] Because the new Republic of Czechoslovakia had placed a high value on religious freedom under the first President, T.G. Masaryk, and a Protestant Theological Faculty had been established in the historic Charles University, the Commissioners naturally looked there, where a promising young Baptist, Henry Prochazka, had recently gained a doctorate.[87] However, no move forward was made on this topic from the 1920 Conference and it was only after the 1948 Conference that an initiative was taken, but not in respect of Prague – then within the communist sphere of influence – but to Zürich-Rüschlikon, though the Seminary did ultimately move to Prague in 1996, seventy-six years after the recommendation of Brooks and Rushbrooke.

Mission in the Post-War Period

When the EBF was founded, an existing agenda was inherited, since the North American mission agencies and the BWA had been cooperating with European Baptists for many years. The first Secretary of the EBF, W.O. Lewis, was also Director of the BWA Relief Department. European Baptists were still much affected by the events of the Second World War with significant issues of displaced persons, the need for church reconstruction and debate as to how to take care of many of the older and retired pastors from Eastern Europe who found themselves in Germany without any means of support. Lewis, travelling around Europe relating to the Unions, also sought to identify needs which could be met by the mission agencies, the British Baptist Continental Committee and the BWA Relief Committee. An important aspect of this work was inevitably coordination. His principal colleague in the USA was R. Paul Caudhill, Pastor of First Baptist Church, Tennessee (Southern Baptist), who was Chairman of the BWA Relief Committee. Lewis wrote to him in May 1951 reporting on various issues in Germany. A decision had been taken to establish a home for old people in Münich in the Maria Ward Strasse, part of the Nymphenberg district of the city. Lewis reported he had set up a Committee of seven to oversee the project.[88] He was also able to report that it was possible for non-German organisations to purchase 'block Marks' at a good rate for building projects and some of these had been used for the home in Münich:

---

[86] *Ibid.*, p. 3.

[87] Dr Prochazka was later to be Dean of the Faculty, though there was some suspicion that he was too cooperative to the communist authorities in the 1950s.

[88] Letter from W.O. Lewis to R.P. Caudhill, 5 May 1951, BWA/EBF Letter File Box 24, Angus Library.

> Norquist[89] has made application for DM 500,000 more of these cheaper marks and has received a licence to use them. We have to report to the authorities each time what we are using the marks for. This is a wonderful privilege. The house in Münich which we expected to cost about US$15,000 has cost us little over US$7,000. No German living inside Germany can buy them legally. It now looks as if the Southern Baptists and Northern Baptists are going to put at our disposal an interesting sum of money to help our German brethren rebuild some important chapels in their cities.[90]

Inevitably, the mission agencies and the BWA, in their desire to help, struggled with the many controls exercised by the German Government and the occupying power. A particular difficulty in which Lewis became involved was in the provision of coffee and cotton to a German Baptist organisation, the Bruderhilfe. Throughout 1950 an investigation was carried out by the Bonn Government and the regional government of Hesse. The German Baptists had to make new arrangements to separate out their own accounting from that of the Bruderhilfe, and Sadler remained in close contact with them, reporting to the BWA in April 1950:

> Our brethren are waiting and hoping that they may finally be told that in view of the good that was done, they are to be excused for any irregularities in accordance with a sort of general amnesty which it is believed the Government officials will soon issue.[91]

The mission agencies, whilst anxious to help and not to dictate in areas such as the reconstruction of European Baptist buildings, were obviously intent on being heavily involved from the beginning and being part of developing plans.

The Seminary in Hamburg was in special need. Re-opening after the war, it had run up debts on re-building and paying salaries. This was, in part, due to a failure of the German Baptist Union to hand over funds intended for the Seminary as these had been diverted to other programmes as an emergency measure and in anticipation that funds for the Seminary would come in future years.[92] However, the situation had become critical when the Seminary was

---

89 Norquist was working in Europe for the Swedish-American Baptists in relief work, and served until 1952, when he was recalled to the USA. Report of W.O. Lewis to the BWA Relief Committee, 17 April 1951, submitted to the BWA General Secretary and Relief Committee. BWA/EBF Letter File Box 24, Angus Library.

90 Letter from W.O. Lewis to R.P. Caudhill, 5 May 1951, BWA/EBF Letter File Box 24, Angus Library.

91 Report on relief work in Germany, W.O. Lewis, April 1951, BWA/EBF Papers Box 24, Angus Library.

92 Lewis had reported this problem to A.T. Ohrn in 1950 and expressed concern about the actions of the German Union leadership, even though he understood the reasons for their actions, BWA/EBF Papers Box 22, Angus Library.

charged 9% interest on the debt. On 7 April 1951, a group of leaders gathered in a hotel at Schwenningen, south east of Stuttgart, where a new chapel was to be dedicated, and the situation of the Seminary in Hamburg was discussed. Amongst those present were Jesse D. Franks and John D. Watts (Southern Baptist missionaries based at Rüschlikon), Edwin A. Bell (ABC representative in Europe), W.O. Lewis (EBF/BWA) and some of the German union leadership. Lewis records:

> Knowing how difficult it is to appeal to our friends in America for money to pay debts, we agreed that it would probably be better for us to pay the running expenses of the seminary for a year, and ask our German brethren to concentrate on paying the debts.[93]

Here can be seen the cooperative relationship operating with three North American-based mission and aid agencies, a relationship which seems to have been a mark of this period and which indicated a desire to uphold the ecclesial integrity of Baptists in Europe.

A continuing need throughout the 1950s was funding for building projects – especially new churches. Both Bell and Sadler, and then later Nordenhaug, sought to support German Baptists in a strategic building plan, but as the German economy improved and other mission possibilities opened up elsewhere, American Baptists sought to indicate to the German leadership that fellowship support for new church and community buildings could not continue as it had in the immediate post-war years. The West German Baptists were conscious of this, but pointed out that 40% of the Baptist membership in Germany was behind the Oder-Neisse line and, with the movement of displaced persons, this had added to the problems they faced. A meeting between the German Baptist Building Commission and Bell in the autumn of 1956 sought to clarify the situation and address possible expectations. This resulted in a three-year programme (1957-1959) asking the German Baptists to match each dollar given by ABC, and expressing the hope that Southern Baptists would do the same. The hope was that such a national challenge to German Baptists to raise a building extension fund would improve national cooperation, as much of the life of German Baptists still focused in the Vereiningung, the district organisation.[94]

There were those, however, who saw the most pressing missional needs as being elsewhere – in Africa for example. In this context Edwin Bell wrote:

---

[93] Report of W.O. Lewis to BWA and BWA Relief Committee, April 1951, BWA/EBF Correspondence Box 24, Angus Library.

[94] Proposals outlined in a letter from E.A. Bell to J.L. Sprigg, 13 October 1956, ABFMS Box 476.

> European lands are not considered mission fields, and our Society [ABFMS] sends no missionaries to these countries in connection with our Baptist work. Rather, we do cooperate with the Baptist groups which are indigenous to the several countries in which we have accepted responsibility for giving assistance and counsel through the representative the Society maintains in Europe.[95]

So Bell articulated a policy – which was not new – that saw mission as including areas such as help with buildings[96] or support for key young leaders in theological development. At times, however, Bell struggled with the attitude of the ABFMS Board. An example was his desire to see a substantial building erected as a seminary and home for the Central Baptist Church in Warsaw. The Board were reluctant to release funds, given the political situation, and questioned the attitude of Polish Baptists. On 11 February 1948 Edwin Bell wrote:

> I am at least dimly aware of the tendency of our countrymen and the Russians to stick out their tongues and throw pebbles at each other. How serious this will get, of course, no one knows. I have never been given to pooh poohing the hazards in the eastern European situation and have never guaranteed the interest on any investment which I have suggested the Society make in Poland.... I think, however, there is as much reason for hope as there is for fear. I trust we are more inclined to take counsel of our faith than of our apprehensions.[97]

Bell clearly felt that the home Board was being too cautious. He recognised it was for the home staff to decide whether it would be an act of faith in God or foolhardiness, but he made his own position clear, writing:

> I can only say that it seems to me that now is the day of opportunity in Poland.... It would in my opinion seriously impair the morale of our Baptists in Poland to demur in our cooperation on the basis of our fears over the international tensions.[98]

This letter from Bell resulted in a reappraisal of the situation and the Board reversed their earlier decision and agreed to release the US$ 35,000 Bell had suggested.[99]

Work with groups of refugees continued through into the mid 1950s. One group that took much of the time of Lewis and Cook and required significant

---

95 Report on ABFMS work in Europe. E.A. Bell, May 1948, ABFMS Archive Box 395.

96 An example of this would be the 1948 decision to assist Polish Baptists by making a substantial grant for the church building and seminary in Warsaw. Letter from M.D. Farnum to E.A. Bell, 4 February 1948, ABFMS Archive Box 395.

97 Letter from E.A. Bell to M.D. Farnum, 11 February 1948, ABFMS Archive Box 395.

98 *Ibid.*

99 Letter from M.D. Farnum to E.A. Bell, 17 March 1948, ABFMS Archive Box 395.

resources to be found by Bell and Sadler, were the Volksdeutsche (German-speaking people from Poland, Czechoslovakia and Hungary). There was a significant number of Baptists amongst them, but they did not assimilate well into the German Union churches, so the officers of the EBF and the two principal North American mission agencies sought to assist them by founding refugee churches. Several of these churches were founded in Catholic-dominant southern Germany, to which a considerable number of the uprooted people had migrated. Traditionally, German Baptists had been strongest in the North Eastern part of the country. Assisted by 'block Marks' to purchase building materials, these groups often erected their own premises. Henry Cook, writing to an Australian Baptist leader in 1954 commented: 'It was very interesting to see old men and women working every day on these chapels, and the male members of the church came and worked for some hours after they had finished their day's toil'.[100] There was a strong emphasis on the Baptist community being committed to helping with the real needs of the people. Baptists saw themselves as community-minded missionaries.

'A unified organ of Baptist life in Europe'

Writing to Henry Cook in 1955, Edwin Bell enclosed lists of assistance being given by ABC, so that the EBF officers would be clear as to what ABC was doing. Bell and ABC shared a concern for continued support and assistance. Support for salaries of national workers, including general secretaries, youth leaders and those involved in theological education, was being provided in Belgium, Finland, France, Germany and Sweden.[101] One interesting development, as a special appropriation, was funding for a fishermen's hostel at Honningsvog (North Cape) in Norway.[102] This northern most Baptist church had been 'utterly destroyed when the Germans retreated from Finland and Norway in 1945'.[103] Three years after Bell produced his list, the Continental Committee of the Baptist Union of Great Britain and Ireland held a session (in October 1958) looking at what had happened in Europe since the war. One source of information was a letter Edwin Bell had sent to the Committee. From this letter, and from their own observations, they noted that many new church buildings had been erected out of the ashes of war.

---

[100] H. Cook, EBF General Secretary to G.H. Blackburn, Victoria, Australia, 28 October 1954, BWA/EBF Letters File 27, Angus Library.

[101] *Ibid.,* ABFMS Appropriations in Europe, 1955.

[102] The Honningsvog connection has continued. This is the most northerly Baptist church in the world and ABC now support the Norwegian pastor based there. He was visited by Bell's then current successor, Reid S. Trulson, in September 2002, and the work is now growing in the building erected in the 1950s.

[103] Report of E.A. Bell to ABFMS, May 1948, ABFMS Archive Box 395.

Country	Reconstructed	New
Germany	60	94
Norway	03	13
Holland	03	24
Denmark	01	13
Austria	02	07
Italy	00	20
Spain	00	24
Sweden	00	09
Great Britain	60	94

The cost of this enterprise was counted in millions of dollars.[104] Though some Unions, especially the British[105] and Germans, had made great efforts to raise money themselves, both the American Baptist and Southern Baptist Mission Boards had been very much involved. It should be noted that the representatives on the ground for both ABC and SBC were clear europhiles. Both had a strong desire to argue the case to help European Baptists recover from the devastation of war and be placed on a footing where the churches could engage in effective mission.

Bell, who had been appointed as ABFMS representative in Europe in 1945, came to the conclusion of his work in 1960. In a candid letter to his ABFMS colleague, Dana Albaugh, in December 1956 he commented on what his successor ought to do, revealing his strong support for the development of the EBF, over against the BWA:

> I would definitely work with the European Baptist Federation. And seek to strengthen it and encourage the present trends towards its development as a unified organ of Baptist life in Europe, taking over even administrative functions in the development of the work as it is able to. I should like to see this organization become something more than simply an arm of the BWA and under its tutelage and domination to the extent that some of our friends in the BWA feel should be the direction of its development. I hope its development would be in directions somewhat different from those of our Southern Baptist brethren vis-à-vis the other Protestant bodies… I grow as impatient as any of you over some of the things that occur in the BWA.[106]

This attitude of Edwin Bell reveals an important approach that ABC has had to

---

[104] Minutes of the Baptist Union of Great Britain Continental Society, Baptist Union Minute Book 1958, p.155, item III, Angus Library.

[105] *Ibid.*, p. 156, item VI. British Baptists had, like the Americans, helped other Unions. For instance a gift of £500 had been made towards the construction of the John Smyth church building in Amsterdam.

[106] Letter from E.A. Bell to D. Albaugh, 15 December 1956, ABFMS Europe Representative Archive.

the life of the EBF. It accords well with a baptistic ecclesiology which always wants to give greater significance to those interdependent forms nearest to the local church. The debate is ongoing between the BWA and the EBF about their relationship,[107] their relative strength, and their programmatic objectives (in mission, relief, dialogue and human rights). However, European Baptists have always greatly valued an approach which was seen as assisting in the work of capacity building within the EBF.

Relief efforts involving both ABC and SBC continued in a modest way from 1960-1985. With a great portion of the EBF community behind the totalitarian wall of communism, what could be done was limited and sporadic, depending on particular personal initiatives. However, this took a dramatic turn in the late 1980s and early 1990s with the collapse of communism. Following the EBF Congress in Budapest in 1989 and the appointment of Karl Heinz Walter as General Secretary, it soon became apparent that an opportunity to engage in significant relief and development work was about to present itself. Immediately Walter took the initiative, calling together European representatives of Baptist mission agencies and relief and development mission agencies. He proposed the formation of a relief and development organisation, Baptist Response-Europe (BRE), at the EBF Executive Committee in April 1990.[108] The proposal had arisen out of a consultation on the situation in Eastern Europe held in Dorfweil, Germany, in January 1990.[109] Again, the two North American mission agencies were pivotal agents in the development, with G. Keith Parker, the SBC representative for Europe, serving on the core group with Karl Heinz Walter and Paul Montacute of Baptist World Aid.[110] An immediate challenge facing the EBF in the light of the bad winter and the collapse of communism was to engage in a response to relief requested in the sum of over US$6 million.

Though British, German and Swedish Baptists, with support from some of the smaller Western European Unions, supported the work of BRE, it was quite clear from the start that the strength of the support given to the EBF for this work came from Keith Parker (SBC) and the ABC representative, Robert Frykolm. Later (in the 1990s), the involvement of two Cooperative Baptist

---

107 The debate has become one involving all the six regions of the BWA as part of the work of the BWA Implementation Task Force charged with engaging in the organisational renewal of the BWA in the period 2005-2010.Minutes of the BWA ITF, October and December 2005 and March 2007, IBTS Archive, Prague. Further consultations between regional officers and the BWA General Secretary, Neville Callam, continue.

108 Minutes of the EBF Executive Committee, Box 809, EBF Archive, Prague.

109 EBF Baptist Response-Europe [BRE], EBF Archive.

110 BRE Report to EBF Council, De Bron, Netherlands, September 1990, Box 809, EBF Archive.

Fellowship missionaries, Paul Thibodeaux and James A. Smith,[111] constituted an added factor. This point is well illustrated in the 1990 account of the EBF, where the BRE fund received 876,141 Deutschmarks, with the largest contributors being the SBC-FMB at 80,946 Deutschmarks and ABC-IM with 25,702 Deutschmarks.[112] It is important to understand these were sums deliberately channelled through the EBF to help develop the concept of BRE. Additionally, both organisations were making direct payments to specific countries and projects where they had a partnership. The mission agencies desired to work through the accepted ecclesial framework of the EBF, and also to continue in what has always been seen as a normally Baptist approach, working with specific national Unions and Conventions, whilst trying to make sure all concerned have some appreciation of the total picture. The issue of more than one organisation funding the same request remained a deep concern, and BRE was the common ground for exchange of information.

The danger was that Europe could be seen simply as 'needy'. This difficulty was understood by Erik Rudén, who wrote, at the beginning of his secretaryship in the EBF, to the FMB leadership pleading the cause of Europe, but also pointing out the positive features in Baptist life. He thanked the FMB for the presence of George Sadler, referred to the fact many Unions were small, and to the problematic actions of the Roman Catholics in Southern Europe and the Lutherans in Northern Europe, and then went on to say:

> But this is not the whole picture. There are many promising characteristics. Our brethren in small countries, living in meagre circumstances, experience the Christian fellowship in such a way that no sacrifice is too great for them if they thereby can confess their love to others of the same faith. There is a great interest in theological education and advanced education. The struggle for religious liberty still goes on. The evangelistic activity is strong in many quarters.... However, I do not think I am overestimating the actual situation when I suggest that we are just now at one of our most critical points of the European Baptist activities. Are we ready to commit ourselves to the great needs of Europe?[113]

He concluded his letter with a plea that Southern Baptists, as such a strong Convention, might have patience with Europeans and continue in the important mission work with them. He copied his letter to George Sadler, who

---

111 Paul Thibodeaux and James A. Smith were both Southern Baptist career missionaries in Europe, but with the defunding of Rüschlikon they resigned from SBC-FMB and joined the first group of missionaries appointed by the Cooperative Baptist Fellowship, as they wished to continue working in Europe and in cooperation with Europeans and not against them.

112 EBF Annual Accounts for 1990, Box 809, EBF Archive.

113 Letter from E. Rudén to C. Goerner, SBC-FMB in Richmond, Virginia, 8 December 1959, Erik Rudén Papers, Box 1, Angus Library.

commented:

> Let me thank you for the copy of your letter of 8th December addressed to Dr Cornell Goerner. It seems to me that you put the matter of the mission of Southern Baptists to Europe admirably. It is my opinion that neither Dr Cauthen[114] nor Dr Goerner sees the importance of Europe from a Baptist point of view as you and I do. It will take impacts such as you made in your letter to convince them.[115]

Rudén had set out major features of Baptist life that were worthy of support: fellowship, training, freedom, evangelism and wider mission.

The concern of both ABC and SBC to assist Europeans in active evangelism within and through the churches was evident in this period. In the earlier years of the life of the EBF there was a willingness both within ABC and SBC to work with the EBF in such cooperation. In 1958 Edwin A. Bell, Joel Sorenson (BWA Youth Secretary based in Europe) and Henry Cook, contemplated organising a Conference on Evangelism at Rüschlikon to be followed by an evangelistic tour of several communities in Europe. This was to be spearheaded by Walter E. Woodbury of the Department of Evangelism of the Pennsylvania Baptist Convention (ABC) and Gaines S. Dobbins of Golden Gate Theological Seminary and representing the Southern Baptist Convention. The Rüschlikon conference was to feature:

> The New Testament Teaching on the necessity of evangelism, proselytising versus evangelism, God's part and Man's part in Evangelism, the importance of human decision, the importance of helping converts to form Christian habits, instruction in the way of Christ and fellowship watch-care and three types of visitation evangelism.[116]

Woodbury and Dobbins then wanted to visit various western European countries to demonstrate the various types of evangelism. As Woodberry commented, 'little is accomplished by simply lecturing about evangelism. Personal soul winning can be taught only to those who are willing to go into the laboratory of life.'[117] The two North Americans recognised that they needed help from Cook, Sorenson and Rudén about the actual situation in Europe. The language of the letter quoted introduced some American phrases, such as 'watch-care', with which the Europeans would not have been familiar. But there was a willingness to engage in mutual learning. Henry Cook wrote to all

---

[114] Baker J. Cauthen, President (Chief Executive Officer) of the SBC-FMB at that time; Cornell Goerner was the Richmond-based executive responsible for Europe.

[115] Letter from G.W. Sadler, SBC-IMB special representative for Europe to E. Rudén, 14 December 1959, Erik Rudén Papers, Box 1, Angus Library.

[116] Letter from W.E. Woodberry to H. Cook, 22 January 1958, Erik Rudén Papers, Box 1, Angus Library.

[117] *Ibid.*

the member Unions in the February asking each of them to appoint two delegates for the event. The two speakers were to remain in Europe until the Berlin Congress and Joel Sorenson hoped they might be used by the Unions to whom the respective Mission Boards related. However, Edwin Bell wrote to Henry Cook saying:

> I have said to Dr Nordenhaug that we [ABC] have no particular desire to have Dr Woodbury's activities confined to areas where we have been especially interested for a long time. We would like everybody concerned to know that, from our point of view, Dr Woodbury would be free to be used wherever the Committee felt he could render best service.[118]

Clearly, Bell did not want to see Woodbury confined to a particular part of Europe, a point Henry Cook acceded to when he wrote to Erik Rudén on 15th January stating, 'it does seem to me we must make use of Dr Woodbury as much as we can'.[119] The Conference itself was overshadowed by preparations for the Berlin Congress of 1958, but the significance of this joint venture in mission training was fully recognised, and as the two mission boards were meeting the expenses of these visiting specialists, Henry Cook and Erik Rudén were most anxious that the Unions should play their full part in welcoming them as 'we invited the Boards to send us these men and they have done so, and we must use them as much as we can'.[120] In the future, however, Europeans would seek to use mission methods that were their own, rather than something imported.

Changing Relationships

As can be seen from the foregoing, the two large mission agencies in the USA – the SBC and ABC – have had long involvement in mission within Europe. With the formation of the EBF in 1949 a new area of cooperation opened up, with a desire to develop the life and work of the EBF, sometimes in preference to the role of the BWA. The pinnacle of this understanding might be seen in the 1988 decision of the SBC-FMB to hand to the EBF the theological education facility in Rüschlikon. This has been fully explored in Chapter 4. The events the following year when the FMB Board of Trustees decided to break a commitment made to the EBF to continue funding Rüschlikon for a further fifteen years until 2005, marked a turning point in the partnership

118 Letter from E.A. Bell to E. Rudén, 23 January 1958, Erik Rudén Papers, Box 1, Angus Library.

119 Letter from H. Cook to E. Rudén, 15 January 1958, Erik Rudén Papers, Box 1, Angus Library.

120 Letter from H. Cook to E. Rudén, 11 February 1958, Erik Rudén Papers, Box 1, Angus Library.

understanding and in the stance of the FMB in support, capacity building and engagement with the EBF. The issue of the defunding started a crisis in the overall relationship between the SBC and the EBF. Though initially there was a desire by both parties to keep the issue of defunding Rüschlikon as a distinct point within a wider relationship, inevitably, the EBF General Secretary, Karl Heinz Walter, and other EBF officers were involved in the discussions, and the wider relationship came under scrutiny. This happened within the EBF Executive Committee and ultimately the EBF Council. The desire for understanding was not aided by criticisms from some within the SBC that European Baptists were 'liberal, not believing the Bible and spreading heresy all over the world'.[121]

There was, in fact, no way that the defunding of Rüschlikon could be kept separate from the general relationship between the SBC and the EBF. This was borne out when the EBF decided to call a consultation on mission at the Dorfweil Conference Centre in Germany in January 1992. This proved to be a defining moment for the beginning of a general change in relationship between European Baptists and SBC. Thirty-seven leaders from twenty-three Baptist Unions participated in the meetings.[122] The leaders wanted to write appreciatively of the FMB Missionaries, Keith Parker and Isam Ballenger, who had served in Europe and who resigned following the defunding of Rüschlikon, but they had also been incensed by a letter written by FMB Trustee Ron Wilson.[123] In a common statement from the Dorfweil consultation they commented:

> We have felt keenly the derogatory remarks made by some members of the Board of Trustees about European Baptists. We dare to believe such remarks would not have been made had there been more personal contact between the trustees and our churches.[124]

Stung by the attacks that had been made upon the faith of European Baptists, the EBF Executive and Council asked the Theology and Education Division to begin work on a statement about the beliefs, practices and identity of European

---

[121] This point is made in J.W. Merritt, *The Betrayal – The hostile takeover of the Southern Baptist Convention and a missionary's fight for Freedom in Christ* (Asheville, NC, 2005), p. 85. Merritt served in Europe with the European Baptist Convention as General Secretary and is a one-time President of the EBF. He was at the heart of the controversy as a Southern Baptist who lived and worked as a respected statesman amongst the Europeans.

[122] EBF Mission Consultation Files, January 1992, EBF Archive.

[123] The text of the Ron Wilson letter is discussed in Chapter 4 on IBTS and will not be repeated here.

[124] Letter from the EBF Dorfweil Consultation to the FMB, EBF Archive. Parts also quoted by Merritt in *The Betrayal.*

Baptists.[125] The theological driving force behind the document was Paul Fiddes of Oxford, then Chair of the EBF Theology and Education Division. A meeting with representatives of the SBC- FMB was held in Hamburg, something that had been proposed at the Dorfweil meeting. The Unions, acting in common through the EBF, wanted to try to establish a future way of relating to the SBC-FMB, and especially their Board of Trustees.

The 'Hamburg Agreement',[126] as it came to be called, sought to lay out five essentials of partnership between the SBC-FMB and Baptists in Europe. It was concluded on 12 September 1992, at a meeting at High Leigh in England. The EBF delegation was led by Peter Barber, the EBF President and General Secretary of the Scottish Baptists, who had a long-standing and effective partnership with SBC-FMB. As North-West Europeans, the Scottish Union had no vulnerability to FMB pressure. Other Unions did perhaps because of issues to do with ownership of property, or the position of SBC-FMB Missionaries (for example John Merritt) or because of long-term agreements with the FMB. In this sense, Peter Barber,[127] a long-serving General Secretary of strong evangelical persuasion, was a good 'honest broker' for the EBF. For their part, the FMB played a master stroke in appointing Samuel M. James as interim Vice-President for Europe in succession to Isam Ballenger, who had resigned from the FMB over these issues. James was a lovely warm-spirited career missionary with a heart for reconciliation and went on a tour around Europe before the EBF Council at High Leigh in 1992.[128]

The principles enshrined in the Hamburg Agreement flowed from a recognition that deep damage had been done to the mission relationship between FMB and European Baptists by the pattern of events surrounding the defunding of Rüschlikon. The five principles had, at their heart:

---

[125] This document 'What are Baptists?' was received by the EBF Council in England in 1992 and then printed and distributed for consideration by the member Unions, Box 811, EBF Archive.

[126] 'The Hamburg Agreement', Appendix to the EBF Council Minutes, September 1992, Hoddesdon, Hertfordshire, Box 811, EBF Archive.

[127] E. Burrows, *To me to live is Christ: A biography of Peter Barber* (Milton Keynes: Paternoster, 2005).

[128] The General Secretary and Deputy General Secretary of the British Baptists met S.M. James from the SBC-FMB at Didcot over the summer of 1992 and warmed to him and his mission spirit. His approach and manner did much to heal the pain of the earlier exchanges with the FMB Board, but the policies eminating out of Richmond and the Board did not appear to change.

- Mutual respect in which the partners deal with each other with candour but with Christian courtesy (Eph 4:1-3).
- Spiritual freedom in which the partners, working within a common commitment, recognise and welcome differences of outlook and diversity of practice (Rom. 15:7; Mark 9:38-41).
- Moral integrity in which partners honour and maintain solemnly-made agreements (2 Cor. 1:12-17).
- Genuine consultation in which the partners confer together and aim for mutual consent (2 Cor. 8:8-9).
- Reciprocal sharing in which the partners learn, work and grow together, giving and receiving (Rom. 1:11-12).[129]

Whilst the document was welcomed by both SBC-FBM and EBF representatives, and the genuine desire to make it work of those actually participating was noted, in reality the SBC-FMB was on a journey away from their erstwhile European partners. Keith Parks, the FMB Chief Executive Officer, soon retired and moved to become head of Global Missions with the Cooperative Baptist Fellowship (CBF). He was replaced by a career missionary from South East Asia, Jerry Rankin, who had little interest in the Hamburg Agreement. The post of Vice-President for Europe was abolished and in a new structure two FMB Regional Leaders were created – John Floyd (Eastern Europe) and Eddie Cox (Western Europe). As the direction of the FMB changed towards a policy of church planting and evangelism, which also involved abandoning connections with theological education and indigenous leadership, so the Hamburg Agreement was placed to one side. Though both Eddie Cox and John Floyd sought to keep good personal contacts with the EBF officers, being missionaries living and serving in the region, in reality, Union after Union discovered that a plan of parallel rather than cooperative mission was being pursued.

Eventually, Jerry Rankin announced a series of world-wide consultations on the FMB, now re-titled International Mission Board (IMB), and it was agreed the European Consultation would be in Dorfweil on 4th and 5th April 2000, before an EBF Executive Committee. All partner Unions were invited and also several members of the Executive Committee, but some were excluded from the meeting, including the Rector of IBTS. The Consultation proved to be something of a sham: Jerry Rankin had come to declare the future policy of the IMB, not to consult. In a tense session at the end of the 'consultation', European Baptist leader after European Baptist leader denounced the non-

[129] 'The Hamburg Agreement'.

partnership style of the IMB. Rankin was visibly shaken.[130] Though it was generally assumed that the Hamburg Agreement was now in shreds, in fact it existed on paper until, in 2005, the new EBF General Secretary, Tony Peck, presented a paper which had been requested by the 2004 EBF Council on the state of relations between the IMB and European Baptists.[131] This document set out the difficult relationships the majority of EBF Unions now had with IMB, especially with Rankin in Richmond. Though Tony Peck sought to emphasise positive elements and there was ready affirmation of individual missionaries who worked well with their local Unions, nevertheless, person after person expressed concern at the new IMB policy. Smaller Unions like Portugal, Lithuania, Latvia and Armenia all commented on a lack of true partnership.[132] In a subsequent meeting of the Executive, Peck reported he had a meeting in London with Jerry Rankin and, whilst they exchanged understandings, Peck commented that 'great differences remain on appropriate mission strategies for our region and on the concept of mission partnership'.[133]

Even apart from these changes, European Baptists were engaging in some re-thinking in areas of mission activity. The use of specialist colleagues from North America was not to be repeated. The British Anglican-developed 'Alpha' package became a preferred evangelism tool for many of the Baptist communities in Europe, being translated into a range of European languages.[134] Though European Baptists were interested in Willowcreek seeker services and the Saddleback Church 'Purpose Driven' approach, what proved to be most valuable, in many cases, was people from American churches coming over to Europe to help run camps and programmes, especially in teaching English language as a tool for pre-evangelism and evangelism. ABC, which consistently argued against having field personnel working as missionaries in Europe, did place one couple in Prague, based on the EBF campus,[135] Pieter and Nora Kalkman, with the aim of facilitating church to church partnership. The

---

130 My conversations, at the time in Dorfweil immediately after the close of the final SBC-IMB session, with those present including K.H. Walter, Zjelko Mraz (Croatia), Samuel Verhaeghe (Belgium), Helen Wordsworth (United Kingdom).

131 Minutes of the EBF Council, September 2005, Prague, Czech Republic, Minute 16, pp. 73-75, EBF Archive.

132 *Ibid.*

133 EBF Executive Committee, Bristol, UK, April 2006, Document E2006/4, EBF Archive.

134 For Alpha see alpha.org.uk, accessed 6 January 2007. This course, originally intended as a discipleship course, but now essentially used in evangelism, is used by churches in 153 countries.

135 ABC took a deliberate decision to move their regional office to the IBTS Prague campus in 1997. Previously, it had been located in Vienna. CBF had established their office in Berlin in the early 1980s and chose to keep it there. SBC-IMB established their Central and Eastern European office in Prague in 1999.

CBF, though having mission personnel working in certain parts of Europe, also used their European Coordinator, James A. Smith, in the work of fostering local church mission trips from the USA to Europe. The IMB, however, moved from partnership to the practice of parallel mission.

The mission boards, especially ABC and CBF, took a particular interest in the EBF Home Mission Secretaries Conference and regularly provided financial assistance for representatives of the EBF Unions in the poorer countries of Europe to gather and discuss issues of evangelism and mission. When the EBF began to develop, from 2000 onwards, the concept of cross-cultural support for indigenous missionaries in a special EBF programme, the then General Secretary, Theo Angelov, approached all the North American mission agencies and invited them to participate financially in this scheme designed to foster indigenous church planting. At a special conference convened at a Hotel near Heathrow Airport, London, in August 2001, the EBF Executive invited the mission boards of ABC, SBC, CBF, BMS, North American Baptist Convention and the State Conventions of Virginia, Texas, Tennessee and North Carolina, to look at four special projects for cross-cultural cooperation. Only one of these, the Indigenous Missionary Project, was developed,[136] with positive support from all the mission agencies assisting in the funding of missionaries and a coordinator.[137] It might be argued that a significant rubicon had been crossed with this development: apparently all the mission agencies had, to a greater or lesser extent, accepted the concept that American mission money might be used to fund indigenous missionaries in Europe who they did not control and who were not in any formal way related to them. The missionaries were nominated by the Unions to an EBF Core Group who agreed to their appointment and provided for their salaries out of a financial resource to which mission agencies contributed. Certain agencies preferred to see their money go to specific countries, but all were given regular reports on progress by the EBF Coordinator.[138]

Clearly, the most significant change in relationships has been between the EBF and the SBC-FBM. The latter organisation has moved through differing missiological and theological phases and, in recent years, the changes have profoundly altered the shape and emphasis of its missiological direction, with

[136] Initial report of meeting in EBF Council Minutes, September 2001, Prague, p. 6, EBF Office Archive.

[137] The development of the EBF Indigenous Missionary Project is looked at more fully in Chapter 7.

[138] The IMB did contribute funds, but in a modest way and out of locally designated moneys, as the overall international policy of the IMB remains to place their own missionaries in the field to follow through their grand strategy and not to cooperate with national evangelists and church planters.

consequent effect upon work within the European context.[139] For those who have examined the approach of the SBC-FMB, there is an emerging view that the Board has had at least two conflicting approaches – what has often been seen as a 'minority' approach around three core values (indigeneity, incarnation and responsible autonomy) and an approach which might be described as centralist, corporate structured institutional mission. Keith Eitel and others argue the first 'underside' approach was best seen in the Gospel Mission Movement[140] and later in the work of R. Keith Parks to establish the Cooperative Services International as a way of doing mission in the unevangelised world.[141] In fact, the argument of Eitel is that the call of the Commission on World Mission and Evangelisation of the WCC for a mortatorium in missions was, 'Really a wake up call for everyone engaged in missions to take indigeneity and contextualization seriously... Southern Baptists fit the generally dismal pattern of failing to achieve the best ideals of indigeneity noted by Bosch'.[142] There is a deeper analysis to be made, however, in that in the European Baptist context the failure has been a failure to continue to espouse an authentically Baptist ecclesial vision – one that takes seriously the integrity of local gathering communities and the inter-church bodies which they create and support.

Conclusion

The two major mission agencies amongst North American Baptists, SBC and ABC, have both had a deep commitment to European Baptist life. Following the 1948 BWA strategy meeting, both agencies presented, and carried forward, major plans to work with European Baptists to rebuild mission life and community in continental Europe, in theological education, church planting, relief and evangelism. Whether it was completely intended by the leadership of the two agencies or not, they permitted their European leaders to play a positive and influential role in both the founding and development of the EBF and in stimulating theological education at a European standard, not only in

---

[139] There are several important works which explore these differing traditions. The most helpful, in analysing the missiological drives, is K.E. Eitel, *Paradigm Wars: The Southern Baptist International Mission Board Faces the Third Millennium* (Oxford: Regnum Books, 2000).

[140] The Gospel Mission Movement 1892-1910 was a break-away from the FMB by missionaries in the FMB North China Mission, influenced by Hudson Taylor and concerned with issues of indigeneity (missionaries living like the locals), local decision-making and the avoidance of incentives to convert.

[141] For a detailed description of the Parks paradigm shift see Eitel, *Paradigm Wars*, pp. 97-99.

[142] D.J. Bosch, *Transforming Mission: Paradigm Shifts in Theology of Mission* (Maryknoll, NY: Orbis, 1991).

Rüschlikon, but in the support of key national seminaries. George W. Sadler and Edwin A. Bell were key figures in the early development of the EBF and both had a desire to see the EBF truly European and were cooperative. Their successors, Gordon Lahrson (ABC) and John Allen Moore (SBC), also proved to be cooperators. Whilst the pattern of leadership within ABC, from Bell through to Reid S. Trulson,[143] remained consistent, SBC-IMB always had more of a centralist policy, though this seemed to allow sufficient flexibility for regional directors and regional vice-presidents. But when fundamentalists took control of the SBC-IMB Board of Trustees, adherence to policies became a priority. Jerry Rankin, in a recent meeting and through exchange of letters with Tony Peck,[144] asserted the freedom of SBC-IMB Regional Leaders to pursue their own strategy, but it is clear that freedom is within narrow boundaries which would not have been recognised by George Sadler.

Early involvement in Europe by ABC-IM and SBC-FMB took seriously the European Baptist desire for an ecclesial reality expressed through the EBF. The approach of both mission agencies was positive, though different strategies emerged at key points. The SBC-FMB policy was to have many field personnel and the ABC-IM policy was to support nationals and institutions and not to have many of their own missionaries 'operational' in Europe. In the 1980s both followed important mission trends[145] in transferring resources from the 'field' mission structure to the 'national' or 'regional' ecclesial organisations. As has been seen, sometimes these moves followed well-thought through mission strategies. ABC-IM sought to draw closer to the ecclesial life represented in the EBF by moving their regional office from Vienna to the IBTS campus in Prague. In reverse, the SBC-IMB, having had their regional office at Rüschlikon, created a new base at Wiesbaden in Germany, though they did establish a second regional office in Prague, but not on the IBTS campus. ABC-IM continued their policy of not having field missionaries in Europe. They committed funding to salaries of nationals engaged in mission at points where they had either previous involvement, or saw of strategic importance.[146] In contrast the SBC-FMB (now IMB) drew away from the Unions and sought to appoint an ever-growing number of field personnel to engage in evangelism and church planting.

---

[143] R.S. Trulson served ABC-IM from the mid 1990s until 2006 as ABC Area Representative until his appointment as Chief Executive Officer of ABC-IM in November 2006.

[144] Reported by Tony Peck to the EBF Executive in document E2006/4, EBF Office Archive.

[145] Classic cross-cultural mission thinking has advocated transferring resources from the mission agencies and in supporting nationals alongside cross-cultural workers from the second half of the twentieth century.

[146] For instance, the salary support for the pastor of North Cape Baptist Church in northern Norway.

Whilst ABC-IM continued to see theological education of Europeans as an important mission strategy and continued to assist the EBF work in Prague, SBC-IMB withdrew from support of theological education, not only at IBTS, but at the Arab Baptist Theological Seminary in Beirut. The Richmond strategy became focused on funding and providing North American church planters and this no longer required the theological education of nationals.[147] Both agencies pulled back from seeking to impose, through special courses, a North American approach to evangelism, choosing to offer support to the EBF Home Mission Secretaries event. Whilst ABC-IM took an active financial part in the EBF Indigenous Missionary Project from the beginning, as this did not fit with SBC-IMB policy, IMB stood at a distance and only later did the IMB Regional Leader for Eastern Europe, Rodney Hammer, commit a modest level of funding to support the post of the EBF Indigenous Missionary Coordinator. It seems clear that a constructive partnership with European Baptists in general, and the EBF in particular, was maintained by ABC-IM and its area representatives over the period under review. They engaged positively in the founding and development of the EBF and sought to respond to assistance requests from the EBF, but not to seek to impose their own agenda. Similar partnership agreements and good cooperation exist between the other significant North American mission agencies and the EBF – the Cooperative Baptist Fellowship, Canadian Baptist International Ministries and the North American Baptist General Conference. The SBC-IMB, however, has now a minimal sense of partnership with the EBF. The period of George Sadler might now be described as a golden age, when a Southern Baptist missionary was committed to working in support of European Baptist ecclesial leadership.

[147] However, some fundamentalists within the Southern Baptist leadership chose direct support of seminaries in line with their thinking in various parts of the world, by-passing the IMB and its global strategy.

CHAPTER 7

Mission in the World

Mission, it is often claimed, is the heart beat of Baptist life. Recent theological reflection on mission has reminded the Christian Church that mission is firstly a response to the *Missio Dei* and it is also properly wide in concept.[1] Baptists are predominantly evangelical in their theological orientation and the majority of European Baptists have responded positively to the Lausanne Covenant (1974).[2] Many are active participants in the varied initiatives of groups and agencies engaged in mission, seeing their involvement as both a commitment to evangelism and an addressing of the social, political and cultural dimensions of the gospel,[3] in the way in which the Covenant outlined these issues. When considering Baptist ecclesiology, mission is always drawn out as one of the essential ecclesial features.[4] In the context of the European Baptist Federation

---

[1] Writings on mission relevant to this approach include D.J. Bosch, *Transforming Mission: Paradigm Shifts in Theology of Mission* (New York: Maryknoll, 1991), J.A. Kirk, *The Mission of Theology and Theology as Mission* (Valley Forge: Trinity Press International, 1997). For a recent European perspective see S. Barrow and G. Smith (eds.), *Christian Mission in Western Society* (London: Churches Together in Britain and Ireland, 2001). For an EBF perspective on the importance of this issue for the life of baptistic churches see P.F. Penner (ed.), *Theological Education as Mission* (Schwarzenfeld, Germany: Neufeld Verlag, 2005).

[2] The Lausanne Covenant is a declaration, agreed upon by more than 2,300 evangelicals during the 1974 International Congress, to be more intentional about world evangelisation. Since then, the Covenant has challenged churches and Christian organisations to work together to make Jesus Christ known throughout the world. See www.lausanne.org.

[3] The Chinese Baptist, Raymond Fung, has been an important figure in helping Baptists have a holistic approach to mission. He was, for several years, Secretary for Evangelism at the World Council of Churches [WCC]. His book, R. Fung, *The Isaiah Vision* (Geneva: WCC, 1992) and also his work in *Your Kingdom Come: Mission Perspectives: The report of the WCC World Conference on Mission and Evangelism, 1980, Melbourne* (Geneva: WCC, 1980), p 83 -92, might be seen as providing a challenging framework for local church mission. This emphasis has been important since the late 18th century.

[4] Baptist World Alliance Study and Research Division, *We Baptists* (Franklin, Tenn.: Providence House Publishers, 1999), J.W. McClendon, Jr, *Systematic Theology: Ethics* (Nashville, Tenn.: Abingdon, 1986), p. 28.

(EBF), there have been important questions to ask as to how baptistic theology works itself out in the mission of the people of God and in the relationships between those engaged in primary theology and mission – the local gathering communities of believers, national unions and the continental organisation. This is a broad topic since it takes in a variety of missional enterprises. Ever since the founding of the British Baptist Missionary Society (BMS), there has been the influence of denominational cross-cultural mission agencies on the life of the churches. Within the EBF context, an increasing role has been played by the child of European Baptists, the European Baptist Mission (EBM). In addition, Baptists have been involved in many evangelical and non-denominational faith missions.[5]

This chapter looks at certain issues which have been prominent in the mission perspective of the EBF – cooperative evangelism and the formation of the EBM, cross-cultural and indigenous mission, mission in context, reconciliation and peace in Europe, and religious freedom and human rights. Generally, the EBF has not engaged with every area of development within the field of mission because it has, in a properly ecclesial way, looked for prompting from its members before becoming involved in specific areas of work. Theologically this is an important point: that primary theology and mission is done in the gathering believing communities and only when they need the help of, or see the value in the involvement of the translocal, national and continental ecclesial realities such as the EBF, do they seek such help. A focus of concern will be to see what were the advantages and disadvantages of a group of European countries working together in this way – despite differences of language and culture. It will be important to note that the Nordic Unions developed separate mission agencies and also why the British BMS was not seen as a platform from which to build wider pan-European cooperation. I will explore why some Unions in the former Soviet bloc[6] chose to join EBM in the post-communist era and why others remained outside, or developed their own cross-cultural mission work. Were decisions at crucial points made on missiological or ecclesiological or cultural grounds? Did they relate more to the history of individual Unions? What was the influence of the views and attitudes of mission partners from overseas? These are issues that will be examined.

'Missionary activity': Europe-Wide Concerns

From the very beginnings of the EBF there was a recognition of the work of Baptist mission agencies within Europe that engaged in cross-cultural mission

[5] On faith missions see K. Fiedler, *The Story of Faith Missions* (Oxford: Regnum Books, 1994).

[6] The history of mission in communist days is helpfully explored in W.W. Sawatsky and P.F. Penner (eds.), *Mission in the Former Soviet Union* (Schwarzenfeld, Germany: Neufeld Verlag, 2005).

both within Europe and elsewhere in the world. The already existing national mission agencies in the British Isles[7] and the Nordic countries were engaged in cross-cultural mission, sustainable development and aid work. Although not primarily committed to placing missionaries in other European countries, their support of indigenous mission by Baptist Unions in other countries was consistent throughout the period under review. The development of the EBF provided a platform for the exchange of views and, in several instances, cooperative activity and support. These factors will be analysed in this chapter. On becoming General Secretary of the EBF in 1959, Erik Rudén wrote to the President of the Baptist World Alliance (BWA) about this tension between being primarily a community of *koinonia* and being more intentionally missional, saying:

> Some people want to strengthen the power of the Federation and make it an organisation of missionary activity. Others look at the Federation as an instrument for 'promoting fellowship'. A good policy might be to choose a middle course.[8]

In fact, EBM had begun seven years earlier. One of the earliest and most important initiatives arising out of the formation of the EBF was the founding of the EBM in 1952. At the meeting held in Paris on 20th and 21st October 1950 to form the EBF, one item raised in the discussion concerned mission:

> Attention was called to the fact that the Baptists in certain countries in Europe have no mission work in non-Christian lands. Those desiring to undertake such work were advised to communicate with the Secretary who would endeavour to guide them in the fulfilment of their desires.[9]

At a meeting in Hamburg in the summer of the following year (August 1951), the EBF Council provided opportunity on the agenda for reports from the various national Unions about the foreign mission work they were undertaking. The work of the BMS was long-standing and extensive throughout the world, and in its early days it drew inspiration from Central Europe. The modern protestant missionary movement arguably began with the Moravian community in Hernhutt, Germany, in the 1730s, and William Carey and others within the

---

[7] The British Baptist Missionary Society [BMS] was engaged principally at that time in cross-cultural mission work in Africa and Asia. However the position was to change in the latter part of the twentieth century. The Baptist Union of Great Britain Continental Committee was, however, very active in Europe in the first seven decades of the twentieth century, but post 1975 it ceased to be an important player in cross-cultural mission work.

[8] Letter of E. Rudén to T.F. Adams, 13 October 1959, Erik Rudén Papers Box 1, Angus Library, Regent's Park College, Oxford.

[9] Minutes of the EBF Council, October 1950, p. 7, Box 801, EBF Archive, IBTS, Prague.

BMS were indebted to the example of the Moravians. 'Have not the missionaries of the *Unitas Fratrum*, or Moravian Brethren', Carey asked, 'encountered the scorching heat of Abyssinia, and the frozen climes of Greenland and Labrador...?' He argued that 'none of the moderns have equalled the Moravian Brethren in this good work'.[10] BMS involvement was particularly strong in parts of South East Asia, in the Caribbean and in parts of Africa. There had been involvement in some specific parts of continental Europe,[11] as noted in the previous chapter, such as Brittany[12] and Italy.[13] Swedish Baptists had engaged in foreign mission work – in China, India, Congo, Brazil, Finland and (until the 1920 comity agreement)[14] Spain. Norway also had eight missionaries in what was then the Belgian Congo.[15] The Minutes of the Hamburg meeting note that 'we were surprised that so much is being done'.[16] Discussion began regarding how Baptist Unions in Europe interested in cross-cultural mission could work more effectively together. Those interested in the possibilities were invited to talk further with W.O. Lewis.[17] It was this which led to the founding of the EBM.

One factor which was to cause much debate and concern within the whole area of cross-cultural mission was how far such work should be undertaken exclusively within a Baptist framework and how much might also be done within ecumenical structures. This was always to be a particular focus in relation to relief and development work, and it was discussed from the very beginning of the EBF. It was important that the EBF should reflect on its relationship to the wider work in this area of the Nordic, Dutch, German and British Unions. Some, within the Baptist world, such as J.H. Rushbrooke, criticised what he felt was the proportionately low level of giving to Baptists from the inter-church aid organisations. A certain tension ensued between advocates of Baptist relief work and ecumenical relief work. This issue has

---

[10] The full text of Carey's 'Enquiry' is in T. George, *Faithful Witness: The Life and Mission of William Carey* (Leicester: IVP, 1991).

[11] The BMS had sent W.H. Angus to tour Europe and visit Mennonite communities to obtain support and partnership. His reports of these travels are in the BMS Archive, Angus Library, Regent's Park College, Oxford.

[12] S. Fath, 'A Forgotten Missionary Link: The Baptist Continental Society in France (1831-1836)', *BQ*, Vol. 40, July 2003, pp. 133-151.

[13] Stanley, *A History of the Baptist Missionary Society*, pp. 220-222.

[14] Baptist World Alliance [BWA] London Conference of 1920, Notes in ABFMS Archive Box 254, American Baptist Historical Society, Valley Forge, Pa.

[15] J.H. Rushbrooke, *The Present Situation in Europe,* 24 April 1928, p. 8, ABFMS Archive Box 254.

[16] Minutes of the EBF Council, August 1951, Hamburg, p. 13, Box 801, EBF Archive.

[17] *Ibid.*

continued to surface within the EBF community through to the present day.[18] In the summer of 1950, as plans were being drawn up for the inauguration of the EBF, C.T. LeQuesne, KC, a prominent British Baptist layman and Joint Treasurer of the BWA, wrote to W.O. Lewis, who was then attending the Central Committee of the World Council of Churches (WCC) in Toronto:

> The General Purposes Committee of the BU met here a little over a week ago and received a resolution from the British Council of Churches who had agreed that the appeal of the new department of Inter-Church Aid and Refugee Services be approved and that the Constituent churches… be asked to commend the appeal.[19]

LeQuesne went on to comment on the strength of the British Council of Churches (BCC) resolution. The officers of the British Union had proposed a grant of one thousand pounds from the post-war British Baptist Victory Thanksgiving Fund, 'with the request that it be used as far as possible for Baptist work through the Inter-Church Aid and Refugee Services'. One member of the British Baptist General Purposes and Finance Committee had proposed the omission of reference to help being given to Baptists, but LeQuesne commented, 'Rushbrooke spoke more than once in my hearing to the effect that our fellow Baptists did not get their fair share, when funds were distributed by some international or undenominational agencies'.[20]

In his letter LeQuesne indicated that he was anxious to know how Lewis saw this issue since he was Director of Relief Services for the BWA and also as Associate Secretary of the BWA for Europe. Lewis was much involved in the relief work going on in this post-war period amongst displaced persons in Europe. For his part, LeQuesne concluded: 'I am sure, I suppose, that we should be able to distribute one thousand pounds through Baptist channels to Baptists and Baptist institutions, who are in great need of help'.[21] The response of Lewis could have simply been 'yes'. Indeed, throughout 1950 he was struggling to raise funds in Europe and the USA for care packages and parcels, especially for displaced persons in Germany and Belgium, and, in this context,

---

[18] From time to time efforts are made to defuse the tension as in the concordat agreement brokered by the Fellowship of British Baptists in 1996 between Christian Aid, Baptist World Aid, Baptist Response-Europe [BRE] and the BMS. This agreement was reneged on in 2001 by the BMS. Minutes of the Fellowship of British Baptists, Angus Library.

[19] Airmail letter from C.T. LeQuesne, KC, to W.O. Lewis in Toronto, 25 June 1950, LeQuesne Papers, Angus Library.

[20] *Ibid.*

[21] *Ibid.*

he had constant requests from European Baptists for more assistance.[22] However, Lewis himself was torn between his own requirements as BWA Director of Relief and his role in the WCC Central Committee discussing the needs of Inter-Church Aid. His reply from Toronto on 14 July 1950 commented:

> I do not think I should appear to intervene in a matter that IS ALMOST PURELY a British Baptist affair. As you know I am now attending a meeting of the Central Committee of the World Council of Churches. The question of Inter-Church Aid has been discussed. I think the WCC makes good use of the funds at its disposal. And I feel that Baptist bodies belonging to the World Council should give something to the work of the Council. It is partly a question of proportion.[23]

There were broader issues being raised by some evangelicals in this period connected with involvement in the WCC,[24] but the discussions within the EBF tended to concentrate on practical rather than theological matters.

The point that Lewis made continues to be important. Several of the Baptist Unions within the EBF were and are also members of the various national, European and world ecumenical organisations and are active in their ecumenical relief and development agencies.[25] But some within the Baptist world, especially certain of the mission agencies and some of the leaders in the BWA, have wanted Baptist communities to give exclusively to Baptist organisations. This narrower view has never been expressed by the European leadership of the EBF, who have held to the W.O. Lewis position that giving should be both denominational and ecumenical; the debate has been about proportions.[26] This proved to be true with the response to the extreme needs in

---

[22] An analysis of his correspondence for 1950 suggests over 60% of his letters were seeking assistance for refugees and displaced persons in the Baptist communities in mainland Europe. BWA Correspondence Box 23, Angus Library.

[23] Letter from W.O. Lewis to C.T. LeQuesne, Toronto, 14 July 1950, Le Quesne Papers, Angus Library.

[24] These issues had been raised in the World Evangelical Fellowship, which was emerging as an alternative for some evangelicals to the WCC.

[25] An example would be the Baptist Union of Great Britain, the Baptist Union of Scotland and the Baptist Union of Wales which are all members of Christian Aid, the British Churches aid and development agency. They have a seat on the Board of the agency, encourage their churches to raise funds and participate in campaigns and, on occasion, jointly promote particular campaigns, for instance 'Trade for Life' (1997) and 'Just Life' (2006). See www.christian-aid.org.uk, accessed 22 January 2007.

[26] W.O. Lewis was succeeded in his work by Archie Goldie, a Canadian Baptist, who developed proper patterns of application for assistance, then later by British Baptist, Paul Montacute, who increased the scope of work and activity and introduced pioneering work, such as providing aid in North Korea during the 1990s. Goldie developed the public relations style of Baptist World Aid.

Europe after the collapse of communism and the EBF development of BRE. The issue has surfaced again in recent years with the Hungarian Baptists creating 'Hungarian Baptist Aid', which has built capacity in what has been called a 'first foot on the ground' strategy in response to global catastrophies and which has been largely funded by Baptist World Aid.[27] This has provoked a major debate within the BWA as to the importance of the BWA developing a fully operational relief and disaster agency aimed at rapid response, using the platform of Hungarian Baptist Aid. Some, especially those seeking to promote the development work of the BWA, have called for this to be a priority for member bodies, seeing in it a device for strengthening the visibility of the BWA.[28] However, European leaders have been sceptical about this and German, British, Danish, Swedish and Norwegian Baptists, in particular, have continued to want to work both through Baptist organisations and ecumenically. This reflected a Baptist vision for mission and at the same time recognition by European Baptists of their part within the mission of the wider church.

'International partnership'

The EBM was clearly intended to be the vehicle for Unions within Europe which did not have their own mission activities enabling them to cooperate together and provide a way of doing cross-cultural mission. The EBM would later refer to this as 'international partnership'.[29] Reference to this idea was made from the very first EBF meetings, although it was usually in the context of 'Europe to elsewhere'. By the mid 1950s the Austrian, Belgian, Finnish, French, German, Italian, Spanish, Swiss and Yugoslavian Baptist Unions were members of EBM, with Henri Vincent (France) as President, Paul Schmidt (Germany) as Secretary and Otto Winzeler (Swiss) as Treasurer,[30] and with Henry Cook (EBF Secretary), Carmelo Inguanti (Italy), Herbert Mascher (Germany) and Karl Reichardt (Germany) as committee members. All these Baptist Unions and their leaders had agreed to cooperate together and a plan

---

27 Baptist World Aid is the relief and development arm of the BWA. It has a turnover of US$3.9 million (2005) per year and can obtain medical supplies and emergency equipment from the US Government, BWA General Council Report Book, Mexico City, 2006, pp. 118-19, BWA Archive, Falls Church, Virginia.

28 I.M. Chapman, Special Assistant to the BWA General Secretary, has been a noted advocate of this point of view, for instance in a submission to the BWA Implementation Task Force. Notes of First Meeting 27-29 October 2005, p. 3, ITF Minutes, BWA Archive.

29 European Baptist Mission [EBM] Council Minutes 2004, EBM Archive, Elstal, Germany.

30 Letter from Henri Vincent calling representatives to the July 1958 annual meeting in Zürich, Erik Rudén Papers, Box 1, Angus Library.

had been advanced to begin mission work in what was then the French Cameroons. The first initiative was developed at Meri in the North Cameroons and Mr Maurice and Dr Farelly were sent there. They made contact with local people and by April 1956 the first mission buildings had been erected. EBM had already identified other people to join them. A young German couple, the Kasssuhulkes, had been sent to Paris for language training and it was hoped, in January 1957, that a young German qualified in building work would also begin language training in Paris. They would be joined in 1957 by two teachers from France.[31]

When the EBM began to work in what was then the French Cameroons in 1957 it did so with support from a good number of Unions – at that stage all of them western Unions.[32] In due course further mission fields were opened in Sierra Leone, Liberia and Argentina. The EBM continued to grow and develop, with significant progress being made in a number of areas.[33] Following the collapse of the communist governments, the Unions in Central Europe especially, also joined EBM and began contributing both funds and personnel. Typically, EBM operated with the classic Baptist societal model established in 1792 by those who founded the BMS. Baptists in one group – normally a nation, but in the case of EBM, something like eighteen European nations, operating through a directional body (the Mission Council) – were involved in recruiting, training and sending missionaries from the participating bodies to another part of the world. This is a classic model in mission history and has been the paramount model for gathering churches and even for some episcopal and synodical churches.[34] However, in response to fresh thinking about cross-cultural mission and the paradigm shift in Christian commitment from the old 'north' to the new 'south',[35] the EBM Mission Council in Berlin in 2004 resolved:

> The Mission Council sees the future of world mission in an international partnership with a shared responsibility of all partners involved. The Mission Council asks the Executive Committee [of the EBM] to establish a task group

---

[31] *European Baptist Federation News Bulletin Number 22*, April 1956, EBF Office, London, Erik Rudén Papers, Box 1, Angus Library.

[32] EBM Minutes and archives, EBM Archive, Elstal, Berlin.

[33] A description of the overseas work of the EBM is not within the purpose of this thesis.

[34] In Europe, the Church Missionary Society [CMS], Anglican, and the Methodist Missionary Society for example. For an early history of CMS see J.A. Evenson, *Yes Magazine*, April-June 1999.

[35] On this see P.H. Jenkins, *The Next Christendom* (Oxford: Oxford University Press, 2002).

> which presents a report and a concept paper.... About the process of changes needed in the structures of EBM/MASA.[36]

The reference to MASA is to the Mission Activities in South America, which was a small separate mission incorporated into EBM in the 1980s.

This EBM Task Force was established, and was led by Ngwedia Paul Msiza, General Secretary of the Baptist Convention of Southern Africa. In the Task Force Report, Msiza and his colleagues told the EBM Council, in February 2006, that the future function of EBM should be 'serving churches to fulfil God's mission in the world'. Here there is no mention of geographical or denominational limitation. Instead, the Task Force Report focused on the task of assisting local gathering communities of believers to engage in mission:

> beyond the church starting in the local context going into cross-cultural work worldwide with a deliberate focus on personal salvation and as well on developing a healing and reconciling community including the subjects of justice and preservation of creation.[37]

Changing the whole focus and method of the work and abandoning the 'Europe to elsewhere approach', the Task Force, whilst, in its wording, abandoning any specific link with Europe, does recommend providing 'information concerning links, activities and possibilities for stronger South-to-South and North-to-North cooperation in supporting already existing initiatives by the Baptist World Alliance (BWA) and its regional fellowships'.[38]

The fact that the Task Force was led by Msiza was a clear indication of the intention of the EBM to move away from the model of the sending society, a model which has served Baptists in Europe from 1792 until today, to a global partner model, picking up particularly on the thinking that is now emerging about world mission, as expressed for example by distinguished missiologist Andrew F. Walls, who comments:

> Christian faith is now more diffused than at any previous time in its history; not only in the sense that it is more geographically, ethnically, and culturally widespread than ever before, but in the sense that it is diffused within more communities. The territorial 'from-to' idea that underlay the older missionary movement has given way to a concept much more like that of Christians within the Roman Empire in the second and third centuries: parallel presences in

[36] EBM Council Minutes 2004, EBM Archive.

[37] EBM Task Force Report to the EBM Council, February 2006, EBM Archive.

[38] *Ibid.*

> different circles and different levels, each seeking to penetrate within and beyond its circle.[39]

It remains to be seen to what extent the EBM Task Force proposals, having been agreed, will be implemented. If the proposals are fully implemented this will see a major mission shift in the nature of the EBM from a regional mission body, working with European ecclesial bodies and sending missionaries to other regions, into a global organism where all partners are both senders and receivers.

As the EBF gained institutional strength in the 1950s and the member Unions began to think in a positive way about mission, they included in their thinking cross-national support in Europe. Mission involved, as has already been clear in this thesis, caring for the needs of others. A distinctly European Baptist dimension began to be developed. Whilst the BWA continued to be the arena in which cross-cultural aid and development was offered, the aftermath of the 1956 uprising in Hungary and its brutal suppression by the forces of the Warsaw Pact, saw the BWA Relief Committee establish a Baptist Relief Committee for Hungary under the chairmanship of the President of the Seminary at Rüschlikon, Josef Nordenhaug. It met in Vienna on 10 November 1956 and faced the issues of how to care for refugees – about 30,000 were in Vienna alone. Over 200 people, 173 of whom were Baptists, were temporarily housed in the Mollardgasse Baptist Church, then later in a refugee home developed at Rekawinkel. Nordenhaug reported they had handled fifty-one tons of clothing, two-thirds from Sweden and one-third from the USA. Some US$ 41,000, a very significant sum, was collected for aid work in the period 26 November 1956 to 10 July 1957.[40] This funding came from many North American and European sources, including the three mission agencies, American Baptist Churches (ABC), Southern Baptist Convention (SBC) and the North American Baptist General Conference.[41] John Allen Moore, an SBC Missionary, was seconded to be full-time Executive Secretary of the Relief Committee for Hungary. Hans Luckey was dispatched in July 1957 to Budapest to meet with Laszlo Szabo, President of the Hungarian Baptists, to learn about the plight of the Hungarian Baptists and to report back to the Committee.[42]

Coordination of appeals became a crucial factor from the later 1950s onwards as many individual Baptist churches and Unions wrote to Baptists throughout the world seeking support for projects they were undertaking. How

---

[39] A.F. Walls, *The Missionary Movement in Christian History: Studies in the Transmission of Faith* (Edinburgh: T&T Clark, 1996), pp. 258-69.

[40] Report of J. Nordenhaug to the BWA Relief Committee and the EBF Officers, 1 August 1957, Erik Rudén Papers, Box 1, Angus Library.

[41] Financial Report of Baptist Relief Committee for Hungary, August 1957, Erik Rudén Papers, Box 1, Angus Library.

[42] BWA Relief Committee Minutes 1956 and 1957, BWA Archive.

these matters were to be handled in Europe was set out in a letter from Frank H. Woyke, BWA Associate Secretary with responsibility for the relief programme, to Reinhold Fandrich, a Canadian Baptist, in November 1970:

> I believe I should now call to your attention a procedure concerning relief appeals by European Baptist groups that has been adopted by the EBF. In the years following World War II it was discovered that some of the Baptist groups in Europe in a time of need sent out many appeals to other Baptists in many parts of the world. As a result of this procedure, those groups who were most aggressive in sending out appeals sometimes received more relief aid than was really needed and those groups who were more reticent received very little or nothing to meet their needs.[43]

Woyke was outlining what was a real problem. What is significant for the purpose of the present study of wider Baptist ecclesiology is that it was the EBF, in its role as an ecclesial body, which addressed the issue. Woyke noted that the EBF Council:

> adopted the policy that all relief appeals on the part of the EBF member unions should first of all be reported to the EBF.... Since all of the Baptist Unions participate in the work of the [EBF] Council, this policy was intended to provide for an evaluation of the appeals and for a decision as to their endorsement. The BWA Relief department sends out appeals for European needs only after they have been cleared through EBF.[44]

In this way, the international Baptist effort in this sphere of mission recognised and cooperated with the regional expression of Baptist life embodied in the EBF.

As noted above, some of the Western European Baptist Unions worked ecumenically in the sphere of relief and development, as well as denominational support. This was true for the Germans, Dutch, Danish, Swedish and British Baptists. Ernest A. Payne noted this point when presenting a paper on British Baptist relief activities to the BWA Relief Committee in August 1969. He noted:

> Since the early days of the BWA, British Baptists have given regular help to their brethren on the Continent of Europe. In 1920 there was a division of spheres of special interest between the British Baptist Union of Great Britain and Ireland and the Northern and Southern Conventions of the USA.[45] Since 1948 there has been more general cooperation in meeting special needs whenever they have occurred,

---

[43] Letter from F.H. Woyke to R. Fandrich, Winnipeg, 16 November 1970, BWA Europe Box 3, Angus Library.

[44] *Ibid.*

[45] See Chapter 6 for a full outline of the 1920 and 1948 agreements.

> though until recently annual grants continued to be made to the Baptists of Finland. Since the formation of the EBF help to the Baptists of the Continent has frequently been channeled through the EBF and always in consultation with its secretary... British Baptists regularly contribute large sums direct to Christian Aid, Oxfam, War on Want and other general appeals.[46]

The point firmly established that member bodies were free to work both denominationally through the EBM, BRE (post 1990), and national Baptist mission agencies and, if they so desired, ecumenically, in keeping with a gathering church ecclesiology which did not impose restrictions on the churches.

'Solidarity and fellowship': Cross-Cultural Mission in Europe

As well as establishing the EBM as an agency of several member bodies of the EBF to do mission work outside Europe, the EBF also began to take on some responsibility for supporting mission work in certain European countries. When the EBF met in Stockholm in 1958, proposals were advanced for the EBF, as such, to take on responsibility for mission work in Belgium and Finland. Edwin Bell wrote to Erik Rudén on these points in January 1959:

> If it is definitely decided that the Federation is to assume responsibility for care and development of the work in Belgium and Finland I think it would be well for the responsible officers of the Baptist Unions in these two countries to be advised of this fact with the confirmation of the budget and provisions therefore for 1959.... I think it would be helpful to you and reassuring to the leaders in Belgium and France if you would pay them a visit as soon as possible, since you are already known in and know Finland quite well.[47]

In the thinking of Erik Rudén, the adoption of a budget for 1959 increasing the demands of the EBF from US$500 per year to US$19,000 per year represented a strategic move from fellowship to mission. On 27 April 1959 he wrote personally to each General Secretary of the member Unions commenting:

> We discussed various mission projects and the financial responsibilities to carry out such a program. We adopted a mission budget... Yes, but this does not mean we have the money we need for the work of the Federation. Some Unions have promised to increase their contributions... It would be wonderful if we could get

---

[46] Report by E.A. Payne, July 1969, to the BWA Relief Committee, BWA Relief Papers, BWA Europe Box 3, Angus Library.

[47] Letter from E.A. Bell to E. Rudén, Erik Rudén Papers, Box 1, Angus Library.

> support from all denominations. Of course I know most groups cannot give very much, but also a small gift is a token of solidarity and fellowship.[48]

The Seminary at Rüschlikon also sought to foster a concern for evangelism and for sharing insights into methods of evangelism by the holding of periodic conferences on the topic. A small Evangelism Group was created in 1966 under the chairmanship of Baungaard Thomsen, arising out of discussions amongst Europeans who were present at a BWA Executive Committee in London in 1966 when reports were received on plans for evangelism in the USA and 'the great success of a crusade in Brazil'.[49] Such a Committee, with a wide reference to promote and encourage evangelism, also encouraged the exchange of ideas and mutual support in the task of mission. This group has been a feature of EBF life ever since, though it has changed its name and construction at many points over the succeeding decades.[50] At a conference on evangelism held at Rüschlikon in March 1967, with a wide attendance from Baptists throughout Europe, it was agreed to recommend that:

> The EBF Committee on Evangelism should be expanded to represent the different linguistic and cultural areas and to help the Unions in their work. Different Unions should share in their evangelistic plans in order to help each other better.[51]

Guenter Wiske, of the German Baptist Union, was invited to chair the Committee and, in 1968, the expanded Committee began its work. An annual meeting of those involved in national mission work was planned[52] for the summer of 1969 in Novi Sad, Serbia, with speakers, including Stephen F. Olford from Calvary Baptist Church, New York.[53]

In the course of the Novi Sad Conference, at which seventy people were present from throughout all of Europe (except East Germany and Bulgaria), it was agreed to hold a further and longer conference in 1970 to analyse the missionary situation throughout Europe, to look at methods and structures and then to set goals and tasks to promote evangelism in the member bodies. A

---

[48] Letter from E. Rudén to M. Ronchi, 27 April 1959, similar to ones in the file to all EBF Unions. Erik Rudén Papers, Box 1, Angus Library.

[49] Minutes of the EBF Evangelism Committee, November 1966, EBF Archive, Angus Library.

[50] It is currently the Division of Mission and Evangelism, which has a Core Group of five members and organises annual conferences for national home mission secretaries. See *EBF Directory 2006* (Prague: EBF Publications, 2006), p. 36.

[51] Recommendations of the Evangelism Conference (1967), EBF Archive, Angus Library.

[52] The annual meeting of Home Mission Secretaries continues up to the present and is now organised by the Core Group of the EBF Division of Mission and Evangelism.

[53] Circular letter from G. Wiske to the Evangelism Committee, December 1968, EBF Archive, Angus Library.

preliminary phase was the circulation of twelve questions to all Unions seeking to gain accurate information about the life of the churches, the methods of evangelism used, types of evangelistic training employed and the settings and possibilities for evangelism.[54] This initiative to set Europe-wide structures and goals, whilst worthy in itself, was not taken forward in a way that had any significant impact on the Unions, or on cooperation between the Unions in this important arena. Discussion of the importance and possible strategies of evangelism continued, not least in the 1980s and 1990s, through the development of an annual conference of those responsible for 'home mission' of the various Unions. These Union representatives were brought together in the late spring each year to exchange information and ideas and often to listen to papers delivered by representatives of Unions developing specific programmes.

With the formation of the EBF Division of Mission and Evangelism in 1990, the responsibility and planning for this event moved to the Division. From this stage onwards more careful thought was given to how ideas might be exchanged and resources provided cross-culturally, as the impact of post-communist and post-modern life began to markedly change the mission scene in Europe. As has been seen, many European Baptist leaders had begun to recognise, at an earlier stage, that it was not simply a matter of taking the latest offering from North America, but that there needed to be careful examination of the European situation, and Europe-appropriate solutions were needed.[55] One effect of globalisation which was experienced in this period was that most of the big cities of Europe became multi-ethnic in character, with an inflow of migrants, especially to Western and some regions in Northern and Southern Europe from other continents or from other parts of the European continent. Thus the 2005 Mission and Evangelism Conference focused on the phenomenon of the establishment of ethnic churches in these cities. In Austria, Belgium and Germany ethnic communities began to represent significant numbers within the Union. In large cities like London, Vienna, Brussels, Paris and Berlin, ethnic churches formed the most significant and vibrant baptistic communities. The conference produced many excellent papers which the International Baptist Theological Seminary (IBTS) published in book form.[56] Here was EBF cross-cultural mission concern at its best, with an issue being identified, and with Europeans gathering together, both to inform each other

---

54 EBF Questionnaire on Evangelism, Autumn 1969, EBF Archive, Angus Library.

55 See Chapter 6.

56 P.F. Penner (ed.), *Ethnic Churches in Europe: A Baptist Response* (Schwarzenfeld, Germany: Neufeld Verlag, 2006).

and to draw on specialist thinkers within the EBF family.[57]

A further significant development took place in 2000 when incoming General Secretary, Theo Angelov, a Bulgarian who had suffered under the Bulgarian communist government, addressed the EBF Council and proposed that the EBF Executive seek to talk with all the North American mission partners of European Baptists about four specific mission priorities which the partners might support and which would be controlled and shaped by the EBF.[58] This represented another significant ecclesial first for EBF, given that to date the role of the EBF had been focused on the area of relief and development through BRE. Discussions with the partners took place at a meeting held at a hotel near Heathrow Airport, London, from 24-25 August 2001. ABC-International Missions Board, SBC-Foreign Mission Board, the Cooperative Baptist Fellowship (CBF), BMS, Baptist State Conventions from Virginia, Texas, Tennessee, North Carolina and the North American Baptist Convention were all present to hear Theo Angelov's presentation. Whilst several ideas were discussed at that meeting – such as continuing support for relief and development and assistance with theological education – one idea that seemed to engender general support was the creation of an indigenous missionary project, which envisaged Unions applying to a coordinating group of the EBF for funding for salaries (at an EBF-set figure) for nationals who would plant new congregations. In turn, the EBF would solicit finances from Unions in Western Europe and from mission partners in the USA to fund this work. Regular reports would be furnished to the funding partners and there would be a declining scale of salary support as the church plants would be expected to become self-supporting or to be funded by their Union within five years.[59]

This Indigenous Missionary Project (IMP), as it came to be known, was an initiative within and overseen by the EBF, involving partners across the EBF and strategic mission partners in the USA. Though some doubted that, in practice, either the mission partners or the Baptist Unions of Europe would be willing to cede key responsibilities and oversight to the EBF, subsequent events proved this to be unduly pessimistic. Theo Angelov already had a coordinator in mind, the vigorous pastor of Wroclau Baptist Church in Poland, Daniel Trusiewicz. Angelov drove the scheme forward, demonstrating again that the EBF General Secretary could, in some circumstances, have a significant amount of personal episcope. After initially meeting some hesitancy within the

[57] The keynote address at this conference was delivered by Paul Weller, University of Derby, a noted expert on ethnic minorities in European society and a member of Broadway Baptist Church, Derby, UK.

[58] T. Angelov proposed this at the EBF Council, September 2000, in Riga. A first meeting with mission partners to explore his ideas was held in London, 24-25 August 2001.

[59] EBF Indigenous Missionary Project Guidelines. EBF web site: www.ebf.org/articles /index, accessed 18 January 2007.

EBF Executive Committee,[60] a smaller Core Group of the President, Finance Chair, General Secretary and Convenor of the Mission and Evangelism Group was given responsibility for both managing the Coordinator, approving the church planting schemes to be supported and soliciting funding into the scheme. In April 2002 a modest start was made with a handful of missionaries in Moldova, but the Report of the Coordinator to the EBF Council 2006 in Lyons, France, revealed that IMP personnel were now supported in Armenia, Belarus, Latvia, Russia, Ukraine, Jordan, Egypt, Lebanon, Syria, the Caucasus region, Romania, Hungary and Iraq.[61] Several Western European Unions and Conventions – Germany, Norway, Scotland, Spain, the International Baptist Convention (based in Germany) and the Czech Republic – had joined forces with the Texas and Virginia (USA) State Conventions and the BMS, CBF and ABC mission agencies. The work of Trusiewicz and the leadership offered by Angelov and his successor, Tony Peck, had made the IMP's success remarkable. By January 2007 over fifty new viable churches have been planted in twenty-one different countries in Europe and the Middle East.[62] This demonstrates that the Unions and mission agencies both trusted and used the EBF to facilitate an exciting programme of church planting by indigenous missionaries, involving cross-cultural support and with training and resourcing offered by the EBF-IMP Core Group.

Cross-Cultural Diversity

To achieve united missional action in Europe was not easy. The IMP initative is an example of a successful venture. In other cases the diversity of the European Baptist family meant that initiatives either had limited success or ended in failure. One of the greatest cross-cultural challenges in the first forty years of the EBF was cooperating with and supporting Baptist communities in Eastern Europe 'behind the iron curtain'. There were many difficulties to be faced in involving those in the communist countries in European Baptist life and in keeping channels of communication open. Questions about how to avoid misunderstandings and support the Eastern European Union leaderships in useful ways beset the EBF officers, especially in the early years of the EBF. In March 1959 Erik Rudén, on the verge of assuming the secretaryship, was able to visit Moscow and make contact with various Russian Baptist leaders, including Jakub and Michael Zhidkov, Alexey Karpov and Ilia Orlov. One topic raised by them was, as Rudén recorded it:

[60] I admit that I was one of those who could not see that the EBF would be sufficiently trusted by either the donors or the Unions to oversee the programme.

[61] EBF Council, Lyon, September 2006, Document C2006/14, EBF Office Archive, Prague.

[62] Updated information is maintained at www.ebf.org/projects, accessed 15 January 2007.

> [t]he election of the new Executive Committee of the EBF. '50% of the Baptists of Europe live in the eastern countries, but we Russians have no representative on the Committee.' At the end of this part of the discussion I sketched out the constitution of the EBF and reminded the brethren that the Council will meet again in 1960, new officers will be elected, and the Russians have the same opportunity as other nations to make their voice heard. I emphasized as my conviction that the Russian Baptists will have a great contribution to give to our Baptist fellowship in Europe.[63]

At that same meeting, the issue of a letter from Russian Baptists to Soviet President Bulganin was taken up by Eric Rudén. Some in the West had seen the letter as unduly supportive of the Soviet system but the Russians insisted that they were simply acting as good citizens. They pointed out that Rudén, a Swede, prayed for his king, and they prayed for the Russian government and leaders. They protested that the translation of their letter circulating in the West was misleading and that the letter had merely been an expression of gratitude and congratulation. But then they came to an ecclesial and cross-cultural dimension. They contended:

> No committee in other countries has the authority to discuss such matters. The privilege to write letters belongs to every citizen. We do not accept the attitude that the actions of the different Unions are to be examined at a meeting of the EBF. We can write letters to our government and still be good Baptists.[64]

Thus the EBF struggled throughout the communist period with the challenge of speaking into diverse political worlds without causing difficulty for one group or another.

Even in the post-communist period, differences of social and political background among the Unions could cause problems, especially when some of the more socio-politically active Unions such as Italy, Sweden and Great Britain wanted to comment on wider social and political issues. In 2005, in Lebanon, a resolution expressing joy at the enlargement of the European Union, which had little contentious political comment, nonetheless resulted in long discussion. After amendment and counter-amendment the following was minuted:

> The council members discussed extensively the proposed resolution, argued for and against having such a resolution and discussed in detail the wording. Finally the council members voted whether to have the resolution or not:

---

[63] Confidential Report on this visit from E. Rudén to H. Cook, 13 March 1959, Erik Rudén Papers, Box 1, Angus Library.

[64] *Ibid.*

33 members voted not to have it.
11 members voted to have it.
12 abstained.
The resolution was not passed.[65]

On the other hand, a resolution criticising the invasion of Iraq by a coalition of the governments of the USA, United Kingdom and some other countries, was clearly passed at the same meeting. In this period there was a desire on the part of some within the EBF to distance European life from some of the tendencies in North American life. Thus the BWA, in some of its operational initiatives, such as the 'Living Waters Conferences',[66] drew widespread criticism on the grounds that it was seeking to impose a North American model and conference style on different parts of the world family. In the social, as well as the political realm, diversity needed to be recognised if mission was to be affective.[67]

Part of the work of the EBF, as it has sought to equip member bodies for mission, has been educational. When the EBF Congress was held in Berlin in 1958, a concern was expressed that the EBF should look at the possibility of developing educational and Bible study material for use across the EBF family. This matter was pursued and the EBF Executive, meeting in Stockholm in the October, spent much time on the topic and agreed a Committee on Bible Study and Membership Training be established. The Committee met in Rüschlikon, 20-24 June 1959, and presented a report to the EBF Executive indicating that a questionnaire on needs had been circulated to member Unions, with the general response that a curriculum guide for young people and adults would be advisable, but not for children.[68] The mixed replies, and lack of replies from Unions, posed some questions for the Committee and it was soon clear that the swift action asked for at the Congress was not going to happen. Most Unions had material already in place for 1960 and many already had partnership agreements with other denominations for the production of joint material. There were other problems: the diverse settings for the teaching (day school, weeknight activities, Sunday activities), the challenges of different environments and backgrounds, and the difficulties involved in adapting the material culturally. Against this, positives were noted: the strong can help the weak; there could be better understanding of Baptist beliefs; material could be

---

[65] Minutes of the EBF Council, Beirut, Lebanon, 2004, p. 13, item 27, EBF Office Archive.

[66] BWA 'Living Waters Conferences' 2005-2010 on evangelistic strategies, funded by a special gift from donors in the USA.

[67] Critical exchanges took place during the BWA Executive Committee in Washington, DC, March 2006, BWA Executive Papers, BWA Archive, and my recollections.

[68] Report of the Bible Study and Membership Training Committee of the EBF, 31 July 1959, Erik Rudén Papers, Box 1, Angus Library.

introduced in situations where there was little available; and *koinonia* within the EBF could be fostered.[69] However, it was seen that the needs of the Unions were diverse and it proved not to be appropriate for the EBF to try to develop material for use by a range of member Unions.[70]

The EBF officers have constantly sought to include within the EBF all who called themselves Baptists in Europe, including the small Baptist groups in Syria, Turkey and Greece, and even single churches in Malta and Iceland. This has been part of the vision for European-wide mission. One group that it has not proved possible to include is the Irish Baptist Association, formerly the Irish Baptist Union. Originally this Union was more closely linked to the, then, Baptist Union of Great Britain and Ireland,[71] but because of the social and theological climate in Northern Ireland,[72] the Baptist Union of Ireland gradually moved away from membership of the BWA[73] and any involvement with the Baptist Union of Great Britain. A major issue of disagreement has been membership of the WCC and other ecumenical instruments. Irish Baptists have taken the view that such links taint the purity of gospel witness, and an attitude of 'guilt by association' has meant they have been unwilling to remain involved with Unions that have ecumenical links. When Rudén was appointed General Secretary of the EBF in 1959, he wrote to the Secretary of the Irish Baptists, Joshua Thomson, describing the ministry of the EBF and his own story and asking if he could visit the Baptist Union.[74] Thomson took the letter to his Council and replied on 5 November, 'While many of our people would welcome closer links with the wider Baptist fraternity, the majority of Irish Baptists do not favour affiliation with other organisations. This attitude arises from the fact that Irish Baptist Churches are solidly conservative in theology

---

[69] *Ibid.*, p. 3.

[70] Some materials produced by Christians in one context did prove capable of transfer to another, such as the Alpha material, but most Unions or evangelicals within a particular setting chose to prepare their own material suitable for their own setting.

[71] In deference to the Irish, reference to 'Ireland' was removed from the title in the 1980s.

[72] The Baptist Union of Ireland predates the creation of the Republic of Ireland, so there are a handful of churches in the Republic. However, the bulk of the churches are in Ulster and heavily influenced by the conservative theological disposition of the larger Presbyterian churches.

[73] The Irish Baptists withdrew from the BWA, but did have observers at the 1955 BWA Congress in London. J. Edwin Orr sought to act as an intermediary to improve relations at the time of the appointment of Erik Rudén. Letter from A.T. Ohrn to J. E. Orr, September 1959, Erik Rudén Papers, Box 1, Angus Library.

[74] Letter from E. Rudén to J. Thomson, 5 October 1959, Erik Rudén Papers, Box 1, Angus Library.

and outlook.'[75]

Erik Rudén did not give up, replying later that month pointing out that many Baptists on the mainland of Europe were deeply conservative in outlook, that the EBF was a simple organisation for fellowship and cooperation, and expressing the view that Irish Baptists no doubt had a very great contribution 'of spiritual power and theological knowledge to give to us in other countries in the future'.[76] However, Irish Baptists continued to stand apart despite other attempts to encourage them to at least send observers to the EBF meetings. Each new General Secretary of the EBF made contact with them and invited participation, but all met with polite, but firm refusal. In 2002 David McMillan, one of the leading pastors in the Irish Baptist Association, took his sabbatical at IBTS, Prague, and was present for the Graduation Ceremony in May when the speaker was Billy Taranger, then Vice-President of the EBF. Billy Taranger had already worked hard to secure the involvement of the highly conservative Baptist Church in Iceland into the life of the EBF. He invited David McMillan to attend the EBF Council in Oslo in September 2002 to observe life in the EBF and report back to the Council of the Irish Baptist Association. David McMillan did attend and realised that the EBF family did include very conservative Unions like his own and promised to encourage Irish Baptists to at least have observer status at EBF Councils.[77] The search for a way to express ecclesial unity in diversity, particularly for the sake of the gospel, continues to be a challenge for the EBF.

European Baptists and Peace

Mission has also been seen by Baptists as involving reconciliation between peoples. From the first tentative steps towards cooperation between Baptists in Europe, there have been those keen advocates who saw one of the most important areas of concern as building bridges of peace between the different nations in the region. J.H. Rushbrooke[78] was married to a German, Dorothea Weber, and had a passionate concern for Anglo-German friendship. In visiting Germany with a delegation of British Christians in June 1909 he spoke of the task in hand:

---

[75] Letter from J. Thomson to E. Rudén, 5 November 1959, Erik Rudén Papers, Box 1, Angus Library.

[76] Letter from E. Rudén to J. Thomson, 16 November 1959, Erik Rudén Papers, Box 1, Angus Library.

[77] Address to EBF Council, Oslo, September 2002, my recollection.

[78] On Rushbrooke and peace see B. Green, *Tomorrow's Man: A Biography of James Henry Rushbrooke* (Didcot: Baptist Historical Society, 1997). On his peacemaking initiatives see also P. Dekar, *For the Healing of the Nations: Baptist Peacemakers* (Macon, Ga.: Smythe and Helwys, 1993), pp. 77-85.

> We...resolve to work earnestly and self-sacrificingly for the cause of international friendship...we are conscious that when we have worked and testified in the interests of peace, our hope is in God...surely our faith is deepened and strengthened knowing Jesus Christ is the King of Peace.[79]

In the lead up to the First World War, Baptists such as Rushbrooke and John Clifford campaigned tirelessly for peace and the easing of tension between Britain and Germany, although the war itself changed attitudes dramatically and had a serious effect on historic German-British Baptist relationships.[80] Beyond the First World War, as editor of the *Goodwill* magazine, Rushbrooke continued to promote concerns for peace in Europe, and in 1934 a Baptist Ministers' Pacifist Fellowship was formed by British Baptists, with 580 ministers becoming members.[81]

Hopes of peace were to be shattered by the rise of the Nazi Party in Germany and the creation of the Third Reich.[82] The effects of this on Baptist communities were devastating. Despite the earlier commitment to peace, there was little evidence of Baptist leaders engaging themselves in peacemaking in a pan-European way through this period of conflict. After the Second World War the division of Europe into communist East and social democratic West[83] was a major issue, as it deeply affected the sense of *koinonia* between Baptists. As a Baptist, Paul Weller has commented:

> As one who, during the Cold War, used to be engaged in work against the threat of nuclear annihilation and to promote east-west dialogue, I remember the arrogance with which politicians and others in the West often used to appropriate the terminology of Europe as if the capitalist societies were the whole of Europe. There were very few bodies or organisations that were genuinely and inclusively European. It was almost as if the countries and peoples of Central and Eastern

---

[79] J.H. Rushbrooke in F Siegmund-Schultze (ed.), *Friendly Relations between Great Britain and Germany* (Berlin: H.S. Herman, 1909), pp. 209-10.

[80] K.W. Clements, 'Baptists and the Outbreak of the First World War', *BQ*, Vol. 26, No. 2, 1975, pp. 74-92; K. Robbins, 'Protestant Nonconformists and the Peace Question', in A.P.F. Sell and A.R. Cross (eds.), *Protestant Nonconformity in the Twentieth Century* (Carlisle: Paternoster, 2003), pp. 216-39; I.M. Randall, *The English Baptists of the Twentieth Century* (Didcot: Baptist Historical Society, 2005), pp. 78-83.

[81] Randall, *The English Baptists of the Twentieth Century*, pp. 196-200.

[82] The complex relationship between German Baptists and National Socialism has been examined by A. Strübind in, 'German Baptists and National Socialism', *JEBS,*Vol 8, No. 3, May 2008. On British Baptists see K.W. Clements, 'A Question of Freedom - British Baptists and the German Church Struggle', in K.W. Clements (ed.), *Baptists in the Twentieth Century* (London: Baptist Historical Society, 1983), pp. 96-113.

[83] This is a generalisation, with obvious exceptions in Spain and Portugal, which had a form of dictatorship, and variant models of social democracy in the Nordic and Latin countries.

> Europe had somehow become non-European because they lived in a different socio-economic, political and military sphere of influence. Among honourable exceptions to this were the European Baptist Federation and Conference of European Churches.[84]

The desire by European Baptists in the post-war period (as well as before) to maintain *koinonia* in the face of adverse political situations, made them naturally interested in every opportunity which arose to have contact between the Baptists of the East and West. Occasionally the communist governments of the East were willing to allow, indeed use, the Christian communions in support of their own purposes. An issue which continued to interest them was the cause of peace, and many communist governments encouraged the churches within their countries to take an active part in a series of conferences related to the theme of peace. This, of course, sounded an obvious note of interest to baptistic churches, and individuals within those churches, many of whom had a pacifist understanding of the teaching of Jesus and saw themselves to be following in the way of earlier European Baptists, like Rushbrooke, who had striven for peace in Europe. The life of the EBF and its member bodies were intimately bound up with these initiatives and, naturally so, as they reflected that important stream of the baptistic form of Christianity concerned with peacemaking.[85]

One of the earliest of these Peace Conferences was held at the Troitse-Sergiyeva Monastery, Zagorsk, in May 1952, with a further one in 1969.[86] Though principally involving all the major Christian churches in the USSR, the 1952 Conference also had representation from Denmark, Bulgaria, Romania (Rumania),[87] Finland, Holland and Austria. Five Baptists participated from the All-Union Council of Evangelical Christians-Baptists (AUCECB), including Jakub Zhidkov (President) and Alexander Karev (General Secretary). In his speech, Zhidkov criticised Baptists in the USA and Britain who had not embraced this call to peace and concluded:

---

[84] P. Weller, 'The Changing Face of Europe: The Nature and Role of Ethnic minorities in European Societies', in P.F. Penner (ed.), *Ethnic Churches in Europe: A Baptist Response* (Schwarzenfeld, Germany: Neufeld Verlag, 2006).

[85] For a biblical and theological justification for this stand see G.H. Stassen, *Just Peacemaking: Transforming Initiatives for Justice and Peace* (Louisville, Ky.: Westminster/John Knox Press, 1992). For biographies of key Baptist activists see Dekar, *For the Healing of the Nations*.

[86] 'Conference in Defence of Peace of all Churches and Religious Associations in the USSR, 9-12 May 1952'. Official transcript in English published by the Moscow Patriarchate, E.A. Payne Papers, Box K/1, Angus Library.

[87] The current spelling is Romania, but under the communists it was often spelt Rumania. To avoid confusion I henceforth use 'Romania'.

> The task of enlisting all Baptists and other Christians of kindred creeds into the cause of peace is far from being achieved. But the All-Union Council of Evangelical Christian Baptists is filled with the hope that the Baptists abroad will recognize the responsibility they bear in defending peace and preventing a third world war and will zealously participate in this cause.[88]

The Stalinist government was anxious to encourage the churches on the topic of peace as the Korean war proceeded and the armaments race between the four nuclear powers developed. The final statement of the conference was a message of greeting to Joseph Vissarionovich Stalin, signed by Zhidkov on behalf of the Baptists, which declared:

> It is with enormous enthusiasm and unanimity that we, representatives of various faiths, express to you, dear Joseph Vissarionovich, our greetings, devotion and very best wishes that you may live long years, bringing joy to the hearts of your people and all peace-loving and progressive mankind.[89]

Russian Baptists found this involvement in the call for peace a way of keeping a tolerable relationship with the Soviet government. It held within it the possibility of relating in some way to the outside world. It was also an important element in the worship life of the Baptist communities, as Ernest Payne was to discover when he joined with F. Townley Lord (BWA President) and W.O. Lewis (EBF General Secretary) in a visit to Russia in June 1954. He commented:

> In all the services at which we were present there were fervent prayers for peace. The Baptist leaders have been active supporters of the World Peace Council and the Stockholm Peace Appeal, as have the present leaders of the Orthodox church. Co-operation in this cause has resulted, we were told, in better relationships between the Orthodox church and the Baptists than have ever been known before.[90]

A year later attention turned to a World Peace Conference planned for Helsinki. Russian Baptists were involved in discussions, possibly one of their number attending a preparatory meeting in Vienna, from where invitations were extended to the BWA and EBF to be represented. Baptist leaders, in a core group working on plans for the BWA Jubilee Congress, turned their minds to the issue at a meeting in London on 10 May 1955. In those discussions the consensus of opinion was that someone ought to go to Helsinki as Lewis, Lord and Payne had been told by the Hungarian Baptists that unless the western

---

[88] *Ibid.*, speech of J. Zhidkov, to the Conference, p. 154.

[89] *Ibid.*, greetings to J.V. Stalin, p. 283.

[90] E.A. Payne, 'The Baptists of the Soviet Union' in *The Ecumenical Review*, January 1955, p. 167.

Baptist community was in some way represented there then no Russian Baptists would be permitted to attend the BWA Congress.[91] It was agreed that H.R. Williamson, the Foreign Secretary of the BMS at that time, should go to the Peace Conference representing British Baptists as he could speak Chinese and could talk with delegates from that country. Also it was noted that he was 'now at the end of his career and association with the Communists would not likely hurt him very much'.[92] W.O. Lewis also agreed to go as he could speak German and Russian and he wanted to try to make some contact with Finnish Baptists. Great care was taken to book in at a 'mission' hotel and take such other steps as would avoid giving the impression that they fully identified with the World Peace Council. They attended as observers so as not to be overtly linked to the communists. However, the Finnish Baptists were unhappy.[93] The Finnish General Secretary commented on 7 June 1955:

> May I inform you confidentially that the so called peace movement in Finland is entirely in communist hands and directed by the communist party. It is a propaganda tool of the communists. It does not enjoy the confidence of our nation.[94]

This letter indicates the dilemma facing the sincere Baptist peace activist. If there is a passionate belief in the cause of peace, and if the various conferences presented, in however limited a way, a contact and *koinonia* between Baptists in the East and the West, then was it right to participate, even knowing that in some measure the event was being used as a tool by communist governments? Many European Baptists took the view that the cause itself, the possibility of contact and the opportunity to engage in dialogue, was worth the risk. This understanding has continued to be part of the experience of many European Baptists until today.[95] In 1958 the Hungarian Ecumenical Council called a Peace Conference, when Christian workers from East Germany, Poland,

---

[91] Report from H. Cook to A.T. Ohrn, 11 May 1955, BWA/EBF Letters Box 27, Angus Library.

[92] Letter from H. Cook to A. T. Ohrn, 11 May 1955, BWA/EBF Letters Box 27, Angus Library.

[93] Various exchanges of correspondence between the General Secretary, M. Kolomainen and W.O. Lewis, BWA/EBF Letters Box 27, Angus Library.

[94] Letter from M. Kolomainen of Vaasa to W.O. Lewis, 7 June 1955, BWA/EBF Letters Box 27, Angus Library.

[95] A more recent example might be Norman Kember, a Baptist from England, who went to Baghdad as part of a Christian peace group in 2006. He was kidnapped and held by a militant group for some time before being released without major harm. He was roundly criticised by the United Kingdom Chief of the Army General Staff, Sir Michael Jackson, for his actions and for failing to thank the military for their involvement in his release. Kember has been a member of the Baptist Peace Fellowship and the Fellowship of Reconciliation most of his adult life.

Czechoslovakia, Hungary, Bulgaria, Romania and the USSR met in Budapest. Zhidkov, President of the AUCECB, attended the meetings in the 'Reformed' city of Debreczen. Here the call was made for a wider conference on peace involving both East and West, and Zhidkov commented:

> A strong confidence was expressed that this work is not only pleasing to God but it is an accomplishable task and very much needed in our time. Further, at the request of the Baptist leadership in Hungary I had an opportunity of visiting eight Baptist churches in Debreczen, Budapest and in Kishkirish to bring greetings and preach the gospel of Christ.[96]

This meeting in Hungary, held at the height of the so-called cold war, duly led to the churches in the then Czeckoslovakia being allowed, indeed no doubt encouraged by the communist authorities, to call a series of Christian Peace Assemblies in Prague. A successor to the Hungarian Conference was held in Prague, 16 - 19 April 1959, and Erik Rudén was invited to attend by the Secretary, Bohuslav Pospíšil, and by the Czech Baptists, hoping Rudén would visit their churches when in the country.[97] He was already committed to visit elsewhere, but Henry Cook was able to be present[98] and used the opportunity to make a radio broadcast.[99] He wrote about his visit to Erik Rudén, saying, 'I met brother Lohn and brother Svenson (Swedish Baptists) who had come to attend the Peace Conference, but who were also present at the (Baptist) meetings I was able to address'.[100] Henry Cook was apprehensive in advance about participating, writing to Rudén:

> I have had a further letter from the brethren [Czechoslovak Baptists] to say that there is to be some kind of Peace Ecumenical meeting held in Prague at which I am to speak, and I must do my best to steer my way through the difficulties of an 'iron curtain' Peace Conference![101]

Edwin Bell visited the USSR in the same year and reported to Erik Rudén:

---

[96] Translation by A. Klaupiks of letter from Y. Zhidjov to T. Adams, BWA President, Erik Rudén Papers, Box 1, Angus Library.

[97] Letters from the Christian Peace Conference and Report of the Conference. Erik Rudén Papers, Box 1, Angus Library.

[98] Disappointingly, Keith Robbins, in his article examining British Free Churches and the peace question, ignores involvement of British Baptists in this European initiative. See K. Robbins, 'Protestant Nonconformists and the Peace Question' in Sell and Cross, *Protestant Nonconformity in the Twentieth Century*, pp. 216-39.

[99] Letter from H. Cook to E. Rudén, 22 April 1959, Erik Rudén Papers, Box 1, Angus Library.

[100] *Ibid.*

[101] Letter from H. Cook to E. Rudén, 6 March 1959, Erik Rudén Papers, Box 1, Angus Library.

> In almost every instance in our conversations with the brethren there were certain stock questions regarding peace presented to us.... In several instances the full conversations including the prayers we had were taken down in recorded fashion by a secretary.[102]

Strains among 'the brethren' were evident, yet given the commitment to a Baptist community across Europe, these very strains constituted a stimulus to seek understanding and reconciliation.

'Against the division of Europe': Central Europe Peace Conferences, 1959-1978

From these basic beginnings, a larger and more representative series of peace gatherings was considered and developed. The 1960 event was one that Erik Rudén was able to attend, though his schedule did not permit him much time to meet with local Baptists.[103] The June 1961 Conference was held under the title '....And Peace on Earth'. The founding members of the Christian Peace Conference were six Czech Protestant churches headed by Josef Lukl Hromádka, one-time Dean of the Comenius Theological Faculty in the historic Charles University.[104] This organisation was encouraged by the State, and a later official Czech socialist government publication recorded:

> The Soviet Union was pursuing a policy which was close to the heart of the broad masses of people and was attractive to the nations then shedding the fetters of colonial oppression. On the other hand, the imperialist circles in the United States tried to reverse the course of history, fed the flames of war in Korea and Vietnam, and fomented the cold war which could have erupted into a hot one at any time..... therefore, the professors and associate professors from the Protestant theological faculties in Czechoslovakia met in October 1957 to express in a new form of ecumenical dialogue theological views on world developments and in particular on the nuclear arms race.[105]

The aims of these Christian peace conferences were to strive for a theological standpoint on nuclear war, to campaign against nuclear weapons, to recognise the struggle for world peace was an ecumenical matter, and to convene a universal Christian assembly to which churches from the whole world would be invited. The first event in 1961 was attended by 680 delegates

---

[102] Letter from E.A. Bell to E. Rudén, 2 August 1959, Erik Rudén Papers, Box 1, Angus Library.

[103] Letter from E. Rudén to J.N. Ondra, COPC Secretary, 11 August 1960, Erik Rudén Papers, Box 2, Angus Library.

[104] Milan Návrat, *Religion in Czechoslovakia* (Prague: Orbis Press Agency, 1984), pp. 87-9.

[105] *Ibid.*, pp. 88-9.

from forty countries. A second event was planned from 28 June – 3 July 1964 in Prague under the title, 'My Covenant is Life and Peace'.[106] The EBF Executive received an invitation and, at the EBF Executive meeting the previous year in Lisbon, resolved:

> That the European Baptist Federation send as observers to the Prague Christian Peace Assembly in 1964, the President of the Federation, the Revd Baungaard Thomsen, and two or more members of the EBF Executive Committee or the EBF Council. The Secretary of the Federation should be included in this delegation if he finds it possible to participate.[107]

An Advisory Committee was created which held a planning meeting in June 1963. The following key people in the EBF were involved – Jakob Zhidkov and A. Karev (AUCECB), Z. Pawlik (Baptist Seminary, Warsaw, Poland), Harvey Cox[108] (Goessner Mission fraternal worker in Berlin and later a major theological writer), Baungaard Thomsen (EBF President) and Glen Garfield Williams (Executive Secretary, Conference of European Churches (CEC)).[109] At a meeting of the EBF Executive Committee on 16 January 1964 it was agreed the actual delegation should be President Thomsen, General Secretary Rudén and Elizabeth Flugge of the European Baptist Women's Union.[110] However, the BWA was anxious about the Conference, no doubt because of pressure from the political right in the USA, and the BWA General Secretary, Josef Nordenhaug, had expressed the view that it would be 'inadvisable for the Associate Secretary of the Alliance to attend any of the meetings of the Christian Peace Conference'.[111] This placed the EBF General Secretary in a dilemma as both offices were combined in one person and whilst the BWA might be unhappy about their Associate Secretary attending, the EBF wanted their General Secretary to participate. Here is a classic example of a problem which has dogged the relationship between the BWA and the EBF. The EBF clearly appoints its General Secretary and then the BWA has taken that person to be its Regional Secretary for Europe. This dilemma, connected with almost every aspect of the work of the General Secretary, has been more fully explored

---

106 *Ibid.*, pp. 95-6.

107 EBF Executive Committee, 1963, Lisbon, Minutes, p. 20, Box 801, EBF Archive.

108 H.G. Cox, an American Baptist, and author of several key books including *The Secular City* (London: SCM Press, 1965), and *On Not Leaving it to the Snake* (New York: Macmillan, 1964), *Fire from Heaven: The Rise of Pentecostal Spirituality and the Reshaping of the 21st Century* (Reading, Mass: Wesley-Addison Publications, 1995).

109 European Baptist Press Service [EBPS], 63:200, Bound vol 2, EBPS Archive, IBTS Library, Prague.

110 Minutes of the EBF Executive Committee, 16 January 1964, Box 801, EBF Archive.

111 Referred to in letter from C.R. Goulding to J. Nordenhaug, 6 September 1966, EBF Christian Peace Conference Files, Angus Library.

in an earlier chapter, but surfaced again here. In the event, illness meant that Erik Rudén could not attend.[112] The EBF delegation did not include anyone holding an official position in the BWA.

At the 1964 Christian Peace Conference, the President, J.L. Hromádka, addressed the meeting, commenting, 'We are a movement and as such we do not stay in one place, but rather attempt at every opportunity to come nearer to one another and clarify our positions'.[113] The 'Message to the Churches', produced at the conclusion of the conference, encouraged churches to support concrete measures aimed at easing tension and at disarmament. The Conference, although essentially a Protestant affair (a Buddhist monk was present), was meeting after the Second Vatican Council and agreed to ask representatives to meet with representatives of the Roman Catholic Church to discuss the possibility of common or parallel witness on this topic. Inevitably the final statement also contained a hint of the agenda of the state: 'Prejudices are not being overcome in all Christian congregations. All too frequently Christian sermons contain cold war tones and slogans of political propaganda.'[114] The message was: stop preaching anticommunist sermons.

Despite the bias of some of the Conference leaders, the Conference itself seemed to strike a chord with EBF representatives and, speaking to the EBF Council in Amsterdam, President Thomsen commented:

> The Christian Peace Conference was most interesting and we feel its message as it will be given later on through the Press was very important. Our Christian responsibility for the underdeveloped countries, the hunger problem, etc were [sic] laid upon our shoulders as a heavy burden in a new way.[115]

An Advisory Committee was established which met in Budapest in the October of 1965. Of the 240 people present, fifteen were European Baptists, including four Russians, six from Hungary, several from Poland, Clifford H. Cleal (Britain) and Glen Garfield Williams (WCC/CEC, Geneva).[116]

The pattern of conferences continued in 1968, 1971 and 1978. Donald D.

---

[112] Telegram, 23 June 1964, to the Czech Baptist Secretary, Stanislav Svec, 'Regret cannot attend Peace Assembly due to illness. Ruden', EBF Christian Peace Conference Files, Angus Library.

[113] EBPS, 63:200, Bound vol 2, EBPS Archive.

[114] In report contained in Návrat, *Religion in Czechoslovakia*, p. 95.

[115] Report of EBF President, Baungaard Thomsen, to the EBF Council in the John Smyth Memorial Church, Amsterdam, 12 August 1964. Minutes of the EBF Council, 1964, Box 801, EBF Archive.

[116] Report from C.H. Cleal to C.R. Goulding, Christian Peace Conference Files, EBF Archive, Angus Library.

Black of the Baptist Union of Great Britain attended the 1968[117] Conference entitled 'Save Man – Seek Peace and Pursue It' and noted that the following European Baptist Unions were represented – Hungary, Holland, Czechoslovakia, East Germany, West Germany, Poland, Romania, Russia, Great Britain and Scotland – as was the EBF[118] and the European Baptist Press Service (EBPS).[119] In the opening section of his report he sought to reflect on the major differences between the WCC and the Christian Peace Conferences. These can be summarised as:

- The CPC is organised by eastern European nations and owes a great deal to the generosity of the Russian (Orthodox) church.
- The WCC is Anglo-Saxon organised and owes a great deal to the generosity of the USA.[120]
- The CPC is concerned almost exclusively with the political situation in the world.
- The WCC is also concerned with faith and order and mission issues.[121]

The 1968 meeting took place in the period now thought of as the 'Prague Spring' and Donald Black reported that Professor Hromádka 'was at pains to point out that this new move had arisen within the Socialist State and was not a departure from the main principles of Democratic Socialism'.[122] Black reflected on the value of the event in a report for the British Baptist Union Council:

> I have always believed that one of the doctrines of the Baptist denomination was 'A Free Church in a Free State'. So much of the work of the Christian Peace conference is concerned with this very concern. It is vital that the Baptists should continue to make their distinctive witness in this context. I hope that the denomination will not only continue to support this movement but will also show an increased interest and concern in this work. Many of our Baptist brothers are

---

[117] It is interesting to note that at this time Emilio Castro of Uruguay was listed as a Vice-President of the Christian Peace Conference. He was later to serve as General Secretary of the WCC.

[118] The EBF was represented by Jacob Broertjes for Haarlem, Holland. Letter from C.R. Goulding to the Revd Boertjes, 2 February 1968. Christian Peace Conference Files, EBF Archive, Angus Library.

[119] Report on Third All Christian Peace Conference, Prague, 31 March-5 April 1968. D.D. Black, EBF Archive, Angus Library.

[120] In fact, J.H.Y. Briggs commented to the author that the WCC has benefited immensely in the past from church tax in Germany and Scandinavia (75% of income). Briggs was a member of the WCC audit committee in the 1990s.

[121] *Ibid.,* Summary of points made in opening paragraphs of Report on Third All Christian Peace Conference.

[122] *Ibid.*

> deeply involved in it. Pawlik (Poland) Stoyan (Russia)[123] are on the Working Committee.[124]

Donald Black's concept of the purpose of the conferences was ecclesiological, and this central Baptist concern for a 'Free Church in a Free State'[125] meant that far more European Baptist Unions sent representatives to the Christian Peace Conferences than to the Conference of European Churches, or to the World Council of Churches. The continuing interest in peace was linked to the advocacy of human and religious rights, especially after the Helsinki Conference on Security and Cooperation in Europe, 1975 with its Final Act[126] including important commitments on Human Rights, which was warmly welcomed in the circles of those who had been involved with the Christian Peace Conferences.

In 1977 a wider religious forum was convened in Moscow with 670 people from 107 countries throughout the world. Of these, forty-one were Baptists. Gerhard Claas, EBF General Secretary, was part of the delegation, and the Baptists attended services at Moscow Central Baptist Church, with Claas preaching in the morning, Donald Black at the second service and Glen Garfield Williams at the evening service. Black, writing a confidential report for British Baptist leaders, stated that the keynote speeches had been typical for such an event, but the group work was rewarding:

> In one group, which was excellently chaired by Karoly Toth [Hungarian Reformed Bishop], of just over ninety people, eighty people took part. Increasingly towards the end the western voice was raised not, I hope, defensively, but with an appeal for understanding.[127]

From the side of the authorities, this involvement in the debate about peace in Europe by the churches continued to have a positive response. When the communist parties of Europe assembled in Berlin in 1976 the final document stated:

---

[123] Stoyan was widely assumed to have a loyalty to the KGB. Comment to the author by J.H.Y. Briggs.

[124] Report of D.D. Black to the Baptist Union General Purposes and Finance Committee and Baptist Union Council, 1968, Baptist Union Archives, Angus Library.

[125] This Church-State issue is explored in N.G.Wright, *Disavowing Constantine* (Carlisle: Paternoster, 2000) and N.G. Wright, *Free Church, Free State: the Positive Baptist Vision* (Carlisle: Paternoster, 2005).

[126] For the Helsinki Accords see http://en.wikipedia.org/wiki/Helsinki_Accords, accessed 2 February 2007.

[127] Report on Moscow Conference, June 1977, D.D. Black, Collection of papers; Religious liberty in the Soviet Union, E.A. Payne Papers, Box K/1, Angus Library.

> Ever broader Catholic forces, members of other Christian communities and adherents to other faiths play an important role in the struggle for the rights of the working people for democracy and peace. The Communist Workers' Parties recognise the necessity of dialogue and joint action with these forces, which is an inseparable part of the struggle for the development of Europe in a spirit of democracy and in the direction of social progress.[128]

Whilst no-one was naïve to believe the communist authorities did not have their own agenda, what is clearly to be noted is that politically astute western European Baptists such as Donald Black, who regularly engaged with British politicians as the then Social Responsibility Secretary of the British Baptists,[129] could write about the positive value of these peace conferences, especially in the interaction in the group work. Paul Weller, attending some of the later meetings as a young man, reflected on the conferences he attended whilst addressing a recent Conference in Prague, organised by the EBF and IBTS, over twenty years after the last such Prague Peace Conference:

> For myself, I became involved in the CPC as a Christian from western Europe who, like the CPC's founder, the Czech (Baptist) pastor and theologian Josef Hromódka, did not think that faithful Christian living was something that required anti-Communism or that it was the business of Christianity to sacralise capitalism. I was a Christian who wanted to take a stand against the division of Europe based on the threat of mutually assured nuclear destruction.[130]

Paul Weller and Donald Black both make clear the importance many Baptists in Western Europe attached to this pan-European adventure. The caution of Baptists at the BWA in Washington DC was generally seen to be from pressure exerted by the SBC, which has often been a strong supporter of the policies of the US Government.[131]

All of this reflected baptistic ecclesiology as the EBF became involved in the Christian Peace Conferences because its member bodies were involved and they wanted the EBF to be involved. It did not remain aloof because the international Baptist body, the BWA, was anxious about causing offence in the

---

[128] 'For Peace Security Cooperation in Europe', Final document of the 1976 Conference of the Communist and Workers' Parties, p. 11, E.A. Payne Papers, Box K/1, Angus Library.

[129] A short article by D.D. Black gives insight into some of his concerns. Don Black, 'The Cassock Club', *BQ*, Vol. 40, July 2004, pp. 436-9.

[130] EBF/IBTS Conference on Ethnic Churches in Europe, Prague, June 2006. The full text is in Penner, *Ethnic Churches in Europe*, pp. 17-46. It should be noted that Hromódka was not a Baptist. Paul Weller is wrong in this assertion.

[131] The United States Department of State Foreign Affairs classified the Prague Christian Peace Conference as a 'A Soviet-backed international front organization'. Archive of the State Department, Washington DC.

USA. The Baptist Unions involved were all member bodies of the BWA, but the BWA applied pressure to its regional body to desist from involvement. The Christian Peace Conference meetings themselves spawned working groups on anti-racism and youth as well as on nuclear disarmament.[132] It is interesting that those who participated from the West see them as important events, whilst recognising that they were partly driven by the political agenda of certain communist national governments. Amongst Baptists, it became possible to hold an international conference on peace in 1988 in Sweden, with representatives from both East and West, featuring mainly people from countries who had been signatories to the Helsinki Peace accords. This event was thoroughly part of the European Baptist community, with the foreword to the report being written by EBF General Secretary Knud Wümplemann and with a range of participants prominent in the work of EBF. The official report, *Seek Peace and Pursue It*, was edited by H. Wayne Pipkin of the Seminary in Rüschlikon.[133] The EBF clearly wanted to show a different approach to the much more cautious BWA or the more politically aligned CPC by taking an active role in events in Europe, using the opportunities to keep alive living links between Baptists and demonstrating an independence, where appropriate, from the policies of the BWA.

Religious Freedom and Human Rights

From the very beginning of cooperation amongst Baptists in Europe there has been a concern to try to ensure that all the Unions and Conventions enjoyed a legal status in their countries and had opportunity to exercise religious freedom in public worship, in community activities, including education and work with children, and in mission. In many countries such rights have not been obtained, but within the life of the EBF they have featured as an important aspiration. During the communist era concerns about the issue were expressed in several countries. It was often difficult for the leadership of EBF to know which was the best way to act. Sometimes, behind the scenes diplomacy secured greater freedom for the believers, and dialogue with officials proved helpful in achieving a modicum of relief. On other occasions a more overt approach was tried with official letters and media publicity. Inevitably, when leaders in the EBF and the larger Western Unions tried less-public ways of securing help for those not enjoying full religious freedom in the East, others within the Baptist

132 Information Department, Christian Peace Conference, 1985, Conference Report, 'Choose Life! The Hour is Late. The Christians in Resistance to the Powers of Death – on the Path to Peace and Justice for all', Documents of the Sixth All-Christian Peace Assembly, Prague. July, 1985.

133 H.W. Pipkin (ed.), *Seek Peace and Pursue It: Proceedings from the International Baptist Peace Conference, 1988* (Memphis, Tenn.: Baptist Peace Fellowship of North America and the Institute for Baptist and Anabaptist Studies, IBTS, 1989).

and evangelical community offered criticism that 'nothing was being done'. Thus, in 1972, the General Secretary of the Baptist Union of Australia came under pressure with regard to material about persecution of Russian Baptists referred to in the newsletter, 'Christian Mission to the Communist World'.[134] Ronald Goulding, as EBF Secretary, set out some of the key initiatives taken within Europe. He advised the Australian General Secretary that:

> We have had to decide what would be the course of action most helpful to the suffering people and we have not been persuaded that public outcry is the most advantageous way.... Indeed, it is quite possible that such public action only links the persecuted people more with the western world and this increases their suffering.[135]

Goulding went on to explain the problem of protesting about the break-away unregistered congregations in the Soviet Union and the need to have sensitivity with the AUCECB (the EBF member body). He concluded: 'I put these points as guidance and in no way thinking that they should determine your action. The whole situation is far too complex for anyone of us to presume that we are wholly right.'[136]

Ronald Goulding had been present at the 1969 Triennial Congress of the AUCECB and had observed the struggles the leadership in Russia had had with this issue of what they described as the 'separated brethren'.[137] He was fortunate at this time to have a meeting with Alexander Karev and Michael Zhidkov, when Karev tried to spell out his own understanding of the reasons for the development of the reform or *Initsiativinki* movement.[138] Goulding went on to describe the process of contact between the two groups commenting:

> One of the difficulties in making progress in reconciliation was the divisions in leadership among the Initsiativinki groups. Certainly some of them were imprisoned during this time, but the 'fall' of Prokoviev (the original leader) was the major factor. He was the original leader of the group who in 1961 had led the separation and excommunicated the leaders of the AUC. Now he himself had

---

[134] This was an organisation run by Richard Wurmbrand. At the 1969 Triennial Conference of AUCECB, Brother Timchenko said, in regard to the papers produced out of the reconciliation discussions with the reformed Baptists, 'men like Wurmbrand use them only for themselves and for evil'. Quoted by C.R. Goulding in his report of the Congress, p. 7, E.A. Payne Papers, Box K/1, Angus Library.

[135] Letter of C.R. Goulding to J.G. Manning, 17 March 1972, Soviet Union Religious Liberty Papers, E.A. Payne Papers, Box K/1, Angus Library.

[136] *Ibid.*

[137] Term used by General Secretary Karev in his report to the 1969 AUCECB Triennial Congress in notes taken by C.R. Goulding, E.A. Payne Papers, Box K/1, Angus Library.

[138] Confidential Interview with A. Karev, with M. Zhidkov translating, in Russia Papers, E.A. Payne Papers, Box K/1, Angus Library.

> been excommunicated by the members of the Council of Churches (the 'Reformed' group) for leaving his wife and taking another woman. The new leader was a disciple of Prokoviev, Krychkov, who was later joined by Vins. Vins is Chairman and Kyrchkov General Secretary.[139]

The AUCECB leadership reported they had held a series of meetings with the unregistered group and had worked through issues of repentance; an earlier action in 1966, having originally been rejected by Vins and Kyrchkov, was accepted on 4 December 1969.[140] In the plenary session, discussing the meetings between the two groups, many wanted to speak. Several were pastors from places as distant as Moldova and Tashkent. They were confessing faults, seeking forgiveness and looking to be readmitted to the AUCECB.[141]

The role of propaganda from independent and para-church organisations also presented problems for the EBF, and in particular the General Secretaries, who wanted to keep contact with all groups in communist countries and to ensure that churches in the West had, as far as possible, accurate information. The time and effort involved in counteracting misleading propaganda from the various groups connected with Richard Wurmbrand can be detected in this letter from Goulding. Wurmbrand had denounced the magazine, *Australian Baptist*, from a public platform in a meeting in Australia, with accusations of printing lies about the number of congregations in Moscow. In fact, the article had referred to Leningrad and it was a prominent Australian Baptist who had visited the Baptists there, but Richard Wurmbrand seemed intent on a path of denouncing EBF and BWA leaders because they sought to work with both the AUCECB and the unregistered congregations, and to engage in quiet diplomacy behind the scenes to assist the believers rather than in public denunciations of the system and public protests of the type associated with Richard Wurmbrand and his various para-church organisations. Goulding wrote to the editor of the *Australian Baptist* in December 1975:

> Once again Mr Wurmbrand has excelled himself in presumption and exaggeration. I would be inclined to take his offer to pay the round trip and all the expenses. The facts are that, apart from the Central Church in Moscow there are **at least** ten churches or 'preaching stations' as they are called in the district of Moscow. Previously we have believed that it was not good to enter into public controversy with fellow believers but there are times when this unfortunately becomes necessary.[142]

---

[139] Notes taken by C.R. Goulding during 1969 AUCECB Triennial Council, p. 6, E.A. Payne Papers, Box K/1, Angus Library.

[140] *Ibid.*

[141] *Ibid.*, pp. 7-8.

[142] C.R. Goulding to T.J. Cardwell, 17 December 1975, C.R. Goulding Papers, EBF Archive Box 33, IBTS.

Goulding struggled throughout his time as EBF General Secretary to deal with correspondence from across the world where Richard Wurmbrand had caused agitation and dissent amongst Baptists regarding the situation in Eastern Europe, especially the USSR and Romania. Writing to the General Secretary of the South African Baptists in 1970 he commented:

> The attacks that Wurmbrand makes upon leaders of our Baptist work in any country are both unjust and unkind... my own estimate is that as a result of persecution and pressure treatment in Rumania, a part of which could well have been because of his Christian commitment but quite a bit was caused in earlier years by political involvement, he has now in his freedom become obsessed with communism to such an extent he makes accusations and statements that simply do not bear the mark of truth.[143]

The continuing issue between the AUCECB and the unregistered Baptists made more problematic the attempts to secure the religious freedoms of the 'reformed' or unregistered Baptists, whilst maintaining cordial relationships within the EBF family with the AUCECB. Nowhere was this more delicate than in the search to secure freedom for the Chairman of the unregistered group, Georgi Vins. He was presented by some connected with Wurmbrand and his underground church as a great hero and martyr. By contrast Wurmbrand spoke of Alexander Karev of the AUCECB as a 'liar and a traitor'.[144] But if it wanted to achieve freedom for all Baptists, the EBF had to avoid such slogans and try to work more behind the scenes, keeping in touch with all parties, not least the AUCECB. The EBF officers and British Baptist General Secretary, David Russell,[145] worked on this from December 1974, when Georgi Vins was first under investigation, through to his release and removal to the USA in April 1979.[146] In August 1977 a delegation of British Baptists[147] were able to go to

---

[143] C.R. Goulding to C.W. Parnell, General Secretary, Baptist Union of South Africa, 22 December 1970, C.R. Goulding Papers, EBF Archive Box 33.

[144] Quote by C.R. Goulding from the writings of Richard Wurmbrand (1909-2001), in notes of confidential meeting with A. Karev, 1969, E.A. Payne Papers, Box K/1, Angus Library.

[145] On D.S. Russell's work in the area of human rights see D.S. Russell, 'Cold War Years', *BQ*, Vol. XXXVI, January 1995, pp. 21-28 and D.S. Russell. 'Baptists in Central and Eastern Europe in the Post-War Years: Recollections and Reflections', *BQ*, Vol. 37, No. 4, October 1997, pp. 193-201. For accounts of some of the more humorous incidents see D.S Russell, *In Journeyings Often* (London: Baptist Union Publications, 1981).

[146] List prepared (3 sides A4 paper) of letters written and meetings held by D.S. Russell, E.A. Payne Papers Box K/1, Angus Library.

[147] When D.S. Russell retired as BUGB General Secretary in 1982 he was awarded the CBE for his advocacy of human rights in Eastern Europe. See I.M. Randall, *The English Baptists of the 20th Century* (Didcot, The Baptist Historical Society, 2005), p. 422.

Kiev and on 29 August they visited the Church of which Vins had been pastor, which was now registered. In his notes on the visit E.A. Payne commented:

> He [Vins] is still in a labour camp, but our friends were assured that charges of deliberate poisoning were false.[148] Relations between the two churches in Kiev are improving (the central registered church and that of Vins) helped by contacts between their young people. Dr Russell's visit is gratefully remembered.[149]

Vins, of course, was far from being the only person suffering and, in 1975, Pastor Janis Smits of Latvia sought to send out a letter from Aizpute to the BWA Congress in Stockholm complaining of his plight and the withdrawal of his permit to preach and serve as a pastor because he had '(u)rged believers to organize petitions on behalf of their brethren in the faith imprisoned for their loyalty to the faith and had permitted the children of believing families to sing in church choirs'.[150]

The EBF continued during the Secretaryships of Gerhard Claas, Knud Wümplemann and Karl Heinz Walter, to approach the situation in the same way: seeking to keep contact with those behind the so-called 'iron curtain' and use every opportunity that presented itself to make representations for the rights of religious assembly and spiritual freedom for Baptist groups who suffered at the hands of communist authorities or national churches. What was clear was that they did not engage in sensational protest or in outright illegal gestures, though inevitably some meetings with believers took place in circumstances where the communist law was flouted. Whilst Karl Heinz Walter was General Secretary he made endeavours to encourage all the Unions to alert their churches to the continuing need for vigilance for religious freedom and human rights. Though the communist oligarchies had been replaced in most of the countries of Eastern Europe, the governments which had been created were not all inclined to introduce laws to protect free assembly for worship and spiritual exercises to a standard likely to impress the European Union, Council of Europe and the Organisation for Security and Cooperation in Europe

---

[148] There had been accusations of mercury poisoning. The Russian Baptist leadership had earlier informed C.R. Goulding that these accusations were false, though there had been a mercury spillage near the prison at some time.

[149] 'Good News from a far country', typescript record of visit by E.A. Payne, W.M.S. West and Peter Clark to the USSR, August 1977, E.A. Payne Papers, Box K/1, Angus Library.

[150] This letter was reported in *Religious Liberty in the Soviet Union*, Keston College, 1976, prepared for the WCC, p. 76. Ultimately Janis Smits left the USSR, but returned to Latvia post 1991 and served for a term as Bishop of the Latvian Baptist Union 1999-2005.

(OSCE).[151] Accordingly, in 1994, Walter proposed to the EBF Council the establishment of an EBF Task Force on Human Rights and the holding of an annual EBF Sunday of Fasting and Prayer for Human Rights and Religious Freedom.[152] This proposal was accepted. Unions such as Bulgaria took up the idea of a special Sunday with enthusiasm, reporting to the EBF Council in Portugal the following year that 100 per cent of their churches participated. Ole Jørgenson, General Secretary of the Danish Baptists, was able to report that the Task Force had met on two occasions. The Task Force was initially led by IBTS staff member, Thorwald Lorenzen, who had done research and delivered lectures on this topic from a theological perspective. However, Lorenzen resigned from IBTS during 1995 to take up the pastorate at Canberra Baptist Church, Australia. Jørgenson reported that work had begun on establishing a network of lawyers and human rights experts who could monitor violations of human rights in Europe. A consultation was planned, aimed at creating a network of Baptist experts in human rights, exchange of relevant information, the development of methods of practical assistance to groups suffering from a lack of religious liberty and the preparation of material to demonstrate the biblical foundations for human rights and religious liberty. The hope was also to establish an Institute for Religious Freedom and Human Rights.[153]

In 1996 the convenorship of the Task Force passed to the Danish lawyer, Ebbe Holm, who, though passionately committed to the work, was not able to give as much time to developing the proposed initiative. The hope for 'a planned communication network ... could not be realised because of the difficult financial situation in the EBF',[154] but Theo Angelov, then EBF President, spoke about the issue wherever he travelled, including making a major presentation at the British Baptist Assembly in Blackpool in May 1996.[155]

At the EBF Council in Croatia in 1997, a special human rights seminar was held with representatives from various countries making presentations. One of the speakers was Ivan Grozdanov from Macedonia, who commented that the new Macedonian law was 'very subtle and it needs detailed interpretation from

---

[151] On these issues see, for instance, M.D. Evans, *Religious Liberty and International Law in Europe* (Cambridge: Cambridge University Press, 1997) and A. Bloed, L. Leicht, M. Nowak, A. Rosas (eds.), *Monitoring Human Rights in Europe* (Dordrecht: Martinus Nijhoff, 1993).

[152] Report of the EBF General Secretary to the EBF Council, Portugal, September 1995, Box 813, EBF Archive, IBTS, pp. 8-9.

[153] Report of the Division of External Relations, EBF Council Report Book, Portugal, 1995, p. 23, Box 813, EBF Archive.

[154] Report from the EBF External Affairs Division, EBF Report Book, Estonia, 1996, p. 43, Box 816, EBF Archive.

[155] Baptist Union of Great Britain Annual Report, 1996, BUGB Archives, Angus Library.

those of us who know just what some of the regulations aim at'.[156] The new law supposedly was aimed to assist the Macedonian government in its desire to join NATO and, one day, the European Union. However, for many ex-communist countries, as Grozdanov commented, 'the new law is more discriminative, more restrictive and more bureaucratic than the previous one!'[157] His comment could easily have been echoed by others, especially in countries where the Orthodox Church was seeking to re-establish itself as the national church with a canonical territory, and laws were often constructed in such a way as to discriminate against gathering, or free churches as opposed to territorial or geographical churches with episkope. To these concerns, repeated in similar ways in other countries, the Task Force gave attention, with letters being written and submissions made. A key member of the Task Force was Anatoly Pchelintsev, a Russian Baptist based at the Slavic Law Centre in Moscow. The Task Force members tried to keep an open perspective on the religious freedom of others and the Report to Council of September 2002 mentioned the work undertaken by Pchelintsev, with the support of the group, to gain registration in Russia for the Salvation Army, who had been proscribed by the Soviet Government in 1923, but had sought to re-establish themselves under the new Russian dispensation.[158]

Another important member of the Task Force was Malcolm Evans of the University of Bristol. An international law expert, he was often used by the OSCE as a specialist investigator on human rights. The Task Force was particularly concerned about the deteriorating situation for religious freedom in Belarus and Georgia at the time.[159] The work of the Task Force was somewhat curtailed in simply reporting events, as the members were not always able to meet in a particular year and, though the overall commitment to the concern for Religious Freedom was high, the Task Force did not achieve all that had been hoped in terms of community activity. The EBF office dropped back from the provision of material for the EBF Day of Fasting and Prayer for Religious Freedom and Human Rights. Tony Peck, as the new EBF General Secretary, was asked to serve on the Conference of European Churches Religious Freedom and Human Rights Group.[160] The concern for human rights and religious freedom remained within the General Secretariat of the EBF, and had

[156] I. Grozdanov, 'What is wrong with the new Religious Law in Macedonia', paper presented to the EBF Council, Novi Vinodolski, Croatia, September 1997, EBF Council Minutes Report Book for 1998, Appendix 3, Box 818, EBF Archive.
[157] *Ibid.*
[158] EBF Division of External Relations Report to EBF Council, Oslo, Norway, September 2002, EBF Council Report Book, 2002, EBF Archive.
[159] *Ibid.* Also EBF External Relations Division Report to EBF Council, Radosc, Poland, September 2003, EBF Council Report Book, p. 43, EBF Office Archive.
[160] EBF External Relations Division Report to EBF Council, Beirut, Lebanon, 2004, EBF Council Report Book, p. 4, EBF Archive.

been a particular concern of Peck's before his appointment, but the Task Force, which brought together key Baptist lay leaders working in this important area from different parts of Europe, ceased to exercise any influence in cross-cultural debate and intervention. In 2006 no reference to the annual prayer event could be found on the EBF web site.[161] In the same year, IBTS offered to host the Thomas Helwys Centre for Religious Freedom and Human Rights when Bristol Baptist College decided it could no longer sustain it. The Centre had been of great interest to Tony Peck, and its move to the same location as the EBF office may signal an opportunity for close EBF involvement in the issue.

Conclusion

As an ecclesial reality, the EBF has had and continues to have some notable successes in providing a platform for European Baptists to work together in mission. The creation of the EBF meant a new channel for contributing to programmes of aid and relief across Europe in the post-war period.[162] The development of the EBM, involving, firstly, a good number of Western European Unions and more recently Unions from Central and Eastern Europe, was and is significant. The EBM is a respected organisation in the family of world mission agencies. The recent developments to create a global partnership, with all participants being both senders and receivers, places the EBM in the forefront of current missiological thinking. It is important to note, within the story of the EBF, the way in which it has wanted to foster unity within diversity and to see the missional dimension in this promotion of unity in diversity. This was difficult in the communist era. The EBF also wanted to do cross-cultural work in other areas such as production of educational material, but it was recognised that this was impractical. However, the EBF was able to take on an important role with Theo Angelov's vision of the Indigenous Missionary Project, which has seen the planting of over 100 churches in fifteen countries across the EBF territory and with expansion being encouraged and fueled amongst those originally sceptical to the plan.

The concern for issues of peace has been one which brought together East and West in dialogue and concern during the communist era, and this was an issue on which the EBF Council could make a resolution as recently as the Iraq war. Though Baptists cannot be counted historically as belonging to the 'peace churches',[163] alongside the Mennonites and Quakers (though many have been

161 www.ebf.org, accessed November and December 2006.

162 W.O. Lewis was succeeded in his work by Archie Goldie. For the account of the development see R.V. Pierard (ed.), *Baptists Together in Christ 1905-2005: A Hundred-Year History of the Baptist World Alliance* (Birmingham, Al.: Samford University Press, 2005).

163 Dekar, *For the Healing of the Nations.*

driven by a vision of peacemaking as Paul Dekar has demonstrated), nevertheless, the story of the EBF illustrates a strong bias within the Baptist communities across Europe towards positive identification with issues of geo-political peace. Linked with the desire for peace and reconciliation has been a commitment to justice for all. The topic of human rights and religious freedom is one which has always been of great concern to the baptistic tradition from Balthasar Hubmaier, through Thomas Helwys to Jimmy Carter and Martin Luther King, Jr. The EBF maintains this concern in its overall life and certainly, through the communist era and until the retirement of Theo Angelov as General Secretary, it had a prominent focus in the meetings of the EBF Council. This has subsequently been less noticeable in the larger setting of the Council, but the concern still continues in the office of the General Secretary, if not so clearly in the Council and the Division of External Relations, following the collapse of the Human Rights Task Force. European Baptists are concerned deeply about peace and justice and recognise it as one of several key areas of mission in which working together within the EBF is more appropriate than working in national isolation.

CHAPTER 8

The Ecclesial Reality of European Baptists

If the Baptist historian, W.T. Whitley, was right that 'the distinctive feature about Baptists is their doctrine of the Church',[1] this suggests that serious attention needs to be paid to that doctrine. The intention of this book has been to contribute to that task. In particular, the focus of the study has been the wider Baptist ecclesiology evidenced in the European Baptist Federation (EBF). This study has sought to demonstrate that Baptist ecclesiology does not assert the independence of each local church at the expense of the interdependency of Baptist communities. The independent position has certainly been a feature of Baptist life and has been defended by some scholars and preachers (especially in the USA),[2] but a thorough-going interdependency, based around a clear identity and with a strong covenantal element, represents the historic Baptist position as seen in shaping Confessions of Faith.[3] This thesis has explored the historical dimension, showing that, in the story of Baptists in Europe up to the present time, there is a sense of the wider, or 'catholic' dimension of the Church.[4] This trans-local understanding of 'being church' has, it has been argued, a theological coherence and significance, at local, regional and national level, but also, in terms of this study of Europe, across a continent.[5] The work has examined in detail the history of the EBF from its founding in 1949, analysing the ecclesial strength of that body and the identity it has both within

---

[1] W.T. Whitley, *A History of British Baptists*, rev. ed. (London: Kingsgate, 1932), p. 4.

[2] A recent example of a strong defence of the idea of the autonomy and independence of local congregations is in T.J. Nettles and R. Moore (eds.), *Why I am a Baptist* (Nashville, Tenn.: Broadman and Holman, 2001).

[3] See, for instance, The London Confession (1644), The Particular Baptist Confession (1689), The General Baptist Orthodox Creed (1679), and The Second London Confession (1677), in W.L. Lumpkin, *Baptist Confessions of Faith*, rev. ed. (Valley Forge: Judson Press, 1969).

[4] A.P.F. Sell, commenting on Congregationalism expresses this as visible sainthood, orderliness and catholicity. See A.P.F. Sell, *Saints: Visible, Orderly and Catholic - The Congregational Idea of the Church* (Geneva: World Alliance of Reformed Churches, 1986), Preface..

[5] It is also true in the Caribbean, Australasia and parts of Asia and Africa, especially where there has been a European Baptist influence in the founding of Baptist causes by travellers or missionaries.

the wider Baptist family in Europe and beyond, and also within the ecumenical community. The core argument that has been pursued has been that the basic unit of Baptist ecclesiology is the local gathering, intentional, convictional community of believers, but that such a community properly understands itself to be in an interdependent relationship with other such communities and that this is expressed through associating locally, regionally, nationally and internationally.[6] This associating is seen internationally in the EBF.

Ecclesiology has been an important topic within the theological world, and ecumenical endeavours have meant that theologians, church leaders and church members have increasingly given attention to the place and contribution of their own communions within the Christian World Communions as a whole.[7] As indicated, however, ecclesiology has not been a topic upon which many Baptists have written at any depth in the last thirty years. There have, however, been exceptions. In the European context Paul Fiddes has examined the features of gathering, covenanted communities, local and regional, in *Tracks and Traces*,[8] and especially in his important essay, 'Walking Together – the Place of Covenant Theology in Baptist Life Yesterday and Today'.[9] Among others who have been concerned to explore aspects of Baptist ecclesiology have been Nigel G. Wright, for example, in *Free Church, Free State*, and John H.Y. Briggs and Stanley K. Fowler, in essays in the book edited by P.E. Thompson and A.R. Cross, *Recycling the Past or Researching History?*.[10] These notable exceptions apart, Baptists have generally not been part of the wider debate on ecclesiology as it applies beyond the local gathering, convictional community. Indeed, Alan Sell rightly comments that it 'would seem that Baptists have not always clearly articulated the practical ways by which the mutuality which they profess as between local church and wider association is actually to be achieved'.[11] Given this weakness, and given the lack of Baptist thinking on the

---

[6] On gathering communities see my article: K.G. Jones, 'Rethinking Baptist Ecclesiology' in *Journal of European Baptist Studies*, Vol 1, No. 1 (Prague: IBTS, September 2000), pp. 4-18.

[7] P. Avis, *The Christian Church: An Introduction to the Major Traditions* (London: SPCK, 2002).

[8] P.S. Fiddes, *Tracks and Traces: Baptist Identity in Church and Theology* (Milton Keynes: Paternoster, 2003).

[9] W.H. Brackney and P.S. Fiddes with J.H.Y. Briggs (eds.), *Pilgrim Pathways: Essays in Baptist History in Honour of B.R. White* (Macon, Ga.: Mercer University Press, 1999), pp. 47-74.

[10] N.G. Wright, *Free Church, Free State: The Positive Baptist Vision* (Milton Keynes: Paternoster, 2005), and essays by J.H.Y. Briggs and S.K. Fowler in P.E. Thompson and A.R. Cross (eds.), *Recycling the Past or Researching History? Studies in Baptist Historiography and Myths* (Milton Keynes: Paternoster, 2005).

[11] A.P.F. Sell, 'Doctrine, Polity, Liberty: What Do Baptists Stand For?', in Brackney et al, *Pilgrim Pathways*, pp. 1-46.

subject from a pan-European viewpoint, this book has sought to contribute to wider ecclesial conversations. It is also important to note that whilst there is a relative lack of recent writing affirming the more-than-local ecclesial dimension amongst Baptists (the more-than-local dimension has been taken up by theologians in the Southern Baptist Convention (SBC), but in order to oppose it) this does not mean that such Baptist ecclesial life has not existed. On the contrary, there have been strong relationships, as Baptist communities have associated in local clusters,[12] relational associations, national Unions and continental bodies. It is the latter that has been explored here.

Thus, this study has brought together history and theology. Bernard Green, a former General Secretary of the Baptist Union of Great Britain, charted the story of the EBF in his important book, *Crossing the Boundaries*.[13] This particular work, while telling the story, has utilised a wide range of primary sources relating to the EBF in order to examine the organic life of the Federation as an ecclesial reality. Within that I have analysed the way European Baptists fit within the context of historical 'Christian Europe', and in the totality of their coverage of Europe. This coverage, as has been seen, is unmatched by any other Protestant World Communion. So I have noted the way in which the EBF has developed a world-class post-graduate theological education centre and its commitment to a range of mission interests. This missional concern has been not only in evangelism and church planting, both in Europe and beyond, but also with concerns for human rights and religious freedom, issues of peace and justice, and involvement in relief and development. This wide range of activity has embraced Baptist Unions and Conventions throughout Europe and the Middle East. In this vibrant expression of Baptist life, the crucial role of the personal episkopal figure, the General Secretary of the EBF, has been scrutinised. I have argued that the General Secretaries have acted as 'living letters', affirmed and valued by the member bodies and authorised to play a pivotal role in developing the life of the EBF, relating to unions and between unions, and taking initiatives in both mission and relationships. The changing relationship between European Baptists and mission agencies based in the USA, key players in the formative years of the EBF, has also been explored. In the developing story of the EBF the evidence is that many of the people who have actively participated in its life or, at one step removed, have been beneficiaries of its work and mission, have seen it not

---

[12] 'Clusters' is a term used now within BUGB for local town or district-wide gatherings of churches, either denominationally or ecumenically. See D. Allan, 'Clustering – a Dynamic for Mission (Didcot: BUGB, undated, but Autumn 1999), and 'Relating and Resourcing – the Report of the Task Group on Associating' BUGB Council, March 1998, BUGB Archives, Didcot.

[13] Bernard Green, *Crossing the Boundaries: a history of the European Baptist Federation* (Didcot: Baptist Historical Society, 1999).

simply as another agency, like a mission agency, but as a genuinely ecclesial body.

It is significant that the well-known international text books on Baptist history give scant attention to the EBF as a crucial ecclesial organism of continental Baptist life, perhaps because most of these major histories have been written by North Americans who come from a tradition which pays little attention to aspects of interdependency. Thus H. Leon McBeth in *The Baptist Heritage: Four Centuries of Baptist Witness* (1987), which was for many years a standard reference book for Baptists, has more references to the Church of England (36) than to the European Baptist Federation (4).[14] William H. Brackney in his book *The Baptists* makes little reference to the Baptist World Alliance (BWA) and the continental federations. In his *A Genetic History* he has twelve references each to Baylor and Harvard[15] Universities, but no reference to the EBF or North American Baptist Fellowship or to the other continental Baptist fellowships that exist throughout the Baptist world, and makes scant reference to the BWA.[16] Bill J. Leonard in *Baptist Ways: A History*, a volume regarded by many as the current principal international Baptist history, does rather better, with ten references to the EBF, but with only one to the All-Africa Baptist Fellowship. However, even Leonard makes no references to the continental groups in Asia, South America, North America or the Caribbean.[17] So, certainly, in these books (all written in North America) – which are concerned to offer a major overview of Baptist life and witness from the 1600s until today, and which are widely regarded as authoritative within the Baptist world – the recognition of the place of wider Baptist fellowship is played down. In dealing with the twentieth century, the attention given to continental federations as a whole is minimal, and given the importance of the life and mission of the EBF within Europe its neglect means that the picture presented of European Baptists has been deficient.

Yet the picture painted here of the EBF is one that is consistent with wider Baptist thinking and practice. This work, in seeking to add to the discourse on wider ecclesial realities from a Baptist perspective, has recognised that such discourse among European Baptists goes back (for example) to the 1611 Confession formulated in Amsterdam, with its reference to the trans-local

---

[14] H.L. McBeth, *The Baptist Heritage: Four Centuries of Baptist Witness* (Nashville, Tenn.: Broadman Press, 1987).

[15] Harvard is not even a Baptist institution, though Baylor is a Baptist University in Texas.

[16] W.H. Brackney, *The Baptists* (Westport, Connecticut: The Greenwood Press, 1988), and *A Genetic History of Baptist Thought: with special reference to Britain and North America* (Macon Ga.: Mercer University Press, 2004).

[17] B.J. Leonard, *Baptist Ways: A History* (Valley Forge, Pa.: Judson Press. 2003).

ministry of apostleship.[18] Almost four centuries later, the BWA Centenary Message (longer version) of 2005, after stating that Baptists seek to be obedient to the plea of our crucified, risen and ascended Lord that his friends 'may all be one' (John 17:20-24), comments:

> We understand that through the Holy Spirit we experience interdependence with those who share this dynamic discipleship of the church as the people of God, whom God is always drawing forward into deeper relationship and mission.[19]

In commenting on the concept of unity, the statement again stresses interdependence, relating this specifically – in part under European Baptist influence – to churches that 'Christ is gathering'. Such unity is:

> both God's gift to us and what God demands of us. It is no static thing, but is present by the dynamic of the Holy Spirit as individuals are confronted by Christ and believe, repent and are baptized. We are called out with others in such churches that Christ is gathering. These, in turn are interdependent with other such churches in associations, unions, conventions, regional federations and in the Baptist World Alliance (Acts 15).[20]

Thus, although some of the historians of Baptist life seem to have neglected the place of wider associations, their place has been and is being recognised in the practice of Baptist life.

An emphasis on a trans-local ecclesial model of Baptist life does not restrict the possibilities for the interaction of Baptists with other Christians who are not Baptists. Indeed I have sought to show in this book that where the ecclesial reality of a Baptist trans-local body (in this case the EBF) is fully recognised and affirmed by the member communities, a weight and authority is given to such a body to relate to, and converse and dialogue with, other such bodies from other traditions. This permits real theological and ecclesial outcomes. At a global level the BWA Centenary Message refers to:

> others within the Christian World Communions who share many attitudes and insights with us. We rejoice that over the past century we have been able to have constructive dialogue with Mennonites (1989-1992, 2002), Lutherans (1986-

[18] 'A Declaration of Faith of English People, Amsterdam, 1611', in Lumpkin, *Baptist Confessions of Faith*, article 22, p. 122.

[19] K.G. Jones (ed.), 'The Baptist World Alliance Centenary Message', (longer version), BWA Centenary Congress Resolutions Committee, Falls Church, BWA, 2005, BWA Library, Falls Church, Va.

[20] *Ibid.*

1989), Reformed (1973-1977),[21] Anglicans (2000-2004), Roman Catholics (1984-1988) and others. We look forward to additional opportunities for dialogue with other Christian communions in the future.[22]

In Europe this has been exemplified in significant ways, as has been shown, not least in substantial dialogue with the Community of Protestant Churches in Europe (CPCE). The EBF has been able to operate ecumenically with the confidence of the member bodies, and to engage in theological discussions regarding issues that have had real consequences for EBF member bodies already engaged with members of CPCE in their own national contexts, such as Germany and Italy. Such dialogue and interaction has also made it possible for Baptist Unions, who have previously had little or no direct contact with the magisterial reformation churches in Europe, to develop such contact.[23] From the side of the CPCE, an invitation was extended by their Assembly in Belfast in 2001 for the EBF to appoint individuals to serve on their study commissions in the period 2001-2006.[24] The EBF has been able to engage at a pan-European level in a way that would not have been possible for individual Baptist Unions.

This ecclesial community of the EBF has been able to develop relationships, not only ecumenically, but also in important internal areas of ecclesial life in Europe. This has been demonstrated in Chapter 4, in which the International Baptist Theological Seminary (IBTS) is examined. In the case of IBTS, the EBF, as a Europe-wide ecclesial body, was able to take ownership of a major educational facility serving the whole of Europe, and carry forward its theological work in new ways, particularly from the 1990s. It has been shown that the EBF, as the body through which the Unions of Europe were acting together as a community of churches committed to contextual theological work, developed the work of the institution away from the form inherited from the North American mission agencies, notably the Southern Baptists (who began the Seminary), and moved it in a more explicitly European direction. This was done in order to meet the needs of the member bodies, and also to gain recognition and meet the standards of the European Union.[25] The development

---

[21] A.P.F. Sell, *Enlightenment, Ecumenism, Evangel: Theological Themes and Thinkers 1550-2000* (Milton Keynes: Paternoster, 2003), though on this, Sell notes that, too frequently, the reports lie dormant, p. 279.

[22] Jones, 'The Baptist World Alliance Centenary Message', (longer version).

[23] W. Hüffmeier and T. Peck (eds.), *Dialogue between the Community of Protestant Churches in Europe(CPCE) and the European Baptist Federation (EBF) on the Doctrine and Practice of Baptism* (Frankfurt am Main: Verlag Otto Lembeck, 2005).

[24] The EBF Executive appointed P.F. Penner, IBTS, to serve on a mission study group and Eric Geldbach, a German Baptist and Professor of Ecumenical Theology at Bochum, to serve on a group looking at the life of the Church.

[25] See http://ec.europa.eu/education/policies/educ/bologna/bologna.pdf, accessed 23 January 2007.

by the Board of Trustees and the IBTS academic staff of relevant post-graduate degrees with a truly European flavour and Baptist context has, from the later 1990s, produced an international multi-cultural, multi-national institution which, through its alumni, five research institutes and publications programme now commands international respect and acknowledgement for its work.[26] This would not have been possible but for the contribution of many within the member Unions of the EBF, and the channelling of these contributions, theological and otherwise, would not have been achieved in the way that it has been without the EBF as an ecclesially active body.

Although many within the member bodies that comprise the EBF have contributed to its corporate life, there has been particular 'oversight'. In terms of classical reflection on translocal ecclesiology, I have sought to show in Chapter 5 that there has been developed, over the decades, an episkopal element within the life of the EBF, and that this oversight has been valued as having personal, collegial and communal insights.[27] The personal element, embodied in the General Secretary, has been seen as operating alongside the 'synodical' element of the EBF General Council and the gathering community element of the churches in membership with the member bodies. From a Baptist point of view, in a modest way this model contributes to the classical discussion in ecclesiology about the nature and shape of the Church. The role of the General Secretary is as a 'living letter' (or in classic General Baptist ecclesiology, a 'Messenger'[28]) and as a representative figure for the wider church. This represents a significant move away from the early assumption that European Baptist life was served by a figure appointed by the BWA. The ecclesial role of the General Secretary has been expressed in ordination of pastors when there has been some break in succession, or when a new national grouping has come into being – as in Georgia, Macedonia and Bulgaria. The role of the General Secretaries as relationship-builders and leaders focused on mission has been demonstrated. These are typical Anabaptist and Baptist aspects of oversight. J.H.Yoder spoke of the Anabaptists as those who cared for one another and supported each other missiologically without regard to narrow ecclesial definitions.[29] In certain specific ways EBF General Secretaries have

---

[26] See, for instance, A. Rifkin, 'Jesus with a Genius Grant', *Los Angeles Times Magazine*, 23 November 2003, pp. 22-40.

[27] P. Goodliff, 'Contemporary Models of Translocal Ministry: A Critical Appraisal', in S. Murray (ed.), *Translocal Ministry: equipping the churches for mission* (Didcot: Baptist Union of Gt Britain, 2005), p. 55.

[28] R.M.B. Gouldbourne, 'Messengers: Do they have a Message for us?', in Murray, *Translocal Ministry*, pp. 24-31. On Waldensian, Lollard and Anabaptist insights for translocal ministry see Murray, 'Translocal Ministry in Post-Christendom', in *Translocal Ministry*, pp. 64-74.

[29] J.H. Yoder, *The Royal Priesthood: Essays Ecclesiological and Ecumenical* (Scottdale, Pa.: Herald Press, 1998).

been able to break down barriers to cooperation that often exist between 'sending agencies', such as the North American and Western European mission agencies, and the receiving communities of faith. Each General Secretary has brought a personal style to the role, as has been demonstrated through looking more particularly at the long-term service of Knud Wümplemann and Karl Heinz Walter, who, between them, served the EBF for almost one-quarter of its life and developed relational and missional aspects in new ways.

Indeed, within the EBF, the accent has been upon relationships as a model for developing real ecclesial community and not upon juridicial imperatives,[30] as has been the case in some other Christian World Communions. This relational perspective helps to illuminate the complex role of the partners of the EBF – the North American mission agencies (especially the American Baptist Churches–International Ministries (ABC-IM) and the Southern Baptist Convention–International Mission Board (SBC-IMB)) – which I have explored in Chapter 6. Their agents in Europe, after the BWA Conference of 1948, Edwin A. Bell and George W. Sadler, played selfless and crucial roles in helping Europeans develop the work of the EBF, but struggles along the way have marked some aspects of these relationships. The goal, from a European perspective and from the perspective of some Baptists in the USA, has been that such mission agencies should engage in true partnership which knows when to contribute to the advancement of the work and when a supportive but less influential position has to be adopted. This has been and remains a crucial missiological and ecclesial issue. For ABC-IM this struggle to understand their relationship to ecclesial communities with whom they are working, in Europe and elsewhere, has been seen to involve careful dialogue and exploration of the concept of partnership. This has been done on the basis of an understanding that the responsibility for directing Baptist work in Europe rests with European Baptists themselves. It is less clear from the research presented in this book that the SBC–IMB and BMS World Mission[31] have been as anxious, in recent years, to engage in such theological reflection and to seek to be sensitive in their responses to the receiving partners' needs.

As is to be expected in looking at the EBF as a Baptist ecclesial body, mission undertaken by Europeans has been a key part of the vision of those involved in the EBF. The most significant out-bound agency of European Baptists working together across the continent has been the European Baptist Mission. In Chapter 7 I argued that the EBF has not only been a forum for discussion and debate amongst the member bodies where ideas and concerns

---

[30] On the juridicial element see M. Reuver, *Faith and Law: Juridicial Perspectives for the Ecumenical Movement* (Geneva: WCC, 2000).

[31] The British Baptist Missionary Society changed its name in the late 1990s to BMS World Mission.

about the life and mission[32] of Baptist communities in Europe can be explored, but has also engaged in many ways in holistic mission. Often such missional initiatives were a response to the wider context, which is, I have argued, an authentically Baptist way of doing mission.[33] The years of the Cold War were years of enormous challenge for Baptists in Europe. In order to engage with the serious issues of this period, Baptists in Europe, some of them EBF leaders, involved themselves in Peace Conferences. At the end of the Cold War, and with the fall of communism, the EBF, under the leadership of Karl Heinz Walter, committed itself to massive relief efforts. More recently, with new opportunities in Eastern Europe in particular, there has been the development of the EBF Indigenous Missionary Project. Issues of human rights have also been addressed. The EBF has both initiated and affirmed specific Europe-wide projects, monitoring their life and effectiveness and establishing a measure of quality control in what has been a range of very varied activities in the area of cross-cultural mission.

This variety has been important within the EBF. What has undoubtedly been the case, and is clear from the wide variety and style of Unions that have been and are covenanted together in the EBF, is that for European Baptists unity does not mean uniformity. Even among those who agree on the essentials of the Christian life as understood by Baptists, there are differences on non-essential matters such as worship style, congregational life, approaches to mission and models of ministry. As the BWA Centenary message says, 'Often times these differences reflect the various cultures and histories of local believers'.[34] There is scope for much more exploration of these histories, in which the lives of specific communities are examined. Baptist scholars across Europe are taking up this challenge and their work is beginning to be published.[35] Much more remains to be done, however, to show the unity that there is within ecclesial diversity. As an example of how the unity operates, ecumenical dialogue, which for some Baptists is a very vexed issue, has been undertaken with confidence. The clearest demonstration of this European-wide dialogue within the last few years has been the conversations with the CPCE, where it is evident that Baptists in Europe are perfectly capable of engaging with other ecclesial families about such important theological and ecclesial issues as entry into the

---

[32] On issues of external missionaries and indigenous mission see R.T. McConnell, *Indigenous Baptists and foreign missionaries: Baptist communities in Romania, Hungary, and Yugoslavia 1872-1980* (Columbia, SC: University of South Carolina, 1996).

[33] On current issues in mission see J.M. Terry, E. Smith and J. Anderson, *Missiology: an introduction to the foundations, history and strategies of world missions* (Nashville, Tenn.: Broadman & Holman, 1998), pp. 301-17.

[34] Jones, 'The Baptist World Alliance Centenary Message'.

[35] K.G. Jones and I.M. Randall (eds.) *Counter-Cultural Communities: Baptistic Life in Twentieth-Century Europe* (Milton Keynes: Paternoster, 2008).

church, in particular baptism, and in the nature and form of relationships between the traditions – what CPCE calls 'church fellowship'.[36] This work has shown that Baptists see the place for real 'church fellowship' which expresses and presents their own gathering baptistic intentional *koinonia*. This is done whilst, at the same time, recognises the reality of variety, both within Baptist life and within the wider Christian community.

Belief in associating, and in the interdependency between local gathering communities, has been part of the Baptist story in Europe from the seventeenth century onwards. The way in which this has been worked out since 1949 in the EBF, through certain specific issues, has been analysed in the course of the book. In its exploration of the EBF, I have sought to contribute to an understanding of who the people called Baptists are, not only as local, gathering, convictional communities, but as communities associating across a continent and internationally in a way which has a clear ecclesial value. It is demonstrably the case that most European Baptist scholars are at odds with many in the USA. The majority of Baptist scholars in the USA appear to be minimalists in terms of the value of more-than-local associating. The withdrawal of the Southern Baptist Convention from the BWA in 2003 is also indicative of a low view of committed Baptist relationships. More recently, however, there has been an initiative by former US Presidents Jimmy Carter and Bill Clinton, both Baptists, who have drawn the majority of Baptist leaders together in the USA to challenge them to a deeper covenantal relationship.[37] It is possible that there could be a reaction against the minimalist understanding of this by a previous generation and a move away from the understanding espoused by Nettles and Moore.[38] The exploration in this book of the reality of wider relationships in a European context has sought to show how Baptists in Europe have developed an appropriate measure of ecclesial interdependency.

---

[36] William Hüffmeier (ed.), *Agreement between the Reformation Churches in Europe* (Frankfurt am Main: Verlag Otto Lembeck, 1993).

[37] Report, 'Baptist Covenant Offers Chance to Heal Racial Wounds', *Associated Baptist Press*, 11 January 2007 (7-5), Carter Center, Atlanta, Ga.

[38] A recent example of the strength of view about the autonomy of local congregations and the independency of churches can be found in Nettles and Moore, *Why I am a Baptist*.

Given that Baptists do stress the local community, it is notable that, at a pan-European level, Baptist ecclesial reality is more substantial than is the case for some other Christian World Communions. It is not the case that Baptists have only an ecclesiology of the local church. This work has shown that a more-than-local ecclesiology exists and has a vibrant part to play within the life and mission of the Church. In Europe it has had an episkopal, conciliar and local gathering community reality which has proved its theological integrity in the accomplishments of the European Baptist Federation.

Appendix

European Baptist Federation Presidents 1950 – 2009

1. Bredahl Petersen, *Denmark*, 1950 – 1952.
2. Henry Cook, *Great Britain*, 1952 – 1954.
3. Manfredi Ronchi, *Italy*, 1954 – 1956.
4. Hans Luckey, *Germany*, 1956 – 1958.
5. Eric Rudén, *Sweden*, 1958 – 1959.
6. F. Ernst Huizinga, *Netherlands*, 1959 – 1960.
7. Ronald Goulding, *Great Britain*, 1960 – 1962.
8. Baungaard Thomsen, *Denmark*, 1962 – 1964.
9. Jacob Broertjes, *Netherlands*, 1964 – 1966.
10. Michael Zhidkov, *Russia*, 1966 – 1968.
11. Rudolf Thaut, *Germany*, 1968 – 1970.
12. Andrew McRae, *Scotland*, 1970 – 1972.
13. Claus Meister, *Switzerland*, 1972 – 1974.
14. José Goncalves, *Portugal*, 1974 – 1976.
15. Alexej Bichkov, *Russia*, 1976 – 1978.
16. Knud Wümpelmann, *Denmark*, 1978 – 1980.
17. David S. Russell, *Great Britain*, 1980 – 1981.
18. Stanislaw Svec̆, *Czech Republic*, 1981 – 1983.
19. David Łagergren, *Sweden*, 1983 – 1985.
20. Pierro Bensi, *Italy*, 1985 – 1987.
21. Vasile Talpos, *Romania*, 1987 – 1989.
22. Peter Barber, *Scotland*, 1989 – 1991.
23. John W. Merritt, *EBC*, 1991 – 1993.
24. Birgit Karlsson, *Sweden*, 1993 – 1995.

25. Theodor Angelov, *Bulgaria*, 1995 – 1997.
26. David R. Coffey, *Great Britain*, 1997 – 1999.
27. Ole Jørgensen, *Denmark*, 1999 – 2001.
28. Gregory Komendant, *Ukraine*, 2001 – 2003.
29. Billy Taranger, *Norway*, 2003 – 2005.
30. Helari Puu, *Estonia*, 2005 – 2007.
31. Toma Magda, *Croatia*, 2007 – 2009.

Bibliography

EBF Archive, IBTS Library, Prague

Minutes of the EBF Council, 1949-1999, Boxes B 801-822.
Minutes of the EBF Council, 2000-2006, awaiting box number.
Minutes of the EBF Executive, 1950-1999, Boxes B 801-822.
Minutes of the EBF Executive 2000-2007, awaiting box number.
Study Paper issued by the Division for Theology and Education of the EBF, Oxford, 1993, Box 811.
EBF Constitution and Statutes (revised), 27 September 2001, waiting to be boxed.
EBF Constitution 1975, Box B 803.
EBF Constitution 1987, Box B 806.
Report of the EBF General Secretary, 1974, Box B 803.
EBF Directory, 1980-2007, Boxes 805-820.
EBF Baptist Response-Europe, Boxes J1-45.
Report of the EBF Structure Review Committee, 1990, Box B 809.
C. Ronald Goulding Correspondence, Boxes B 1-38.
Gerhard Claas Correspondence Boxes, B 39-71.
Knud Wümplemann Correspondence, Boxes B 72- 90.
Karl Heinz Walter Correspondence, Boxes B 91-163.
Tony Peck Documents, awaiting box number.
EBF/CPCE Dialogue Papers, awaiting box number.
IBTS Board of Trustees Minutes and Documents, Boxes A 1-16 and E 1-11.
The European Baptist, Boxes B 901-902.

EBPS Archive, IBTS Library, Prague

European Baptist Press Service Press Releases 1961-2001, Boxes D 1-16.
European Baptist Press Service News Clips 1977-2000, Boxes D 201-234.
European Baptist Press Service Photo and Events Archives, Boxes D 501-525.
European Baptist Press Service Reports of EBF Councils, Boxes D 801-809.

IBTS Archive, IBTS Library, Prague

Baptist Theological Seminary, Trustees Minutes 1950-1988.
Baptist Theological Seminary, EBF Trustees Minutes 1985-1998, Archive Boxes A 1-12.
International Baptist Theological Seminary of the EBF, Trustees Minutes 1994-2006.
International Baptist Theological Seminary of the EBF, Relocation Group, Bs016 Archive.
J.D. Franks, 'Our Seven Years in post war Europe', 1954, duplicated Report, Bs016.
J.D. Franks, 'Baptist Theological Seminary', commentary for slide presentation, undated

duplicate, Bs016.
G.W. Sadler, 'Historical sketch of the Baptist Theological Seminary, Rueschlikon-Zuerich, Switzerland', Unpublished notes, 1960, Bs016.
Minutes of the Baptist Theological Seminary Administrative Committee, 1948, Bs016.
Programme of the Inauguration Ceremony and Dedication, 1950, Bs016.
Interview in film 'Rüschlikon – Bridge for the Future', SBC-FMB film, 1985, Box 201 LS.
Rüschlikon Letters Archives 1949-1960, Bs016.
Faculty Minutes, 1949-1996, Bs016.
Leaflet on the new Rüschlikon Chapel, miscellaneous papers, Bs016.
'Proposed International Baptist Lay Academy, Budapest Hungary, East Branch, Rüschlikon Seminary', Document submitted to the Seminary Executive Committee, February 1988, Bs016.
IBTS Opening Celebrations Programme, 19 April 1997, Archive A, Box 16.
Submission and Quinquennial Review Report, University of Wales, 2004, Bs016.
G. Keith Parker Documents and Correspondence, Boxes G 1-10.
Wiard Popkes Papers, Boxes H 1-19.
Keith G. Jones personal papers for IBTS, BWA, BWA–ITF, EBF, Archive Boxes L 1-14.
IBTS Magister Degree Submission, Czech Ministry of Education Accreditation Commission 2001 and 2006, Bs016.

BWA Archive, Falls Church, Virginia, USA.

BWA General Council Report Books 1950-2007.
BWA Executive Committee Minutes 1950-2006.
Baptist World Aid Executive Committee Minutes 1990-2006.
Baptist World Alliance Relief Committee Minutes 1950-1980.
BWA Year Books and Directories 1970-2006.
Document presented by C.R. Goulding to the Commission on Cooperative Christianity of the BWA, July 1973.
BWA Baptist World Congresses *Record of Proceedings: 1st to Centenary World Congress*, 2005.
K.G. Jones (ed.), 'The Baptist World Alliance Centenary Message', (longer version), BWA Centenary Congress Resolutions Committee, 2005.

Angus Library, Regent's Park College, Oxford

BWA Correspondence Boxes 22-27.
BWA Europe Boxes 2, 3.
Baptist Union of Great Britain Annual Reports 1980-1998.
Baptist Union of Great Britain Council Papers 1955-1998.
D. Allan, 'Clustering – a Dynamic for Mission', undated, but Autumn 1999, and 'Relating and Resourcing – the Report of the Task Group on Associating', both Baptist Union of Great Britain Documents and Papers, 1990-1998.
Baptist Union of Great Britain Ministerial Recognition Committee Papers 1981-1983.
Baptist Mission Society Minutes, 1870 volume.

EBF Evangelism Committee Papers 1966-1969.
EBF – Christian Peace Conferences, unnumbered box.
Fellowship of British Baptists Minute Book 1992-1998.
C. Ronald Goulding BWA Papers, unnumbered box.
David S. Russell Papers, EBF Boxes 1, 2.
Erik Rudén Papers, Boxes 1, 2.
Ernest A. Payne Papers, Boxes 64, K/1.
Le Quesne Papers, unnumbered folder.

ABFMS Archive, American Baptist Historical Society, Valley Forge, Pa, USA

BWA Minutes of the London Conferences 1920, 1948, Box 3.23H.
BWA Executive Committee Minutes 1939-1956.
W.O. Lewis, 'Northern Baptists and Post War Europe', 5 January 1943, typescript, BWA, Washington DC, Box I 2.1.
Letters from M.E. Aubrey to W.O. Lewis, Box I 2.2.
ABC FMS Boxes 254, 395, 476.
Report of the Board of the American Baptist Foreign Mission in the *American Baptist Magazine 1835*.

FMB Archive, SBC-IMB, Richmond, Va, USA

FMB Minutes, 6 April 1948.
G.W. Sadler, 'Report to the Board', FMB Minutes, 1948.
Poster 'Southern Baptists Can Make These Dreams Come True! You and the Future of Missions', 1948.
The 'Missionary Family Album', 1948.

EBM Archive, Elstal, Germany

EBM Council Minutes 1950-2005.
EBM Task Force Report to the EBM Council, February 2006.

Periodicals/Newspapers

Associated Baptist Press.
The Alabama Baptist.
The Baptist Times.
The Baptist World.
The Commission.
Fellowship News (CBF).
The Religious Herald, Virginia.
Highlights, news journal of the European Baptist Convention.
Berlingske Tidende, Denmark.
Yes Magazine, 1999.

Los Angeles Times Magazine, 2003.

Articles

Don Black, 'The Cassock Club', *The Baptist Quarterly*, Vol. 40, July 2004.

W.H. Brackney, 'An Historical Theologian Looks Anew at Autonomy', unpublished paper presented at the BWA Symposium on Baptist Identity and Ecclesiology, Elstal, Berlin, 21-24 March 2007.

I. Braznik, Moscow University, was printed in *Science and Religion*, December 1969.

J.H.Y. Briggs, 'Baptists and the Ecumenical Movement', *Journal of European Baptist Studies,* Vol. 6, No. 1, September 2005.

W.R. Burrows, 'Reconciling all in Christ: An old new paradigm for mission', Mission Studies, *Journal of the International Association for Mission Studies*. Vol. XV, 1, 29, 1998.

K.W. Clements, 'Baptists and the Outbreak of the First World War', *The Baptist Quarterly*, Vol. 26, No. 2, 1975.

S. Fath, 'A Forgotten Missionary Link: The Baptist Continental Society in France (1831-1936)', *The Baptist Quarterly*, Vol. IV, No. 2, (July 2003).

H.E. Fey, *World Confessionalism and the Ecumenical Movement*, 1970. Mimeographed draft, IBTS Library, Prague.

A. Golloshi, 'Leadership in the Albanian Evangelical Community: A Theological Assessment of Paradigms, Practices and Vision', MTh Dissertation, IBTS, Prague, 2003.

N.M. Healy, 'Karl Barth's Ecclesiology Reconsidered' in *Scottish Journal of Theology* 57 (2004).

J.D. Hughey, 'The Baptist Theological Seminary of Rueschlikon, Retrospect and Prospect', *Quarterly Review*, April-June 1963.

B. Hylleberg, 'Knud Wümplemann', *Journal of European Baptist Studies*, Vol. 2, No. 3 (Prague: IBTS, May 2002).

K.G. Jones, 'The International Baptist Theological Seminary of the European Baptist Federation', *American Baptist Quarterly*, Vol. XVIII, No. 2, June 1999.

— 'Rethinking Baptist Ecclesiology' in *Journal of European Baptist Studies*, Vol. 1, No. 1, September 2000.

— Editorial in *The Journal of European Baptist Studies*, Vol. 2, No. 3, 2002.

— 'Towards a Model of Mission for Gathering, Intentional, Convictional Koinonia', *Journal of European Baptist Studies*, Vol. 4, No. 2, January 2004.

M. Kinnamon, 'Assessing the Ecumenical Movement' in *A History of the Modern Ecumenical Movement Volume 3*.

Ken Manley, 'The Right Man in the Right Place: W.T. Whitley in Australia (1891-1901), *The Baptist Quarterly*, Vol. XXXVII, No. 4, October 1997.

J.F.V. Nicholson, 'The Office of Messenger amongst British Baptists in the Seventeenth and Eighteenth Centuries', *The Baptist Quarterly*, Vol. XVII, No. 5, January 1958.

— 'Towards a Theology of Episcope Amongst Baptists', *The Baptist Quarterly*, Vol. XXX, No. 6, April 1984, pp. 265-81.

E.A. Payne, 'The Baptists of the Soviet Union' in *The Ecumenical Review*, January 1955.

A.A. Peck, 'Grace and Law: Baptists and Religious Freedom: Historical Antecedents and Contemporary Context', *The Baptist Quarterly*, Vol. XXXIX, No. 7, July 2002.

I.M. Randall, 'The Blessing of An Enlightened Christianity: North American Involvement in European Baptist Origins, *American Baptist Quarterly*, Vol. XX, March 2001, No. 1.

— 'Evangelicals and European Integration', *European Journal of Theology*, Vol. XIV, No. 1, 2005.

— '"Pious Wishes": Baptists and wider renewal movements in nineteenth-century Europe', *The Baptist Quarterly*, Vol. XXXVIII, No. 7, July 2000.

E. Rudén, 'The Baptist Witness in Scandinavia and the North', *BQ*, Vol. XXVII, No. 2, April, 1979.

D.S. Russell, 'Cold War Years', *The Baptist Quarterly*, Vol. XXXVI, January 1995

— 'Baptists in Central and Eastern Europe in the Post-War Years: Recollections and Reflections', *The Baptist Quarterly*, Vol. XXXVII, No. 4. October 1997.

R.E. Schlosser, 'Chronological History of the Board of International Ministries', *American Baptist Quarterly*, Vol. XIV, June 1995, No. 2.

I. Sellers, 'W.T. Whitley – A Commemorative Essay', *The Baptist Quarterly*, Vol. XXXVII, No. 4, October 1997.

S. Slade and R.S. Trulson, 'Planning and Partnering at American Baptist International Ministries', *American Baptist Quarterly*, Vol. XX, March 2001.

A. Strübind, 'German Baptists and National Socialism', *Journal of European Baptist Studies,* Vol. 8, No. 3, May 2008.

Documents

Constitution of the World Alliance of Reformed Churches, Offices of the WARC, Geneva, Switzerland.

Constitution of The Lutheran World Federation as adopted by the LWF Eighth Assembly, Curitiba, Brazil, 1990, including amendments adopted by the LWF Ninth Assembly, Hong Kong, 1997.

The Meissen Agreement, The Council for Christian Unity of the General Synod of the Church of England, 1992, Church House, Westminster.

An Introduction to the Anglican Communion, Anglican Consultative Council, Lambeth Palace, London, 2002.

Guidelines for CEC/CCEE Cooperation adopted in Guernsey, March 1999, and signed in Prague, February 2000, CEC/CCEE, Geneva/St Gallen, Switzerland, May 2000.

Documents from the Second European Ecumenical Assembly in Graz, CCEE/CEC, Switzerland, 1998.

Statement on Conciliar Self-consciousness by the Ecumenical Patriarch, 2002, Ecumenical Patriarchate, Constantinople.

Statement by the Ecumenical Patriarch on initiating the common search for convening a Panorthodox Holy and Great Council in which the entire ecclesiastical body of Orthodoxy would be represented, Constantinople 2000.

CEC Information Document 91/33, 1991, Geneva.

Baptism, Eucharist and Ministry, Faith and Order Paper 111, WCC, 1981, Geneva.

CEC Central Committee Minutes 1 to 13, May 1990, Geneva.

CEC/CCEE Final Communiqué from the 5th Encounter, Santiago de Compostela, November 1991, CEC, Geneva.

CEC Document 91/08, 14 May 1991, CEC, Geneva.

CEC Official Study Document, Vol. 17, No. 3, June 1992.

CEC 12th Assembly Trondheim, Norway, Official Report, 2003.

Document of Mutual Recognition, The Baptist Union of Italy, the Waldensian Church of Italy, the Methodist Conference in Italy, Rome, 2-4 November 1990.

Christian Peace Conference, 1985, Conference Report, 'Choose Life! The Hour is Late. The Christians in Resistance to the Powers of Death – on the Path to Peace and Justice for all', Documents of the Sixth All-Christian Peace Assembly, Prague. July, 1985.

CEC Documentation Service, Vol. 17, No. 33, June 1992.

'The Place of World Confessional Families in the Ecumenical Movement', in *Study Encounter IV*, Geneva, 1968.

Official Statement of Mission and Purpose of the Pentecostal World Fellowship.

Agreement between Reformation Churches in Europe (Leuenberg Concordat) (Frankfurt am Main: Verlag Otto Lembeck, 1973). The official English translation copyright the United Reformed Church in the United Kingdom.

Consultation between the churches of the Leuenberg Church Fellowship and the churches Involved in the Meissen Agreement and the Porvoo Agreement (Frankfurt am Main: Verlag Otto Lembeck, 1995).

Dialogue between the Community of Protestant Churches in Europe (CPCE) and the European Baptist Federation (EBF) on the Doctrine and Practice of Baptism (Frankfurt am Main: Verlag Otto Lembeck, 2005).

Interpretive essays: A Reader Designed to Introduce American Evangelicals to the Complexities of the European World (Pasadena, Cal: Fuller Theological Seminary and Trinity Evangelical Divinity School, 1987).

Books

Nancy Tatom Ammerman, *Congregation and Community* (New Brunswick: Rutgers University Press, 1997).

A.H. Anderson and W.J. Hollenweger, *Pentecostals after a Century: Global Perspectives on a Movement in Transition* (Sheffield: Sheffield Academic Press, 1999).

P. Avis, *The Christian Church: An Introduction to the Major Traditions* (London: SPCK, 2002).

— *A Church Drawing Near: Spirituality and Mission in a post-Christian culture* (London: T&T Clark, 2003).

— *Pushing at the Boundaries of Unity: Anglicans and Baptists in Conversation* (London: Church House Publishing, 2006)

G. Balders, *Theurer Bruder Oncken: Das Leben Johann Gerhard Onckens* (Wuppertal und Kassel: Oncken, 1978).

The Baptist Union of Great Britain, Doctrine and Worship Committee, 'The Nature of the Assembly and the Council of the Baptist Union of Great Britain' (Didcot, 1994).

— *Baptist Union Documents 1948-1977* (London: Baptist Historical Society, 1980).

S. Barrow and G. Smith (eds.), *Christian Mission in Western Society* (London: Churches Together in Britain and Ireland, 2001).

K. Barth, *Church Dogmatics,* vols. I, IV (ET G.W. Bromiley and T.F. Torrance (eds.)

(Edinburgh: T&T Clark, 1960).
J.F. Baugh, *The Battle for Baptist Integrity* (Austin, Tx.: Battle for Baptist Integrity Inc. 1997).
Paul Beasley-Murray, *Radical Believers: The Baptist Way of Being the Church* (Didcot: The Baptist Union of Great Britain, 1992).
D.W. Bebbington, *Evangelicalism in Modern Britain: A History from the 1730's to the 1980's* (London: Unwin Hyman 1989).
— *Patterns in History* (Leicester: Inter-Varsity Press, 1979).
— *The Baptists in Scotland: A History* (ed.) (Glasgow: Baptist Union of Scotland, 1988).
— *The Nonconformist Conscience: Chapel and Politics 1870-1914* (London: Allen & Unwin, 1982).
— *The Gospel in the World: Studies in Baptist History and Thought*, (ed.), Vol. 1 (Carlisle: Paternoster, 2002).
H. van Beek (ed.), *Handbook of Churches and Councils: Profile of Ecumenical Relationships* (Geneva: WCC, 2006).
T.J. Beeson, *Discretion and Valour* (London: Fontana Books, 1974).
A.J. van der Bent (ed.), *Historical Dictionary of Ecumenical Christianity (*Metuchen: Scarecrow Press, 1994).
T.F. Best and G. Gassman (eds.), *On the Way to Fuller Koinonia* (Geneva: WCC, 1994).
E. Bethge, *Dietrich Bonhoeffer* (London: Collins, 1970).
— *Friendship and Resistance: Essays on Dietrich Bonhoeffer* (Geneva: WCC, 1995)
A. Bloed, L. Leicht, M. Nowak, A. Rosas (eds.), *Monitoring Human Rights in Europe* (Dordrecht: Martinus Nijhoff, 1993).
L. Boff, *Church Charism and Power: Liberation Theology and the Institutional Church* (London: SCM, 1985).
— *Ecclesiogenesis: The Base Communities Reinvent the Church* (Glasgow: Collins, 1982).
D. Bonhoeffer, *The Cost of Discipleship* (English Translation from German original; London: SCM, 1948).
— *Life Together* (ET from German original; London: SCM, 1954).
M. Bordeaux, *Opium of the People: The Christian Religion in the USSR* (London: Faber and Faber, 1965).
— *Faith on Trial in Russia* (London: Hodder and Stoughton, 1971).
D.J. Bosch, *Transforming Mission: Paradigm Shifts in Theology of Mission* (Maryknoll, NY: Orbis, 1998).
Faith Bowers, *A Bold Experiment: Bloomsbury Central Baptist Church* (London: Bloomsbury Central Baptist Church, 1999).
W.H. Brackney, *The Baptists* (New York: Greenwood Press, 1988).
— *Baptist Life and Thought*, rev. ed. (Valley Forge, Pa.: Judson Press, 1998).
— *A Genetic History of Baptist Thought: with special reference to Britain and North America* (Macon Ga.: Mercer University Press, 2004).
— *The Believers Church: A Voluntary Church* (ed.) (Ontario: Pandora Press, 1998).
W.H. Brackney and P.S. Fiddes with J.H.Y. Briggs (eds.), *Pilgrim Pathways: Essays in Baptist History in Honour of B.R. White* (Macon, Ga.: Mercer University Press, 1999).
W.H. Brackney with Ruby J Burke (eds.), *Faith, Life and Witness: The Papers of the Study and Research Division of the Baptist World Alliance 1986-1990* (Birmingham,

Al: Samford University Press, 1990).
W.H. Brackney and L.A. (Tony) Cupit (eds.) *Baptist Faith and Witness: The Papers of the Study and Research Division of the Baptist World Alliance 1990-1995* (Birmingham, Al: Samford University Press, 1995).
Timothy Bradshaw, *The Olive Branch: An Evangelical Anglican Doctrine of the Church* (Carlisle: Paternoster, 1992).
Peter Brierley, (ed.) *Christianity in Europe* (Eltham, London: MARC Europe, 1988).
J.H.Y. Briggs, *The English Baptists of the 19th Century* (Didcot: The Baptist Historical Society, 1994).
— *A Russian Journey: Summer 1989* (Brightwell, Wallingford: Gem Publishing, 1989).
J.H.Y. Briggs and I. Sellers, *Victorian Nonconformity* (London: Edward Arnold, 1973).
C.A. Brooks and J.H. Rushbrooke, *Report of the Commissioners of the Baptist World Alliance* (London: Baptist Union Publications, 1920).
E. Burrows, *To me to live is Christ: A biography of Peter Barber* (Milton Keynes: Paternoster, 2005).
BWA Study and Research Division, *We Baptists* (Franklin, Tenn.: Providence House Publishers, 1999).
Barry L. Callen, *Radical Christianity: The Believers Church Tradition on Christianity's History and Future* (Nappanee, Ind: Evangel Publishing House, 1999).
Jean Calvin, *Institutes of the Christian Religion* (ET from Latin by Ford Lewis Battles, Grand Rapids, Mich: Eerdmans, 1986).
James E. Carter, *The Mission of the Church* (Nashville: Broadman, 1974).
T.G. Carter, *The Journal and Selected Letters of William Carey* (Macon, Ga.: Smyth & Helwys, 2000).
K.W. Clements (ed.), *Baptists in the Twentieth Century* (London: Baptist Historical Society, 1983).
— *A Patriotism for Today: Dialogue with Dietrich Bonhoeffer* (Bristol: Bristol Baptist College, 1984).
— *What Freedom? The Persistent challenge of Dietrich Bonhoeffer* (Bristol: Bristol Baptist College, 1990).
— *Lovers of Discord: Twentieth Century Theological Controversies in England* (London: SPCK, 1988).
J.E. Colwell, *Promise and Presence: An Exploration of Sacramental Theology* (Milton Keynes: Paternoster, 2005).
J.R. Coggins, *John Smyth's Congregation: English Separatism, Mennonite influence and the Elect Nation* (Scottdale, Pa: Herald, 1991).
H. Cook, *What Baptists Stand For* (London: Carey Kingsgate Press, 1947).
G.C. Cothen, *The New SBC: Fundamentalism's Impact on the Southern Baptist Convention* (Macon, Ga.: Smythe and Helwys, 1995).
H.G. Cox, *On Not Leaving it to the Snake* (New York: Macmillan, 1964).
— *The Secular City* (London: SCM Press, 1965).
A.R. Cross, *Baptism and the Baptists: Theology and Practice in Twentieth-Century Britain* (Carlisle: Paternoster, 2000).
— (ed.) *Ecumenism and History: Studies in Honour of John H.Y. Briggs* (Carlisle: Paternoster, 2002).
Hubert Cunliffe-Jones, *A History of Christian Doctrine* (Edinburgh: T & T Clark, 1978).
L.A. (Tony) Cupit (ed.) *Baptist Faith and Witness Book 2: The Papers of the Study and Research Division of the Baptist World Alliance 1995-2000* (McLean, Va: Baptist

World Alliance, 1999).

— *Baptist Faith and Witness Book 3: The Papers of the Study and Research Division of the Baptist World Alliance 2000-2005* (ed.) (Falls Church, Va: Baptist World Alliance, 2005).

Arthur Dakin, *The Baptist View of the Church and Ministry* (London: Baptist Union, 1944).

D. Davie, A Gathered Church: *The Literature of the English Dissenting Interest, 1700-1930* (London: Routledge and Kegan Paul, 1978).

G. Davie, *Religion in Modern Europe* (Oxford: Oxford University Press, 2000).

N. Davies, *Europe: A History* (London: Pimlico, 1997).

— *The Isles* (London: Macmillan,1999).

P. Dekar, *For the Healing of the Nations: Baptist Peacemakers* (Macon, Ga.: Smythe and Helwys, 1993).

R.K. Downton, *Authority in the Church* (New York: University Press of America, 2006).

A. Dulles, *The Catholicity of the Church* (Oxford: Clarendon, 1985).

— *Models of the Church: A Critical Assessment of the Church in all its Aspects* (Dublin: Gill and Macmillan, 1976).

James D.G. Dunn, *Unity and Diversity in the New Testament* (London: SCM Press, 1977).

D.F. Durnbaugh, *The Believers' Church: the History and Character of Radical Protestantism* (New York: The MacMillan Company, 1968).

N. Ehrenström and G. Gassmann, *Confessions in Dialogue* (Geneva: WCC, 1975).

K.E. Eitel, *Paradigm Wars: The Southern Baptist International Mission Board Faces the Third Millennium* (Oxford: Regnum Books International, 2000).

Christopher J. Ellis, *Gathering: A Theology and Spirituality of Worship in the Free Church Tradition* (London: SCM Press, 2004).

— *Together on the Way: A Theology of Ecumenism* (London: British Council of Churches, 1990).

Millard J. Erickson, *Christian Theology*, sec.ed. (Grand Rapids: Baker Books, 1998).

Gillian R. Evans, *The Church and the Churches: Towards an Ecumenical Ecclesiology* (Cambridge: Cambridge University Press, 1994).

M.D. Evans, *Religious Liberty and International Law in Europe* (Cambridge: Cambridge University Press, 1997).

The Faith and Unity Executive Committee, the Baptist Union of Great Britain, 'Spiritual Leadership in the Baptist Union', *The Nature of the Assembly and the Council of the Baptist Union of Great Britain* (Didcot: BUGB Publications, 1994).

Walfred J Fahrer, *Building on the Rock: A Biblical Vision of Being Church Together from an Anabaptist-Mennonite Perspective* (Scottdale: Herald Press, 1995).

P. Fiddes, *Tracks and Traces: Baptist Identity in Church and Theology* (Carlisle: Paternoster, 2003).

K. Fiedler, *The Story of Faith Missions* (Oxford: Regnum Books, 1994).

S.K. Fowler, 'Churches and the Church' in P.E. Thompson and A.R. Cross (eds.), *Recycling the Past or Researching History? Studies in Baptist Historiography and Myths* (Milton Keynes: Paternoster, 2005).

Howard Foreman, *A New Look at Protestant Churches in France* (Bromley, Kent: MARC Europe, 1987).

R. Fung, *The Isaiah Vision* (Geneva: WCC, 1992).

James Leo Garrett, Jr, *Systematic Theology: Biblical, Historical and Evangelical*, 2 vols. (Grand Rapids: Eerdmans, 1990 and 1995).

— *The Concept of the Believers' Church: Addresses from the 1967 Louisville Conference* (ed.)(Scottdale, PA: Herald Press, 1969).

T. George, *Faithful Witness: The Life and Mission of William Carey* (Leicester: IVP, 1991).

Timothy and Denise George (eds.), *Baptist Confessions, Covenants and Catechisms* (Nashville, Tenn: Broadman and Holman, 1996).

Alec Gilmore (ed.), *The Pattern of the Church: A Baptist View* (London: Lutterworth Press, 1963).

Rollin G. Grams and Parush R Parushev, *Towards an Understanding of European Baptist Identity* (Prague: International Baptist Theological Seminary, 2006).

B. Green, *Tomorrow's Man: A Biography of James Henry Rushbrooke* (Didcot: Baptist Historical Society, 1997).

— *Crossing the Boundaries: A History of the European Baptist Federation* (Didcot: The Baptist Historical Society, 1999).

S.J. Grenz, *Theology for the Community of God* (Carlisle: Paternoster, 1994).

— *The Baptist Congregation: A Guide to Baptist Belief and Practice* (Vancouver, BC: Regent College Publishing, 1985).

J. Gros, H. Meyer and W. Rusch (eds.), *Growth in Agreement II: Reports and Agreed Statements of Ecumenical Conversations on a World Level 1982-1998* (Geneva: WCC, 2000).

R. Gurney (ed.), *CEC at 40: Celebrating the 40th Anniversary of the Conference of European Churches 1959-1999* (Geneva: CEC, 1999).

F.M.W. Harrison, *It All Began Here* (London: East Midland Baptist Association, 1986).

R. Hayden (ed.), *Baptist Union Documents 1948-1977* (London: Baptist Historical Society, 1980).

T. Helwys, *The Mistery of Iniquity*, Extant copy in Bodleian Library, University of Oxford.

Eric Hobsbawn, *Age of Extremes: The Short Twentieth Century, 1914-1991* (London: Michael Joseph, 1994).

— *The Invention of Tradition* (Cambridge: Cambridge University of Press, 1983).

Walter J. Hollenweger, *The Pentecostals* (London: SCM Press, 1972).

Ladislav Holy, *The Little Czech and the Great Czech Nation: National Identity and the Post-communist Social Transformation* (Cambridge: Cambridge University Press, 1996).

D.M. Howard, *The Dream that would not Die* (Exeter: Paternoster, 1986).

W. Hüffmeier and T. Peck (eds.), *Dialogue between the Community of Protestant Churches in Europe (CPCE) and the European Baptist Federation (EBF) on the Doctrine and Practice of Baptism* (Frankfurt am Main: Verlag Otto Lembeck, 2005).

J.D. Hughey, *Baptist Partnership in Europe: The HOW of Christian Missions in Europe today* (Nashville, Tenn.: Broadman Press, 1982).

Samuel P Huntington, *The Clash of Civilisations and the Remaking of the World Order* (London: Simon and Schuster, 1997).

Keith Jenkins, *Re-thinking History* (London: Routledge, 1991).

P.H. Jenkins, *The Next Christendom* (Oxford: Oxford University Press, 2002).

K.G. Jones, *A Believing Church: Learning from some contemporary Anabaptist and Baptist perspectives* (Didcot: Baptist Union of Great Britain, 1998).

K.G. Jones and I.M. Randall (eds.) *Counter-Cultural Communities: Baptistic Life in Twentieth-Century Europe* (Milton Keynes: Paternoster, 2008),

R.L. Kidd (ed.), *Something to Declare* (Oxford: Whitley Publications, 1996).

— *On the Way of Trust* (Oxford: Whitley Publications, 1997).

J.A. Kirk, *The Mission of Theology and Theology as Mission* (Valley Forge: Trinity Press International, 1997).

J.K. Lee, *The Theology of John Smyth: Puritan, Separatist, Baptist, Mennonite* (Macon: Mercer University Press, 2003).

B.J. Leonard, *Baptist Ways: A History* (Valley Forge, Pa.: Judson Press. 2003).

— *Baptists in America* (New York: Columbia Press, 2005).

T. Lorenzen, *Freedom of Religion as a Human Right* (Hamburg: EBF, 1995).

— *Resurrection and Discipleship: Interpretive Models, Biblical Reflections, Theological Consequences* (Maryknoll, NY: Orbis Books, 1995).

D. Lotz (ed.) *Baptist Witness in the USSR* (Valley Forge: ABC, 1987).

W.L. Lumpkin, *Baptist Confessions of Faith* (Valley Forge, Pa: Judson Press, 1969).

H.L. McBeth, *The Baptist Heritage: Four Centuries of Baptist Witness* (Nashville, Tenn.: Broadman Press, 1987).

— *A Sourcebook for Baptist Heritage*, (Nashville, Tenn: Broadman Press, 1990).

D.K. McCall with A.R. Tonks, *Duke McCall: An Oral History* (Brentwood, Tenn: Baptist History and Heritage Society/Nashville: Fields, 2001).

J.W. McClendon, Jr., *Systematic Theology: Ethics*, vol. 1 (Nashville, Tenn.: Abingdon, 1986).

— *Systematic Theology: Doctrine*, vol. 2 (Nashville, Tenn.: Abingdon, 1994).

— *Systematic Theology: Witness*, vol. 3 (Nashville, Tenn.: Abingdon, 2000).

R.T. McConnell, *Indigenous Baptists and foreign missionaries: Baptist communities in Romania, Hungary, and Yugoslavia 1872-1980* (Columbia, SC: University of South Carolina, 1996).

J.W. Merritt, *The Betrayal of Southern Baptist Missionaries by Southern Baptist Leaders 1979 –2004* (Ashville, North Ca.: Published by the author, 2004), later reprinted as Merritt, *The Betrayal: The hostile takeover of the Southern Baptist Convention and a missionary's fight for Freedom in Christ* (Ashville, North Ca.: R. Brent and Co, 2005).

H. Meyer 'Christian World Communions', A *History of the Ecumenical Movement Volume 3, 1968-2000* (Geneva: World Council of Churches, 2004).

— *That All May be One: Perceptions and Models of Ecumenicity* (Grand Rapids: Eerdmans, 1999).

Paul S Minear, *Images of the Church in the New Testament* (Philadelphia: Westminster Press, 1960).

J. Moltmann, *The Church in the Power of the Spirit: A contribution to Messianic Ecclesiology* (New York: Harper and Row, 1977).

S. Murray (ed.), *Translocal Ministries: Equipping the Churches for Mission* (Didcot: Baptist Union of Great Britain, 2004).

Milan Návrat, *Religion in Czechoslovakia* (Prague: Orbis Press Agency, 1984).

S. Neill, *A History of Christian Missions* (London: Penguin, 1986).

T.J. Nettles and R. Moore (eds.), *Why I am a Baptist* (Nashville, Tenn.: Broadman and Holman, 2001).

L. Newbigin, *The Household of God: Lectures on the nature of the Church* (New York: Friendship, 1954).

J. Novotny, *The Baptist romance in the Heart of Europe: The Life and Times of Henry Novotny* (New York: Czechoslovak Baptist Convention in America and Canada, undated).

Tim and Ivana Noble, Martien E. Brinkman and Jochen Hilberath (eds.), *Charting Churches in a Changing Europe: Charta Oecumenica and the Process of Ecumenical Encounter* (Amsterdam: Rodopi B.V., 2006).

G.F. Nuttall, 'Assemblies and associations in Dissent', *Studies in Church History* 7 (1971).

G.K. Parker, *Baptists in Europe – History and Confessions of Faith* (Nashville, Tenn.: Broadman Press, 1982).

L.P. Patterson, *Anatomy of a Reformation: The Southern Baptist Convention 1978-2004* (Fort Worth: Southwestern Seminary Publications, 2006).

E.A. Payne, *Out of Great Tribulation: Baptists in the USSR* (London: Baptist Union of Great Britain, 1974).

— *The Baptist Union: a short history* (London: The Baptist Union of Great Britain and Ireland, 1958).

— *Free Churchmen: Repentant and Unrepentant* (London: The Carey Kingsgate Press, 1965).

P.F. Penner (ed.), *Theological Education as Mission* (Schwarzenfeld, Germany: Neufeld Verlag, 2005).

— *Ethnic Churches in Europe: A Baptist Response* (Schwarzenfeld, Germany: Neufeld Verlag, 2006).

— *Anabaptism and Mission* (Schwarzenfeld, Germany: Neufeld Verlag, 2007).

R.V. Pierard (ed.), *Baptists Together in Christ 1905-2005: A Hundred-Year History of the Baptist World Alliance* (Birmingham, Al., Samford University Press, 2005).

H.W. Pipkin, *Seek Peace and Pursue It: Proceedings from the International Baptist Peace Conference, 1988* (Memphis, Tenn.: Baptist Peace Fellowship of North America and the Institute for Baptist and Anabaptist Studies, IBTS, 1989).

H.W. Pipkin and J.H. Yoder (ed.), *Balthasar Hubmaier: Theologian of Anabaptism* (ET from German original, Scottdale, Pa.: Herald Press, 1989).

Stephen Plant, *Bonhoeffer* (London: Continuum Books, 2004).

Colin Podmore (ed.), *Community-Unity-Communion: Essays in Honour of Mary Tanner* (London: Church House Publishing, 1998).

P. Pressler, *A Hill on Which to Die: One Southern Baptist's Journey* (Nashville, Tenn.: Broadman and Holman, 1999).

Y. Pusey, *European Baptist Women's Union: Our Story 1948-1998* (Oakham, Rutland: EBWU, 1998).

I.M. Randall '"Days of Pentecostal Overflowing": Baptists and the Shaping of Pentecostalism', in D.W. Bebbington, ed., *The Gospel in the World: Studies in Baptist History and Thought*, Vol. 1 (Carlisle: Paternoster, 2002).

— Baptists and Orthodoxy: On the way to understanding (ed.) (Prague: IBTS, 2003).

— *The English Baptists of the 20th Century* (Didcot: Baptist Historical Society, 2005).

I.M. Randall and D. Hilborn, *One Body in Christ: The History and Significance of the Evangelical Alliance* (Carlisle: Paternoster, 2001).

I.M. Randall, T. Pilli and A.R. Cross (eds.), *Baptist Identities: International Studies from the Seventeenth to the Twentieth Centuries* (Carlisle: Paternoster, 2006).

M. Reuver, *Faith and Law: Juridical Perspectives for the Ecumenical Movement* (Geneva: WCC, 2000).

P. Rietbergen, *Europe: A Cultural History* (London: Routledge, Second Edition, 2006).

F. Rinaldi, *The Tribe of Dan: The New Connexion of General Baptists 1770-1891* (Carlisle: Paternoster, 2008).

J. Rippon, *Baptist Annual Register 1 (1790- 1793)* (London: Dilly, Button and Thomas, 1793).

K. Robbins, 'Protestant Nonconformists and the Peace Question', in A.P.F. Sell and A.R. Cross (eds.), *Protestant Nonconformity in the Twentieth Century* (Carlisle: Paternoster, 2003).

H. Wheeler Robinson, *The Life and Faith of the Baptists* (London: Carey Kingsgate Press, 1966).

Michael Root and Risto Saarinien (eds.), *Baptism and the Unity of the Church,* (Geneva: WCC Publications, 1998).

R. Rouse, S.C. Neill and H.E. Fey (eds. vols.1 and 2), J.H.Y. Briggs, M.A.Oduyoye, G. Tsetsis (eds. Vol. 3), *The History of the Ecumenical Movement*, vols.1, 2 and 3 (Geneva: WCC, 1967, 1998 and 2005).

J.H. Rushbrooke in F Siegmund-Schultze (ed.), *Friendly Relations between Great Britain and Germany* (Berlin: H.S. Herman, 1909).

J.H. Rushbrooke (ed.), *The Baptist Movement in the Continent of Europe* (London: Kingsgate Press, 1915).

— *Some Chapters of European Baptist History* (London: Kingsgate Press, 1929).

D.S. Russell, *In Journeyings Often* (London: BUGB, 1981).

W.W. Sawatsky and P.F. Penner (eds.), *Mission in the Former Soviet Union* (Schwarzenfeld, Germany: Neufeld Verlag, 2005).

Frank Schimmelfennig and Ulrich Sedelmeier, *The Europeanization of Central and Eastern Europe* (Ithaca, New York: Cornell University Press, 2005).

A.P.F. Sell, *Saints: Visible, Orderly and Catholic - The Congregational idea of the Church* (Geneva: World Alliance of Reformed Churches, 1986).

— *Confessing and Commending the Faith* (Cardiff: University of Wales Press, 2002).

— *Enlightenment, Ecumenism, Evangel: Theological Themes and Thinkers 1550-2000* (Milton Keynes: Paternoster, 2005).

— *Testimony and Tradition: Studies in Reformed and Dissenting Thought* (Aldershot: Ashgate Publishing, 2005).

— *Nonconformist Theology in the Twentieth Century* (Milton Keynes: Paternoster, 2006).

A.P.F. Sell and A.R. Cross (eds.), *Protestant Nonconformity in the Twentieth Century* (Carlisle: Paternoster, 2003).

I. Sellers (ed.), *Our Heritage: The Baptists of Yorkshire, Lancashire and Cheshire 1647-1987* (Leeds: Yorkshire Baptist Association and Lancashire & Cheshire Baptist Association, 1987).

P. Shepherd, *The Making of a Modern Denomination: John Howard Shakespeare and the English Baptists. 1898 -1924* (Carlisle: Paternoster, 2001).

W.B. Shurden, *Proclaiming the Baptist Vision*: *The Church* (Macon, Ga.: Smyth and Helwys, 1996).

— *Proclaiming the Baptist Vision: Baptism and the Lord's Supper* (Macon, Ga.: Smyth and Helwys, 1996).

— *Proclaiming the Baptist Vision: The Priesthood of All Believers* (Macon, Ga.: Smyth and Helwys, 1996).

— *Baptist Identity: Four Fragile Freedoms* (Macon, Ga.: Smyth and Helwys, 1993).

F. Siegmund-Schultze (ed.), *Friendly Relations between Great Britain and Germany* (Berlin: H.S. Herman, 1909).

F.W. Simoleit (ed.), *Offizieller Bericht ueber den 1. Kongress der europaeischen Baptisten* (Kassel: Oncjen Verlag, 1908).

C.A. Snyder, *Anabaptist History and Theology: An Introduction* (Kitchener, Ont: Pandora, 1995).

R. Wayne Stacy (ed.), *A Baptists Theology* (Macon, Ga: Smyth and Helwys, 1999).

B. Stanley, *The Baptist Missionary Society 1792-1992* (Edinburgh: T&T Clark, 1992).

G.H. Stassen, *Just Peacemaking: Transforming Initiatives for Justice and Peace* (Louisville, Ky.: Westminster/John Knox Press, 1992).

P.P. Streiff, *Methodism in Europe: 19th and 20th Century* (Tallinn, Estonia: Baltic Methodist Theological Seminary, 2003).

A. Strübind, *Die unfreie Freikirche, Der Bund der Baptistengemeinden im, Dritten Reich* (Wuppertal/Zürich: Neukirchen-Vluyn, Neukirchener, 1995).

A. Taylor, *Memoirs of Dan Taylor* (London: Baynes and Son and Whittemore, 1820).

J.M. Terry, E. Smith and J. Anderson, *Missiology: an introduction to the foundations, history and strategies of world missions* (Nashville, Tenn.: Broadman & Holman, 1998).

P.E. Thompson and A.R. Cross (eds.), *Recycling the Past or Researching History? Studies in Baptist Historiography and Myths* (Milton Keynes: Paternoster, 2005).

Bernard Thurogood, *One wind, many flames: Church Unity and the diversity of the Churches* (Geneva: WCC, 1991).

Derek J. Tidball, *Who are the Evangelicals? Tracing the roots of today's movements* (London: Marshall Pickering, 1994).

A.C. Underwood, *A History of the English Baptists* (London: Carey Kingsgate Press, 1947).

D. Van Broekhoeven, *The Baptist River* (Macon, Ga: Mercer University Press), forthcoming

P. Veselá, *Fit for a King* (Prague: IBTS, 2004).

M. Volf, *After Our Likeness: The Church as the Image of the Trinity* (Cambridge and Grand Rapids, Mich: Eerdmans, 1998).

— *Exclusion and Embrace: A theological Exploration of Identity, Otherness and Reconciliation* (Nashville: Abingdon, 1996).

W.L. Wagner, *New Move Forward in Europe* (South Pasadena, Ca.: William Carey Library, 1978).

A.F. Walls, *The Missionary Movement in Christian History: Studies in the Transmission of Faith* (Edinburgh: T&T Clark, 1996).

A.W. Wardin (ed.), *Baptists Around the World* (Nashville, Tenn.: Broadman and Holman, 1995).

— *Gottfried F Alf: Pioneer of the Baptist Movement in Poland* (Nashville Tenn.: Baptist History and Heritage, 2003).

J.B. Weatherspoon, *M Theron Rankin: Apostle of Advance* (Nashville, Tenn.: Broadman, 1958).

W.M.S. West, *To Be A Pilgrim: A memoir of Ernest A Payne* (Guildford: Lutterworth Press, 1983).

B.R. White, *The English Separatist Tradition* (London: Oxford University Press, 1971).

— *The English Baptists of the 17th Century* (London: The Baptist Historical Society, 1983).

W.T. Whitley (ed.), *Minutes of the General Assembly of General Baptists*, 2 vols. (London, 1910).
— *A History of British Baptists*, rev. ed. (London: Kingsgate, 1932).
G.H. Williams, *The Radical Reformation (*Philadelphia: Westminster, 1962).
Haddon Willmer (ed.), *20:20 Visions – The Futures of Christianity in Britain* (London: SPCK, 1992).
N.G.Wright, *Disavowing Constantine* (Carlisle: Paternoster, 2000).
— *Challenge to Change: A Radical Agenda for Baptists* (Carlisle: Paternoster, 1990)
— *New Baptists, New Agenda* (Carlisle: Paternoster, 2002).
— *Free Church, Free State: The Positive Baptist View* (Milton Keynes: Paternoster, 2005).
— *The Radical Evangelical: seeking a Place to Stand* (London: SPCK, 1996)
S. Wright, *The Early English Baptists, 1603-1649* (Woodbridge, Suffolk: The Boydell Press, 2006).
J.H. Yoder, *The Royal Priesthood: Essays Ecclesiological and Ecumenical* (Scottdale, Pa.: Herald Press, 1998).
— *Body Politics: five practices of the Christian community before the watching world* (Nashville: Discipleship Resources, 1989).
J.D. Zizioulas, *Being and Community: Studies in Personhood and the Church (*Crestwood, NY: St Vladimir's Seminary Press, 1985).
— *Eucharist, Bishop, Church: The Unity of the Church in the Divine Eucharist and the Bishop during the first three centuries* (ET, Elizabeth Theoritoff, Brookline, Ma: Holy Cross Orthodox Press, 2001).

Websites

www.ibts.eu
www.ebf.org
www.abps.org
www.bwanet.org
www.ecupatriarchate.org
www.europe.anglican.org
www.Keston.org
www.lutheranworld.org
http://warc.jalb.de
www.wcc-coe.org/wcc/wh
www.sbc.net/bfm/bfmcomparison
www.imb.org
www.alpha.org.uk
www.christian-aid.org.uk
http://ec.europa.eu/education/policies
http://www.pctii.org/pwf/
http://lkg.jalb.de
http://blog.ibts.eu

Theses

R. Lysenkaite, 'The Place of Cultural Heritage in the Context of Contemporary Baptist Identity: A Case Study of Klaipeda Baptist Church', unpubl. MTh dissertation (International Baptist Theological Seminary, Prague, 2003).

William Lyle Wagner, 'North American Protestant missionaries in Western Europe: A Critical Appraisal', unpubl. D.Theol dissertation (University of South Africa, 1989).

Brian N Winslade, 'Prioritising Mission Within a Baptist Polity', unpubl. D.Min dissertation (Bethel University, St Paul, Min, USA, 2007).

C.G. Woodfin, 'Rueschlikon: The Establishment and Early Development of an International Baptist Theological Seminary in the Heart of Post-War Europe', unpubl. MA dissertation (Wake Forest University, Texas, USA, 1987).

Index

Studies in Baptist History and Thought

(All titles uniform with this volume)
Dates in bold are of projected publication
Volumes in this series are not always published in sequence

David Bebbington and Anthony R. Cross (eds)
Global Baptist History
(SBHT vol. 14)

This book brings together studies from the Second International Conference on Baptist Studies which explore different facets of Baptist life and work especially during the twentieth century.

***2006** / 1-84227-214-4 / approx. 350pp*

David Bebbington (ed.)
The Gospel in the World
International Baptist Studies
(SBHT vol. 1)

This volume of essays from the First International Conference on Baptist Studies deals with a range of subjects spanning Britain, North America, Europe, Asia and the Antipodes. Topics include studies on religious tolerance, the communion controversy and the development of the international Baptist community, and concludes with two important essays on the future of Baptist life that pay special attention to the United States.

2002 / 1-84227-118-0 / xiv + 362pp

John H.Y. Briggs (ed.)
Pulpit and People
Studies in Eighteenth-Century English Baptist Life and Thought
(SBHT vol. 28)

The eighteenth century was a crucial time in Baptist history. The denomination had its roots in seventeenth-century English Puritanism and Separatism and the persecution of the Stuart kings with only a limited measure of freedom after 1689. Worse, however, was to follow for with toleration came doctrinal conflict, a move away from central Christian understandings and a loss of evangelistic urgency. Both spiritual and numerical decline ensued, to the extent that the denomination was virtually reborn as rather belatedly it came to benefit from the Evangelical Revival which brought new life to both Arminian and Calvinistic Baptists. The papers in this volume study a denomination in transition, and relate to theology, their views of the church and its mission, Baptist spirituality, and engagements with radical politics.

***2007** / 1-84227-403-1 / approx. 350pp*

July 2005

Damian Brot

Church of the Baptized or Church of Believers?

A Contribution to the Dialogue between the Catholic Church and the Free Churches with Special Reference to Baptists

(SBHT vol. 26)

The dialogue between the Catholic Church and the Free Churches in Europe has hardly taken place. This book pleads for a commencement of such a conversation. It offers, among other things, an introduction to the American and the international dialogues between Baptists and the Catholic Church and strives to allow these conversations to become fruitful in the European context as well.

***2006** / 1-84227-334-5 / approx. 364pp*

Dennis Bustin

Paradox and Perseverence

Hanserd Knollys, Particular Baptist Pioneer in Seventeenth-Century England

(SBHT vol. 23)

The seventeenth century was a significant period in English history during which the people of England experienced unprecedented change and tumult in all spheres of life. At the same time, the importance of order and the traditional institutions of society were being reinforced. Hanserd Knollys, born during this pivotal period, personified in his life the ambiguity, tension and paradox of it, openly seeking change while at the same time cautiously embracing order. As a founder and leader of the Particular Baptists in London and despite persecution and personal hardship, he played a pivotal role in helping shape their identity externally in society and, internally, as they moved toward becoming more formalised by the end of the century.

***2006** / 1-84227-259-4 / approx. 324pp*

Anthony R. Cross

Baptism and the Baptists

Theology and Practice in Twentieth-Century Britain

(SBHT vol. 3)

At a time of renewed interest in baptism, *Baptism and the Baptists* is a detailed study of twentieth-century baptismal theology and practice and the factors which have influenced its development.

2000 / 0-85364-959-6 / xx + 530pp

July 2005

Anthony R. Cross and Philip E. Thompson (eds)

Baptist Sacramentalism

(SBHT vol. 5)

This collection of essays includes biblical, historical and theological studies in the theology of the sacraments from a Baptist perspective. Subjects explored include the physical side of being spiritual, baptism, the Lord's supper, the church, ordination, preaching, worship, religious liberty and the issue of disestablishment.

2003 / 1-84227-119-9 / xvi + 278pp

Anthony R. Cross and Philip E. Thompson (eds)

Baptist Sacramentalism 2

(SBHT vol. 25)

This second collection of essays exploring various dimensions of sacramental theology from a Baptist perspective includes biblical, historical and theological studies from scholars from around the world.

2006 */ 1-84227-325-6 / approx. 350pp*

Paul S. Fiddes

Tracks and Traces

Baptist Identity in Church and Theology

(SBHT vol. 13)

This is a comprehensive, yet unusual, book on the faith and life of Baptist Christians. It explores the understanding of the church, ministry, sacraments and mission from a thoroughly theological perspective. In a series of interlinked essays, the author relates Baptist identity consistently to a theology of covenant and to participation in the triune communion of God.

2003 / 1-84227-120-2 / xvi + 304pp

Stanley K. Fowler

More Than a Symbol

The British Baptist Recovery of Baptismal Sacramentalism

(SBHT vol. 2)

Fowler surveys the entire scope of British Baptist literature from the seventeenth-century pioneers onwards. He shows that in the twentieth century leading British Baptist pastors and theologians recovered an understanding of baptism that connected experience with soteriology and that in doing so they were recovering what many of their forebears had taught.

2002 / 1-84227-052-4 / xvi + 276pp

July 2005

Steven R. Harmon
Towards Baptist Catholicity
Essays on Tradition and the Baptist Vision
(SBHT vol. 27)

This series of essays contends that the reconstruction of the Baptist vision in the wake of modernity's dissolution requires a retrieval of the ancient ecumenical tradition that forms Christian identity through rehearsal and practice. Themes explored include catholic identity as an emerging trend in Baptist theology, tradition as a theological category in Baptist perspective, Baptist confessions and the patristic tradition, worship as a principal bearer of tradition, and the role of Baptist higher education in shaping the Christian vision.

***2006** / 1-84227-362-0 / approx. 210pp*

Michael A.G. Haykin (ed.)
'At the Pure Fountain of Thy Word'
Andrew Fuller as an Apologist
(SBHT vol. 6)

One of the greatest Baptist theologians of the eighteenth and early nineteenth centuries, Andrew Fuller has not had justice done to him. There is little doubt that Fuller's theology lay behind the revitalization of the Baptists in the late eighteenth century and the first few decades of the nineteenth. This collection of essays fills a much needed gap by examining a major area of Fuller's thought, his work as an apologist.

2004 / 1-84227-171-7 / xxii + 276pp

Michael A.G. Haykin
Studies in Calvinistic Baptist Spirituality
(SBHT vol. 15)

In a day when spirituality is in vogue and Christian communities are looking for guidance in this whole area, there is wisdom in looking to the past to find untapped wells. The Calvinistic Baptists, heirs of the rich ecclesial experience in the Puritan era of the seventeenth century, but, by the end of the eighteenth century, also passionately engaged in the catholicity of the Evangelical Revivals, are such a well. This collection of essays, covering such things as the Lord's Supper, friendship and hymnody, seeks to draw out the spiritual riches of this community for reflection and imitation in the present day.

***2006** / 1-84227-149-0 / approx. 350pp*

Brian Haymes, Anthony R. Cross and Ruth Gouldbourne

On Being the Church

Revisioning Baptist Identity

(SBHT vol. 21)

The aim of the book is to re-examine Baptist theology and practice in the light of the contemporary biblical, theological, ecumenical and missiological context drawing on historical and contemporary writings and issues. It is not a study in denominationalism but rather seeks to revision historical insights from the believers' church tradition for the sake of Baptists and other Christians in the context of the modern–postmodern context.

***2006** / 1-84227-121-0 / approx. 350pp*

Ken R. Manley

From Woolloomooloo to 'Eternity': A History of Australian Baptists

Volume 1: Growing an Australian Church (1831–1914)

Volume 2: A National Church in a Global Community (1914–2005)

(SBHT vols 16.1 and 16.2)

From their beginnings in Australia in 1831 with the first baptisms in Woolloomoolloo Bay in 1832, this pioneering study describes the quest of Baptists in the different colonies (states) to discover their identity as Australians and Baptists. Although institutional developments are analyzed and the roles of significant individuals traced, the major focus is on the social and theological dimensions of the Baptist movement.

*2 vol. set **2006** / 1-84227-405-8 / approx. 900pp*

Ken R. Manley

'Redeeming Love Proclaim'

John Rippon and the Baptists

(SBHT vol. 12)

A leading exponent of the new moderate Calvinism which brought new life to many Baptists, John Rippon (1751–1836) helped unite the Baptists at this significant time. His many writings expressed the denomination's growing maturity and mutual awareness of Baptists in Britain and America, and exerted a long-lasting influence on Baptist worship and devotion. In his various activities, Rippon helped conserve the heritage of Old Dissent and promoted the evangelicalism of the New Dissent

2004 / 1-84227-193-8 / xviii + 340pp

July 2005

Peter J. Morden

Offering Christ to the World

Andrew Fuller and the Revival of English Particular Baptist Life

(SBHT vol. 8)

Andrew Fuller (1754–1815) was one of the foremost English Baptist ministers of his day. His career as an Evangelical Baptist pastor, theologian, apologist and missionary statesman coincided with the profound revitalization of the Particular Baptist denomination to which he belonged. This study examines the key aspects of the life and thought of this hugely significant figure, and gives insights into the revival in which he played such a central part.

2003 / 1-84227-141-5 / xx + 202pp

Peter Naylor

Calvinism, Communion and the Baptists

A Study of English Calvinistic Baptists from the Late 1600s to the Early 1800s

(SBHT vol. 7)

Dr Naylor argues that the traditional link between 'high-Calvinism' and 'restricted communion' is in need of revision. He examines Baptist communion controversies from the late 1600s to the early 1800s and also the theologies of John Gill and Andrew Fuller.

2003 / 1-84227-142-3 / xx + 266pp

Ian M. Randall, Toivo Pilli and Anthony R. Cross (eds)

Baptist Identities

International Studies from the Seventeenth to the Twentieth Centuries

(SBHT vol. 19)

These papers represent the contributions of scholars from various parts of the world as they consider the factors that have contributed to Baptist distinctiveness in different countries and at different times. The volume includes specific case studies as well as broader examinations of Baptist life in a particular country or region. Together they represent an outstanding resource for understanding Baptist identities.

***2005** / 1-84227-215-2 / approx. 350pp*

James M. Renihan

Edification and Beauty

The Practical Ecclesiology of the English Particular Baptists, 1675–1705

(SBHT vol. 17)

Edification and Beauty describes the practices of the Particular Baptist churches at the end of the seventeenth century in terms of three concentric circles: at the centre is the ecclesiological material in the Second London Confession, which is then fleshed out in the various published writings of the men associated with these churches, and, finally, expressed in the church books of the era.

***2005** / 1-84227-251-9 / approx. 230pp*

Frank Rinaldi

'The Tribe of Dan'

A Study of the New Connexion of General Baptists 1770–1891

(SBHT vol. 10)

'The Tribe of Dan' is a thematic study which explores the theology, organizational structure, evangelistic strategy, ministry and leadership of the New Connexion of General Baptists as it experienced the process of institutionalization in the transition from a revival movement to an established denomination.

***2006** / 1-84227-143-1 / approx. 350pp*

Peter Shepherd

The Making of a Modern Denomination

John Howard Shakespeare and the English Baptists 1898–1924

(SBHT vol. 4)

John Howard Shakespeare introduced revolutionary change to the Baptist denomination. The Baptist Union was transformed into a strong central institution and Baptist ministers were brought under its control. Further, Shakespeare's pursuit of church unity reveals him as one of the pioneering ecumenists of the twentieth century.

2001 / 1-84227-046-X / xviii + 220pp

July 2005

Karen Smith

The Community and the Believers

A Study of Calvinistic Baptist Spirituality in Some Towns and Villages of Hampshire and the Borders of Wiltshire, c.1730–1830

(SBHT vol. 22)

The period from 1730 to 1830 was one of transition for Calvinistic Baptists. Confronted by the enthusiasm of the Evangelical Revival, congregations within the denomination as a whole were challenged to find a way to take account of the revival experience. This study examines the life and devotion of Calvinistic Baptists in Hampshire and Wiltshire during this period. Among this group of Baptists was the hymn writer, Anne Steele.

***2005** / 1-84227-326-4 / approx. 280pp*

Martin Sutherland

Dissenters in a 'Free Land'

Baptist Thought in New Zealand 1850–2000

(SBHT vol. 24)

Baptists in New Zealand were forced to recast their identity. Conventions of communication and association, state and ecumenical relations, even historical divisions and controversies had to be revised in the face of new topographies and constraints. As Baptists formed themselves in a fluid society they drew heavily on both international movements and local dynamics. This book traces the development of ideas which shaped institutions and styles in sometimes surprising ways.

***2006** / 1-84227-327-2 / approx. 230pp*

Brian Talbot

The Search for a Common Identity

The Origins of the Baptist Union of Scotland 1800–1870

(SBHT vol. 9)

In the period 1800 to 1827 there were three streams of Baptists in Scotland: Scotch, Haldaneite and 'English' Baptist. A strong commitment to home evangelization brought these three bodies closer together, leading to a merger of their home missionary societies in 1827. However, the first three attempts to form a union of churches failed, but by the 1860s a common understanding of their corporate identity was attained leading to the establishment of the Baptist Union of Scotland.

2003 / 1-84227-123-7 / xviii + 402pp

July 2005

Philip E. Thompson
The Freedom of God
Towards Baptist Theology in Pneumatological Perspective
(SBHT vol. 20)

This study contends that the range of theological commitments of the early Baptists are best understood in relation to their distinctive emphasis on the freedom of God. Thompson traces how this was recast anthropocentrically, leading to an emphasis upon human freedom from the nineteenth century onwards. He seeks to recover the dynamism of the early vision via a pneumatologically-oriented ecclesiology defining the church in terms of the memory of God.

***2006** / 1-84227-125-3 / approx. 350pp*

Philip E. Thompson and Anthony R. Cross (eds)
Recycling the Past or Researching History?
Studies in Baptist Historiography and Myths
(SBHT vol. 11)

In this volume an international group of Baptist scholars examine and re-examine areas of Baptist life and thought about which little is known or the received wisdom is in need of revision. Historiographical studies include the date Oxford Baptists joined the Abingdon Association, the death of the Fifth Monarchist John Pendarves, eighteenth-century Calvinistic Baptists and the political realm, confessional identity and denominational institutions, Baptist community, ecclesiology, the priesthood of all believers, soteriology, Baptist spirituality, Strict and Reformed Baptists, the role of women among British Baptists, while various 'myths' challenged include the nature of high-Calvinism in eighteenth-century England, baptismal anti-sacramentalism, episcopacy, and Baptists and change.

***2005** / 1-84227-122-9 / approx. 330pp*

Linda Wilson
Marianne Farningham
A Plain Working Woman
(SBHT vol. 18)

Marianne Farningham, of College Street Baptist Chapel, Northampton, was a household name in evangelical circles in the later nineteenth century. For over fifty years she produced comment, poetry, biography and fiction for the popular Christian press. This investigation uses her writings to explore the beliefs and behaviour of evangelical Nonconformists, including Baptists, during these years.

***2006** / 1-84227-124-5 / approx. 250pp*

July 2005

Other Paternoster titles relating to Baptist history and thought

George R. Beasley-Murray

Baptism in the New Testament

(Paternoster Digital Library)

This is a welcome reprint of a classic text on baptism originally published in 1962 by one of the leading Baptist New Testament scholars of the twentieth century. Dr Beasley-Murray's comprehensive study begins by investigating the antecedents of Christian baptism. It then surveys the foundation of Christian baptism in the Gospels, its emergence in the Acts of the Apostles and development in the apostolic writings. Following a section relating baptism to New Testament doctrine, a substantial discussion of the origin and significance of infant baptism leads to a briefer consideration of baptismal reform and ecumenism.

2005 / 1-84227-300-0 / x + 422pp

Paul Beasley-Murray

Fearless for Truth

A Personal Portrait of the Life of George Beasley-Murray

Without a doubt George Beasley-Murray was one of the greatest Baptists of the twentieth century. A long-standing Principal of Spurgeon's College, he wrote more than twenty books and made significant contributions in the study of areas as diverse as baptism and eschatology, as well as writing highly respected commentaries on the Book of Revelation and John's Gospel.

2002 / 1-84227-134-2 / xii + 244pp

David Bebbington

Holiness in Nineteenth-Century England

(Studies in Christian History and Thought)

David Bebbington stresses the relationship of movements of spirituality to changes in their cultural setting, especially the legacies of the Enlightenment and Romanticism. He shows that these broad shifts in ideological mood had a profound effect on the ways in which piety was conceptualized and practised. Holiness was intimately bound up with the spirit of the age.

2000 / 0-85364-981-2 / viii + 98pp

July 2005

Clyde Binfield

Victorian Nonconformity in Eastern England 1840–1885

(Studies in Evangelical History and Thought)

Studies of Victorian religion and society often concentrate on cities, suburbs, and industrialisation. This study provides a contrast. Victorian Eastern England—Essex, Suffolk, Norfolk, Cambridgeshire, and Huntingdonshire—was rural, traditional, relatively unchanging. That is nonetheless a caricature which discounts the industry in Norwich and Ipswich (as well as in Haverhill, Stowmarket and Leiston) and ignores the impact of London on Essex, of railways throughout the region, and of an ancient but changing university (Cambridge) on the county town which housed it. It also entirely ignores the political implications of such changes in a region noted for the variety of its religious Dissent since the seventeenth century. This book explores Victorian Eastern England and its Nonconformity. It brings to a wider readership a pioneering thesis which has made a major contribution to a fresh evolution of English religion and society.

***2006** / 1-84227-216-0 / approx. 274pp*

Edward W. Burrows

'To Me To Live Is Christ'

A Biography of Peter H. Barber

This book is about a remarkably gifted and energetic man of God. Peter H. Barber was born into a Brethren family in Edinburgh in 1930. In his youth he joined Charlotte Baptist Chapel and followed the call into Baptist ministry. For eighteen years he was the pioneer minister of the new congregation in the New Town of East Kilbride, which planted two further congregations. At the age of thirty-nine he served as Centenary President of the Baptist Union of Scotland and then exercised an influential ministry for over seven years in the well-known Upton Vale Baptist Church, Torquay. From 1980 until his death in 1994 he was General Secretary of the Baptist Union of Scotland. Through his work for the European Baptist Federation and the Baptist World Alliance he became a world Baptist statesman. He was President of the EBF during the upheaval that followed the collapse of Communism.

2005 / 1-84227-324-8 / xxii + 236pp

Christopher J. Clement

Religious Radicalism in England 1535–1565

(Rutherford Studies in Historical Theology)

In this valuable study Christopher Clement draws our attention to a varied assemblage of people who sought Christian faithfulness in the underworld of mid-Tudor England. Sympathetically and yet critically he assess their place in the history of English Protestantism, and by attentive listening he gives them a voice.

1997 / 0-946068-44-5 / xxii + 426pp

July 2005

Anthony R. Cross (ed.)
Ecumenism and History
Studies in Honour of John H.Y. Briggs
(Studies in Christian History and Thought)

This collection of essays examines the inter-relationships between the two fields in which Professor Briggs has contributed so much: history—particularly Baptist and Nonconformist—and the ecumenical movement. With contributions from colleagues and former research students from Britain, Europe and North America, *Ecumenism and History* provides wide-ranging studies in important aspects of Christian history, theology and ecumenical studies.

2002 / 1-84227-135-0 / xx + 362pp

Keith E. Eitel
Paradigm Wars
The Southern Baptist International Mission Board Faces the Third Millennium
(Regnum Studies in Mission)

The International Mission Board of the Southern Baptist Convention is the largest denominational mission agency in North America. This volume chronicles the historic and contemporary forces that led to the IMB's recent extensive reorganization, providing the most comprehensive case study to date of a historic mission agency restructuring to continue its mission purpose into the twenty-first century more effectively.

2000 / 1-870345-12-6 / x + 140pp

Ruth Gouldbourne
The Flesh and the Feminine
Gender and Theology in the Writings of Caspar Schwenckfeld
(Studies in Christian History and Thought)

Caspar Schwenckfeld and his movement exemplify one of the radical communities of the sixteenth century. Challenging theological and liturgical norms, they also found themselves challenging social and particularly gender assumptions. In this book, the issues of the relationship between radical theology and the understanding of gender are considered.

***2005** / 1-84227-048-6 / approx. 304pp*

July 2005

David Hilborn

The Words of our Lips

Language-Use in Free Church Worship

(Paternoster Theological Monographs)

Studies of liturgical language have tended to focus on the written canons of Roman Catholic and Anglican communities. By contrast, David Hilborn analyses the more extemporary approach of English Nonconformity. Drawing on recent developments in linguistic pragmatics, he explores similarities and differences between 'fixed' and 'free' worship, and argues for the interdependence of each.

***2006** / 0-85364-977-4*

Stephen R. Holmes

Listening to the Past

The Place of Tradition in Theology

Beginning with the question 'Why can't we just read the Bible?' Stephen Holmes considers the place of tradition in theology, showing how the doctrine of creation leads to an account of historical location and creaturely limitations as essential aspects of our existence. For we cannot claim unmediated access to the Scriptures without acknowledging the place of tradition: theology is an irreducibly communal task. *Listening to the Past* is a sustained attempt to show what listening to tradition involves, and how it can be used to aid theological work today.

2002 / 1-84227-155-5 / xiv + 168pp

Mark Hopkins

Nonconformity's Romantic Generation

Evangelical and Liberal Theologies in Victorian England

(Studies in Evangelical History and Thought)

A study of the theological development of key leaders of the Baptist and Congregational denominations at their period of greatest influence, including C.H. Spurgeon and R.W. Dale, and of the controversies in which those among them who embraced and rejected the liberal transformation of their evangelical heritage opposed each other.

2004 / 1-84227-150-4 / xvi + 284pp

July 2005

Galen K. Johnson

Prisoner of Conscience

John Bunyan on Self, Community and Christian Faith

(Studies in Christian History and Thought)

This is an interdisciplinary study of John Bunyan's understanding of conscience across his autobiographical, theological and fictional writings, investigating whether conscience always deserves fidelity, and how Bunyan's view of conscience affects his relationship both to modern Western individualism and historic Christianity.

2003 / 1-84227- 151-2 / xvi + 236pp

R.T. Kendall

Calvin and English Calvinism to 1649

(Studies in Christian History and Thought)

The author's thesis is that those who formed the Westminster Confession of Faith, which is regarded as Calvinism, in fact departed from John Calvin on two points: (1) the extent of the atonement and (2) the ground of assurance of salvation.

1997 / 0-85364-827-1 / xii + 264pp

Timothy Larsen

Friends of Religious Equality

Nonconformist Politics in Mid-Victorian England

During the middle decades of the nineteenth century the English Nonconformist community developed a coherent political philosophy of its own, of which a central tenet was the principle of religious equality (in contrast to the stereotype of Evangelical Dissenters). The Dissenting community fought for the civil rights of Roman Catholics, non-Christians and even atheists, on an issue of principle which had its flowering in the enthusiastic and undivided support which Nonconformity gave to the campaign for Jewish emancipation. This reissued study examines the political efforts and ideas of English Nonconformists during the period, covering the whole range of national issues raised, from state education to the Crimean War. It offers a case study of a theologically conservative group defending religious pluralism in the civic sphere, showing that the concept of religious equality was a grand vision at the centre of the political philosophy of the Dissenters.

***2007** / 1-84227-402-3 / x + 300pp*

Donald M. Lewis

Lighten Their Darkness

The Evangelical Mission to Working-Class London, 1828–1860

(Studies in Evangelical History and Thought)

This is a comprehensive and compelling study of the Church and the complexities of nineteenth-century London. Challenging our understanding of the culture in working London at this time, Lewis presents a well-structured and illustrated work that contributes substantially to the study of evangelicalism and mission in nineteenth-century Britain.

2001 / 1-84227-074-5 / xviii + 372pp

Stanley E. Porter and Anthony R. Cross (eds)

Semper Reformandum

Studies in Honour of Clark H. Pinnock

Clark Pinnock has clearly been one of the most important evangelical theologians of the last forty years in North America. Always provocative, especially in the wide range of opinions he has held and considered, Pinnock, himself a Baptist, has recently retired after twenty-five years of teaching at McMaster Divinity College. His colleagues and associates honour him in this volume by responding to his important theological work which has dealt with the essential topics of evangelical theology. These include Christian apologetics, biblical inspiration, the Holy Spirit and, perhaps most importantly in recent years, openness theology.

2003 / 1-84227-206-3 / xiv + 414pp

Meic Pearse

The Great Restoration

The Religious Radicals of the 16th and 17th Centuries

Pearse charts the rise and progress of continental Anabaptism – both evangelical and heretical – through the sixteenth century. He then follows the story of those English people who became impatient with Puritanism and separated – first from the Church of England and then from one another – to form the antecedents of later Congregationalists, Baptists and Quakers.

1998 / 0-85364-800-X / xii + 320pp

Charles Price and Ian M. Randall

Transforming Keswick

Transforming Keswick is a thorough, readable and detailed history of the convention. It will be of interest to those who know and love Keswick, those who are only just discovering it, and serious scholars eager to learn more about the history of God's dealings with his people.

2000 / 1-85078-350-0 / 288pp

July 2005

Jim Purves

The Triune God and the Charismatic Movement

A Critical Appraisal from a Scottish Perspective

(Paternoster Theological Monographs)

All emotion and no theology? Or a fundamental challenge to reappraise and realign our trinitarian theology in the light of Christian experience? This study of charismatic renewal as it found expression within Scotland at the end of the twentieth century evaluates the use of Patristic, Reformed and contemporary models (including those of the Baptist Union of Scotland) of the Trinity in explaining the workings of the Holy Spirit.

2004 / 1-84227-321-3 / xxiv + 246pp

Ian M. Randall

Evangelical Experiences

A Study in the Spirituality of English Evangelicalism 1918–1939

(Studies in Evangelical History and Thought)

This book makes a detailed historical examination of evangelical spirituality between the First and Second World Wars. It shows how patterns of devotion led to tensions and divisions. In a wide-ranging study, Anglican, Wesleyan, Reformed and Pentecostal-charismatic spiritualities are analysed.

1999 / 0-85364-919-7 / xii + 310pp

Ian M. Randall

One Body in Christ

The History and Significance of the Evangelical Alliance

In 1846 the Evangelical Alliance was founded with the aim of bringing together evangelicals for common action. This book uses material not previously utilized to examine the history and significance of the Evangelical Alliance, a movement which has remained a powerful force for unity. At a time when evangelicals are growing world-wide, this book offers insights into the past which are relevant to contemporary issues.

2001 / 1-84227-089-3 / xii + 394pp

Ian M. Randall

Spirituality and Social Change

The Contribution of F.B. Meyer (1847–1929)

(Studies in Evangelical History and Thought)

This is a fresh appraisal of F.B. Meyer (1847–1929), a leading Free Church minister. Having been deeply affected by holiness spirituality, Meyer became the Keswick Convention's foremost international speaker. He combined spirituality with effective evangelism and socio-political activity. This study shows Meyer's significant contribution to spiritual renewal and social change.

2003 / 1-84227-195-4 / xx + 184pp

Geoffrey Robson

Dark Satanic Mills?

Religion and Irreligion in Birmingham and the Black Country

(Studies in Evangelical History and Thought)

This book analyses and interprets the nature and extent of popular Christian belief and practice in Birmingham and the Black Country during the first half of the nineteenth century, with particular reference to the impact of cholera epidemics and evangelism on church extension programmes.

2002 / 1-84227-102-4 / xiv + 294pp

Alan P.F. Sell

Enlightenment, Ecumenism, Evangel

Theological Themes and Thinkers 1550–2000

(Studies in Christian History and Thought)

This book consists of papers in which such interlocking topics as the Enlightenment, the problem of authority, the development of doctrine, spirituality, ecumenism, theological method and the heart of the gospel are discussed. Issues of significance to the church at large are explored with special reference to writers from the Reformed and Dissenting traditions.

2005 / 1-84227330-2 / xviii + 422pp

Alan P.F. Sell

Hinterland Theology

Some Reformed and Dissenting Adjustments

(Studies in Christian History and Thought)

Many books have been written on theology's 'giants' and significant trends, but what of those lesser-known writers who adjusted to them? In this book some hinterland theologians of the British Reformed and Dissenting traditions, who followed in the wake of toleration, the Evangelical Revival, the rise of modern biblical criticism and Karl Barth, are allowed to have their say. They include Thomas Ridgley, Ralph Wardlaw, T.V. Tymms and N.H.G. Robinson.

2006 */ 1-84227-331-0*

July 2005

Alan P.F. Sell and Anthony R. Cross (eds)

Protestant Nonconformity in the Twentieth Century

(Studies in Christian History and Thought)

In this collection of essays scholars representative of a number of Nonconformist traditions reflect thematically on Nonconformists' life and witness during the twentieth century. Among the subjects reviewed are biblical studies, theology, worship, evangelism and spirituality, and ecumenism. Over and above its immediate interest, this collection provides a marker to future scholars and others wishing to know how some of their forebears assessed Nonconformity's contribution to a variety of fields during the century leading up to Christianity's third millennium.

2003 / 1-84227-221-7 / x + 398pp

Mark Smith

Religion in Industrial Society

Oldham and Saddleworth 1740–1865

(Studies in Christian History and Thought)

This book analyses the way British churches sought to meet the challenge of industrialization and urbanization during the period 1740–1865. Working from a case-study of Oldham and Saddleworth, Mark Smith challenges the received view that the Anglican Church in the eighteenth century was characterized by complacency and inertia, and reveals Anglicanism's vigorous and creative response to the new conditions. He reassesses the significance of the centrally directed church reforms of the mid-nineteenth century, and emphasizes the importance of local energy and enthusiasm. Charting the growth of denominational pluralism in Oldham and Saddleworth, Dr Smith compares the strengths and weaknesses of the various Anglican and Nonconformist approaches to promoting church growth. He also demonstrates the extent to which all the churches participated in a common culture shaped by the influence of evangelicalism, and shows that active co-operation between the churches rather than denominational conflict dominated. This revised and updated edition of Dr Smith's challenging and original study makes an important contribution both to the social history of religion and to urban studies.

***2006** / 1-84227-335-3 / approx. 300pp*

July 2005

David M. Thompson

Baptism, Church and Society in Britain from the Evangelical Revival to *Baptism, Eucharist and Ministry*

The theology and practice of baptism have not received the attention they deserve. How important is faith? What does baptismal regeneration mean? Is baptism a bond of unity between Christians? This book discusses the theology of baptism and popular belief and practice in England and Wales from the Evangelical Revival to the publication of the World Council of Churches' consensus statement on *Baptism, Eucharist and Ministry* (1982).

***2005** / 1-84227-393-0 / approx. 224pp*

Martin Sutherland

Peace, Toleration and Decay

The Ecclesiology of Later Stuart Dissent

(Studies in Christian History and Thought)

This fresh analysis brings to light the complexity and fragility of the later Stuart Nonconformist consensus. Recent findings on wider seventeenth-century thought are incorporated into a new picture of the dynamics of Dissent and the roots of evangelicalism.

2003 / 1-84227-152-0 / xxii + 216pp

Haddon Willmer

Evangelicalism 1785–1835: An Essay (1962) and Reflections (2004)

(Studies in Evangelical History and Thought)

Awarded the Hulsean Prize in the University of Cambridge in 1962, this interpretation of a classic period of English Evangelicalism, by a young church historian, is now supplemented by reflections on Evangelicalism from the vantage point of a retired Professor of Theology.

***2006** / 1-84227-219-5*

Linda Wilson

Constrained by Zeal

Female Spirituality amongst Nonconformists 1825–1875

(Studies in Evangelical History and Thought)

Constrained by Zeal investigates the neglected area of Nonconformist female spirituality. Against the background of separate spheres, it analyses the experience of women from four denominations, and argues that the churches provided a 'third sphere' in which they could find opportunities for participation.

2000 / 0-85364-972-3 / xvi + 294pp

July 2005

Nigel G. Wright

Disavowing Constantine

Mission, Church and the Social Order in the Theologies of John Howard Yoder and Jürgen Moltmann

(Paternoster Theological Monographs)

This book is a timely restatement of a radical theology of church and state in the Anabaptist and Baptist tradition. Dr Wright constructs his argument in dialogue and debate with Yoder and Moltmann, major contributors to a free church perspective.

2000 / 0-85364-978-2 / xvi + 252pp

Nigel G. Wright

Free Church, Free State

The Positive Baptist Vision

Free Church, Free State is a textbook on baptist ways of being church and a proposal for the future of baptist churches in an ecumenical context. Nigel Wright argues that both baptist (small 'b') and catholic (small 'c') church traditions should seek to enrich and support each other as valid expressions of the body of Christ without sacrificing what they hold dear. Written for pastors, church planters, evangelists and preachers, Nigel Wright offers frameworks of thought for baptists and non-baptists in their journey together following Christ.

2005 / 1-84227-353-1 / xxviii + 292

Nigel G. Wright

New Baptists, New Agenda

New Baptists, New Agenda is a timely contribution to the growing debate about the health, shape and future of the Baptists. It considers the steady changes that have taken place among Baptists in the last decade – changes of mood, style, practice and structure – and encourages us to align these current movements and questions with God's upward and future call. He contends that the true church has yet to come: the church that currently exists is an anticipation of the joyful gathering of all who have been called by the Spirit through Christ to the Father.

2002 / 1-84227-157-1 / x + 162pp

Paternoster: thinking faith

Paternoster
9 Holdom Avenue,
Bletchley,
Milton Keynes MK1 1QR,
United Kingdom
Web: www.authenticmedia.co.uk/paternoster

July 2005